OUTRAGE

OUTRAGE

The Story Behind the Tawana Brawley Hoax

Robert D. McFadden
Ralph Blumenthal
M. A. Farber
E. R. Shipp
Charles Strum
Craig Wolff

of

The New York Times

BANTAM BOOKS
NEW YORK · TORONTO · LONDON · SYDNEY · AUCKLAND

To the crowd at Edgar's

OUTRAGE

A Bantam Book / September 1990

Designed by Susan Hood

Library of Congress Cataloging-in-Publication Data

Outrage: the story behind the Tawana Brawley hoax / by Robert D.
McFadden . . . [et al.].
   Includes bibliographical references.
   ISBN 0-553-05756-1
   1. Rape—New York (State)—Investigation—Case studies. 2. Rape—
New York (State)—Wappingers Falls—Investigation—Case studies.
3. New York (State)—Race relations—Case studies. 4. Brawley,
Tawana. I. McFadden, Robert D.
HV6565.N7T39   1990
364.1'532'0974733—dc20   90-32338
                                                              CIP

Published simultaneously in the United States and Canada

Bantam Books are published by Bantam Books, a division of Bantam Doubleday
Dell Publishing Group, Inc. Its trademark, consisting of the words "Bantam
Books" and the portrayal of a rooster, is Registered in U.S. Patent and Trademark
Office and in other countries. Marca Registrada. Bantam Books, 666 Fifth Avenue,
New York, New York 10103.

PRINTED IN THE UNITED STATES OF AMERICA

BOMC offers recordings and compact discs, cassettes
and records. For information and catalog write to
BOMR, Camp Hill, PA 17012.

Acknowledgments

This book would not have been possible without the cooperation and assistance of many public officials and private individuals who played major roles in the Brawley case and who generously gave us their time and insights. We wish to express our gratitude in particular to Governor Mario M. Cuomo of New York; Attorney General Robert Abrams; Deputy Attorney General John M. Ryan; Timothy Gilles, the director of policy and communications for the attorney general's office; Dutchess County district attorney William V. Grady and assistant district attorney Steven A. Pagones; Russell Crawford of the New York State Police; Reverend Al Sharpton; Perry McKinnon; Daryl T. Rodriguez; Anthony Montanari; and Rosemary Dean. Of course, none of these people are responsible for the conclusions drawn in this book.

We are not at liberty to name some of the people who shared their knowledge and made crucial contributions to our work, but their anonymity in no way limits our gratitude.

Although their roles in the Brawley case were largely peripheral, the regulars at Edgar's Food Shop in Brooklyn were important to us and to the tenor of this book. Ethelyn Smith, William Mackey, Jr., Roy Canton, William Bradfield, and Hampton Rookard provided us with insights on the case and on racism in America, and for these we are grateful.

At Bantam Books, the enthusiasm of former editor-in-chief and publisher Steve Rubin and the advice of editor Charles Michener

Acknowledgments

were crucial in guiding us through this project. Henry Ferris also helped in the early stages.

We wish also to express our profound appreciation to *The New York Times* for allowing us the time and opportunity to carry what began as a fascinating reportorial assignment for the newspaper to full fruition in this book. Most especially, for their invaluable advice, we wish to thank Max Frankel, the executive editor; Arthur Gelb, the former managing editor; John Darnton, the metropolitan editor; Dennis Stern, the deputy metropolitan editor; and reporters Don Terry and Fox Butterfield.

Not least, we must apologize to and deeply thank our families and friends, whose patience and gentle encouragements were crucial to the completion of this volume.

Robert D. McFadden
Ralph Blumenthal
M. A. Farber
E. R. Shipp
Charles Strum
Craig Wolff

New York, N.Y.
April 1990

Introduction

In November 1987, Tawana Brawley fabricated a tale of abduction and rape by white racists. In succeeding months, millions of people embraced her lie as a paradigm of racism in America, and many later clung to it in the face of overwhelming evidence of a hoax. How could all this have happened?

The authors of this book set out to learn the truth about the girl, but the journey took us inevitably into larger realms. This volume is, accordingly, far more than a comprehensive account of the Tawana Brawley mystery. It is also the story of simmering racial hatreds, a flawed criminal justice system, a distortion-prone press, and the charlatans who exploited these problems. It is the story, too, of ordinary Americans who felt deeply about the case.

We found the voices of some of those people in a little diner in Brooklyn called Edgar's Food Shop. Through the feelings and words of its black patrons came insights on racism and a fresh perspective on the case. Though they played no direct role in it, they are characters in the Brawley story as surely as the girl and the governor, for they are the ordinary people whose private lives are affected by the public dramas of the day.

The authors of this book covered the Tawana Brawley story for *The New York Times* throughout much of 1988. But hundreds of interviews with key figures and many confidential official documents have produced a wealth of additional detail and new insights. Governor Mario M. Cuomo, Attorney General Robert

Abrams, chief prosecutor John M. Ryan, the Reverend Al Sharpton, and Tawana Brawley's boyfriend at the time, Daryl T. Rodriguez, are only a few of the many key figures who provided us with extensive new information. With a transformed vision, we have critically reexamined the events, characters, and crosscurrents of the case from its obscure origins to its troubling consequences. We have stepped behind the scenes to examine the motives of the protagonists, the work of investigators and prosecutors, the conduct and aims of the Brawley advisers, and the actions of the police, the press, and the political leaders. Similarly, we have taken the opportunity to reevaluate the actions of the state's highest public officials, including Cuomo and Abrams, and many nationally prominent blacks and whites, people as disparate as Mike Tyson, Bill Cosby, Minister Louis Farrakhan, Phil Donahue, the Reverend Jesse Jackson, and New York City's mayor, David N. Dinkins.

Our investigation, finally, has given us the opportunity to approach the elusive truth about what happened to Tawana Brawley. The whole story may never be known, since the girl and her family have to date refused all entreaties to provide a verifiable account. This book sets forth a version of events based on the authors' own investigation, as well as the material compiled by the New York State grand jury. It is, to the best of our knowledge, what actually happened.

HOT
COFFEE

"Hey, Bradfield," the old Professor shouted.

Down the counter of the little diner, the Professor's longtime pal, William Bradfield, could tell the razzing was coming. He looked up from his cup of coffee, a feigned innocence on the witty face.

"Squire," intoned the Professor, "we are about to have a serious confrontation here now. So you are dismissed. You may take a walk around the block. Don't you have to go to the bathroom or something?"

Laughter like clattering dishes erupted along the counter, along the single row of white tables and from the back where the steam rose in puffs from the coffee urns and the griddle. They loved it: the gentle obligatory ribbing that always came before they got down to the serious talk, the seismic opinions on black affairs.

"I want to partake of your great knowledge," Bradfield retorted, trying not to be upstaged in front of the regulars. "I want to drink from the fountain of your great erudition."

But no one high-hatted Professor William Mackey, Jr. "Shit!" he said, faking a frown, and they all roared with great guffaws.

The name of the place was Edgar's Food Shop, but the regulars called it "Mrs. Smith's," after the proprietor, Ethelyn Smith, who arrived at four o'clock every morning to get the coffee going, to bake the biscuits and stoke up the fires for plates of sizzling grits, bacon and sausage, home fries, and pancakes.

The regulars—Professor Mackey, Hampton Rookard, Squire Bradfield, Oswald Cumberbatch, Sterling Johnson, Wayne Chinnery, and others—came every day to swap gossip, read the newspapers, and cut earth-shaking events down to size. Edgar's was America's front porch, the old-fashioned stoop, the barbershop, wherever ordinary people gathered to talk about the world and what mattered to them. It was beyond the reach of presidents and hucksters, for here the people decided things for themselves. Like members of a club, they spent hours at the table under the hand-lettered sign: The Over-the-Hill Gang. And it was true: Cumberbatch was seventy-four and most of the others were in their sixties, though a couple were much younger.

There were other places in Brooklyn where people talked about football and *glasnost* and business. And many New Yorkers in November 1987 were preoccupied with the stock market crash, the Iran-Contra scandal, and the tragic death of battered little Lisa Steinberg.

But at Edgar's Food Shop on Nostrand Avenue, between the Starlite Bar and Dick Tracey's Bicycle Shop, there was only one topic every day of the year for the regulars: anything black.

Nostrand Avenue courses through the heart of one of the nation's largest black ghettos, the Bedford-Stuyvesant section of Brooklyn. It is a throbbing, vibrant thoroughfare—like 125th Street in Harlem, Auburn Avenue in Atlanta, 47th Street in Chicago, or Central Avenue in Los Angeles long ago. Meat markets sell goat, duck, and country hams. Greengroceries, many owned by Koreans, spill over with Georgia peaches, collard greens, mangoes, raw peanuts, yams, and sweet potatoes. A record shop called Buy Something International offers newspapers and magazines from the Caribbean, aromatic incense, lucky powders, and exotic sprays. There are Caribbean restaurants, vegetarian eateries run by Muslims seeking converts, hamburger and fried-chicken outlets; and there are churches, beauty shops, hardware and variety stores, fish markets, and shops that specialize in religious articles.

The angry face of Malcolm X scowls from many shop windows,

along with posters of Bob Marley, Haile Selassie, and Martin Luther King, Jr. Booksellers spread their wares out on the sidewalks: black nationalist tracts, comic books, novels, history. People eddy around or stop to peruse or talk. Old men on ancient chairs watch over the sidewalk merchandise and keep an eye out for friends, for the children, for the drug pushers. On the corners, clusters of men jive good-naturedly for hours while women head briskly to the subway for Manhattan or stroll in and out of the shops. Speakers outside the record shops blare gospel or jazz or calypso, including the popular dance form known as *soca*—soul calypso. At every subway entrance, on every spare wall, the signs tell of gospel shows, *soca* concerts, dances, the great and small tempos of a flourishing black community.

Professor Mackey and the other regulars sometimes sat and talked for hours behind the steamy windows, warmed by Ethelyn Smith's coffee and soothed by the soft wail of jazz drifting from the radio. The radio was usually tuned to WBGO, a Newark jazz outlet, but on special occasions it was switched to WLIB, a Manhattan station whose talk-show format made it a good source of ideas and information about black goings-on. And for those who had not caught up on the day's news before coming in, Mrs. Smith put out copies of *The New York Times*, the *Daily News*, the *New York Post*, and, on Wednesdays, *The City Sun*, a weekly published in Brooklyn for a black readership in the New York metropolitan area.

Professor Mackey often led the seminars. At sixty-seven, he was not the oldest, but he was like an elder statesman with awesome knowledge and penetrating insights. He had been a professor for over twenty years and still taught literature, history, and black affairs at Empire State College in Manhattan and the College of New Rochelle. He also counseled young people four nights a week at Empire State. Years ago, he had been a professional photographer and in the early 1960s had been the proprietor of a bohemian coffeehouse in Greenwich Village where young poets, including LeRoi Jones, later known as Amiri Baraka, read from works. It was at the coffeehouse, Les Deux Mégots (the two cigar butts), that Mackey first began holding informal seminars. He called it "speak out night," and customers held forth on McCarthyism, the FBI, radioactive fallout, the civil rights struggles in the South, and other issues of the day. Mackey was a chess player, a frustrated poet, a lover of European classical music. He took long walks through Brooklyn's black neighborhoods, where he picked up news and stopped to chat, and he often found himself in demand, like a grizzled village *griot*, among people who wanted his wisdom to settle disputes and points of debate. His hair had gone gray, but he was an imposing six-footer: a man of power with a caustic wit.

Hampton Rookard provided vivid counterpoint: a sixty-year-old man bedecked with red, black, and green liberation beads, with neck chains and bracelets, with rows of rings across the knuckles and a headband of cowrie shells circumnavigating the spiked gray dreadlocks. His radical appearance said something about his beliefs, but not everything. And he resisted attempts to stereotype him politically. "I've been a lot of things," he told them. "I was with Malcolm. I was with the Panthers. I was with the Revolutionary Army Movement. I've been in jail behind the political scene a number of times."

Bill Bradfield was another of the old-timers. He, too, was sixty. They called him the Squire of St. Mark's Avenue, and in an allusion to independence rather than indolence, Mackey liked to say that Bradfield was "the only black man you've ever seen that's never held a colored person's job."

Sterling Johnson had the distinction of being the first black man ever to become a motorman on New York City's BMT subway system; he also had the distinction of being the father of Sterling Johnson, Jr., New York City's special prosecutor for narcotics cases. With just a bit of prompting, Johnson would tell of one of his first days as a motorman. As his train pulled into a subway station, he recalled, a startled little white boy tugged at his mother's arm and shouted: "Look, Mama, a nigger stole the train."

Oswald Cumberbatch—"a classic Belgian name!" Mackey would

exclaim—had been one of the first blacks hired as a railroad clerk in the New York City subway system.

Wayne Chinnery, a lawyer in his thirties who had migrated to New York years ago from the Virgin Islands, provided legal interpretations whenever they were needed.

Roy Canton, a forty-five-year-old custodial engineer in the city school system, was also from the Virgin Islands. He was a new member of the group, Rookard's protégé and Chinnery's cousin. In two decades in the United States, he had undergone a metamorphosis concerning whites and, especially, white police officers. Once he had risked his life to save a white officer from a black mob; but he had seen too much white contempt for blacks, and after the police mistook his brother for a robbery suspect and shot at him, he no longer trusted whites or the law.

Every day at Edgar's Food Shop, the shifting cast of regulars met for hours, and the "anything black" agenda produced spirited discussions that sometimes drew other customers into the circle, especially when the erudite Professor Mackey was there. After ten o'clock each morning, when the rush of breakfast was over, Ethelyn Smith would take off her apron, pour a cup of coffee, and join the gang.

The topics were legion—the death of Chicago's first black mayor, Harold Washington; the violence in Haiti and the drought in Ethiopia; the reelection of Wilson Goode as mayor of Philadelphia; the drumbeat for a black district attorney in the Bronx and a black chancellor for New York City's troubled schools. There was much talk, too, of Mayor Koch's legal battle with a homeless black woman who insisted the city had no right to take her off the streets and put her in a mental ward.

But more than anything these days, they talked about the Howard Beach case. It had been the racial outrage of the decade in New York. A year earlier, several black men passing through the white neighborhood near Kennedy Airport had been attacked by a white mob, and one of the blacks had been chased to his death on a highway. Several white youths had been accused of homicide and other crimes, and their trial was now under way in neighboring Queens. (Three were later convicted of manslaughter and lesser offenses.) The case dominated the conversations at Edgar's now. Hampton Rookard and Roy Canton were even attending the trial every day and reporting back.

Rookard had badgered Canton into going.

"Even if you can't put in but twenty minutes, show your face, show your body," Rookard had urged him.

So, usually on his lunch hour and often double-parking, Roy Canton joined Rookard and scores of other black people who made the daily pilgrimage to the Queens County Courthouse to see the white boys who had killed Michael Griffith, to see how the white criminal justice system would find a way to let them go free.

Every morning, Rookard and Canton reported to Edgar's, telling what they had seen, comparing their observations with the accounts in the white newspapers. Later in the day, when they got there, Chinnery offered legal interpretations and Professor Mackey gave the historical perspective.

Why were white people the way they were? Rookard's explanation was the most blunt: "Caucasians are programmed to be pillagers, murderers, cheaters," he insisted. "This comes with their mother's milk."

Closing time at Edgar's was around three P.M., but they would be back tomorrow.

Part One

THE GIRL IN THE GARBAGE BAG

1
___

It was fickle chance, the mere turn of her head, that provided a witness, that changed everything about the sordid affair. The little drama out on the lawn might have come to nothing. But at the critical moment, Joyce Lloray glanced out the sliding-glass doors at the rear of her apartment and saw the black girl.

Intrigued, she switched off the whining vacuum cleaner and stared out across the broad expanse of leaf-strewn lawn that was the common yard for scores of residents at the Pavillion Condominiums.

It was so strange. The girl, perhaps a teenager, was crouching like a burglar or a child in hiding under an air conditioner at the rear of a building across the way. She seemed dirty, her hair was disheveled, and her clothes were in tatters. Lloray's husband, Lorenzo, had just come home for lunch and she called him to the window.

As they watched, the crouching girl glanced around furtively, as if to see whether anyone was observing her. She was holding a big green plastic garbage bag. Suddenly, she spread the bag open and climbed in, pulling it up so that just the top of her head was sticking out. Then she hopped twice, moving along the edge of the building until she was near the rear sliding-glass doors of a vacant apartment, where she toppled headlong onto the wet, mushy ground and lay there, still as death.

The Llorays watched her for a few minutes, but there was no

more movement. Alarmed, Joyce Lloray called the Dutchess County Sheriff's Department, and Lorenzo Lloray put on an overcoat and went out for a better look. On the way, he met a neighbor, Gary Lanza, and together they walked toward the figure in the bag. Joyce Lloray put on a coat and followed them.

It was chilly that day, but autumn was resplendent in the hills above the Hudson: a painter's dream of earth tones and tangled woods and small-town serenity beside the flowing river. The afternoon sun, a pale disk in a pale sky, cast its light across the stubbly fields and crimson-gray woodlands, across the Town of Wappinger and the fading lawns of the Pavillion Condominiums. They had to step carefully because the wet grass was strewn with dog droppings. The remnants of forgotten summer littered the lawn as well: a charcoal grill, an infant's rusting playpen, a broken tricycle.

There was no one around but the girl in the distance. It was too cold for children to be out playing. Teenagers were off to the malls, and many residents were busy with Saturday housework, watching football games on television, or shopping in Wappingers Falls or nearby Poughkeepsie. A quiet mood enveloped the setting. A line of trees to the west swayed gently in the wind like dancers. A lone car passed on a road, tires singing on the pavement. In a field, a squadron of birds shot into the air and beat away toward the river.

They approached cautiously, as if something sinister lurked in the unmoving form on the ground, as if she might spring up and attack them. She was curled in a fetal position, and they could see only her head sticking out of the green plastic bag; even that was partly hidden under a black turban of some kind. Her eyes were closed. She seemed unconscious.

Then, close up, it hit them: a powerful odor of excrement rising from the bag. They looked at one another, puzzled.

"Hello? Hello?" Joyce Lloray called softly.

There was no response.

It occurred to Lorenzo Lloray that the girl might be hurt, that the plastic bag might conceal some terrifying sight. With the police on the way, they decided not to touch the girl or the bag.

It was Gary Lanza who noticed the beads of sweat on the girl's face. Strange, he thought: it was quite cold out. It occurred to him that she must have just come outside from some warm interior.

While they waited for the police, a blue-gray Lincoln Continental that had been parked for half an hour in front of the vacant apartment slowly pulled away, unnoticed, and drove out of the Pavillion complex.

Behind the wheel was a heavyset black woman with thick arms, strong hands, and an uncompromising demeanor. She had the experienced eyes of a woman who has seen too much trouble, heard too many excuses. She looked much older than thirty-two: her face was creased with poverty, missed opportunities, and a mother's hard tenderness. She had an infant boy and a teenaged girl, and she lived with a man whose past had been tainted by guns, drugs, violence, and even a killing. She herself had a criminal record for welfare fraud and had taken and given vicious beatings. Her name was Glenda Brawley.

Two weeks earlier, she and her family had been evicted from 19A Carnaby Drive at the Pavillion for failing to pay the rent. They had moved to a larger apartment in Wappingers Falls. To anyone who wondered what she was doing at her old apartment this Saturday, Glenda Brawley had a ready explanation: she had come back to pick up unforwarded mail and to see if her daughter, who had been missing for four days, was there.

But after parking out front, she had not taken the mail from the hallway box. Instead, she had gone straight into the apartment, for which she still had a key. The place was vacant except for the soiled beige carpet and the memories. You could remove the furniture, the china, and the cheap pictures, but the angry fights and the gentle affections stayed behind like grit on the wall. The apartment was not quite as she had left it. The refrigerator was humming and there was some clothing lying around, including a pair of white boots that did not belong to anyone in her family. And the place was like a steam bath. She had opened the windows to let out the heat.

The rear windows looked out on the lawn where the neighbors were clustered around the girl in the bag, just a few feet away. Glenda Brawley had not joined them, however. Instead, she had hurried in the opposite direction, out the front door, and had sat in the car pretending to read a letter while she pondered the complex situation.

Abruptly the flashing light of a police car in the distance caught her eye. She started the engine and pulled away. For days, she had been worrying about her headstrong teenaged daughter, who had run away several times before. But now, as she drove into Wappingers Falls, her nagging concerns deepened. Perhaps it was time to file a missing person's report: after what had just happened, it might look peculiar if she didn't go to the damn cops.

Deputy Sheriff Eric Thurston arrived in a white patrol car, its siren wailing at no one, its flashing red dome light lurid against the woods. He didn't know where to go at first. The complex sprawled over ten acres and had eighteen identical two-story buildings that looked more like army barracks than country condominiums.

Thurston finally found the right place and walked over to the little cluster of people. The girl on the ground was still curled up in the plastic bag. Her eyes were closed, but she was breathing softly. He, too, noted the strong smell of excrement.

He stooped down and peeked into the bag, but did not try to remove it. There were no obvious injuries, no grotesque gunshot wounds or protruding bones, no splotches of blood. He wondered if the girl was conscious.

"Hello," he said. "Hello."

She did not reply. But a strange thing happened. The girl opened her eyes momentarily, then quickly closed them.

The deputy tried once more.

"Hello? Hello?"

The girl again opened and shut her eyes.

Thurston looked up at the little circle of neighbors. Did they know who she was?

They shrugged.

Did they know what had happened to her?

They shook their heads.

Did anyone have any idea how she had come to be here?

The Llorays said they had spotted her about one-thirty and had watched her crawl into the plastic bag and flop over onto the ground. But they knew nothing else.

Thurston didn't know what to make of it. A cold west wind whipped around them, feathering the grass and hurling dead leaves between the legs of a charcoal grill. The girl on the ground shivered suddenly. The deputy reached down and pulled the plastic covering back over her. He was beginning to get an uneasy feeling. He decided to radio for an ambulance.

The Wappingers Falls police headquarters, a rustic old log cabin on the village green, might have been a set for Smokey the Bear or the home of some reclusive mountain trapper, with little wisps of smoke curling out a chimney into the overhanging pines. Officer Paul Lysko was on duty when Glenda Brawley walked in.

There was no urgency in her manner. As if reporting a minor traffic accident, she told him calmly that her daughter, fifteen-year-old Tawana Brawley, had been missing for four days, since Tuesday.

"Since Tuesday?" he asked.

Perhaps it was Monday, five days ago, that the girl had disappeared, Glenda said. She was not sure. In any case, some acquaintances thought they had seen her across the river in Newburgh early in the week.

Why, the officer wondered, had she waited so long to report this?

Glenda Brawley said she worked nights at the IBM plant in East Fishkill and did not have a car to come to the police station. (It was less than the truth. She apparently had not been at work all week and her family had three cars. Besides, she could have telephoned and had a police car at her door, or she might have walked over. The police station was only seven blocks away and it was open around the clock.)

The officer did not press the matter. He scribbled a few notes and recorded the time and date: 2:02 P.M., November 28.

Glenda Brawley gave him her daughter's photograph and a description of the clothes she was wearing the day she disappeared—a denim skirt, a black top, black shoes, and a gold chain. She told him that the girl had run away before.

The implication was clear: the mother was not very worried and perhaps the police should not be either. It seemed she only wanted to get her report on the record.

"She's over there," Deputy Thurston told the ambulance crew, and they hurried onto the lawn with their medical bags.

The girl was still lying on her right side in a fetal curl and not moving. They could smell the feces, and the first thing they did was cut away the plastic bag to have a look at her.

She was a lanky, light-skinned black teenager with a narrow face, delicate features, and slender, youthful limbs. Excrement was smeared on her arms and legs. It was in her hair and on her feet, and it encrusted much of her clothing too. Her acid-washed jeans had been burned away in the crotch, in the seat, and along the inner thighs. No underclothing was apparent, and she was wearing no socks and only one pink slip-on shoe. Some lettering had been scrawled with charcoal or felt-tipped pen on her torn and dirty pink blouse, and letters had been carved into the side of her shoe, but the sense of the lettering escaped them. Another blouse, a black one, was wrapped around her head like a turban, and a corner of it was clamped between her teeth.

The paramedic, Sharon Brantingham, checked her vital signs

and found nothing unusual beyond a slightly irregular pulse. She removed the black wrap to inspect the girl's head, but when she tried to pull the end of it from her teeth she met resistance.

Was the girl conscious? Brantingham and Raymond Strohm, a medical technician for the Sloper-Willen Ambulance Service, exchanged a puzzled glance. Brantingham rubbed the girl's breastbone, a painful test that causes most conscious patients to show discomfort, but the girl did not seem to react. Strohm wafted ammonia under her nose. Again there was no response. But they now noticed another strange thing: wads of cottonlike material had been stuffed into the girl's nostrils and ears. Her failure to react to the ammonia did not necessarily mean she was unconscious. And there were other bizarre signs: when they tried to open the girl's eyes and straighten her legs, she resisted. She seemed to be responding from some netherworld.

They brought a stretcher from the ambulance. As Brantingham reached under to turn her over, another weird thing happened. The girl grabbed her hand with a firm grip—so tightly that the paramedic could not free herself. They got her onto the stretcher anyway, and on the way to the ambulance Brantingham wrenched her hand free.

In the ambulance, they cut open her blouse and jeans and found that the excrement was caked inside as well as outside her clothing. Her legs were red too. This and the scorched jeans suggested she might have been burned, and they radioed the Sheriff's Department to ask that a deputy be sent to meet them at St. Francis Hospital in Poughkeepsie.

Before setting out, they tried again to straighten her legs. Again, she resisted. But when they jabbed a needle in her arm to give her fluids to counteract shock and a medication to counteract a possible drug overdose, there was no reaction. The signs were so confusing. The vein holding the needle collapsed and some fluid ran under the skin, which swelled up. Brantingham saw this and removed the needle. The rest of the trip to St. Francis was uneventful.

They rolled her into the emergency room on the ambulance

stretcher. The rest of her clothing was cut away, and as they lifted her onto a bed, the remnants of the clothing fell to the floor. So did her shoe, the one with the lettering cut in the side. Brantingham kicked the clothing and the shoe under the bed.

The girl seemed to relax abruptly. They rolled her onto her back without difficulty and the fetal curl vanished. The legs they had been unable to straighten out moments ago now extended easily.

Just before they covered her with a sheet, Brantingham noticed there was something scrawled on her chest. But it was obscure, half hidden by the fecal matter caking her torso, and the paramedics left before learning what the writing was.

They admitted the girl as "Jane Doe, address unknown."

The girl's eyes were still closed, but Nurse Kathleen Hickman found no signs of injury, exposure, dehydration, or undernourishment. She inserted a new intravenous needle and the girl reacted with a jerk to the pain. Tests showed no alcohol or drugs in her system. Blood samples were taken, but they could not get a urine sample. The girl urinated twice in the bed, though there was no apparent reason for incontinence.

To prepare her for a doctor's exam, the nurses began cleaning the feces off her chest. That's when they discovered the writing. It was on her chest and torso in block letters, written with a black substance like charcoal or a felt-tipped pen. One of the slurs was misspelled and some were only fragments of words: "KKK," "NIGG," "ETE SHI," "NIGGER," and "BITCH."

The startled nurses immediately stopped cleaning her and called the Dutchess County Sheriff's Department. It was the department's third call of the day about this girl.

At the Pavillion Condominiums, Deputy Eric Thurston had been joined by a stout, shambling sheriff's detective, Carl Amburgey. They walked the grounds, trying to learn who the girl was and what had happened. Their searches were cursory: a look about the lawn, a walk in the woods, a bit of poking in a garbage container. It was hard to say what such a search might yield, a shoe or a purse, perhaps, a thing that meant nothing at the start, but that might have enormous significance later.

It had begun to look as if they would find nothing. But when they went back to the spot where the girl had been found, several clues turned up. Under the plastic bag that had encased her, they found a pair of black leather gloves smeared with excrement, several pieces of burned cloth, and a piece of gray material like the wads found in the girl's nostrils and ears. They put it all into evidence bags.

They began questioning neighbors and quickly got a lead. A black couple, Ralph King and Glenda Brawley, and their children, a teenaged girl and an infant boy, had recently moved out of 19A Carnaby Drive, the apartment closest to the spot where the girl had been found. At the management office, they learned that the King-Brawley family had rented the place for a year and been evicted.

The manager gave them a key, but when they returned they found the front and back doors and all the windows unlocked and partly open, as if someone had been airing the place out. Even so, it was extremely hot inside. An electric baseboard heater, turned on high, had been tipped over and was burning the rug, giving off a foul smell. There were other signs of life in the deserted apartment. In the cold refrigerator, they found a nearly empty carton of milk. There was a cracker on the floor, and some burned material like denim was scattered all over the living room rug. They also found a wad of gray cottonlike material and singe marks on the carpet. A pair of white boots turned up in a closet; one boot had been cut and some of its gray cottonlike insulation had been removed. They bagged all these items.

After a last look around, they locked the doors and windows, but they found it impossible to lock one window. Its latch had been broken, so that anyone could go in or out anytime. They drew no conclusions except the obvious ones—that someone had been camped in this vacant apartment and that the interloper had just left, apparently in a hurry.

Aware that the police were on the way, Dr. Alice Pena, the emergency room physician, did not touch the excrement or the racial slurs, which might be evidence. But she went ahead with a general physical exam and neurological and pelvic observations.

She detected no injuries other than a small bruise on the back of the girl's head and the swelling in the left forearm where the IV had blown. There was no need for X rays. There were no burns; the redness on her legs had been due to the cold. The head bruise was the size of a quarter, but it was not tender and looked at least several days old.

Throughout the exam, the girl lay quietly on the bed with her eyes closed, showing no reaction to the voices or activity around her. But when Dr. Pena tried to open her eyes, the girl resisted.

The doctor immediately suspected she was faking.

Dr. Pena removed the gray wads from the girl's ears and nostrils and discarded them, not realizing they might be important. Dr. Pena then ran an ammonia inhalant under her nose.

The girl immediately opened and closed her eyes.

Suspecting she was fully awake, Dr. Pena tried another test. She lifted the girl's arm directly over her face and let it fall. The test is nearly always foolproof: if a person is unconscious, the arm will strike the face. But the arm did not strike the girl's face.

"I know you can hear me," Dr. Pena said sharply, "so open your eyes!"

Her eyes opened, blinking into the bright light.

Quickly reinforcing this success, Dr. Pena told her to follow the moving finger with her eyes—up, down, across, around in a circle.

She did so.

To see how well she could move, the doctor had her wiggle her fingers and hands, lift her arms and legs, sit up and lean forward, lie back and push herself down on the bed.

She did all these things easily.

Whatever had happened to her, the girl was not seriously hurt and had not been unconscious, the doctor concluded. Later, Dr. Pena had her put her feet into stirrups for an examination of the vaginal, rectal, and pelvic areas. The examination revealed no cuts, dried blood, bruises, swelling, deep redness, or other indications of injury. There were no signs of trauma to the mouth or throat either. Indeed, the girl's teeth were surprisingly clean and her mouth did not even have a bad odor.

Dr. Pena decided to forego the use of a rape-detection kit, at least for a while. There weren't enough signs to warrant it, and she wanted to talk to the police before proceeding.

For a sleepy Saturday, the Dutchess County Sheriff's Department came to life with surprising speed. Detective George Brazzale was first to reach the hospital; he was a fire-arson specialist and had been called because of reports that the girl might have been burned. Soon he was joined by Detectives Paul Lahey and Jerry Schmidt and their commander, Lieutenant James J. Thompson.

Brazzale took nine photographs of the girl with a 35-millimeter camera. These showed her partly disrobed, with remnants of dried feces on her upper body and in her hair and racial slurs on her chest and torso. Lahey also took photos, but these were Polaroid shots of her face; they were sent to Detective Amburgey at the Pavillion to show to neighbors who might identify the girl.

Nurse Katheryne Ryan, taking over for Nurse Hickman, found the girl subdued but awake and still caked with fecal matter. She decided to do something about it, to make the girl more comfortable. Laboriously, she began washing her. She removed most of the fecal matter, except what was tangled in her hair and the pubic-perineal region, where it had dried and was hard to get out. Some of the charcoallike substance that had been used to write on the girl's body was also washed down the drain, but the racial slurs themselves were not obliterated.

There was no immediate interview with the girl. Brazzale did not even try to talk to her. And when Thompson and Schmidt approached her for information, she did not respond. The detectives got busy anyway. As often happens, they began collecting evidence even before it was clear that a crime had been committed. They found the girl's clothing under the emergency room bed, and they swept the surrounding floor for hairs and fibers. On the pink blouse, they found "KKK" and "NIGGER" written in block letters with a substance like that used on her body. And on the girl's shoe, they found "NIGGER" carved into the instep; the lettering was sharp and slender, as if cut in with a razor blade.

There was no mystery about the meaning of these things. Howard Beach and other episodes of racial violence were fresh in their minds, and it seemed certain that some federal civil rights laws had been violated. They called the Federal Bureau of Investigation. Much of the evidence gathered at the hospital—the girl's clothing, the fibers and hairs, the results of medical tests—was sent to FBI labs in Washington.

But for all their eagerness, the investigators missed some important clues. The wads from the girl's ears and nostrils were not recovered from the wastebasket where Dr. Pena had discarded them. Nor did anyone think to save flecks of the substance used to write on the girl's chest and the feces smeared on her body, though samples of both were recovered from the pink blouse.

Glenda Brawley drove south, dutifully spreading the word of her daughter's disappearance. For days, she had stayed home while her companion, Ralph King, and her sister, Juanita Brawley, had searched the streets of Newburgh, Wappingers Falls, and Poughkeepsie for the missing girl. Now, Glenda Brawley had suddenly taken up the quest.

She sped along the slate-gray Hudson and across the Beacon Bridge into Newburgh and was immediately swallowed up in a tangle of streets ruled by crack peddlers, prostitutes, and children with guns. The danger was palpable. Some twenty-eight thousand people lived here, and a large percentage of them were hostages of poverty, living among criminals and addicts. Hopeless eyes watched Glenda Brawley from the shattered tenements. Crack wraiths slept in the darkened doorways or drifted like ghosts along streets that surrendered at nightfall to drugs and violence. A few blocks from the river, she found the police department, a two-story brick fortress that stood in the squalor like a relic of civilization in the jungle.

Inside the station, Glenda Brawley spoke to the desk officer, Ben Coleman, who sat behind a shield of bulletproof glass that protected him from the murderous rabble.

The woman was as cool as she had been at the station in Wappingers Falls, and her message was the same: her daughter had been missing from Wappingers Falls for four days. Friends had last seen her Tuesday in Newburgh, near South and Liberty Streets, one of the toughest corners in town.

The officer heard her out, but did not bother to write up a missing person's report. Glenda's sister, Juanita, had tried twice in recent days to file such a report at this station, but had been turned away both times. It was the bureaucratic mind at work: Wappingers Falls was another world, and Newburgh had problems of its own. But Coleman did take notes and accepted a snapshot of the girl. It showed a lanky, light-skinned girl with a narrow face and delicate features.

There was an unfeigned fatherliness about Detective Carl Amburgey. The white hair, the paunch under the sport coat, the unhurried gait, the plain words in a slow drawl, all spoke of a careful, patient man hard to fool. He was a good listener: it encouraged others to speak, to give information, to reveal themselves. He went doggedly from door to door at the Pavillion, asking about the girl in the Polaroid pictures. It didn't take long: a neighbor, Deborah Daniels, recognized her.

Her name was Tawana Brawley.

Daniels said the girl's family had recently moved into Wappingers Falls. Her own daughter, Dinha, a high school friend of Tawana's, had the new address and telephone number. Amburgey called.

Glenda Brawley was talking on the phone to her sister, Juanita, when she heard a beep, indicating another call.

Amburgey knew little about the case and did not want to alarm her, so he said vaguely that her daughter had a problem and was at St. Francis Hospital.

Glenda did not sound perturbed.

Would it be all right if he stopped at her apartment to show her a photo of the girl for positive identification?

Of course, she said.

After Amburgey hung up, Glenda resumed the conversation with Juanita and passed on the news that Tawana had been found. Juanita, a counselor at a state home for troubled juveniles in nearby Kingston, had helped raise Tawana from infancy and was in many ways closer to the girl than her mother. Juanita had fretted over Tawana throughout her disappearance and was greatly relieved. She immediately set out for St. Francis Hospital to be with her niece. But Glenda stayed home, awaiting the police.

As evening fell, Amburgey and Thurston found the Leewood Arms Condominiums, a red-brick, garden-apartment complex at the south end of the village. The place had the forlorn look of an out-of-the-way motel, with rows of doors and cars nosed up out front. They knocked at 4-D Carmine Drive.

Glenda Brawley let them in. She was alone with a sniffling, coughing infant. They sat around an octagonal coffee table amid a jumble of boxes half unpacked from the family's move.

The detective showed her three Polaroid pictures.

"Is this your daughter?" Amburgey asked.

She confirmed it.

They talked awhile, about the girl, about where and when she had been found and how she had been taken to St. Francis. Amburgey asked a few questions—the girl's age, birth date, parentage, and school. He wanted to know where and when the family had last seen her and whether she had had any problems lately.

Glenda said Tawana had skipped school Tuesday and had not been home since. Amburgey knew nothing about the girl's medical condition or the condition in which she had been found. But Glenda did not press for any details. To Amburgey, she seemed oddly incurious.

Amburgey and Thurston offered to take her to the hospital, but she declined. She said she had to stay home with her little boy, who had a cold.

As the sheriff's men got up to go, the telephone rang.

Glenda Brawley answered it. Juanita was on the line from St. Francis Hospital, and Glenda listened to her briefly. Then, as the officers watched, Glenda Brawley's impassive face hardened into a mask of anguish, and she shrieked.

2

It's just a short walk through town, a dozen blocks from Wappinger Lake at the north end to the schools on the south, where the homes of Wappingers Falls give way to the playing fields and woods. On an autumn day at midafternoon you can see the yellow school buses at the corners, red lights winking, traffic backing up, children with backpacks dashing up the sidewalks tossing Nerf balls, shouting after one another, heading home with yapping dogs at their heels.

Wappingers Falls is a quiet place where the descendants of Italian and Irish immigrants work hard and raise families, live their lives, and die without much notice from the outside world. Great oaks and elms and maples arch over the slumbering streets and modest homes, some in need of paint or repair. The village green, with its gazebo and benches, is free of litter. If there are no particularly affluent neighborhoods, no rows of doctors' homes or lawyers' offices, no colony of artists, there are no slums either.

Up on Main Street, you can stop in at Miller's Upholstery, where there might be a half-price sale on fabric. Sal's Music Center is an inviting place: it's possible to arrange piano or organ lessons, and there's a layaway plan for Christmas gifts like a guitar or a horn. Sal Ditrocchio's wife, Barbara, sometimes helps out behind the counter, and her little baby, Jennifer, is likely to be playing on the floor. She represents the third generation here: Sal's father owned the store before him.

Shubert's Auto Parts down the block is already a third-generation place. Farther on are Tommy's Barber Shop and O'Toole's Bar and Grill. Just inside the Plaza Pharmacy, there's an old-fashioned glass globe that will eject a big colored gumball for twenty-five cents. There are apartments in the old red-brick building above the coffee shop (a good place for a snack; hours are seven A.M. to three P.M.). Howard Walker's insurance office is over there, and All Country Kitchens has a white picket fence out front. A lot of the businesses in town are in homes: the doctors' and dentists' offices, the Roberts & Straub Funeral Home, even Pinky's Construction Company. Main Street boasts a community theater as well; a favorite production is *Hello Dolly!*

Village Court is over on East Main Street. It handles only traffic violations and other misdemeanors. The accused sit on folding chairs while Raymond C. Chase, Jr., the justice of the peace, ponders the evidence under an American flag and a village banner with a green and black embroidery of the falls; it was donated by the Rotary Club.

The heart of the village, though, is Mesier Park, a green surrounded by the statelier Victorian homes, with brass plaques proclaiming the year they were built. Outside the police station on the green is another plaque, We Honor Those Who Honor Us, naming the men of the village who died in World War I.

Across the way, a sign outside the United Methodist Church tells of a roast beef dinner Saturday: Home Style Cooking. Donation: $6 adults, $2.50 children. And around the corner is the public library, with a bin under an old-fashioned cast-iron lamppost for leaving books at night. Inside you find a homey warmth— plants in the windows, carpets of soft reds and browns, leather armchairs in a cozy corner, and a children's reading room upstairs, where someone has put up framed copies of "The Star-Spangled Banner" and the Emancipation Proclamation.

It is—almost absurdly—a vision out of Norman Rockwell or Thornton Wilder, a town where teenagers sip sodas in a drugstore with a zinc-topped fountain, where sleds course down hillsides in snowy winters and shouts rise from a swimming hole in hot leafy summers.

The name "Wappingers" was taken from a local Indian tribe. A tributary called Wappinger Creek meanders down from the Berkshire Mountains to Dutchess County, and after a swift plunge at the north end of town and a winding sojourn through the village, it empties into the Hudson about a mile farther south.

Most of the early settlers in Wappingers Falls, Dutch men and women who started arriving about forty years before the American Revolution, made their living in mills along the creek, cutting wood and weaving textiles. Their successors did much the same for two centuries. The mills are gone now, some of them renovated as homes, but most of the adults in the village call themselves blue-collar. They are factory workers and shopkeepers, people who drive trucks or pump gas or sell clothing or insurance and patronize the local Irish bars and Italian restaurants. For fellowship they favor the Elks Club or the Ladies' Auxiliary of the Veterans of Foreign Wars. They parade proudly on the Fourth of July. Although religious and politically conservative, for the most part, they are not, as Reverend Michael Webber, the pastor of Zion Episcopal Church, likes to observe, "on the fringe."

The values of small-town America run deep in Wappingers Falls. There is among the townspeople a gratitude to fate that they live fifty miles north of the glitter and chaos of New York City. What they care about cannot be found on the front pages or the lurid evening news programs: homes and families, a Saturday night party down the block, Sunday morning in church, and back to work on Monday.

They are the kind of people who mail in contributions for the upkeep of the Statue of Liberty, the kind of people who are truly shocked by a crime or a scandal. Walking through town, you might see three men sitting on a porch drinking beer in the afternoon. They wear boots and plaid lumberjack shirts and baseball caps that sport ads for tractors. If you ask them to recall the last murder in town, they'll tell you it was a half-dozen years ago around Halloween: happened outside a bar; two men who knew each other got in a fight and one stabbed the other to death. They all have to think hard to remember the last one before that. It was at least seventeen years ago, one fellow thinks, but none of them can recall any of the details.

People in Wappingers Falls go about their business quietly and securely, and the sense of peace seems to them as real, as timeless, as the aroma of damp soil and decaying leaves. On any afternoon in this pretty village in upstate New York, the terrible problems of America—its racism and brutal crime, its betrayals of trust—seem little more than faraway echoes, like drums on a distant battlefield.

Dutchess County lies on the east bank of the Hudson River between the suburban sprawl of Westchester and Putnam counties and the vast open tracts that march toward Albany and Canada. The county has just over a quarter million residents, all but fifteen thousand of them white. A land of rolling hills, of apple orchards and industries, it is prosperous without being rich, a county of Roosevelts and rednecks and a great middle class in between who are mindful of a distinguished Revolutionary-era history, but eager, almost always, for the manifestations of progress. The biggest employer in the county is IBM, with twenty-five thousand jobholders; only a third as many people work for the other major employers, the government-run prisons, state hospitals, and homes for the disabled and retarded. The unemployment rate in Dutchess County in 1987 was only two percent, the lowest in the state; the average family income, a healthy forty-two thousand dollars.

Poughkeepsie, best known as the home of Vassar College, is the hub and county seat. Most of the county's blacks live there. They are disproportionately poor and jobless, and few occupy positions of influence in the county; fewer still have positions of power. Of the county government's forty-three top administrators in 1987, only two were black, and there was only one black in the thirty-five-member county legislature. Blacks were vastly underrepresented in every police agency, corporate management, school faculty, and civil hierarchy in the county; not a single black held a job in the county's fire, recreation, or parks departments. The district attorney had only two blacks on his staff of nineteen prosecutors, and there was only one black among ten full-time lawyers in the public defender's office, which counseled poor defendants in criminal cases. None of the county judges was black, and there was only one black justice of the peace in the local townships.

The semirural Town of Wappinger, with twenty-thousand people, is just south of Poughkeepsie. Once pastureland with dairy herds, it is now dotted with boxy apartments like the Pavillion Condominiums and the kind of split-level, ranch-style houses that can be found anywhere in the country. Route 9, a broad and busy state highway that cuts through the township, is a garish mecca of shopping malls and fast-food restaurants, discount outlets and service stations. It, too, might be anywhere in America. In the northwest corner of the township, sheltered from its heavy traffic, is the older Village of Wappingers Falls.

Wappingers Falls has never had many blacks. Including Tawana Brawley and her family, they numbered only about a hundred of the village's 5,300 residents. The first black man in the village, in the late eighteenth century, was a slave called Black Tom. He belonged to the man whose log home, built on five acres in what became the village green, was now the police headquarters where Glenda Brawley reported her daughter missing. Perhaps because blacks had always lived in town—or had lived there in such small, nonthreatening numbers—or perhaps because its settlers had themselves fled from intolerance, Wappingers Falls has no documented legacy of overt ethnic hatred or sustained racism.

In 1928, according to a local story, a near riot erupted when a Ku Klux Klan chapter in the Hudson Valley tried to stage a parade through Wappingers Falls to celebrate the defeat of Al Smith, the first Roman Catholic candidate for president. People in Wappingers Falls were said to have pelted the marchers with tomatoes. But if there has been no gross mistreatment of blacks, bigotry has always been an undercurrent in the life of the village. Local human-rights officials will point out that, over the decades, many whites either have been ignorant or have chosen to be ignorant of the snubs and insults blacks suffer daily in the stores, on the streets, and in their dealings with the police.

"Used to be a time when you couldn't get out of your car around here if you were black," recalls Frank McCray, an elderly black man who has owned a gas station on the edge of town for twenty-six years. "Things haven't changed much here. There are still some stone racists carrying some deep hatred. There are white people who still can't face the fact that I own this place."

Carlos Rosewhite, a generation younger than McCray and one of the few black corrections officers in Dutchess County, traces his ancestry in Wappingers Falls back more than a century and a half. Rosewhite's grandfather was one of two village policemen in the nineteen-twenties and was a member of the volunteer fire department, a mark of social distinction in communities along the Hudson. His father was a 33rd Degree Mason and, like his mother, who was superintendent of a church Sunday school, became a leader in local civic organizations. But the Rosewhites' long and rich association with Wappingers Falls has not precluded incidents of racism against them. As a boy, Carlos Rosewhite was occasionally beaten by white youths on the school bus; his sister, Sheila, was the target of stone throwers. Both remember being ejected from the Wappingers Hotel one Halloween night in the nineteen-fifties while out trick-or-treating.

More recently, a black woman named Elaine F. Disnuke, who had moved to Wappingers Falls in 1970 and operated a telephone answering service in her home, complained that she was the brunt of crank calls, bomb threats, obscene messages, and many other racial harassments. But authorities disputed most of her claims about being a victim of racism and suggested that her dwarfism might have been a factor. The authorities proved that she had even fabricated some of her complaints, and she pleaded guilty in village court to two counts of disorderly conduct for filing false reports with the police. "This is not Alabama in the sixties," said Lieutenant William J. McCord, the Wappingers Falls police chief.

It wasn't Alabama, but in the autumn of 1987 there was plenty of cause for concern over racism in the Hudson Valley. There was talk about physical, even sexual, abuse of blacks by white police officers and others, and there were hints of Klan activity. In a few towns, it was rumored that white night riders prowled the streets in cars looking for blacks to terrorize. In letters to local newspapers, in comments on radio talk shows, in interviews, Hudson Valley whites often portrayed blacks as lazy ne'er-do-wells, if not drug dealers and criminals. And that view was reinforced by the predominance of blacks as inmates in municipal and county jails and in the eleven state prisons clustered in the region.

If educated, well-dressed, middle-class blacks in Dutchess and neighboring counties experienced racism only in its subtler forms, the poorer blacks in the area had a litany of complaints, ranging from job discrimination to rent gouging, from being patronized by white social workers to being eyed with suspicion by white store clerks. Many of these wounds, real or perceived, were nursed in private or aired mainly in the security of black churches and clubs. The official forums remained all but closed to blacks. In 1984, Sherwood Thompson, the only black ever to sit on the Dutchess County legislature, managed to push through a bill establishing a county human rights commission. But its only powers were advisory, and it took the legislature three more years to allot money for a director and a secretary.

What really aroused the region's civil rights movement from dormancy was the death of a twenty-year-old black man, Jimmy Lee Bruce, Jr., in Orange County, directly across the Hudson from Dutchess County. Bruce was choked to death on December 13, 1986, outside a movie theater in the Town of Wallkill in a scuffle with two white off-duty police officers who were moonlighting as guards at the theater. Before the fatal scuffle, Bruce and several friends had caused a commotion in the theater.

Many blacks in the Hudson Valley were soon comparing Bruce's death to the more widely publicized incident later that month in

Howard Beach, Queens, in New York City, where a black man, Michael Griffith, was run down on a highway trying to escape from a mob of bat-wielding white youths. To Hudson Valley blacks, the death of Jimmy Lee Bruce was outrageously consistent, as well, with incidents in New York City that had cost the lives of Michael Stewart and Eleanor Bumpurs. Stewart, a young black artist and model from Brooklyn who had done nothing but scrawl graffiti on a Manhattan subway wall, had died in a coma on September 28, 1983, of injuries inflicted by six transit police officers who, in what they said was necessary force to subdue Stewart, hog-tied and handcuffed him and forced a nightstick down on his neck as he lay on a step. Needless to say, the officers had been acquitted of any wrongdoing in his death. Eleanor Bumpurs, a sixty-six-year-old black woman with medical and emotional problems, had been killed by two point-blank shotgun blasts fired by a white policeman, one of six officers who went to her apartment on October 29, 1984, to evict her for failing to pay the rent. The police said Bumpurs had lunged at them with a knife; of course, the officer who fired the shotgun was acquitted of all charges.

A grand jury's refusal in March 1987 to indict the officers who had choked Jimmy Lee Bruce had spawned protest rallies, marches, and a host of fruitless appeals to Governor Mario M. Cuomo and state Attorney General Robert Abrams. It was not until late 1987 that the governor asked the State Investigation Commission to review the case, and not until much later that the commission found flaws in the prosecutor's presentation to the grand jury and Cuomo appointed a special state prosecutor. (In October 1989, a second grand jury refused to indict the officers or bring any criminal charges in Bruce's death.) As the case festered throughout 1987, the Jimmy Lee Bruce Justice Committee had been formed, the Poughkeepsie chapter of the NAACP resurrected, and the Dutchess County Committee Against Racism established. The ordinary black people of the Hudson Valley were more than ready to voice their outrage when, in November 1987, three white men brandishing bats and pipes tried to attack a black Peekskill man named Alphonso Smith.

And they were ready again, later that month, when a black teenaged girl from Wappingers Falls was found in a garbage bag, smeared with excrement and racial slurs.

Life began with profound disadvantages for Tawana Vicenia Brawley on December 15, 1971, in Seat Pleasant, Maryland, where her teenaged mother was a high school student. Tawana's father, Robert Knox, was from Statesville, North Carolina. He and Glenda Brawley were unmarried and not willing to form a family. Like the children of countless unwed mothers, Tawana from infancy was drawn into the vortex of dependency and instability that characterizes single-parent families in the United States. Her mother was sixteen and unprepared for motherhood. From the time of Tawana's birth, Robert Knox had little involvement in her life. Indeed, it was not until many years later, when she became a teenager and she visited him occasionally in the summer, that the girl got to know her father.

Glenda Brawley had been born into a working-class family on March 7, 1955, the youngest of seven children of Leon and Bertha Brawley, of Statesville. Her father was a carpenter and upholsterer, and her mother, who worked in a textile factory, died in a car accident in 1968. After her death, Leon Brawley moved his family to Seat Pleasant, in Prince Georges County, near Washington, D.C. Glenda was still living at home when she became pregnant in 1971. She had to quit school, and her father helped make the arrangements for the child's birth. He also supported Glenda and the baby and gave them a home.

They called the baby "Bird" and the nickname stuck. "When she was born she had this gorgeous little patch of hair right on the top, and the rest of her head was bald," Juanita Brawley would recall. "So a friend of Glenda's, Clara Dawson, started calling her Tweetie Bird. And that's what everybody in the family started calling her—Bird."

Glenda struggled for six months to raise the child in her father's home. But the cumulative effects of financial strains, isolation, and the inability of a teenager to cope with the demands of an infant soon doomed the effort. So Glenda, in June 1972, took her six-month-old daughter north to Monticello, New York, a resort village in the Catskill Mountains. There she moved in with her older sister and Juanita's husband, Matthew Strong, a policeman in the village. In the years before Tawana's birth, Glenda had often spent summers with the Strongs in Monticello. She was close to Juanita and made herself useful by baby-sitting the couple's son, Shean. Now, however, her arrival made a household of six, for Juanita and Matthew Strong had a new baby of their own, a girl named Kenya, in addition to Shean, who was now fourteen.

"She was my little sister," Juanita said of Glenda. "I loved her and she had this ol' funny-looking girl with her patch of red hair. It was great because I was in New York by myself. To have my sister here and her little girl was fine."

Glenda began attending school in Monticello and over the next few years earned her high school diploma while her older sister helped care for her infant daughter. Many of the demands of motherhood that should have fallen to Glenda during this period were thrust upon Juanita, who willingly accepted them. Still, Glenda felt guilty. "I could not work because of the baby," she would recall years later for *The City Sun*. "But I wanted to work to take the load off Juanita. Tawana was growing up and she needed a few things. I went on welfare."

When Tawana was three years old, Glenda enrolled as a part-time student at Sullivan County Community College, taking a liberal arts program as a prerequisite to nursing. "I made the dean's list," she told *The City Sun*. "I made the honor roll several times. I was going to college part-time and taking care of my daughter." But caring for the child and keeping up with her schoolwork proved to be too much. She decided to separate herself from her baby. Glenda moved to another apartment in

Monticello and for the next few years left Tawana in the care of her sister and brother-in-law. In 1977, when Tawana was five, Glenda left Monticello, moving to Poughkeepsie, where she rented a room and transferred her credits to Dutchess County Community College.

"When I went to Poughkeepsie, I had to find a place to stay and all that, so Tawana stayed with Nit," Glenda said, referring to Juanita by the family nickname.

"She was doing well," Juanita recalled. "I just told her, 'You have to try to make a life for yourself.' But I said, 'You're not taking the baby yet.' I had gotten so attached to Tawana."

Juanita Brawley was older than Glenda by seven years and was far more capable of nurturing Tawana. Though more emotional, Juanita was tougher, more mature, a woman without illusions, and she had an earthy kindness and sensitivity toward children. By temperament and experience she was well equipped to raise another child along with her own.

Her husband, Matthew Strong, was a large, soft-spoken, easygoing man, gentle to the point of passivity. There was about him also a quiet, upright sturdiness that inspired confidence. His duties as a police officer made him a well-known figure in Monticello, but he was more than a police officer to most of his neighbors; he was a respected black man in a predominantly white community.

The Strongs' home, a pleasant two-story house with a patch of lawn and a narrow porch on Garden Drive in Monticello, wrapped Tawana in a warm, stable environment. Tawana and Kenya, who was only a few months younger, hit it off from the start, and they grew up more like sisters than cousins, sharing clothes and the attentions of parents who cared about them and conscientiously guided their passage through the tender years. Tawana came to think of her surrogate parents as real parents. She called Juanita "Nita-Mom" and Matthew Strong "Daddy." On a wall of the foyer, a succession of photographs of Tawana and Kenya, growing up together, began to appear.

By 1978, Glenda had moved to an apartment at the Charles Street public housing project in Poughkeepsie. She also had a job in a day-care center and was learning a lot about children and their needs. She soon regarded her situation as stable enough to have another try at motherhood. She sent for Tawana, who was now nearly seven years old. It was difficult for the girl to leave the Strongs. She had never known any other home, and now she had to enter second grade in a new town among children who were strangers—and live with a mother she hardly knew. But she was an adaptable child, and over the next five years she remained with Glenda and performed well at school. She is remembered as a bright, quick, and friendly pupil, who liked singing in the chorus and playing games, particularly basketball, on the playgrounds. She also got to know the man upstairs, a man named Ralph King.

As Tawana grew, so did Glenda's expenses. She found it hard to make ends meet. In 1980, though working, she applied for and accepted $1,775 in welfare payments intended for nonworking single parents. She was caught, taken to court, and convicted of fraud. She was not jailed, but got five years' probation, and she was made to pay back the money. By 1983, with poverty again closing in, and finding it increasingly difficult to cope with the child's emotional needs, Glenda gladly accepted an offer by her sister and Matthew Strong to once again take Tawana into their household. Tawana, now eleven, was happy to go.

With Glenda's blessing, Juanita and Matthew Strong now adopted their niece, becoming her legal as well as spiritual guardians. For the next two years, she lived in Monticello, attended junior high school with Kenya, and found love and stability in the home of her aunt and uncle. Tawana flowered in their custody. She grew into a tall, gregarious, pretty girl with a pug nose and large, hazel eyes. She also learned to dance and acquired a flirtatious way with boys.

Only one untoward incident occurred in her two years in Monticello. It happened on a spring night in 1985, when her mother happened to be in town. Tawana, thirteen at the time, slipped out to a pizza parlor and met a fifteen-year-old boy she had been sweet on for several months. According to the boy, she told him she didn't want to go home and asked if she could go home with him.

"She knew she was supposed to go home, but she didn't want to go," the boy recalled.

They went to his grandmother's apartment and watched television.

"I asked her what time she was going home," he said, "and she kept saying, 'Soon.' "

But the youngsters fell asleep on the floor, and the next morning they were awakened by pounding on the door. Glenda and Juanita Brawley had arrived and were hunting for her.

Tawana was panic-stricken.

"Don't tell them I'm here," she said, and hid in a closet.

As the women barged in, cursing the boy and demanding to know where Tawana was, the girl emerged from the closet and ran out the front door, pursued by her mother and aunt. Her mother tried to hit her, but Juanita intervened to calm ruffled feelings. While the indications were that Tawana had not wanted to see her mother, Juanita later made light of the incident, calling it more a night of childish escapade than teenage intrigue.

"She was a real tomboy," Juanita recalled. "She loved sports—basketball, track, soccer—and she used to climb trees all the time. She liked the outdoors and she loved animals." Tawana kept several pets, a dog and caged birds, and in the evenings she did her homework, played records and games with Kenya, and sometimes went to the movies or watched television. Tawana's favorite program was *The Cosby Show*, starring Bill Cosby. The NBC hit revolved around an upper-middle-class black family, with a father who was an obstetrician, a mother who was a lawyer, and articulate children who filled their New York City brownstone home with laughter and a steady stream of friends. To Tawana, it was an idealized picture of what life could be like for blacks in America: all it took was courage, a good sense of humor, a will to succeed, and wonderful, loving parents.

Tawana was about to start the ninth grade at Monticello High School in the autumn of 1985 when the wrenching summons came. She would not be going to Monticello High with Kenya after all. She would have to leave her wonderful, loving surrogate family and move back with her mother—and the man from upstairs, Ralph King.

3

"They cut my baby's hair!" Glenda Brawley shrieked. "They cut my baby's hair!"

Detective Carl Amburgey was amazed. She had been so calm. Glenda quickly left for St. Francis Hospital.

It was well past dark when she arrived in Poughkeepsie and located the emergency room. Juanita Brawley was waiting for her, and the sisters fell into a brief conversation. Moments later, as they were about to go in to see Tawana, one of the sheriff's investigators spotted them.

"You people—wait over there," he said brusquely, motioning to a reception area for visitors.

It was, at best, grossly insensitive. The investigator had not asked the women who they were or why they were there. But from their point of view, it was worse—a bald expression of racism by a white officer contemptuous of black people who had come to the hospital, for all anyone knew, to find a child who might be seriously injured. The incident left the Brawleys bitterly angry.

The investigator walked away, and Glenda and Juanita, ignoring him, went in to see Tawana.

They found her in bed, apparently asleep. Earlier, the nurses and doctors had seen her awake and sitting up. She had taken some ice cream and milk, had moved her arms and legs easily and had given no signs of pain or other difficulty. Now as her mother and aunt stood at her side, she lay back, covered with a sheet, only her head above the drift, her eyes closed and the excrement-matted hair flattened on the pillow. It was the condition of her hair, which seemed considerably shorter than it had been before her disappearance, that had shocked Juanita and been passed on, with hysterical effect, to Glenda.

Softly, Glenda and Juanita called her name until she slowly opened her eyes. She looked at her mother, but said nothing.

Then Glenda pulled the sheet back from the girl's shoulders.

"Look at this!" Juanita gasped, pointing at the letters "KKK" written in black across the top of the girl's breasts, and "NIG-GER" written on her stomach.

Juanita, grasping the bedclothes, pulled them down farther and checked Tawana's vaginal area. Then she quickly examined the girl's back, arms, legs, and feet. Nurses had washed away most of the fecal matter hours earlier, and Tawana's appearance now was not the excrement-smeared spectacle that hospital personnel and the police had seen.

Still, the racial slurs and the flecks of feces were visible, and they were the main source of Juanita Brawley's initial concern. Tawana, submitting quietly to inspection by her mother and aunt, said nothing.

While Glenda and Juanita Brawley waited and worried, two white detectives entered the room—back for a second time to interview the silent girl. Ignoring the women, they passed a white curtain partway around Tawana's bed, apparently to get some privacy, and then tried to talk to her.

"Tawana, you're not still mad at me," one detective said. It could have been merely a bit of playful coaxing, a reference to the girl's previous unresponsiveness. But Tawana seemed suddenly agitated. Glenda did not react, but Juanita was downright shocked. To her, the remark suggested an inexplicable familiarity, even a relationship between the detective and the girl.

Glenda and Juanita Brawley insisted that a black officer be brought in to interview Tawana.

But wanting a black officer was one thing; finding one in Dutchess County was another.

The framed letter from Ronald Reagan seems to shine of its own light on the wall of the Dutchess County sheriff's office in Poughkeepsie.

"Yours has been a career marked by achievement," the 1985 letter from the President proclaims. "You have given so much of yourself over the years to protect the lives of those who live in your community."

Another letter, tacked up beside the first, is even more effusive.

"The name of Frederick Scoralick has been synonymous with ability, leadership and dedication," it trumpets over the signature of United States Senator Alfonse M. D'Amato of New York. "Under your sagacious leadership, the Dutchess County Sheriff's Department has been admired by comparable departments throughout the country."

Frederick A. Scoralick was as proud of these letters—given for loyal GOP campaign work—as if they were the testaments of close friends in high places. It was perhaps an understandable vanity in a man of humble beginnings and limited education and accomplishment.

Born and raised on a farm near Poughkeepsie, the son of a German father and an Irish mother, Fred Scoralick had won a college scholarship through 4-H activities, but did not attend college because his parents needed him to work the dairy herd. He stayed on the farm until he married in 1960. A year later, at the age of twenty-six, he became a part-time deputy sheriff. It was a job he liked: it gave him authority and the freedom to roam the county roads, nabbing speeders and an occasional thief. He was a part-time deputy for fifteen years, and he also worked for a small construction company until 1976, when he was appointed under-sheriff, a reward for loyal service under the longtime sheriff, his friend Lawrence Quinlan. In 1978, when Quinlan got embroiled in a legal problem, Scoralick beat nine Republicans for the sheriff's nomination and then easily defeated a Democrat for the post.

By 1987, after nearly a decade under Scoralick, the department was handling thirty thousand cases a year, ranging from noise complaints to murder, in a county growing rapidly as a center of life in the Hudson Valley, a couple of hours' drive north of New York City. To most whites, who made up the vast majority of the county's 256,000 residents, Scoralick was a tough, capable man worthy of reelection. But to most of the county's blacks, whose growing numbers still made up only six percent of the population, the sheriff's name was anathema and there was a deep mistrust of his deputies and the county jail under his jurisdiction. Critics cited numerous complaints by black inmates of brutality by white guards at the jail and insensitive and abusive treatment of black residents by white deputies. Many black community leaders regarded the entire law-enforcement apparatus in the county as suspect and charged that Scoralick's department was riddled with racism.

"Institutional, traditional racism permeates the whole county," declared Clarence McGill, a retired urban-renewal specialist who was chairman of the Dutchess County Committee Against Racism, a group of thirty blacks and whites who had come together to support Jesse Jackson's presidential campaign. "It's significant that there are no blacks on his staff. He's a loser. He has failed the people of this county."

It was not quite true that Scoralick had no blacks on his staff. The Sheriff's Department employed four hundred people—two hundred in the jail, one hundred fifty as deputies and detectives, and the rest as maintenance workers, clerks, and support staff. There was not a single full-time black on the sheriff's staff, although there were four black part-time deputies.

"Color don't mean a thing to me," Scoralick said, relaxing at his desk under the letters from Reagan and D'Amato. The fifty-two-year-old sheriff denied that his department excluded blacks from its ranks or mistreated black residents or inmates of the jail; he said he would not tolerate such conduct. There were no full-time blacks on his staff, he said, because they did not apply or score high enough on civil service exams to qualify for the jobs. Yes, he did recall dismissing a black corrections officer after the man was caught twice asleep on the job: "I gave him a second chance. He was caught twice. I don't pay people to sleep." And he wanted it noted that he had personally hired the four black part-timers: "They do an excellent job. They are well-dressed, clean-cut gentlemen."

The Sheriff's Department was hardly alone in its hiring patterns. Among nine police agencies in Dutchess County, only two had full-time black officers: the State Police, with twenty-six blacks among 167 troopers in the county, and the Poughkeepsie Police Department, with seven blacks on a force of seventy-eight.

So when the call went out for a black police officer to respond to St. Francis Hospital that night, the authorities discovered that there was only one on duty in all of Dutchess County.

Officer Thomas Young, a tall, slender man, stepped out of the patrol car with an amused smile that seemed to say: "Okay, folks, here I am."

Glenda and Juanita Brawley were waiting for him. They immediately took him aside and told him that Tawana was terrified of the two white detectives who had been assigned to the case. They said they wanted him to interview the girl.

Officer Young had been on the Poughkeepsie force for twelve years, but he had no extensive experience interviewing witnesses or victims of crimes. He was a street cop who wore a uniform and rode in a patrol car and who sometimes answered calls for help and arrested punks in the housing projects where he grew up. Now, because he was black, he was being asked to do a job that required skills and training he didn't have. But he was willing to try.

They took him into Tawana's room and shut the door. Only the girl, her mother, and her aunt were present. The girl was awake, but her eyes had a glazed faraway look, as if she were in a daze.

When Young started asking questions he discovered that she could not, or would not, talk. She communicated, when she answered at all, by nodding or shaking her head, by shrugging her shoulder or scrawling in his notebook.

Things went wrong immediately.

Young asked her what had happened, and she did not respond. Thus, it was not first established whether a crime had been committed and, if so, what it might be. Instead, the officer made an elaborate series of assumptions that she had endured some kind of an ordeal.

"Can you say who did it?" he asked.

In answer, the girl grabbed the silver police badge on his uniform jacket.

Puzzled, he asked what she meant.

She did not respond.

He asked if she had seen a badge like his. Again, she didn't answer. But when he offered her his notebook and pen, she wrote: "White cop."

Now, seeing these words, Juanita Brawley flew into hysterics and Young told an orderly to escort her out of the room until she calmed down. Glenda remained by the bedside, taking it all in.

Resuming his interview, Officer Young asked Tawana if she meant that a white cop had done something to her.

She nodded. It was like a guessing game: when he got it right, she'd reward him with a nod.

Still nothing had been established about what had happened to the girl. Instead, the officer referred to the unknown event as "it" and asked where "it" had happened.

"Woods," she wrote.

Young asked where the woods were located.

There was no response.

It now occurred to Young that he had not established what it was that had happened to the girl. He asked if she had been raped.

"A lot," she wrote.

Young, zeroing in again, asked who had done it.

She drew an arrow toward the words "white cop." Then, as an afterthought, she wrote "first"—seemingly indicating that a white police officer had been the first of a series of men who had raped her.

"Can you give me any description?" Young asked.

She stared off into space.

"Was the person black?"

She did not respond.

"Was the person white?"

She nodded yes.

"Was there one person?"

She did not respond.

"Were there two?"

She did not respond.

"Were there three?"

The girl nodded.

"Was the person's clothing dark?"

She nodded.

"Was the person's clothing black?"

She nodded.

Officer Young, who was thirty-two, then asked if the assailant's age was about the same as his.

She nodded.

Assuming that the girl had been abducted in a vehicle, Officer Young asked: "Was the person's vehicle light or dark?"

She wrote, "Dark."

"Do you know the person who was driving?"

The girl wrote, "No."

He then asked if the men had called one another by any names or had said anything that might help to identify any of them.

For the first time since she had been found at the Pavillion, Tawana Brawley spoke. In a faint voice, she said one word: "Son."

"Did someone call the white cop 'son'?"

She shook her head no.

"Did the white cop call someone else 'son'?"

She nodded.

Young paused. A nurse had come in with some medication for Tawana. They broke off for a short while, and Young left the room. He returned then, and the interview resumed briefly.

"Were they as tall as me?" asked Officer Young, who was six feet four inches tall.

She nodded.

"Was he thin?"

She nodded.

Finally, he asked the color of the assailant's hair.

The girl pointed to the nurse in the room, who had strawberry blond or reddish-brown hair.

That ended the interview.

In many ways, it was unsatisfactory. It had lasted twenty minutes and elicited only one spoken word from the girl. It had begun with the easy assumptions that the girl had been abducted and sexually attacked and proceeded in no logical sequence. While interrogators usually try not to lead a witness, both to elicit more information and to minimize the effects of their own biases, Young's questions had been extremely leading, and the answers he got back had been vague or obviously suggested by the appearance of people in the room. Thus, one assailant had the same hair color as the nurse and was the same height and age as the officer, and also had a badge like his. An experienced black detective, not a street officer, should have been drafted for the interrogation, even if one had to be brought from a distance.

From the start, investigators who reviewed Officer Young's interview with the girl were suspicious of it. But they could hardly discard it. It was almost all they had to go on, and the potential explosiveness of the case, with its sensational sexual and racial overtones, made it imperative to get facts and move quickly. Because of the racial slurs and excrement on Tawana's body, it was natural to assume that something terrible had happened to her. In her responses to the black officer, however, the white investigators saw only a tale full of gaping holes and doubts.

But to Juanita Brawley, whose bond to Tawana was the result of years of surrogate motherhood, there were no troubling doubts, no confusion except that in the minds of the unsympathetic white investigators. Juanita had not yet spoken to Tawana at the hospital and was not even aware of all that had been said in the interview with Young, who had put her out of the room. But to her, the girl's reaction to the white detectives had been spontaneous and pure. To her, Young's interview had been a conscientious effort by a black man to get at the truth, and Tawana's responses— limited by the trauma she must have endured—were a model of clarity: the shocking revelations had been there in every gesture of the shaking hand, every nuance of the frightened eye and the trembling lip.

To Juanita Brawley, heinous crimes had been committed against her beloved niece, and the white cops seemed to be involved all the way—first as kidnappers and assailants in a four-day spree of abduction and gang rape, now as actors in an outrageous plot to conceal the crimes. It was any woman's worst nightmare: rape and sexual humiliation, here in the hands of redneck deputies, and with a lynching of justice as well. But, Juanita Brawley vowed, they weren't going to get away with it this time.

Ralph King seemed drunk when he arrived at the hospital shortly before nine P.M. King was Glenda's companion and the nominal head of the Brawley household. Detectives Brazzale and Schmidt and Officer Young all smelled alcohol on his breath, and as they watched, King slurred his words and moved through the corridors with an unsteady gait.

Juanita Brawley took him to one side. She filled him in on what she knew, telling him that Tawana had written "white cop" when asked who had attacked her. She voiced her suspicion that the white officers at the hospital were attempting a cover-up.

King flew into a rage.

"Don't talk to those white fucking cops," he yelled. "They're not going to help us. We're going to hire a lawyer and get all those cops in court and make them tell us what they know."

Stalking through the hospital, glaring at the officers around him, he shouted: "Cops, you're not going to do this. You jammed up my daughter before. You're not going to cover it up. I'm not an ignorant nigger. I will call the lawyer."

But for all its unseemly appearance, his rage was legitimate. He believed that the girl he called his stepdaughter had been violated and that white police officers were responsible. Now, unaware that Tawana had been interviewed by Young, King approached a white detective and demanded that a black officer be brought to the hospital.

The detective told him a black officer had already interviewed his daughter. He was somewhat pacified, but continued to shout up and down the hallways.

All evening, Dr. Alice Pena had had doubts about administering the rape kit, a standard protocol consisting of a physical exam, questions, and the taking of body samples for analysis by the authorities. Her exam in the afternoon had found no signs of rape, no bleeding, injuries, or obvious trauma. Nor had the girl said anything to her about being raped. Tawana was resting now and the doctor saw no need for the test.

But the investigators were worried. The racial slurs and excrement, the tattered and scorched clothing, Tawana's dazed look, all suggested something bad had happened. If they ignored these signs and failed to insist on medical tests to show whether the girl had been sexually attacked, they would lay themselves open to allegations of incompetence or worse.

It often happens that officers and doctors find themselves at odds over how to proceed in a delicate case. A patient's medical welfare is not an investigator's primary interest; nor is evidence uppermost in the minds of doctors. Compromises are forged by the circumstances, and so it happened in Tawana Brawley's case. After the girl had indicated to Officer Young that she had been attacked by several men in a woods, Dr. Pena relented. She began performing the rape-kit protocol more than six hours after the girl's arrival at the hospital, a time lapse that troubled the family.

Dr. Pena started by asking questions. The girl, reposing on a bed with the sheet drawn up to her chin, did not answer questions orally. Instead, in another exchange that proved sketchy at best, she nodded yes or shook her head no or shrugged her shoulders. The latter gesture was sometimes ambiguous, indicating either uncertainty or perhaps a negative response.

"I understand you said you were assaulted?" the doctor said.

Tawana nodded.

"Was this by three men?"

She nodded.

"Were they white men?"

Again, she nodded.

"Were there more?"

She shrugged her shoulders.

"Did they hit you?"

The girl pointed to an area of her scalp behind her left ear, where the doctor had earlier found a small bruise that had not appeared to be fresh or tender to the touch.

"Does anything hurt?"

Again, she pointed to the bruise.

The doctor asked if the girl had been grabbed, pushed, twisted, or hurt anywhere else.

The girl shrugged, indicating what Dr. Pena took to be a negative answer.

Dr. Pena asked if anal sex had occurred.

The girl shrugged and shook her head from side to side.

Dr. Pena asked if oral sex had occurred.

The girl nodded yes.

The doctor then asked if the girl had voluntarily engaged in vaginal sexual relations in the last seventy-two hours.

She shook her head no.

Finally, Dr. Pena asked if involuntary vaginal sex had occurred.

The response was ambiguous. The girl shook her head in a sort of half 'no' and at the same time shrugged her shoulders. At the end of the questions, it was only clear that Tawana had not indicated, clearly and directly—as she had for Officer Young—that she had been raped.

The physical exam by Dr. Pena, repeating some earlier observations, showed no bruises, lacerations, tenderness, or blood in the vaginal or rectal areas. There also were no signs of trauma to the mouth or back of the throat.

Next, the doctor took wipings and cultures from the girl's vagina. These were immediately examined microscopically for the presence of sperm, but none was detected. Pubic hair was combed for any materials trapped in it. None were found. Pubic hair was pulled. Vaginal swabs and smears were taken and placed on slides. Similar swabs and smears were taken from the rectal area and placed on slides. Swabs of the mouth were also put on slides, a saliva sample was taken and a sample of a white substance found in the girl's mouth was taken and cultured. The girl's fingernails were clipped and saved, along with the material embedded in the nails. Hair was pulled from different areas on her head. And finally, blood samples were drawn.

When the rape-kit protocol was completed, the written results and the collected slides, swabs, and other materials were all sealed in a package by Nurse Ryan, who turned it over to Detective Brazzale. He put the package in a refrigerator at the sheriff's office until it could be sent to the FBI labs in Washington for detailed analysis.

Dr. Pena sat at a desk to write her report for the hospital records. Under the heading of diagnosis, she wrote: "Possible sexual assault." But thinking about it, she had her doubts. She believed that the girl had endured some severe emotional trauma, but there was no sign that she had suffered physical injury. This was striking: how could Tawana Brawley have been abducted, raped, and subjected by racists to prolonged brutality without having been injured?

Perhaps only the girl could answer that, and so far she had said virtually nothing.

As Dr. Pena wrote out her report, Elizabeth Seton Grundy, a

staff social worker, went in and introduced herself to Tawana. Her approach was soft and kindly, full of sympathy for troubled souls, and it struck a responsive chord in the girl.

For the first time all day, Tawana began hesitantly to open up. She told Grundy that she was having trouble speaking because her throat hurt. She said she did not want to talk anymore to the police, but that she did not mind having a few words with the social worker.

She answered questions about her family, her school, and herself, nodding or speaking softly.

Finally, Tawana asked a question. She wondered if Thanksgiving had come yet. The touching question seemed to imply that her recent days had been a blur, that Thanksgiving, with its warm aura of family and feasting and love, had been spent in the clutches of savage men who had celebrated with rape and racial horrors.

Yes, Grundy said, Thanksgiving had passed two days ago.

When the social worker had gone, Glenda and Juanita Brawley asked that Tawana be kept in the hospital, at least overnight. But Dr. Pena and other staff members said they had found nothing to justify that. The paperwork was completed and Tawana was discharged at 10:15 P.M.

She did not walk to the car. At her family's request, she was rolled out in a wheelchair.

Juanita Brawley was incensed, and as she drove home to Kingston that night she resolved to sound the alarm. She called WCBS-TV in New York City, one of the most important news outlets in the East, and set the hook for coverage of a sensational racial story, explaining it in some detail. The station was interested not only because it sounded like a good story, but also because of its timing: the first trial in the Howard Beach case was under way, public awareness of racism was running high, and racial news was getting big play. It was also a long holiday weekend—little else was happening.

Juanita called the Brooklyn office of Alton H. Maddox, Jr., the black lawyer whose name she knew as the champion of the black victims in the Howard Beach case. She did not reach him. Finally, she called the FBI. She told an agent that Tawana had been abducted for four days and raped by local white police officers and that some of them were now engaged in a diabolical cover-up.

Glenda and Tawana Brawley drove home to Wappingers Falls with Ralph King. When they arrived at Carmine Drive, King carried Tawana into the apartment and Glenda gave her a bath, washing away the racial slurs and the last flecks of excrement.

What could not be washed away was the troublesome sense that things had gotten out of hand this afternoon and tonight—a mess that threatened to get worse with the fuss that Juanita, in her confounded kindly concern, was making.

4

Governor Mario M. Cuomo, in sneakers and sweat clothes, padded slowly down the drafty second-floor hallway between the ghastly paintings and the artifacts of New York industry and headed for his trappist's cell.

A lucid Sunday morning peace filled the Executive Mansion in Albany, and he paused at the railing to savor it. Autumn sunlight streamed through the windows, illuminating the ancient rugs and woodwork, animating the landscapes in the gilded frames, the old sewing machine, the products of sixty-two counties installed for the weekend visitors in the Family of New York Room.

Duty called him from the cell down the corridor, but he resisted like a servant luxuriating in his master's surroundings. The forty-room gingerbread mansion on Eagle Street, a nineteenth-century landmark, had once been home to Grover Cleveland, Theodore Roosevelt, Franklin Delano Roosevelt, Charles Evans Hughes, Alfred E. Smith, Thomas E. Dewey, W. Averell Harriman, and Nelson A. Rockefeller, all men who had won or waged serious campaigns for the White House. It was a great claptrap of a building where the staircases creaked and the heating system clanked like a ghost in the basement, where icicles collected under the eaves and curtains moved in a storm.

It was already midmorning, late for a man who often got up before dawn to begin the day's work. Today he had gone, as usual, to seven o'clock mass with his wife, Matilda, and after a cup of coffee had swapped the suit for sneakers and blue sweat clothes. Now he hurried on.

The small library-den on the second floor was his sanctuary. It was a sparsely furnished cell fit for a monk: a plain rolltop desk made by high school students, one chair, and books covering every inch of wall. There were two windows behind the chair, but the shades were always drawn against day, night, and the nosy. There was a telephone, but it almost never rang: his staff knew not to call here unless it was an emergency.

Cuomo loved the solitude and peace of this place on Sundays. It was more than a refuge from political battles and administrative duties, from the marble corridors and cold formalities of the capitol. It was a place to get things done. There were no reporters. No cameras. No staff assistants. Not even any household help. On days like this, after mass and coffee with Matilda, he retreated here to read, write, and ponder. There was always an enormous stack of paper to move. There were always problems of state, legislative conundrums, and moral issues to grapple with. And in the next few months, he would have to make the most important decision of his life: whether to run for the presidency of the United States.

The third child of Italian grocers from Salerno who settled in Queens, New York, Mario Cuomo liked to twit patrician dinner crowds with the apocryphal tale of how his father, too, had lost everything on Wall Street in the 1929 crash: a stockbroker had leaped from a window and crushed Andrea Cuomo's pushcart. Mario Cuomo had gone to St. John's University Law School and as an ambitious young lawyer displayed extraordinary skills as a conciliator, defusing some bitter community fights in Queens. These successes had propelled him up the road to Albany. He had won the governorship in 1982 and been easily reelected in 1986. As governor, he had won a reputation for sensitive political antennae and sharp debating skills, and many credited him with high principles for refusing to impose on others his church's abortion views—which he said he shared—and for rejecting demands for the death penalty as a solution to epidemic crime.

But behind the image was a cerebral, brooding, contradictory man, a spiritualist with a strong streak of vanity; a onetime minor league outfielder who lusted for victory but was flayed by conscience for wanting too much to win; a veteran of bruising political wars who worried about appearances like a thin-skinned alderman. He venerated the French Jesuit philosopher Pierre Teilhard de Chardin, the Catholic martyr Sir Thomas More, and Abraham Lincoln. Yet he sometimes roused reporters at dawn with calls of complaint over a phrase or a characterization that had kept him awake half the night. Then he was bothered by having been bothered. He was tormented by the guilt of a Roman Catholic upbringing. It troubled him that he spent so much time selling himself rather than learning and contemplating life's real problems. "What does God want of me?" he had written in his celebrated diary.

Politics was his living, but the law was his love. He had an almost mystical faith that the law would protect the innocent, punish the guilty, stifle tyranny. "The law is the law," he would say. "Stick to the damn law. It makes more sense than people." But he had to make a living too, and his was the classic dilemma of a liberal politician in a conservative era. It was most apparent in the abyss between his ambitious pronouncements and his modest social accomplishments. On political swings across the country, he was an eloquent champion of programs for the poor and for equal opportunity. But in Albany, he was a sparing administrator, presiding over a state with vast needs and limited resources, balancing budgets over choruses demanding welfare, jobs, school aid, police officers, and housing.

Cuomo embodied another contradiction as well: he was a very private man who longed for high office. He preferred his monk's cell and his wife's company to starlit banquets in Manhattan. When out of town, he took pains to fly back to Albany, even in bad weather, to spend the night at home. He had only two real political allies: Matilda and Andrew, his son. Now he was fifty-five, a great orator and a formidable campaigner who might be the runaway favorite for the Democratic presidential nomination in 1988. Democrats everywhere admired his rhetoric and remembered his keynote address to the last Democratic National Convention. They were impressed by his confidence, his appeals to reason, and his political savvy. And while the 1988 primaries were still months away, a lot of smart money was saying he would be hard to beat. But still he hesitated, agonizing over the imponderables.

For all his inspirational speeches about equality and justice, for all his popularity across the country, his liberal image had been tarnished by the series of racial episodes that included the deaths of Michael Stewart, Eleanor Bumpurs, and Jimmy Lee Bruce at the hands of the police, and the most notorious case of all, Howard Beach. Cuomo's appointment of a special prosecutor for Howard Beach, Charles (Joe) Hynes, had been a kind of defeat. He opposed the appointment of special prosecutors generally. He had appointed one in this case only under inflammatory pressure by the black lawyers Alton H. Maddox, Jr., and C. Vernon Mason, and the Reverend Al Sharpton, and by the decision of the black victims to withhold their cooperation, so that the Queens prosecutor could not complete an investigation. With national attention focused on Howard Beach, the state—and Cuomo as its leader—had for a time seemed impotent, unable to resolve the worst case of racism in years. The shock waves were still reverberating: the trial of the first group of white youths charged in the case was even now drawing to a close, and the whole thing was once again on television and the front pages.

Cuomo was reading at his rolltop desk when the telephone rang, an offense against humanity. He snatched up the receiver.

"Hello?"

It was Kurlander.

"Larry. What's up?"

Cuomo's eyes narrowed thoughtfully as the voice of his director of criminal justice services, Lawrence T. Kurlander, came up the wire. The voice was calm, but what he had to say was unnerving.

There had been a call from the sheriff down in Poughkeepsie, a guy named Scoralick. It was about a troubling case, a tale of abduction and rape over four days, told by a black teenaged girl with nods and shrugs and grunts. She had been found yesterday near a little Hudson Valley village called Wappingers Falls, south of Poughkeepsie.

Wappingers Falls. Cuomo knew it well. Thirty-five years earlier, he had worked there as a counselor at Camp IBG, run by the Italian Board of Guardians for wayward boys who liked to smoke cigarettes and gaze at the reflections in girls' black patent-leather shoes. It was a place where you could smell the cut grass of the infield and take the shock of a dive into icy waters, the home of Guy Kibbee's oldtime radio character Scattergood Baines, who dispensed homespun wisdom from a front-porch rocker.

But there was nothing nostalgic in what Kurlander had to say. It was downright gruesome. The girl had been smeared with excrement and daubed with racial slurs, "KKK" and "NIGGER," and somebody had apparently butchered her hair. What's more, she had hinted that white police officers had been in on it.

And, Kurlander went on, the reaction of the local authorities was bizarre, too: the sheriff was saying that as far as he could tell there had been no crime.

A rush of anger seized Cuomo. No crime? Who were they kidding? It almost sounded like a cover-up. But then, why would the sheriff have called Albany? It was very strange. Whatever happened, Cuomo immediately recognized that it had an enormous potential for trouble.

In the poisonous atmosphere left by Howard Beach and other racial cases, many blacks were willing to believe any black's account of abuse by whites; and no account by a white, especially by a white police officer or public official, could shake them. Indeed, the word of a black teenaged girl could be far more persuasive than the promises of the highest white official. Howard Beach had been a damaging blow to his prestige, and every new racial outrage rubbed the wound open again; he knew that most blacks in the state regarded the criminal justice system with suspicion, and he was the symbol of it all.

There was something else about this episode, something achingly personal for Cuomo: it was the memory of an attack on one of his daughters by a demented fiend who had burned her breast with a cigarette and fled. The man had never been caught.

"Look," he told Kurlander, "I don't know anything about this case, but you can't tell me"—he sounded exasperated—"she's covered with defecation, her hair is shorn, she has 'NIGGER' on her breast—you can't tell me she did it to herself unless you give me some exotic motive."

Kurlander agreed. What should they do about it?

Cuomo was still perplexed over the sheriff. "Is that right?" he persisted. "Is that what the guy said?"

"Yes," said Kurlander. "I checked it myself. That's what the man said."

The governor thought for a moment. Then he said: "You better get your tush down there."

5

On Sunday, the cars began to multiply like parasites outside the Brawley apartment on Carmine Drive. Relatives, reporters, a television crew, detectives, even a social worker joined the throng that crowded into the small, cramped rooms. By early afternoon, a circus atmosphere of hysteria and speculation had enveloped the place: the doorbell and telephone rang constantly; a crescendo of conversations filled the living room; television cameras and tape recorders whirred, strobes flashed, and tantalizing clues and theories floated up in the cigarette smoke.

At the center of it all, Tawana Brawley lay becalmed, face down on a tan sofa under a maroon blanket, her eyes shut against the cacophony, a brown teddy bear clutched in her slender arms. She seemed on the verge of tears, and all the wonders of adolescence, the enormous cunning, the defiant wit, the foolish pride, and unplumbed intellect, were gone. Innocence and vulnerability ruled the childlike face, an illusion enhanced by tiny earrings and a little gold necklace. Her mother sat alongside her like a Buddha, stroking her hair with a pudgy, comforting hand and watching over her with wary, protective eyes.

Juanita Brawley had gotten there early for a private chat with Glenda and Tawana. Tawana still seemed dazed. Then Elizabeth Grundy, the social worker from St. Francis Hospital, had arrived with her soothing voice and kind intentions for a friendly chat. Then Mary Murphy, a reporter for WCBS-TV in New York City, and her camera crew, and Jonathan Saltzman, a reporter for the *Poughkeepsie Journal*, along with a photographer. Finally, Detectives Carl Amburgey, Paul Piastro, and Christine Williams of the Dutchess County Sheriff's Department had arrived, hoping to clear up the mystery at last. Now they were all in discussions with Ralph King and Glenda and Juanita Brawley. Tawana's infant brother, Tyice, bawled into the din.

The crowd, the noise, and the heat made the apartment seem even smaller than it was. It was a five-room duplex with a living room, kitchen, and dining area downstairs and a couple of bedrooms tucked away upstairs. The clutter of boxes from the family's move was still visible. Things had not been put away, and the thin pasteboard partition walls needed decoration.

Everyone wanted to talk to Tawana, but she seemed wan, almost in a swoon, so they settled for the others, moving around the octagonal coffee table to put a question to Glenda, clustering around Juanita and Ralph King for little revelations. Juanita, who had made the calls that brought in the press, dropped some haunting clues: Tawana had seen a badge and a shoulder holster on one of the abductors.

Across the room, another knot of outsiders listened to King speculate on the identity of the assailants. "The Ku Klux Klan— there's no question who it is," he said, nodding sagely. "They sent a message to us."

Glenda's version was slightly different: "One was a white police officer who belongs to the KKK. It had to be somebody who showed her a badge to stop her because Tawana doesn't talk to too many strangers."

Amid the comings and goings, Juanita slipped away and telephoned Sharon Cherven, of the Kingston *Daily Freeman,* and confided: "We don't want her to talk too much to the local police because her attacker may be one of them. We want to let her talk to the media first, which she is willing to do because she wants to help others. She is still in shock and doesn't remember too much of what happened."

Out in the living room, Tawana was perking up, at least with

Elizabeth Grundy, to whom she spoke again of school, sports, and other harmless matters. Only once did she make any reference to the case: yes, she and her family believed that the police could not be trusted.

Finally the press turned to her—and she wasn't so self-contained. Now her heavy-lidded eyes brimmed with tears and her voice cracked with emotion—especially when Mary Murphy of WCBS-TV ordered the cameras turned on to capture an eloquence of wracking sobs and shaking shoulders and choked accusations.

Then, after the cameras stopped whirring, Tawana said that she did not want the interview shown on television. Elizabeth Grundy sided with her: a teenaged victim of a sex crime might have trouble coping with publicity. But Juanita firmly disagreed. The airing of the television report, she argued, would ensure that the police could not cover up for the guilty—this was the important thing. Tawana would just have to be strong. To this, the girl had no answer.

The detectives, when their turn came, expected no less cooperation than was given the press, although they were prepared for a difficult and delicate interview. Carl Amburgey was ready with a string of delicate questions, and Christine Williams was there in case the girl wanted to talk privately about intimate details. At the very least, they hoped to come away with a clearer picture of what had happened. But it was not to be: Tawana was too weak now.

And so Juanita, and to a lesser extent Glenda and Ralph King, did all the talking. As Tawana listened behind closed eyelashes, her staunch aunt gave an account that, she said, had been obtained from the girl herself, albeit in bits and pieces. It went like this:

On Tuesday, November 24, Tawana had skipped school and gone to Newburgh. It was not yet clear what she did there. But in the afternoon the girl had caught a Short Line intercity bus for home and gotten off between four and five P.M. on Route 9D near an Exxon station a mile south of Wappingers Falls. As Tawana started walking home, north along Route 9D, a dark-green "police-type" car had pulled up beside her. One of the two white men in the car got out and grabbed Tawana by the hair and pulled her into the car. When she started to scream for the police, the man said, "I am the police," and struck her on the back of the head. Then, Tawana had been driven to a wooded area, where four or five other white men were waiting. She was sexually abused, defecated and urinated on, and tortured for four days. The torments had included rape and sodomy. In a final act of degradation, the assailants had cut Tawana's hair, smeared excrement on her body, and written "NIGGER," "KKK," and other racial slurs across her chest.

And that was it. That, said Juanita, was all they knew. How had Tawana gotten herself to the Pavillion? Well, the girl had no idea. She simply couldn't remember.

Then it was Glenda's turn: On Wednesday, she began, the day after Tawana vanished, Trayon Kirby, a high school friend who sometimes drove her to school, had told the family that he had taken her to Newburgh on Tuesday to visit a friend. After hearing this, said Glenda, the family had spent the next few days searching the streets of Newburgh.

That's right, Juanita interrupted angrily. She had tried to file a missing person's report with the Newburgh police and been rebuffed—been told the report would have to be filed in Wappingers Falls and by a parent, not an aunt.

Everyone looked at Glenda Brawley and Ralph King: why had they not gone to the police?

Glenda did not repeat her fib about being unable to get to the police station because she had no car. That seemed silly now. But King volunteered an explanation: he did not trust the police. The Poughkeepsie police had harassed him in May. That was when he went to the station to get Tawana after a shoplifting incident in which she had been detained.

Through it all, Tawana lay silently on the couch, the teddy bear cuddled against her cheek, her eyes closed.

———

The truth is often what people say it is—especially if they say it on television. Nothing could have made this point more forcefully than the images that flickered across TV screens throughout the New York metropolitan region that night. For millions of viewers, the truth about what had happened to Tawana Brawley became what Mary Murphy's report for WCBS said it was—and a more sickening tale would be hard to imagine than the one told so graphically by the image of the limp black girl sobbing on a couch, while her grief-stricken family sat there hopelessly, painting a picture of abduction, gang rape, and humiliation by white racists in a small town. Making it even more memorable was the fact that the TV report identified Tawana Brawley by name, as Juanita had insisted, even though it was highly unusual for any news account to name the victim of a sexual assault.

It was certainly a far more detailed account than had been given to the authorities. Indeed, some of it had even come from Tawana, who, Mary Murphy solemnly averred, was "recovering from an ordeal of sexual torture and racial abuse," and who responded to the reporter's gentle prodding with, "He told me to shut up. . . . He was a cop. He showed me a badge." All straight into the camera.

Murphy quoted the family as saying that, yes, one of the assailants had worn a shoulder holster. The girl had been pushed into a dark unmarked car, taken into the woods, and surrounded by a gang of men who "raped and sodomized" her. To the contrary of what the doctors' examinations had revealed, and heedlessly in advance of any result from the laboratory, Murphy went on to say: "Medical evidence shows her vaginal area was bruised. Lab tests will confirm the degree of sexual assault."

The details got worse, nearly unbearable: "They called me 'nigger,' " Tawana said, barely audible through her sobs. In response to a question about the number of attackers, she mumbled, "A lot of men."

Then Juanita was on: "She had feces smeared all over her, in her hair. Her pants were burned. She was incoherent. I saw 'KKK' scrawled on her, on her chest right over her breast. Further down, it was 'NIGGER, NIGGER' written on her stomach."

Finally, Sheriff Frederick Scoralick's face suddenly appeared, Murphy's microphone under his nose. He immediately began casting doubt. Officer Thomas Young "couldn't make out heads or tails" of his interview with Tawana. And, "We don't know whether someone put her in the garbage bag she was found in or whether she got into the bag herself."

But it no longer mattered what the sheriff said—just as it no longer mattered that the Murphy report was full of holes and unfounded assertions. For what other "truth" could banish the you-are-there image of the sobbing face of a pretty black teenage girl with the catchy name of Tawana Brawley, a girl who had somehow lived to recount this nightmare?

At her home in Newburgh that night, Lillian Howard wrinkled her brow as the news of Tawana Brawley came on her TV screen. When it was over, she was outraged. She did not know Tawana or her family, but she was a spirited activist in the Newburgh chapter of the National Association for the Advancement of Colored People and she cared deeply about black people.

It was the second time in a week that Howard had been angered by a reported racial incident. On the previous Sunday, there had been a disturbance at the Orange County Jail at nearby Goshen. It had started when inmates refused to return to their cells for an eleven P.M. lock-in because, they said, excessive heat was being piped into their cellblock. What happened next was in dispute.

The authorities said the heat had been lowered but the inmates still refused to go into their cells. Instead, some had started a small blaze in waste paper, and twelve guards had entered and used a low-powered hose to put out the flames. The hose had also been turned on prisoners when some of them, wielding broomsticks, poked a guard. The prisoners had finally been put back in their cells with a minimum of force.

But the inmates had told a different story. Thirty white guards in riot gear, they said, had swarmed into the cellblock, swinging clubs and shouting racial slurs, blasting inmates with high-powered water hoses and driving them back with a snarling police dog. After the inmates had finally been locked in, a group of guards, including three who donned white sheets like members of the Ku Klux Klan, had entered the cells of nine black and Hispanic inmates, who were all shackled and beaten. The claim of a Klan assault had gained credence from a recent study by a Vassar professor on KKK activity at prisons in the region.

One of those injured had been Howard's twenty-three-year-old son, Timothy, who had been accused of attempted murder. (The charge was later dismissed.) He and eight other inmates had been charged with rioting in the fracas. Civil rights activists were now claiming that these allegations had been made to cover up the brutality of the guards.

A few days later, Lillian Howard had attended a hearing in the Orange County Court at Goshen on the riot charges. It happened that at the same courthouse that day, another hearing was being held in an unrelated case involving a group of radicals known as the New York Eight, who had been arrested in the county. An ally of the New York Eight, a firebrand from Brooklyn named Robert "Sonny" Carson, had met Lillian Howard in a corridor of the courthouse that day. They had talked about their respective cases, and Carson had told her of his plans for a protest in Newburgh over the New York Eight case. She, too, had been planning a protest, and they talked of joining forces. They also had exchanged telephone numbers.

So now, upon hearing the news of Tawana Brawley that Sunday night, Lillian Howard went to her phone. Sonny Carson was at his number, and he heard an earful: another black victim, another cover-up by white police.

Carson did more than share her anger. He asked her to go to the Brawley home in the morning—perhaps the family needed lawyers and advice. If so, he knew just the right man—the hero of the Howard Beach case, Alton Maddox.

———

Later, back home in Kingston that Sunday evening, Juanita Brawley made a few calls herself.

Having failed to reach Alton Maddox the night before, her first call now was to the Newburgh chapter of the NAACP. There was nothing surprising in Juanita's decision to turn to the organization for help. Many blacks in America would have done the same thing. The nation's best-known black civil rights group had been a source of help and assistance to blacks for nearly eight decades. And while it had become one of the more conservative organizations in the broad spectrum of civil rights activism in recent years, it was still an effective presence in many small towns, where the winds of change blew too gently for the more confrontational groups that thrived in the cities.

Juanita said she wanted a lawyer and was told that the chapter's president, B. Harold Ramsey, was a lawyer and a member of the Dutchess County Public Defender's Office. Juanita called him. The authorities would probably want to question the girl again tomorrow, she said, and the family needed guidance. Would he come to the Brawley home to talk about the case and observe any questioning of the girl?

Of course, said Ramsey, whose first name was Bolivar—"Bob" to his friends. He'd be glad to do it.

6

They sat at a table at Edgar's Food Shop and stared through the steam and cigarette smoke like hopeless men back from a lynching they had been unable to stop. The lunatic mob, the murdered men, the raped women: they had heard this horror story all their lives—in Birmingham and Jacksonville and Neshoba County, even here in Brooklyn. Still, the news of Tawana Brawley had robbed them of words.

"Oh no! Oh no!" Ethelyn Smith kept saying.

The Monday morning customers came and went, but the regulars sat and stared into the coffee cups.

The door opened and the roar of Nostrand Avenue came in with Roy Canton.

"Did you hear what they did to that girl?" he shouted.

They all knew. On news reports or in telephone calls from friends, they had heard that a black girl—an "honor student and cheerleader"—had been abducted upstate for four days and repeatedly gang-raped by white policemen who had written racial slurs on her and dumped her.

Once again, Ethelyn Smith wailed "Oh no! Oh no!"—not in disbelief, but in an excess of belief that it was happening again. As a child in South Carolina, she had been raped by an uncle and propositioned many times by white men for whom she worked as a maid or baby-sitter. She never told their wives: the men would deny it and she would lose her job. In 1963, she had come to

New York, where it was hardly any better. One of her sons had been brutally attacked by whites, and she worried constantly that the other might be shot by the trigger-happy police. As she liked to say: "If children don't know where the danger lies, they don't know that danger exists."

Professor Mackey looked across the table. "I'd be a rich man," he said, "if I had a hundred dollars for every time a white man tried to have sex with one of my sisters." In Savannah and Jacksonville, where he had grown up the oldest of thirteen siblings, many white men had assumed that his sisters and other black girls were theirs for the taking. Indeed, when Mackey was fourteen, a truckload of tobacco-chewing white men had offered him a quarter if he would let them have sex with two of his sisters, who were nine and eleven. When one began to fondle the younger girl, Mackey, who was big for his age, punched him and shouted to his sisters to "get in the wind"—to run. The men had then turned on him. "I got the shit kicked out of me," he recalled. "Time and time again this happened all over that South I grew up in."

Mackey had learned of the Brawley case that morning in a telephone call from a cousin in Greenburgh, New York, who had read him an article in the *Poughkeepsie Journal.* "Falls Girl Found Dazed, 'KKK' Written on Her Body," the headline said. Mackey's cousin had read on:

"A Ketcham High School student was found lying dazed in a road, with racial epithets scrawled on her body, and the girl's family said Sunday that white policemen belonging to the Ku Klux Klan kidnapped and molested her."

From somewhere long ago, Mackey could hear his grandmother's voice saying, "Lord, Lord, what these white folks gon' do next?"

The voice on the phone continued: "However, Detective Lieutenant J. J. Thompson of the Dutchess County Sheriff's Department said there is no evidence that Tawana V. Brawley, fifteen, of Wappingers Falls, was molested."

"We're in trouble," Mackey had told his cousin, thinking: another cover-up.

He had made a series of telephone calls, to ministers and other community leaders, to see what might be done, to organize rallies and maybe protest marches. And he had gone to Edgar's to see his friends.

Roy Canton, too, had heard about the case in a telephone call. He had been at the end of a chain of calls that had begun with Lillian Howard and gone through Sonny Carson and Viola Plummer, a longtime black activist associated with the New York Eight.

When Canton hung up, he was enraged. "White people is at it again," he told his wife. "I'm tired of all these acts happening in our community, the disregard and the disrespect of my people. I'm going to *hurt* these people."

Canton had come to this country from St. Thomas in the Virgin Islands in 1963 to try to break into major league baseball. It had been different when he arrived. In fact, he and his brother had won a commendation from New York City for aiding a white police officer who had been surrounded by a black mob in Brooklyn. But one day in 1976, officers mistaking his brother Alric for a bank robber had shot out the tires of his car. Roy's daughter, Loryn, had been in that car, and Canton had lost all respect for the police. Now he advised Loryn and his nine-year-old son, Darren, that there were only two things to be afraid of: muggers and police officers. "The policeman's duty is to confine black people," he had told them. "Don't even think when you get in trouble that you run for the police."

Hampton Rookard, who had heard about the case on WLIB, was caught up in the outrage as well: they could count on him. Years ago, Rookard told them, he had spent a lot of time in the Hudson Valley—summers as a Boy Scout, autumns as a hunter in the woodlands. He had come to know the people in the little towns where the mayor and the sheriff and the judge were all related. "I am into the psyche of those white people up there," he said to his friends at Edgar's. "Black people are living in a state of subservience just to survive. These aren't the descendants of a black sophisticated group. They're the descendants of sharecropping potato pickers that have been up there for a hundred years."

To Rookard, the news of Tawana Brawley had the ring of truth. "I know it has to be real because I know the area," he said. "I know what those white people are capable of and what the white world in general is ashamed to admit."

It was a crazy afternoon at 4-D Carmine Drive. Reporters, camera crews, community leaders, law-enforcement officials, relatives of the family, all flocked to the Brawley apartment for another day of questions, commiserations, and advice.

Lillian Howard got there early to propose that the family retain Maddox as its lawyer. Glenda Brawley and Ralph King seemed reluctant, but Juanita was enthusiastic. Howard called Sonny Carson from the Brawleys' living room, and he promised that they would hear from the lawyer soon, perhaps as early as tomorrow.

Glenda wanted to put the whole thing to rest. So later in the morning, she called the sheriff's office and asked that investigators come to her apartment at one o'clock. Perhaps everything could be cleared up. Tawana, she said, was ready to talk.

Hoping for a breakthrough, Detective Carl Amburgey arrived with Hilda Kogut of the FBI and two Dutchess County senior prosecutors, J. Otto Williams, who was black, and Marjorie Smith, a white woman who specialized in child sex-abuse cases. Waiting for them were Tawana, Glenda and Juanita, King, and Tawana's cousin, Kenya Strong. Bob Ramsey, of Newburgh's NAACP, whom Juanita had called, came in a little later.

Reclining on the living room couch, clutching her teddy bear and snuggling her head in Kenya's lap, Tawana still looked dazed, although it had been two days since she had been found. She seemed to lapse in and out of consciousness. Even when her eyes were open, she did not appear fully aware of what was going on around her. Her apparent pain was like a suit of armor: there was no point even trying to get through it.

Over the next hour and a half, Carl Amburgey asked the questions, but the girl scarcely answered. Sometimes she nodded or shook her head, often in a way that left it unclear whether she meant yes or no. Occasionally, she whispered a word or two to Juanita or Kenya, who passed on the answers to the waiting group.

In this way, a story—told primarily by Juanita—began to emerge. It went like this:

On Tuesday, November 24, Tawana had gathered up her school-books and, about seven A.M., left her apartment and met seventeen-year-old Trayon Kirby, a friend who was to drive her to school. Instead, she had him drive her to Newburgh, to the apartment of Sandra Buxton, a sister of her boyfriend, seventeen-year-old Todd Buxton. Tawana remembered that Sandra Buxton lived in a turquoise-colored house at Clinton and Liberty Streets. She indicated that she then went to the home of Geneva Buxton, Todd's mother, and accompanied her by taxi and bus to the Orange County Jail at Goshen, where Todd Buxton was serving six months for firing a gun at another youth. She visited Todd in a reception room for about two hours and then took the bus back to Newburgh with Geneva Buxton. She spent a few hours at Geneva Buxton's house, and it was after dark when she caught a bus home to Wappingers Falls.

About eight-forty P.M., she got off the bus near Paino's Mobil station and the Norstar Bank on Route 9 at Myers Corners Road, just southeast of Wappingers Falls. She started walking toward home, about a mile away, along Middlebush Road, the westward extension of Myers Corners Road. She did not remember how far she got. Suddenly, a dark four-door car with two men inside drew up. A white man got out. He was wearing a black nylon jacket, a silver badge, and some sort of strap that might have been a shoulder holster. He pulled her by the hair into the back seat and hit her when she started screaming. Lying on the back seat, she could not see what the driver looked like, but the man who had grabbed her was tall and had brownish-blond hair and a mustache. She did not know whether she would recognize him if she saw him again.

She could not recall whether the car went straight or turned right or left. She could not remember how long the car was in motion. The next thing she knew she was in a place with three white men in dark clothes. She did not remember if some of the men were bald, but indicated for purposes of comparison that they were older than her schoolmates. She did not know where she was, but she saw trees and thought it was in a woods. She remembered no lights and heard no running water or passing cars. All the men joined in calling her "nigger," "black bitch," and other names. She was struck again on the head by the man who had hit her in the car. She felt cold. The men urinated on her. Juanita said they urinated into Tawana's mouth.

The girl had no recollection of what happened after that, no idea of what happened to her Wednesday, Thursday, Friday, or Saturday, no idea if she was indoors or outdoors, no idea if anyone had written anything on her and no idea as to how she had ended up at the Pavillion. She did not remember the people who found her, or the deputy sheriff who came, or the ambulance crew that took her to St. Francis Hospital. Her first recollection was the pain of an intravenous needle being inserted into her arm at the hospital.

It was an astounding story: at first an apparently straightforward account of the facts of her day; then, from the point of abduction, an increasingly vague sequence of men and woods and horrors, and finally an almost dreamlike epilogue as the night and the mists closed in on her memory.

There were no assertions that she had been raped or sodomized. And her story was very different from the one Juanita had told on Sunday. Tawana's account of when and where she got off the bus was three hours different and one mile distant from the time and place given by her aunt. Tawana said there were three assailants; Juanita had said there were six. And Juanita's version was far more specific and inflammatory; it had included charges of gang rape and sodomy, portrayals of racists smearing feces and writing racial slurs on the girl's body, and other torments that Tawana herself had not mentioned. Indeed, the girl could recall almost nothing of the assailants, except that one was tall and blond and had a badge and maybe a holster. She could not recall what had happened to her books, how she had come to be in different clothes, or what had happened to the clothes she was wearing when she vanished. She could not recall being smeared with fecal matter or scrawled with racial slurs. She could not recall where she had been or what had happened to her during almost the entire ninety hours she had been missing. There were nothing but questions and more questions.

Ramsey, on his way out, told the family he would call an NAACP attorney, George Hairston, who might contact them in a few days. He also said he would try to counteract the skepticism toward Tawana's story being expressed in the press by the authorities.

"One of the things I have tried to do is not pass judgments about this case," he cautioned a reporter later. "There's a lot of wild speculation going on. The fact remains, we have a victim. The family was cooperating. They made Tawana available for questioning. It's not their fault that she was in a traumatized state."

Morning brought another wave of visitors to the Brawley apartment, but these were allies and their presence had a liberating effect on the household. Bob Ramsey came back. So did Clarence McGill and Lorraine Jackson Ordia of the Dutchess County Committee Against Racism, and Reverend Walter Henderson, president of the Poughkeepsie Ministerial Alliance. Ralph King and Tawana, Glenda, and Juanita Brawley were all there.

Everyone seemed to be talking at once and the house was a chaos of ringing telephones and jabbering voices. Tawana was sprawled on the couch again, silent, ignored in the turmoil, a child in the midst of adult conversations. Someone said it might not be a good idea to discuss the case in front of the girl, but they had already been going for hours and the suggestion was ignored.

Much of the talk revolved around the family's reaction to seeing Sheriff Scoralick on television the previous night saying the Brawleys were still refusing to cooperate. The family was incensed. And while the talk was critical of all the investigators, Scoralick in particular was denounced. Juanita was especially vociferous: Scoralick and his investigators were skeptical and unresponsive, they had not given Tawana a chance, they were racists covering up for someone in the police, they were lying to the press to outmaneuver and discredit the family.

Eventually, the conversation returned to Tawana and her condition. There was a general consensus that she had been discharged prematurely from the hospital, but the Brawleys were adamant about not going back to St. Francis. It was decided that she should see another doctor. Dr. Angela A. Crosdale, a black gynecologist in Fishkill, was suggested. A phone call was made and an appointment within the hour was set.

Meantime, Lorraine Jackson Ordia, a young black woman who was sometimes carried away by her enthusiasms, asked Tawana a few questions about how she felt. The girl still seemed unable to talk. She nodded, shook her head, or wrote short notes, just as she had done for the police. She was left-handed, but scribbled the notes with her right hand, ostensibly because her left arm was still stiff from the intravenous needle. She wrote on a pad of lined white paper that Jackson Ordia had brought along. No one was expecting any revelations.

"The sooner you get better, then we can concentrate on catching the people who did this to you," Jackson Ordia told the girl. It was an innocuous comment, intended to assuage Tawana's feelings, not to elicit any specific information, let alone a revelation.

But the girl responded with a short note that startled everyone. "I want him dead," she wrote on Jackson Ordia's notepad.

The adults looked at one another.

"I can understand how you can feel that way," Jackson Ordia

told her soothingly. "You must be full of hate right now. Let's concentrate on getting better first."

No more was said.

Tawana, in a long nightshirt, was wrapped by Glenda and Juanita in a sheet and a bedspread. Then King carried her out to his van to take her to the doctor's office. He put her in the back seat. Jackson Ordia climbed in beside her and they sat there awhile, waiting for the others. Jackson Ordia again mentioned the importance of getting well before worrying about the search for her attackers.

Again, it seemed to trigger a reaction.

Tawana reached over for the notepad. "I want him dead," she wrote.

Puzzlement crossed Jackson Ordia's face.

They all drove to the doctor's office at Fishkill, and King carried Tawana inside. While he, Glenda, and Tyice waited in a reception room, Juanita and Jackson Ordia went into the examining room with Tawana. Jackson Ordia again spoke to Tawana about getting well and capturing her attackers. It was like a cue for a conditioned response. Jackson Ordia held the notepad in front of the girl, as if to demonstrate the effect for Juanita's benefit.

Tawana picked up the pen. "I want Scoralick," she wrote.

The sight of the name stunned Juanita and Jackson Ordia. Juanita took the note out to the waiting room and showed it to King and Glenda. What did the girl mean? That Scoralick had personally attacked her? How else would she even know the name of the Dutchess County sheriff? It did not seem to occur to any of them that his name had been denounced at the coffee table only an hour earlier as the girl lay on the couch, listening silently.

Back in the examining room, Juanita told the gynecologist that her niece could not walk or talk as a result of her experience. She also said the girl had pain in her pelvis, her head, and the left side of her neck.

The exam was limited. Tawana did not talk, but answered questions by nodding or shaking her head. She made pained expressions when moving her head or trying to raise her legs into the stirrups, and would not cooperate in the cervical exam. She nodded when asked if she had been sexually molested and when asked if she had been hit on the head. She showed less hesitancy now about these points.

The doctor found nothing wrong, but recommended X rays and a CAT scan to rule out neurologic injury and fractures, and she suggested a psychiatric evaluation.

When they got back to the Brawley-King apartment, Juanita leaped out of the car and practically flew inside, triumphantly waving the note that said "I want Scoralick." It was as if the note proved all she had been saying about the case and the sheriff. She showed it to Ramsey, who gave it to King, who showed it to everyone in the apartment. After that, it vanished, along with the two "I want him dead" notes.

Late in the day, after the crowd had left 4-D Carmine Drive, the doorbell rang. King answered it. The man on the doorstep was black, middle-aged, and solemn. His name, he said, was Alton Maddox.

7

An early photograph of Alton Maddox shows a plump-cheeked, wide-eyed boy with shoulders thrown back, his spine ramrod straight like a cadet at attention. His father looms up behind him, a stern-looking man with a silver belt buckle gleaming over the boy's shoulder. When Maddox occasionally shows this snapshot to friends, he says that his boyhood was filled with a joyful discipline. The picture indeed captures the sense of a rigid ten-year-old, but there is no joy in it: the haunted young eyes seem to convey an enormous sadness, as if the boy even then had foreseen a life of struggle and sorrow.

As a teenager in Newnan, Georgia, he was chased by a white mob and beaten bloody. He fought off the attackers with the help of a young neighbor, Leola Weaver, who later became his wife, but the terrifying assault left Maddox with more than a lifelong eye injury: from that day on, he dedicated himself to fighting whites and their racist ways. Many whites who years later felt Maddox's lash never knew that they were paying for a beating long ago in a dusty little redneck town. He never forgot the trauma. Sometimes, before an encounter with hostile whites, he would murmur to Al Sharpton or C. Vernon Mason: "Here comes the white mob at me again."

Maddox was born in Inkster, Michigan, near Detroit, in 1945, but his father, a Baptist minister, and his mother, a teacher, soon moved the family to Newnan, a segregated town of eleven thousand near Atlanta. It was a community where blacks lived in slums and textile barons lived in mansions. Newnan had been spared by General Sherman in the Civil War and left with the highest concentration of antebellum houses near Atlanta. The town had a history of humiliations and even lynchings that dated back to the era of slavery, and most of its customs had the underpinnings of law. The Supreme Court had given its imprimatur to segregation in a notorious 1896 case, *Plessy v. Ferguson*. Homer Plessy, who looked white but had black ancestors, sued after being taken off a whites-only railroad car. But the court ruled against him, saying segregation was constitutional if facilities for blacks and whites were equal. That became the basis for a vast network of "Jim Crow" laws—named for a minstrel-show caricature—that resulted in the establishment of "separate but equal" schools, restaurants, and other facilities across the South.

Maddox's teachers in the all-black schools of Newnan stressed hard work and success, not society's barriers. Maddox's family also helped imbue in the boy a strong sense of discipline and self-esteem. "My parents," he recalled, "would never let me work for white people as I was growing up, because they didn't want me exposed to that way of instilling the racial superiority of whites."

Newnan was run by a rich white elite, and most of its black citizens were lucky to find work. Maddox's educated parents stood somewhat above the rest of the black community, and they sheltered him from its harsher realities, as well as from the ugliness of white supremacy. But the truth filtered through. The boy would sometimes accompany his mother out into the country, to the one-room schoolhouses where she taught the children of black sharecroppers. There he saw a depth of poverty and hopelessness that he and his family had never known. The tattered farm children eyed his clothes and his big lunch as they gnawed fatback sandwiches, and while he perused lessons in history and mathematics, they struggled over the alphabet. Guilt and anger rode home with him.

In high school, he campaigned to have a dark-skinned student elected prom queen, and for the first time there was no light-skinned girl on the throne. He participated in one of Newnan's first civil rights protests in the early 1960s. He and other blacks sat in at the whites-only front counter of King's Drug Store, demanding service. Employees pelted them with eggs and tomatoes before the police arrived and threw the protesters out. It was always that way, he realized: the victims were mauled and the violent were ignored.

He learned young about white politics. When he was eighteen, his father told him that blacks must use their growing numbers to elect blacks and build a base of power. "Son," he said, "the only person that you should ever vote for is a black man. In my lifetime, the only people I ever voted for was white folks, and you see we haven't gotten anywhere."

Maddox's ideas about how to change the system were still unformed when he began college at Howard University in Washington. He soon found his way: it was a place seething with intellectual ferment. His companions were people who would be activists in the black movement of the sixties. It was not hard to subscribe to their ideas: there was nothing theoretical about a beating, and faint blacks who urged restraint were the enemy as much as the white overseer.

But his classmates and teachers only provided definitions. It was the writings of Charles Hamilton Houston that set the course. Houston was the black lawyer and legal scholar who had built the Howard University Law School into a training ground for black lawyers who had launched a broad attack on segregation in American life, winning a series of landmark cases. His sense of mission and his ideas pervaded the university. In his view, educated American blacks had only two choices in life—to become parasites or to become architects of social change.

There was never any doubt in Maddox's mind about *his* course. The theoretical lessons were always being reinforced by violence, by humiliation, by discrimination. On a Christmas break from Howard in 1967, Maddox went back to Newnan to visit his ailing uncle in the hospital. He left his car parked in an emergency zone. When he got back, by Maddox's account, there was a policeman waiting.

"Boy, can't you read?" The officer had his nightstick out.

Maddox moved the car, but was ordered by the officer to get out. The blows fell without warning. He was beaten severely and then arrested for what the officer said was an attack against him. Maddox spent five days in the hospital and then went to jail briefly. He sued the city, but his claim was dismissed when he failed to post a $250 bond to appeal his conviction.

After he and Leola Weaver were married, she worked to help put him through Boston University Law School. In Boston, the Maddoxes settled defiantly in the notorious working-class section of South Boston, where blacks were the damned. Bricks shattered their windows, and taunts and threats chased them down the streets. But these only hardened Maddox's resolve. In 1971, he took his law degree and two years later moved to New York to begin the struggle in earnest.

His first job was with a citizens' rights organization, Harlem Assertion of Rights, where some white colleagues found him virulently—almost irrationally—antiwhite. They were right. He had no white friends. And he bad-mouthed whites at every turn. In time, he even branded the management of Harlem Assertion of Rights as racist, and in 1977 he was dismissed. He ignited controversy everywhere he went.

Later, while working on a juvenile rights project for the National Conference of Black Lawyers, Maddox clashed with the organization's leadership. He decided to get out of the small and close-knit legal community in Harlem and strike out on his own. It was during his work with the NCBL that he met C. Vernon Mason. Both men were from the South; both were outsiders fighting injustice in New York. They liked and understood each other at once. In 1983, Maddox and Mason first used the old technique of having a client refuse to cooperate with the authorities in the case of the Reverend Lee Johnson, a Baptist minister who claimed that the police, after stopping him for a traffic infraction, had beaten him. After the mayor expressed skepticism about his claim, he refused to testify before the grand jury. The case against the police was dropped, but the episode was well publicized.

Maddox had no interest in leading an organization or running for public office. He opened a private law practice and soon began defending black people, especially those who had been beaten by the police. In the courtroom, he had the cold stare of a zealot, and as with the rest of his persona, it was a calculated effect. He had developed it after a juror told him his lack of eye contact had made him seem distant and ineffectual. His locution, too, was distinctive and deliberate. He spoke in a Deep South rural patois of "dey's" and "dat's," flaunting his roots and renegade bravado.

He wanted to be the best black lawyer in town. He could often be found on a Saturday night poring over court cases and statute books in the Columbia University Law Library. He worked at a furious pace, absorbing huge volumes of material and sometimes taking on more cases than he could handle. But he could get fifty things done in eight hours, while other lawyers worked around the clock to accomplish one or two. He wasn't all work. With his friends, he displayed a keen sense of humor, and he liked to go to basketball games and the theater.

But his life was in court. Known since his days in the juvenile rights project as a tenacious fighter against police brutality, Maddox first established a name for himself in the case of Michael Stewart, the graffiti writer strangled by officers. Maddox showed how the case was badly mishandled by the police, the medical examiner, and the Manhattan district attorney's office. Even before that, Maddox had had many such run-ins with the authorities. While defending Willie Bosket, a teenaged murderer who became one of New York's most incorrigible prisoners, he was accused of throwing his briefcase at a judge in a courtroom scuffle. Maddox insisted he was framed, and he was acquitted in a jury trial. And in 1986, he unsuccessfully defended a black man charged with razor-slashing the face of the model Marla Hanson in Manhattan. In a brutal cross-examination, Maddox tried to show that the victim's charges were tainted by racism.

"When you saw two black men walking in a civilized manner down Dyer Avenue, it ran across your mind that you were about to be raped—isn't that correct?" he asked Miss Hanson.

"Yes," she admitted, "that thought ran through my mind."

It was that way in all his defenses: racism, not his client, was on trial. In the Michael Stewart case he first adopted the technique of prolonging the proceedings by filing a string of motions. It seemed he was protesting unfairnesses, but he was really just delaying the trial to gain a forum in which to hammer at themes of racism.

Maddox's prowess was demonstrated anew in his defense of Jonah Perry, a Cornell University sophomore from Harlem who had been accused of trying to help his brother, Edmund Perry, mug an undercover police officer in June 1985. Edmund Perry, a Stanford University–bound graduate of the prestigious Phillips Exeter Academy, had been shot dead by the officer. The case made headlines because of the involvement of the two outstanding Harlem youths. Maddox, who was assisted by Mason in the defense, claimed it was a frame-up against Jonah, but he produced no evidence to support his allegation that the police officer was drunk. Still, Jonah Perry was acquitted of robbery and assault charges.

And when the Howard Beach racial attack rocked the conscience of the city and the nation in late 1986, it was Maddox who again seized control and escalated the confrontation. He entered the case as the lawyer of a surviving victim, Cedric Sandiford, the state's key witness. His first ploy was to accuse the police of a "bad faith" investigation into the death of the black victim, Michael Griffith, who had been chased by a white mob onto a highway and killed by a passing car that left the scene. He said the authorities had suppressed portions of Sandiford's account and that the driver of the car was a willing accomplice of the mob. When the authorities denied his allegations, Maddox then raised the stakes by refusing to let Sandiford testify before a grand jury. That led to the dismissal of charges against some of the accused white youths, and an enormous public outcry. Next, Maddox demanded that the floundering Queens prosecutor, John J. Santucci, step aside and that Governor Cuomo name a special prosecutor for the case. Maddox's allegations against the police and the driver of the car were ultimately disproved, but his pressure—the spectacle of the state being unable to pursue the worst racial case in decades—forced Cuomo to name a special prosecutor, and convictions in the case ultimately seemed to vindicate Maddox's strategy.

The case made Maddox one of the best-known lawyers in New York, but he cared little for fame. He cared more about the answer to one question: what would it take to get justice? The answer seemed somehow to lie not in battering the white faces filled with hate, but in retrying the Dred Scott decision of 1857, which had made the Civil War all but inevitable. In that case, the Supreme Court had held that Congress had no power to forbid slavery in the American territories as it had tried to do in the Missouri Compromise.

"Every time I go to court, I'm trying to dismantle the Dred Scott decision," Maddox proclaimed. "All my cases are just camouflaged Dred Scott." The Supreme Court had written that in the history and law of the United States, "the Negro had no rights that the white man was bound to respect." Maddox often paraphrased that language, saying: "The black man *has* no rights that the white man is bound to respect."

Alton Maddox stood on the doorstep of 4-D Carmine Drive with a little briefcase in his hand. His hair was close-cropped, his face jowly and astute, and behind the glinting, wire-rimmed spectacles were the world's most solemn eyes. He introduced himself as a lawyer from New York City, but he came in like a revolutionary with a satchel of explosives, and when he took off his coat and started talking, it was clear that this was an implacable zealot: it was in the unflinching eyes, the orator's voice, the compact fighter's body. He might have been a maniac or a messiah—either way it was his agenda that mattered.

To Maddox, it was brutally simple: the white mob had struck again. So he did not ask Glenda Brawley and Ralph King any troublesome questions about Tawana; the facts could wait. He explained his mission: to prove to the world that Tawana Brawley had been molested and that the police had been involved all the way and were engaged in a cover-up. The whole criminal justice system was corrupt in its treatment of black Americans, he said. He wanted justice, nothing less.

There were no other black attorneys in New York State who had his record for fighting and winning civil rights cases, he said. The Howard Beach case that had made him famous was merely the tip of the iceberg.

It went without saying, he pointed out, that he was as independent as any lawyer in the nation, that he had the training, background, and dedication to see that black clients like the Brawleys got justice. His influence reached all over New York and out to Albany and Washington, and his clients were the disenfranchised, the powerless, the victims of American injustice. And he pointed out further that whereas the authorities could not be trusted, he had the expertise and clout to investigate the case properly himself. It would be his facts, not the authorities' lies, that would ultimately count. The authorities could not be relied upon for anything; indeed, they were obviously trying to block a thorough inquiry. But Alton Maddox would not let them get away with it. The Brawleys could rely on that.

His only condition was that they trust him completely.

They were dazzled. But there was a hitch. They had already agreed with Bob Ramsey to consider bringing in an NAACP lawyer. They told Maddox they would have to think about it.

Maddox did not try to hide his distaste for the NAACP. That bunch, he said, was far too timid for the struggle now being waged. But whatever their decision, he went on, they must have no further contacts with officials or agencies of law enforcement. That must be done by a lawyer, and he would be glad to do it, even while they were making up their minds about retaining him.

This line appealed to Glenda and to King, who did not trust the authorities. Maddox did not mention it, but he had already taken the liberty of making one contact in the case. He had called Thomas Young, the Poughkeepsie police officer who had interviewed Tawana at the hospital. Maddox had asked him if he had encountered any retaliation from his superiors as a result of his interview with the girl. Young had been dumbfounded at the suggestion.

As night fell over the Hudson Valley, Alton Maddox left the Brawleys and sped down the highway to Newburgh, to a protest rally at the New Hope Baptist Church. The place was packed. Many of the people had come by bus from New York City to hear about outrages against upstate blacks and to vent their anger and plan wider protests. A couple of the regulars from Edgar's Food Shop were there—Roy Canton and Hampton Rookard.

At times it was like an old-fashioned revival meeting; they clapped and sang chorus after chorus of "Jacob's Ladder." But the mood swung from jubilation to anger to grim determination as the rally went on. It had been called by Lillian Howard to protest resurgent racism in Orange and Dutchess counties, specifically in the treatment of inmates, including her son, at the Orange County Jail.

"What has started here this evening is going to snowball," Lillian Howard vowed as the crowd roared its approval. "Policemen and guards are always found not guilty whenever they maim, brutalize or kill minorities."

Angry shouts erupted: "Freedom or death!" "Whose streets? Our streets!" "Black people," someone screamed, "get some arms and start fighting back!"

Even moderates like Bob Ramsey sounded fiery: "My question to you is: How much is enough? If we, as a people, can't protect our young people, who can?"

Then Maddox got up and the crowd fell silent. They remembered him as the defender of the victims in Howard Beach, as the black man who had stood up to Cuomo and the other big shots, who had faced them down and gotten his way. There had been rallies like this before, but now there was a sense that this was something special—like Martin Luther King's appearance in Montgomery on the night of the bus boycott.

Maddox told them that a black girl in Wappingers Falls needed their help. He said she had been kidnapped, savagely raped, brutally beaten, and tortured for four days by a gang of white bigots who had smeared excrement and scrawled racial slurs on her body and dumped her for dead. And it wasn't just a pack of rednecks who had done it: the attackers had included police officers, he said, and already the rapacious, white-ruled criminal justice system was at work, trying to silence the black victim and protect the guilty whites.

He urged the crowd to turn out for a giant protest in Newburgh in a week. "We have nothing to lose," he shouted, "and on the twelfth we're going to rumble."

It was his crowd and they roared for revenge.

The Newburgh rally had not been that big an event as rallies go. But when they came to talk about it at Edgar's Food Shop, the regulars found that their resolve had been hardened by its passions.

Hampton Rookard, with his beads and dreadlocks, said he had gone to Newburgh not only to find out more about Tawana Brawley, but also to see if his recollections from years ago as a Boy Scout and hunter in the Hudson Valley were still accurate. "I found exactly what I thought I would find," he said. It was much like the Hudson Valley of long ago: white people dominating life, black people too timid to stand up for themselves. "The black people living up there were afraid to even try to protect themselves," he reported to his friends. It angered him, and he vowed to do what he could for Tawana to change all that.

Roy Canton, too, had become determined to get involved in the Brawley case—not only for Tawana Brawley's sake, but for the sake of his own children. "I spend a lot of time with my children," he told his friends over a cup of Ethelyn Smith's coffee. His

Loryn and Darren were talented, academically and musically—that's why he and his wife sent them to a private school. They also saw to it that the children participated in black studies programs after school, and on vacations they took them to Africa and the Caribbean or to places in the United States where their black heritage had meaning. Canton had worked hard and sacrificed a great deal to make his children strong "African-Americans." But it was not enough. "The one thing I cannot give them is safety," he reminded his listeners. He said it again: "Safety!" Maybe he couldn't change that, but he could work for those who were trying to help that girl up in Wappingers Falls, a girl who might have been his own daughter. "They can help me give my children what I can't give them," he said. The others agreed.

In a quiet house on South Remsen Avenue in Wappingers Falls, only a few blocks from the Brawley-King apartment, a young man who worked for IBM sat down at his desk a few hours after the rally in Newburgh. He took up a pen and began writing a rambling note. His name was Harry Crist, Jr.

As it happened, he was white and twenty-eight years old. He was tall and had brownish-blond hair and a light mustache, and he generally fit the one vague description of an assailant that Tawana had given the authorities. Crist also carried a badge and holster because he was a part-time police officer in the nearby village of Fishkill.

As it happened, his closest friends were law-enforcement officers and police buffs, some of whom cruised around in refurbished surplus police cars and hung out at a service station on Route 9 at Myers Corners Road, the spot where Tawana had last been seen. One of Crist's closest friends was an assistant prosecutor in the office of Dutchess County's district attorney, William V. Grady.

And as it happened, Crist had been a passenger in a dark, four-door car driven by a white state trooper on the previous Tuesday night, the night Tawana had disappeared, and that car had passed near the spot where the girl had last been seen—and at just about the time she vanished.

Harry Crist finished his note and signed it.

Then, from his uniform holster, he slipped out the powerful .357 Magnum revolver that he always carried on the job. It was fully loaded.

He stood beside his bed now, grasping the long-barreled gun in his right hand, coming to terms with the thing he had to do. He raised the weapon and placed the barrel under his chin, pointing the muzzle up into the brain case. With his left hand, he gripped his right wrist to steady the aim.

The bullet crashed through Crist's skull, killing him instantly. He pitched backward and sprawled across the bed, the gun falling beside him, the coverlet growing dark with the spreading bloodstains.

Downstairs, his landlady, Rose Vincentin, thought that a car had backfired.

Harry Crist's body lay all night on the bed. The next morning— Wednesday, December 2—the telephone on the desk beside the suicide note rang and rang, unanswered.

Scott Patterson was worried. He knew his moody friend had been deeply depressed for days. A couple of times Crist had even taken out his gun and pointed it at his pals for no apparent reason, or at his own head, saying he planned to kill himself. Patterson, a young state police trooper, had taken it seriously and skipped work the past few days to spend time with his friend.

Now, getting no answer on the phone, Patterson drove over to Crist's place. He arrived at ten-thirty and knocked, but there was no answer. The apartment had its own entrance, and Patterson had a key because he often used Crist's weight-lifting equipment. He let himself in.

He half suspected what he would find, but the grisly tableau took his breath away. Crist's .357 Magnum lay beside him, and nearby was the note. It was a rambling farewell that spoke of a confluence of disappointments: the failure of his dream to become a state trooper, his unhappiness with his job at IBM, his inability to handle personal problems, and the collapse of his relationship with Rosemarie Hurtt, the young woman he had hoped to marry.

Patterson telephoned the state police. He called an assistant district attorney, Steven A. Pagones, to tell him that their mutual friend had killed himself. Crist's parents, Harry Sr. and Cornelia O'Rourke Crist, were in Florida, off on the first real vacation they had ever taken, and could not be located immediately.

In a little while, the investigators arrived. They found no signs of a struggle. The body and the gun had apparently not been moved, though Patterson acknowledged that he had picked up the note.

The case had all the earmarks of a suicide. Gunshot residue— tiny particles from the muzzle and breach—were found on Crist's hands and neck in patterns that showed how he had held and fired the gun. Crist's blood had obliterated his fingerprints on the grip, but ballistics showed that the fatal bullet had come from the weapon, which was registered to Crist. Three members of his family and a handwriting expert, Joseph P. McNally, concluded that the suicide note had been written by Crist, and investigators confirmed its contents.

To those who had known him, the explanation of Crist's taking his own life was tied up with recent disappointments. Crist's hope of becoming a state trooper had been dashed in a civil service examination, and there would never be another chance because he would soon have passed the cutoff age of twenty-nine. Fellow workers quoted him as saying he could no longer tolerate his job as an IBM technician in Poughkeepsie, which he had held nine years, and his police job in the town of Fishkill was only part-time. Rosemarie Hurtt told investigators that at nine-thirty the previous night, a few hours before Crist died, she had informed him by phone that she was breaking off their relationship to marry Scott Bierce, a friend of Crist's. An autopsy by the Dutchess County medical examiner, Dr. Joseph D. Ross, ruled the death a suicide. And Dr. Michael M. Baden, a forensic pathologist and former New York City medical examiner, who reviewed the findings, said: "It isn't even a close call."

But all these findings were not enough to dispel public suspicions. There were too many things about Crist that suggested he might have left something unconfessed out of his note. And killing himself like that, just as the Brawley case was gathering steam—that was the most suspicious thing of all.

8

They knew him only as the mysterious stranger upstairs. He lived alone, a man with a past, rarely talking to anyone. They would see him in the hall coming home or waiting at the corner for a bus in the morning, and sometimes they heard him moving around upstairs late at night. His name was Ralph King.

He had the big shoulders and powerful hands of a quarry worker, and there was something menacing about him. Wisdom, temperance, mildness were scarcely to be read in the wary eyes or the desperado's mustache and goatee. His manner and movements were rough, and there was a sense of unfocused fury about him, as if people all around were somehow responsible for the way his life had turned out.

But toward Tawana Brawley he was different. She was only seven when they met, and when she encountered him at the corner where she caught the school bus each morning she saw only a conspiratorial wink and a crooked kindly smile. Eventually they spoke, little pleasantries about the weather and school and home. He began waiting for her in the mornings, and soon she was telling her mother about the man upstairs who met her at the bus stop and told her wonderful stories about flying ducklings and talking pigs.

Glenda Brawley had paid little attention to him. But now she took another look. There were conversations in the building and on the street, and they had a cup of coffee together. What she discovered was a quiet, lonely man with a shady past who was trying to rebuild his confidence in a threatening world, finding it easier perhaps to befriend a little girl. She concluded that his gentle overtures to Tawana were benign, perhaps even sweet, and she allowed King's friendship with the girl to flower. Sometimes he took Tawana swimming, sometimes to the store or to a restaurant for hamburgers and milk shakes. Occasionally, he even began to look after Tawana in the afternoons or evenings while Glenda Brawley worked or went shopping. They laughed together and told each other stories, and for the first time in a decade Ralph King felt the glow of human affection that had been stifled by the killing and by his years in prison.

Born June 22, 1945, one of thirteen children of a poor family, King had dropped out of school and taken a series of dead-end jobs until going to work in 1965 for a printing establishment in Poughkeepsie. Two years later, he was married and he and his wife, Wanda Ann, had a baby boy. The elements of happiness appeared to be within reach, but he had a persistent drinking problem. He had beaten his wife a number of times and had been arrested twice for attacks on her. Eventually he abandoned both wife and baby.

In April 1969, King got drunk and broke into his wife's apartment in downtown Poughkeepsie. They quarreled violently about the child. Blows fell, and during the struggle, King drew a stiletto and stabbed Wanda fourteen times. Afterward, leaving her bleeding on the floor, he walked six blocks to the Mid-Hudson Bridge. He had probably killed her, he knew. The neighbors had no doubt heard the fight and called the police. There was no way out. He walked out onto the bridge in despair and was leaning over a railing, looking down at the dark inviting waters, when a patrol car approached. King was arrested.

But Wanda King survived the brutal knife attack. King was indicted on two counts of first-degree burglary for breaking into her apartment, one count of first-degree assault, and one count of unlawful possession of a weapon. While he was being held in the Dutchess County Jail without bail, his wife obtained a divorce.

After three months behind bars awaiting trial, King began to show signs of what his lawyer called mental instability that might make him unable to assist in his defense. His lawyer, Charles Phillipbar, Jr., a public defender, expressed his concern to the court, saying King was "incoherent as to the events of April 2, 1969."

Two court-appointed psychiatrists found that his emotional problems, aggravated by heavy drinking, made him dangerous to himself and others. His problems with his wife, they said, dated to the start of their marriage. Despite these assessments, the court released him on one thousand dollars bail. By the following summer, the case had still not come to trial. But King had been reconciled with his wife and was living with her and their son once again.

He had promised to reform, but it was hopeless. On July 11, 1970, after another violent quarrel with his wife, King began drinking again. The episode reached a crisis at four A.M. There were conflicting accounts about what happened. The authorities said that as Wanda lay sleeping, King fired four .38-caliber bullets into her head, killing her instantly. But King said he awoke to find his wife pointing the gun at him. He said they struggled for it and that he took the gun away and shot her. Indicted on a murder charge, he was allowed to plead guilty to first-degree manslaughter in the killing and second-degree assault in the earlier knife attack on her. At King's sentencing in November, his court-appointed lawyer told Judge Raymond E. Aldrich, Jr., that the crimes arose from marital problems. The judge gave King seven to twenty years in prison.

The sentence raised no public notice. But to those who reexamined it during the Brawley case a decade later, questions leaped out. Why was a plea bargain offered to a defendant whose only defense to murder was that he had "marital problems"? Was it reverse racism? Did the system regard black life as cheap and treat crimes against blacks less seriously? Blacks might be treated unfairly by the courts, but the criminal justice system sometimes looked the other way when blacks attacked blacks.

King served the minimum—seven years. Released in 1977, he returned to Poughkeepsie to try to put his life back together. He was unable to find steady work at first. But by 1978, he had a job at an IBM plant and had rented a small apartment above Glenda Brawley's. He soon got to know Tawana and her mother.

The girl, he discovered to his surprise, was something of a stranger to her own mother. They had been separated most of Tawana's life and had only recently begun living together again. It was the old story: a lovely child, fatherless and insecure, bounced from home to home by an undereducated, immature, often-unemployed mother, who had been unable to keep her for long stretches of time.

Glenda Brawley kept her daughter in Poughkeepsie for nearly five years, but found it increasingly difficult to be a working mother, to make ends meet and cope with the emotional needs of the growing girl. In 1983, beset by financial and other troubles, she accepted her sister's offer of help. Once again, Glenda sent her daughter back to Monticello to live with her aunt and uncle, Juanita and Matthew Strong. King was sorry to see the girl go. But Glenda was relieved. She could again try to make a life on her own. But it was different this time, for Ralph King was upstairs.

For two years, Tawana Brawley had found a refuge in the Catskills. Now she watched their majestic contours fade in the blue autumn haze as the car carried her down the highway, out of the Catskills, past farmhouses and weathered stables, away from the family and the home where she had been happy.

It was a quick trip from Monticello to Poughkeepsie, a couple of hours from safety into the unknown. She had grown into a tall, outgoing girl of thirteen with strong attachments to her aunt and uncle. She had developed a crowd of good friends and a solid sense of herself. Now, all this was threatened.

During the two years Tawana had been in Monticello, there had been great changes in her mother's life. Glenda Brawley had a new job at the IBM plant in East Fishkill that paid twenty thousand dollars a year. And Ralph King, the man upstairs, had moved downstairs and was now living with Glenda. He had become a Short Line bus driver, working the daily route between Poughkeepsie and New York City, so there were two incomes in the household and three cars, new furniture, a bank account, and lines of credit. And there was a baby, Tyice.

Glenda had found the new situation stimulating. Duty and success had taken root in a life that had been nomadic and insecure. But responsibility still did not come as easily to King. His name had appeared in police reports involving guns and drugs. And there was an ominous reminder of the patterns that had shattered his life fifteen years earlier: he was drinking heavily again, and he had begun beating Glenda.

It was into this household of upward mobility and nagging turmoil that Tawana had been summoned from her idyllic refuge in Monticello in the autumn of 1985.

The reality in Poughkeepsie was even harsher than she had feared. Tawana felt needed more than wanted: with Glenda and King both working full-time, someone had to help clean the apartment and care for baby Tyice. Tawana enrolled as a high school freshman in Poughkeepsie, but her time and activities outside school were sharply restricted by her duties at home. To her friends, she confided that her mother and King had turned her into a virtual house slave.

Shortly after Tawana's return, Alicia Dean, a friend, saw her bleeding profusely from the mouth. Tawana said that Glenda had hit her. "All the kids knew that Tawana's parents were strict," another friend said. "They didn't let Tawana go anywhere. She had to baby-sit her brother all the time. Her parents didn't like her to hang out or to have boys over to her house."

The following spring, in May 1986, Tawana ran away from home a second time. With Lana Stansberry, who lived in a group foster home, Tawana fled to Beacon, a Hudson River village five miles south of Wappingers Falls. They partied with a gang of teenagers at the home of a boy named Charlie Williams. They spent Friday night at the home of Williams's cousin, Chris Horton. Lana Stansberry went home the next day, but Tawana returned to Williams's house and spent Saturday night there. On Sunday, the game was up: Lana Stansberry, under duress, took Glenda to Tawana's hideaway.

Glenda flew into a rage at the sight of her runaway daughter. She grabbed her by the hair and dragged her out into the street. She pulled out some of the girl's hair and, while neighbors watched, beat the girl severely, striking her face a dozen times with her fist. "She closed her fist," said a youth who saw it, "and gave Tawana hard hits to the cheek, about twelve hits, hand to bone. It was whomp, whomp, whomp!" Glenda also lashed the girl with an electrical cord, raising welts on her arms and legs, and inflicted more blows in the car driving home.

The summer of 1986 was a bitter one for Tawana, but gradually she came to be reconciled to her Spartan life and heavy duties. And there was a refreshing change of residence. Escaping from the crumbling old streets of Poughkeepsie, the family moved to the Montclair Town Houses, south of Wappingers Falls. Tawana still had to clean house and care for her baby brother, but she began to find a new circle of friends in the suburban setting, including Trayon Kirby, a neighbor. September and the start of the school year came as a relief. She enrolled as a sophomore at Roy C. Ketcham High School in Wappingers Falls.

Shortly after the school year began, something ugly happened: Tawana was arrested in Wappingers Falls for hitting another girl during an argument and for pulling a knife and making threats. A juvenile delinquency report was filed in Dutchess County Family Court.

But it seemed an aberration. In school, Tawana worked hard, taking a college preparatory curriculum that included mathematics, Spanish, English, and chemistry, and she showed scholastic promise. She loved to read. She devoured *Flowers in the Attic* and other novels by V. C. Andrews that were popular among teenage girls. They were the kinds of stories that appealed to pubescent adolescents with vivid imaginations, drawing upon elements of gothic horror and greed, rape and revenge, brother-sister incest, and the fairy-tale agonies of children locked away by wicked adults.

She loved playing basketball and scrimmaged often at school and on the outdoor courts. That fall, she tried out for the junior varsity cheerleading squad at Ketcham and became the squad's only black member. Marie Caruso, her coach, said she saw problems in the Brawley family. Tawana was often late for practice, and Glenda sometimes appeared angry when she picked her up. Sometimes she failed to pick her up at all.

Friends called Tawana intelligent, sweet, friendly. "She's a damn nice girl," said a boy who knew her as a sophomore. "The girl doesn't smoke. She doesn't drink. In my book that makes her a nice girl. She's the kind of girl you'd take home to mom." The youth added that, like other teenagers, Tawana spent her spare time at the malls.

But her life at home was increasingly bleak. She told Trayon Kirby one day that welts on her body were the result of a beating inflicted by Glenda and King. They used her like a household servant, she said, and they shackled her outside life as well, telling her where she could go, whom she could see, and what time to be home.

One of Tawana's social outlets was a weekly trip to a Pentecostal church in Newburgh, where she became the mascot of a singing group. The House of Joy was a storefront church, with peeling paint and creaky floors and a sign over the door proclaiming: The First Born Church of the Living God. On Sunday nights, dressed in her best Sabbath clothes and adorned with gold jewelry, she joined an eight-person gospel group called the Mighty Jubilaires, who belted out spirited songs. "She would be sitting right up front, clapping her hands and stomping her feet," recalled Coleman Larson. "She was like our little sister," said Kermit Thorpe. "She knew all the songs and would sing along with us. She really gave us a boost." They named Tawana their queen and she sold raffle tickets and pictures of the singers in supermarkets, laundries, and beauty shops.

At home, things were not going well between Glenda and King. Glenda told a coworker that she and King each had "relationships" with other people. For a time, they separated, but were soon reunited.

King continued to be plagued by trouble. His friends were alcoholics and drug addicts; he got into fights, and the Poughkeepsie police listed him as a suspected dealer in marijuana and other drugs. A state police task-force report quoted witnesses as saying that King once had fifty bags of marijuana in his apartment. King admitted to Lorraine Jackson Ordia of the NAACP and the Dutchess County Committee Against Racism that he sometimes carried a gun.

Late that fall, Tawana and her family moved to the Pavillion Condominiums, a mile southeast of Wappingers Falls. It was in a quiet countryside of woods and fields. The new home was in the John Jay Senior High School district, but Tawana finished her sophomore year at Ketcham before transferring. She did well in classes and talked of being a model. Ketcham was a good school. Seventy percent of the seventeen hundred students went to college, while less than five percent dropped out. (In New York City's public schools, a third of all students dropped out, and such a small percentage went on to college that the school system didn't even bother to keep track of their numbers.)

At the Pavillion, where many other teenagers lived, Tawana's circle of friends and activities expanded. Her interest in boys grew avid, too. She went out dancing and began to attend parties, usually with older teens. "She liked attention from guys," said a seventeen-year-old girl who knew her at school and saw her at parties. "That was Tawana's style." Lewis Taylor, who had known Tawana since elementary school, agreed: "She had a posse of boyfriends."

Other acquaintances were less flattering. "A tease," "fast," "wild," they called her, and said she was aggressive and flirtatious. Some girls regarded her with jealousy, and she sometimes fought with girls over boys. Friends said she did not use drugs, but had a tendency to exaggerate, even to lie. "She didn't get into drugs or anything like that that I knew of," said Lewis Taylor. "The only thing about her is she used to lie sometimes. She'd stretch the truth."

Her increasing interest in boys and a new streak of independence led to more strains at home. She sometimes refused to baby-sit or do housework. Neighbors said that family quarrels audible through the thin walls erupted at least three times a week in the Brawley-King apartment and that the police sometimes had to be called. To a coworker at IBM, Glenda revealed that Tawana and King often had fights, and that she was worried about them. The fights were becoming increasingly violent, and they carried overtones of sexual jealousy: the battles seemed always to stem from Tawana's increasing involvement with boys and her demands for greater freedom.

Tawana did have a series of boyfriends, but the most serious of these relationships was with Todd Buxton. She met him in the fall of 1986 when, as a cheerleader, she went to Newburgh for a basketball game. He was a sixteen-year-old junior guard on the Newburgh varsity. After the game, he struck up a conversation with the pretty out-of-town sophomore, imagining at first that she was older than fourteen. They exchanged phone numbers. Soon they were dating. It was an emotionally trying relationship, sometimes on, sometimes off, with frequent quarrels and reconciliations.

"I liked Tawana a lot—she was fun," Buxton said. "But if she got mad, she was the kind of person who would let you know it. She would yell. She liked to dance and I didn't, so she would usually go out without me."

Dinha Daniels, who lived at the Pavillion and was a classmate at John Jay and Tawana's confidante, recalled the girl's infatuation with Todd Buxton: "We used to go down by the pond after school and she would talk about her boyfriend, Todd. She would talk about him all the time. She said she wanted to marry him."

By the spring of 1987, Tawana was beginning to make evening forays into Poughkeepsie, and on weekends she went with Buxton and other friends into the black sector of Newburgh, where prostitutes worked the seedy hotels and drug pushers and crack addicts ruled the streets. Weapons and hard cash were the currency of these streets, and Buxton knew his way around. Tawana's steady relationship with him had lasted only five months, into early 1987, but it had been so intense that they continued to see one another even after they broke up. Friends said that Tawana's emotional attachment to Buxton continued to be extremely strong, while his feelings for her were more moderate.

Tawana's mother and Ralph King, meantime, responded to her growing independence by imposing ever tighter controls. King insisted that she be in before dark. Glenda wanted to screen her boyfriends. There were ugly warnings and threats that sometimes ended in violence. It was difficult to enlist the girl for household duties anymore. Silence and resentment marked the truces.

And there would be no more escapes to Monticello. Juanita Brawley and Matthew Strong had recently been divorced, shattering Tawana's idealistic image of them. Kenya Strong remained with her father in Monticello, but Juanita had moved to Kingston for her job as a state counselor of juveniles. Kingston was only twenty-five miles from Wappingers Falls, and Juanita more often got to see the niece she loved. That was some consolation to Tawana, who was deeply attached to the aunt who had been a mother to her. But the dominant themes Tawana struck among her friends were still negative: Glenda and her common-law husband were mean and grossly unfair to her.

Trying to break the chains, she began making more out-of-town excursions—and began getting into trouble. Friends said she now drank beer often. There were at least two occasions in the spring of 1987 when, they said, she smoked marijuana. In May, she and some other teenagers were detained for shoplifting at a mall in Poughkeepsie.

Finally, during the summer, Tawana ran away from home a third time. She was gone several days, and there were hints from friends that she was with Todd Buxton. But it was never established where she went or what she did. During her absence, Juanita Brawley went to the Buxton family to ask about her. They said they had not seen the girl, who then reappeared without explanation.

Tawana confided to Buxton that she had run away a couple of times before. "She didn't like her stepfather," Buxton recalled. "She said they didn't get along. She didn't tell me why."

There were several reasons, and they went beyond the mere chafing of a teenager under parental restraints. King, Tawana complained to friends, often watched her doing her exercises. And sometimes he discussed her, as one acquaintance put it, "in a real sexual way," calling her, among other things, a "fine fox." To friends, Tawana referred to King as a "filthy pervert." Daryl Rodriguez, a classmate at John Jay who became her next boyfriend, said Tawana suggested that King's sexual interest in her went beyond leering, that he was jealous of her relationships with boys, and that there had even been attempts at a physical relationship.

And there were other resentments that any teenaged girl might have harbored. It was hypocritical for King, an ex-convict and killer who beat women, kept guns and drugs, got into street fights, and stumbled home drunk, to tell Tawana to be in before dark. It was outrageous that Glenda, who had borne her out of wedlock, now preached to her of morality and told her which boys she might and might not see.

In the late summer of 1987, Tawana told Todd Buxton that she was pregnant and that he was the father. According to Malika Holder and Sandra Buxton, Tawana borrowed a Medicaid card and had an abortion.

That autumn, as she was entering the eleventh grade at John Jay, she saw Buxton rarely. Nonetheless, she told friends that her feelings for him were still strong. But by then, Buxton had another girlfriend, Angela Colon. And any hopes Tawana had of winning him back soon were dashed, on October 7, when Buxton fired a shotgun at another youth in a fight. He got six months in the Orange County Jail.

Tawana, meanwhile, took up with Daryl Rodriguez and soon started calling him her boyfriend. They dated and went to parties together. There were more late nights out. And at home there were more fights. "There were always arguments there," recalled a neighbor. "About a month before they moved out, there was a very violent one. They were throwing things. Things were breaking. Ralph's and Glenda's voices were booming."

Now, defiance was Tawana's answer to all parental restraints. She went to a Saturday night party with Rodriguez at Fishkill on November 7 and did not get home until five A.M. She tried to sneak in a window, but King was waiting for her. There was no violence this time, but she was "grounded" for two weeks, denied the privilege of going out evenings or using the telephone. These pressures only intensified her rebelliousness. Tawana was late for school twenty-one times in the first fifty-two school days and she skipped school several times. Her mother gradually forgave her, but King continued to scold her, day after day, even after her punishment was supposedly over. He was angry at her for a whole range of offenses: laziness in housework, ignoring studies, skipping school, running with punks, late-night partying. The vehemence of his outbursts seemed far more than expressions of a fatherly concern, and his simmering anger seemed close to an explosion.

About this time, Tawana and other girls in her circle heard the bizarre story of how a friend, sixteen-year-old Tawana Ward Dempsey, had tried to conceal a late-night escapade with a boy. Tawana Dempsey had gone to the police and told them that, as she was walking home one night along a quiet road in Poughkeepsie, two white men in a green car had pulled up, dragged her inside, driven her into the woods, and raped her. The police discovered discrepancies in the story, and an investigation revealed that she had fabricated the tale to cover up her rendezvous with a boy.

On November 14, the King-Brawley family moved from the Pavillion to the Leewood Arms Condominiums in Wappingers Falls. They had planned it for months, ignoring the rent bills, and had finally been evicted. Two days later, Tawana transferred from John Jay High back to Ketcham, where she had attended classes as a sophomore. She took her troubles with her. A week later, on November 23, Tawana skipped school. She and Trayon Kirby, who also skipped, drove to Poughkeepsie High and to John Jay, where they spent the morning seeing friends. Tawana seemed happy. After lunch, they went to Kirby's apartment at the Montclair Town Houses, where they talked until two-thirty P.M. Then Kirby dropped Tawana at the spot where she usually got off the Ketcham school bus. She walked home, completing the charade to keep King from finding out.

That night, Tawana received a telephone call from Sandra Buxton, Todd's twenty-three-year-old sister. Sandra said her brother wanted to see Tawana at the Orange County Jail. Tawana agreed. No date was set, but after hanging up, Tawana decided to go the next day. At about nine P.M., she called Daryl Rodriguez. The conversation ended—not surprisingly—in a fight and the decision to break up. The way for a renewal of her relationship with Buxton had been cleared.

Tawana then telephoned Chimene Lewis, a school friend, and told her she intended to skip school again the next day to visit Buxton in jail. Tawana was thrilled at the prospect. King would be furious when he found out, but to hell with him; she would cross that bridge when she came to it. She told Chimene she planned to be home around six o'clock the next evening.

But it was not until five days later that she reappeared, streaked with excrement and racial slurs.

Now, like a paralytic, she had spent almost all of the last three days on the couch in the living room, taking her meals and telephone calls, receiving visitors, summoning Ralph King whenever she wanted to be carried upstairs, going to sleep when the police came.

But she was alert and gossipy when several friends dropped in to see the convalescing victim, whose name was on every newscast in three states. They found the celebrity girl on the couch.

Glenda and Juanita Brawley and Ralph King were in the kitchen, paying no attention.

It was mostly small talk around the octagonal coffee table, but there were a few memorable moments. At one point, Tawana whispered that she was afraid of her parents—they had lied, she said, lied to the police. Of course, the police, too, had lied.

Suddenly vague, she mumbled something about "six cops"—and nobody knew what she was talking about.

9

The Reverend Al Sharpton got up and left the room. The meeting of activists at a United Auto Workers hall in Lower Manhattan had been tediously quarrelsome, droning on and on about racism and Tawana Brawley. They had wanted to get up a protest rally, but all they had done all afternoon was argue about coalitions, publicity, and speakers, and talk dreamily about a nationwide movement.

Before they were done talking, Sharpton thought, he might have the whole thing set up.

From a small office in the back, he made a phone call.

"Saul?"

His old friend, the Reverend Saul Williams, pastor of the Baptist Temple in Newburgh, recognized the distinctive growl immediately. As a boy, Sharpton had made a good show of preaching at Williams's former church in Tarrytown, New York, although he was too short to be seen behind the pulpit and had to stand on boxes.

"We want to hold a rally," Sharpton said, and he mentioned the Tawana Brawley case. He did not bring up questionable cases of racism, like the Orange County Jail fracas, for he knew that Williams was a conservative preacher who chose his causes carefully. Sharpton asked if they could use Williams's church.

Williams liked Sharpton and was sympathetic to Tawana Brawley, but he was wary of the radicals Sharpton sometimes associated with.

"You're not bringing all those crazies in my church, are you?" Williams asked.

"Of course not," Sharpton fibbed. They sealed the arrangements.

Afterward, Sharpton had a talk with another preacher—Minister Louis Farrakhan of the Nation of Islam, in Chicago.

Sharpton was the whole circus—part lion, part barker, part clown, and part Houdini. He loved to roar and bellow, mug for laughs, juggle fact with fancy, and delight crowds with slick illusions and vanishing acts. Just when exasperated critics thought they had him bound and gagged, padlocked in a steamer trunk at the bottom of a water tank, he would pop up again, waving to his fans, not even wet.

The rotund preacher with the semiautomatic mouth straddled the worlds of news and entertainment, promotion and boxing, religion and community activism, the media and the mob. Stuffed into running suits like a plump sausage, his long hair straightened and permed, Sharpton cut an outrageous figure—but one that had made him an easily recognizable celebrity on the evening news.

There was something wonderfully comical, even vulnerable, about this blustering rogue who was never at a loss for words, something that fascinated the media despite his broken promises and blatant lies. Sharpton liked to say he didn't hold reporters at gunpoint and force them to cover him. That was true—they were like moths drawn to the flame. His wit was ever ready, as when a reporter asked whether the large Martin Luther King, Jr., medallion Sharpton always wore around his neck was heavy.

Sharpton barely paused. "To me," he rejoined, "it's not."

During the Howard Beach case, Alton Maddox and C. Vernon Mason had allied themselves with Sharpton, taking full advantage of his growing reputation as a tough man in the civil rights cause.

Within hours of the death of Michael Griffith, Sharpton had appeared shortly after dawn at the Griffith home in Brooklyn and met with Griffith's brother, Christopher. Maddox had followed. It was quickly agreed that Maddox and Mason would handle the legal aspects of the case while Sharpton would do what he called the "community work," organizing protest demonstrations and marches and talking to the press. As the legal strategy of withholding the cooperation of the surviving black victims from the authorities evolved, it was Sharpton's role to sell it to the public, a task he relished. With racial tensions at a high pitch and with Sharpton's ready access to the press, it was not a difficult task. He did it with words and demonstrations that outflanked and outmaneuvered the authorities, who seemed to be sitting ducks for his high-profile antics.

When Mayor Koch called a New Year's Day meeting of twenty-three influential blacks at City Hall in an attempt to ease racial tensions in the city, Sharpton held a news conference at a Brooklyn church and described the City Hall meeting as "a coon show." A week later, Sharpton led a march outside police headquarters, calling for the resignation of the black police commissioner, Benjamin Ward, over his handling of the Howard Beach investigation. "He is of our color, but he is not of our kind," Sharpton told the press.

Later in 1987, Sharpton organized high-tension marches of black demonstrators through white Howard Beach. And when the first trial of white youths in the case began in the autumn, Sharpton brought busloads of protesters to court on days of crucial testimony and made sweeping pronouncements from the steps of the Queens courthouse. He filed a complaint with a state judicial panel that disciplines wayward lawyers, charging that Stephen Murphy, one of the defense attorneys, had "repeatedly and incessantly harassed, argued with, and viciously attacked prosecution witnesses despite repeated judicial warnings and in transgression of legal rules of evidence and procedure." The complaint got nowhere, but it caused a stir—like everything Sharpton did.

Sharpton's rise to fame was all the more impressive because he had no apparent constituency, not even a church. But he knew how to use television. Flaunting bad grammar and filling the camera eye with his great bulk, he eschewed sober, predictable homilies for venomous one-liners, pithy catch phrases, and inflammatory charges delivered with delicious bombast.

And if he was a buffoon, he was also shrewd and unrelenting, with more lives in him than a roomful of cats.

In philosophical moments, Sharpton liked to quote the historian James MacGregor Burns, who divided leadership into two types, transactional and transforming. Transactional leaders, Sharpton said, were the traditional politicians who attend cocktail parties and "go to the window to bid for services and goods and concessions for their community." He, on the other hand, classified himself as a transforming leader, one of those who seek to change the rules with marches and sit-ins and confrontations. "I think," he said, "that in an era where almost daily black kids are being beaten or killed and no one is doing time for it, that the cocktail party route is not going to stop it. We have to yell as loud as we can that we are being brutalized and killed in New York, until somebody comes and makes New York deal with its image." Whenever he could get a microphone, he took the occasion to scream: "They're killing blacks in New York. Help!"

"You use whatever means you can when you're talking about life or death," he would explain. As for the traditional politicians, he said disdainfully, "The only thing I've ever seen them come out of the cocktail parties with is intoxication."

Sharpton might easily have fallen into obscurity, like many poor black youngsters who grow up in fatherless homes. But he had two assets: an irrepressible gift for public speaking and a keen eye for influential mentors. From his childhood in Brooklyn's Brownsville section, he was a natural showman. "I have been screaming ever since the doctor slapped me," he liked to say. He was born in 1954 and was four years old when he gave his first sermon at the Washington Temple Church of God in Christ in the Bedford-Stuyvesant section of Brooklyn. At ten, he was a Pentecostal minister, and the following year he toured with the legendary gospel singer Mahalia Jackson. Soon he was being hailed as a "wonder boy" preacher. His father, a building contractor who bought a new Cadillac every year, abandoned the family when Sharpton was ten, leaving his wife, a seamstress and housekeeper, to provide for the boy and his older sister. Sharpton's only childhood recollection of his father was of standing in line with him at the Apollo Theater in Harlem to see the soul singer James Brown.

When Sharpton was twelve, his sister took him to hear Representative Adam Clayton Powell, Jr., preach at Powell's Abyssinian Baptist Church in Harlem. Sharpton was transfixed: he thought he had seen God. Afterward, Sharpton followed Powell to his office, where the forbidding preacher, shirtless, reached down to shake the hand of the wonder boy.

"What do you drink?" Powell asked gravely.

"Drink?" the boy stammered. "I'm twelve years old."

Powell became the first of Sharpton's many mentors. He took Sharpton to his first Broadway show—*Hello Dolly!*—and introduced him to Lucille Ball at Sardi's. Powell took him to Bimini, his Caribbean island retreat, where the congressman refreshed himself with women and rum colas. It was from Powell that Sharpton learned of early job-discrimination protests in Harlem in the years between the wars, when blacks paid electricity bills in pennies and jammed telephone lines by dialing the operator.

Sharpton got another bit of advice from Powell: when your time has passed, don't fight it. "Leadership goes, kid," he told his protégé shortly before his death in 1972. "It never waits for you to sign a permission slip. You know, kid, you got to know when to hit it and you got to know when to quit it and when it's quittin' time, don't push it. Get your fishing pole and go to Bimini and relax."

But Sharpton was just beginning to hit it. While he was still a fifteen-year-old student at Brooklyn's Tilden High School, Sharpton was named youth director for the Southern Christian Leadership Conference's Operation Breadbasket in New York City, an arm of the movement that was coordinating boycotts of businesses whose doors were closed to blacks.

Taking Sharpton under his wing was a former aide to Dr. King, the Reverend Jesse Jackson. He called Sharpton a "young buck" and a "whippersnapper" and counseled him: "Turn on the pressure and don't ever turn it off. Don't ever forget: once you turn on the gas, you got to cook or burn 'em up." With Jackson, Sharpton led boycotts and sit-ins to gain jobs for blacks at Robert Hall clothiers, Coca-Cola, Pepsi-Cola, and the A & P supermarkets. During one of the protests, a white woman in an A & P shoved her shopping cart into Sharpton and called him "nigger." He was surprised. In all his fifteen years, no one had ever called him that.

While alternately picketing City Hall and serving as an intern to the New York City human resources administrator—he had no problem working for the city while at the same time denouncing it—he formed the National Youth Movement with a five-hundred-dollar grant from the civil rights leader Bayard Rustin. The organization promised to promote job training, voter registration, and other programs for blacks, but by 1987 it seemed mostly devoted to combating drugs by publicizing the location of peddlers' dens. It once boasted a membership in the thousands in as many as twenty-five cities, but by this time the organization had only a single cramped, rent-free office in a Brooklyn hospital and several hundred members at most. The chapters scattered around the country had vanished, if indeed they had ever existed.

After graduating from Tilden High in 1972, Sharpton supported the pioneering presidential candidacy of Representative Shirley Chisholm, carrying her pocketbook as she campaigned. Sharpton's own single bid for public office, a race for state senator from Brooklyn in 1978, was ended by a judge's ruling that he was not a resident of the senatorial district.

The following year, Sharpton met another of his hero-mentors: James Brown, the godfather of soul. If he thought he had seen God with Adam Clayton Powell, he *knew* he had with Brown. Sharpton became a disciple, not only copying Brown's hairstyle, but following him around like a puppy. Once, he trailed Brown down a corridor, through a door, and, to his astonishment, onto a stage flooded with spotlights. He immediately went into a wiggle and dance.

When Brown's son Teddy was killed in a car crash in upstate New York, Sharpton became Brown's surrogate son. Brown gave thousands to Sharpton's youth movement, and together they formed a company to promote concerts. They often noshed at the Stage Deli near Times Square. And on Dr. King's birthday in 1981, Sharpton accompanied Brown to the White House to meet Vice President George Bush. Through Brown, Sharpton met top artists and entertainers, including the singers Lloyd Price and Michael Jackson. Sharpton handled some of the publicity for Michael Jackson's 1984 national tour, and he threatened protest actions unless more black promoters were used in cities on the circuit.

Along the way, he met boxing promoter Don King, who had staged the Muhammad Ali–George Foreman fight in Zaire, with James Brown as an added attraction. When Mike Tyson fought Larry Holmes in the Atlantic City Convention Center in January 1988, one party of celebrity guests included Don King, casino owner Donald Trump, the actor Kirk Douglas—and Al Sharpton.

But there was a shady side to Sharpton's associations as well. Through his new friends, Sharpton was drawn into an underworld of mob investors and FBI undercover agents. In one venture in the early 1980s, Sharpton sought to buy into the Mafia-dominated New York–area carting industry, ostensibly as a way of creating job opportunities for blacks. Sharpton and some backers were told that they could purchase the company that held the contract to pick up the garbage of New York City's big utility, the Consolidated Edison Company. According to federal prosecutors, the hauler, Consolidated Carting Company, was controlled by a reputed captain in the Genovese crime family, Matthew (Matty the Horse) Ianniello, and the dealings were an underworld effort to use Sharpton as a front. Sharpton later maintained that he had no knowledge of Ianniello's involvement. Sharpton's role emerged in the 1986 trial of Ianniello and five others on charges of using mob influence in the private garbage-collection industry. The defendants were acquitted. Sharpton was not accused of any wrongdoing and did not testify at the trial.

Sharpton also acquired a controversial connection with the FBI. In 1983, Sharpton was visited by FBI agents who showed him a secret videotape they had made of Sharpton discussing what they said was a drug deal. As Sharpton told it, the agents warned him he could be in a lot of trouble and suggested he cooperate with the government and provide information on Don King. Sharpton said he suggested instead that the FBI investigate two other boxing and entertainment promoters. This tape of Sharpton's supposed drug deal was never made public, but Sharpton insisted it would not incriminate him. At no time, Sharpton contended, did he wear or carry a concealed recording device —an assertion that drew laughter from one ex–FBI agent. Sharpton later acknowledged that he had installed a government-monitored telephone in his house to receive calls about drug dealers. Despite his best efforts, however, Sharpton said the phone produced no information of value to prosecutors, and the tapped telephone was cut off in January 1988, after Sharpton, owing $283, paid with a check that bounced. The government, which had not been paying for the line, let the tap lapse because it was unproductive.

Later, investigators of the New York State Organized Crime Task Force questioned Sharpton about whether he had sold Lionel Richie concert tickets to a reputed Genovese mobster. Sharpton denied it, but acknowledged he had provided tickets for an agency in New Jersey that had trouble getting good seats. The New Jersey outfit called the seats a partial repayment for charity work done for Sharpton's National Youth Movement.

Sharpton's puzzling dealings with the FBI were revealed in an article in *New York Newsday* on January 20, 1988, just two days before he left town for the Tyson-Holmes fight. The account caused consternation among many blacks in New York, and the FBI heard that a contract for a "hit" may even have been put out on Sharpton. Sharpton insisted that political enemies were trying to blunt his influence in a resurgent civil rights movement. As he told the audience of New York's radio station WLIB: "I think the idea of this setup is either killing me or scaring me into running out of town. But I won't back down. When God made me, he forgot to put reverse in my transmission."

Was Sharpton an informant? Clearly he had collaborated with the FBI. And for an organizer who prided himself on his street smarts and shrewd judgments, he displayed an astonishing naiveté about mingling with underworld figures. But beyond that, as with so much involving Sharpton, all was murky. The most striking question was why he had agreed so readily to secret arrangements with the FBI, which had long regarded black activism—indeed, all activism—as subversive. What did the feds really have on him?

Despite his flirtations with enemies of the civil rights movement, Sharpton lost little ground. It was a tribute to his dexterity. But it was also the fault of the media and the black political leadership. The media, particularly television, needed him for his access to the movement. It was easier to reach Sharpton than to seek out diverse views among blacks; reporters didn't waste time wondering whom he spoke for. And the various civil rights groups, in turn, needed him for his access to the media. For nobody knew better what buttons to push to get on the six o'clock news, to get on Oprah and Phil and Downey and Koppel.

He stood at the podium looking out over the assembled reporters like a dictator on a balcony, with folded arms and pouting lips. There were no campaign ribbons across the puffy chest, but the Martin Luther King, Jr., medallion hung like a grapefruit over his breastbone. His helmet was a reddish-brown coiffure that had been tinted and straightened and blow-dried in a beauty shop.

It was a Saturday, December 5, a strange day, perhaps, to hold a news conference, but Al Sharpton knew that weekends were slow news days and that events on Saturday, in particular, were destined for prominent play in the high-circulation Sunday papers. It was always easy to grab a headline on Saturdays, when skeleton news teams were scratching around for stories. Sharpton had put out the word, and the reporters had dutifully appeared in droves, as they always had after Howard Beach. From all over New York City, from far up the Hudson Valley, they were there at the United Auto Workers hall to hear what Sharpton had to say. There were others there, too, a whole phalanx of ministers and lawyers and human rights officials and other community leaders, but the focus, as always, was on Al Sharpton—a master of condensing everything he had to say into ten-second sound bites.

"Governor Cuomo has had laryngitis about Tawana Brawley."

There it was. Television cameras whirred, pens scratched.

"New York is now the Mississippi and Alabama of the eighties."

Whirrrrrr. Scratch, scratch.

"The most shameful act of racism of our times . . ."

Whirrrrrrrr. Scratch.

"Tawana Brawley . . ."

Whirrrrrrrrr . . .

". . . is a traumatized, raped woman."

Whirrrrrrrrrrrrrrrrrrrrr.

Alton Maddox was there, too, and at one point succeeded in nudging Sharpton aside to announce that he had cracked the case. He said Tawana Brawley had been abducted and sexually assaulted by attackers who had followed her from the jail in Goshen.

"Unbeknownst to Tawana, she'd been trailed from the Orange County facility," he said. "She was lured into an automobile by the representation—note that I didn't say misrepresentation—that he was a police officer." The Brawleys had said earlier that she had been dragged in by the hair, but if anyone caught the contradiction they didn't say so.

Maddox went further: guards dressed as Ku Klux Klansmen had attacked inmates at the jail two days before the girl vanished, and Tawana's jail visit with Todd Buxton had "upset the authorities." Again, no one disputed him, even though the State Corrections Commission and the State Division of Human Rights had already concluded that there was no evidence that guards had donned sheets and brutalized the inmates.

Then Maddox repeated one of the earliest charges against the authorities: they were covering up for the men who had attacked Tawana. Again, he offered no proof—not the name of a witness, not the color of a car, not the barest shred of evidence. Unchallenged, he thundered on: "There has been a complete breakdown in the legal and criminal justice system in the state of New York." Tawana would not talk until Governor Cuomo named a special prosecutor for the case. Black people should invoke their constitutional rights: the right to keep and bear arms, the right of self-defense—including, he said, "the right to kill, if necessary."

Before closing, Maddox reminded his listeners of the rally in Newburgh a week hence and a massive protest to be held in New York City a week after that. And by the way, he added, there would be no help required from "the National Association for the Advancement of Coon People." All *they* wanted, he sneered, was to put blacks "back in chains and back on plantations."

As with a pebble dropped in a pond, the ripples began. Sharpton's skillful exploitation of television and the press, Maddox's inflammatory charges, the involvement of a coalition of groups with plans to stage wider and more disruptive protests—the momentum was becoming irresistible.

Thus far, the story had been largely local news, a shocking case that had made headlines in the Hudson Valley and been aired a couple of times on New York City television. But now the New York City newspapers were getting interested. And when the New York press jumped on a story, the national press and the national networks were never far behind.

Part Two

"NO
JUSTICE!
NO
PEACE!"

10

Dutchess County District Attorney William Vincent Grady—
the man in charge of the Brawley investigation—did not cut an
inspiring figure. He was small and slightly built, with thinning
hair. Wire-rimmed spectacles framed his puckish face. He wore
conservative suits, lived plainly, and devoted himself to his family
and his work. He had only one visible extravagance: an ice-blue
Jaguar that he drove to and from his assigned parking space at the
Dutchess County Courthouse in Poughkeepsie. But, lest anyone
get the wrong idea, Grady hastened to explain that it was just a
used car, 1982 vintage, and that he had done a lot of gritty work
out in the garage to fix it up.

Grady was a man who cared about appearances, a small-town
lawyer who kept trim with four-wall handball and did a bit of
sailing on weekends. He was forty-five and had spent most of his
life close to home. He had been born in Beacon, just down the
Hudson a few miles, and had grown up in the county. His father,
Vincent, whose picture he kept in the office, had been the district
attorney in the 1940s and later had been a justice of the state
supreme court—which, despite its name, is not an appellate
court but a trial court for murders and other felonies. Young
Grady had gone off to war and college—he had won a Bronze Star
as a captain in an armored unit in Vietnam and graduated from
New York Law School. In 1971 he had returned to Dutchess
County to become an assistant district attorney.

His ambitions were narrowly focused. In Dutchess County, where position and power were often dynastic, passing from father to son, he had only to hang on to improve his prospects. Eventually he became chief assistant prosecutor. He lost his first bid to become district attorney in 1975, but he ran again in 1983 and won, a careful Republican in a Republican county, and was reelected in 1987. Grady was a local politician, and statesmanship was not requisite. Nuclear war might be the issue of the age, but what counted in Poughkeepsie, as in many other small communities in America, was yesterday's mugging and the prosecutor's angry reaction. Grady's office, which had nineteen assistant district attorneys, prosecuted eight thousand crimes a year and had a respectable conviction rate. Grady liked to talk grimly about drugs and crime, and he was good at it.

On any weekday, seeking Grady out at the courthouse was like stepping back in time. Behind the oak doors of the historic old coral-and-gray fortress at Main and Market streets stretched a cool marble lobby out of the cobblestone-and-gaslight era: soft voices echoing under a lofty tin ceiling, clerks lacking only eye-shades and sleeve garters working at oversized ledgers in the offices, a bulletin board papered with notices of foreclosures and sheriff's sales. The DA's office was up the marble stairs on the third floor, and there was Grady's name, neatly lettered like Sam Spade's on the frosted glass. Inside, it was somber, busy, cluttered with files and people making more files: each one a life's tragedy.

The corner office was Grady's refuge. The chairs were brown, the table black, the rug burgundy. Pale lamps glowed in the daylight. Grady's maxim from Supreme Court Justice Robert H. Jackson yellowed on an antechamber wall: "The qualities of a good prosecutor are as elusive and impossible to define as those which mark a gentleman." True to form, Grady had a knack of sounding tough, but there was often a wariness behind his words. "There's no question in my mind that a crime has been committed," he told a reporter who asked about the Brawley case one day. "We are making every effort to solve that crime, but we will not be prodded into taking hasty action unless there is sufficient evidence to warrant an arrest." It sounded assertive, but it was all in doubt; there *was* a question whether a crime had been committed, *many* people doubted that the authorities were making every effort, and the police *often* rounded up *black* suspects on the flimsiest of guesses.

In nearly two decades as a prosecutor, Grady thought he had seen every vile thing that one human being could do to another. He had prosecuted killers, rapists, and robbers by the score. He had seen torn bodies and desperate victims and had glimpsed some of the darkest corners of the criminal mind. But nothing had prepared him for the Brawley case.

Despite the violence it touched, Grady's world was an orderly one: usually crime victims willingly filed complaints and gave evidence; suspects were nearly always ferreted out and sent to jail. Cases were opened and closed like file drawers. But the Brawley affair, with its uncommunicative victim, its explosive racial politics, was a diabolical thing—not a single case, really, but a maze of stupefying, interlocking mysteries that could not be solved with the usual plodding legwork or even with dazzling Sherlock Holmesian deductions.

"You're not going to believe this," Lieutenant James J. Thompson, the sheriff's chief of detectives, had warned Grady after Tawana was found at the Pavillion. And since then it had only become weirder and weirder.

Grady rarely got personally involved in a case at the start. It was easier, and it was his prerogative, to delegate responsibility for the hard investigative work, to come in later for the coup de grace and the big publicity. To the Brawley case, he had immediately assigned two of his top assistants: Otto Williams and Marjorie Smith. But they had hardly gotten anywhere with Tawana— if anything, their investigation had come up with bits and pieces that seemed to contradict the girl's sketchy account, not confirm it.

At the Pavillion, the investigators had found witnesses who had seen lights and heard music and other sounds in 19A Carnaby

Drive while Tawana had been missing. In 19A, they had found the girl's fingerprints, a candle, a pair of denim jeans, a denim jacket, and other evidence that she had been there. Outside in the yard, they had found dog feces, a charred washcloth, some fragments of burned denim, and a pair of boots with torn cotton insulation. They had questioned Tawana's friends and learned that before her disappearance she had been wearing a hairpiece that gave her the look of shoulder-length tresses, when in fact her hair was quite short. This suggested that, by the time she reappeared, the hairpiece had merely been removed, that her hair had not been brutally chopped off, as her family had said. Added to the assertions by the neighbors who had seen Tawana climbing into a bag and the medical tests that showed no signs of an attack, these findings caused Grady to believe that there was something gravely wrong with the girl's story. Still, it all fell far short of proving what had really happened.

And so Grady was in a bind. The political pressure on him was all in the other direction: to come up with proof confirming Tawana's story, to find and arrest suspects, to show that the authorities were not covering up. But there could be no suspects without a crime, and the only evidence of a crime lay in that sketchy tale, in the bizarre condition in which the girl had been found.

The pressure was building fast. It hit Grady every time he opened a newspaper: a drumbeat of cover-up charges, widening protests, and growing demands for justice. The rumors were flying like boomerangs—about the KKK, about the suicide of Harry Crist, about the ferocity of the attack on Tawana and the horrendous injuries she had suffered.

Heat was coming from the governor as well. "The recent assault of fifteen-year-old Tawana Brawley in Wappingers Falls concerns me deeply, as it should all New Yorkers," Cuomo had said. It was not hard to read between the lines. The populist Democrat in Albany cast a long shadow, especially in a presidential election year. Grady could not help wondering whether he was being set up for a political fall.

It seemed even more so when Cuomo formally ordered the state police in on December 7. By then, as Grady knew, the state police had been working on the case informally for five days. Now, there would be thirty state and county investigators on it, and the state crime laboratory in Albany would be available to analyze forensic evidence. Cuomo's intervention might be good for the investigation—and it was certainly good politics for the governor. But for Grady it made matters worse. For if the governor himself was so worried, then surely there must be a basis for grave concern. Therefore Tawana *must* have been attacked, and perhaps the local authorities—some might even conclude Grady himself—were not to be trusted, just as the Brawleys were saying.

Lucille Pattison, the Dutchess County executive, had chimed in too. She had publicly promised to meet with, among others, Clarence McGill, the chairman of the Dutchess County Committee Against Racism. And she had promised that Sheriff Scoralick and District Attorney Grady would be there with her. The implication was clear: the foot-dragging law-enforcement officials would soon be brought into line.

Grady, like Scoralick, doubted Tawana's tale of rape and abduction. But how could he challenge the account of a black girl who had been found covered with excrement and racial slurs? He would look like a racist unless he had conclusive proof that she had faked the episode, and he did not have that. No, the only way to look good to the voters was to subscribe—temporarily at least—to Tawana's story. And while it would be best to do nothing, he had to do something. And so Grady made another stab at getting the truth out of the Brawleys. First, he decided, he'd better speak to Maddox.

No, said the secretary in Alton Maddox's Brooklyn office, the lawyer was not in. Grady hung up, but he persisted. He called Maddox's office every day for a week. Every time, he got the same story. He left messages. Maddox never called back. Finally, Grady sent two officers to Brooklyn. They found only the secretary, who told them that Maddox would respond when he was good and ready.

Grady decided to go to the Brawleys himself. On December 8, with his black assistant, Otto Williams, he went to 4-D Carmine Drive. Glenda Brawley opened the door. She eyed them skeptically, as if they might be bill collectors, salesmen, or reporters. They explained who they were and produced identity cards. Finally, she let them in.

There was no sign of Tawana. She might have been upstairs, keeping out of sight, but there was no telling. Grady and Williams kept looking around, listening for a cough or the creak of a floorboard, but there was nothing. Glenda seemed to be home alone.

They sat around the dining room table, talking uncomfortably, sizing one another up like boxers in the first round. Grady, perhaps letting hope cloud his judgment, tried to convey that he was impressed by her motherly sincerity. But Glenda made no effort to hide her distaste for these men with expensive suits and polished manners.

The investigation was well under way, Grady told her, trying to sound resolute. And it would go forward whether Tawana cooperated or not, he added. It was like calling the dealer's bluff: it had no effect at all. But Grady tipped his hand—a hand full of low cards—when he said he "sincerely" wanted Tawana's help. Of course, he went on, he and the other officials were sensitive to the importance of the case and had never intended to offend the family with all that talk about their not cooperating. Yes, he regretted remarks by the sheriff and others—including himself— that suggested the family was deliberately withholding help. He told Glenda of his unsuccessful efforts to reach Maddox, and going out on a limb, he explained how hard it was to conduct an inquiry without the victim's help. He said he hoped Tawana was feeling better. His remarks were full of courtesy and hopefulness. But as Glenda Brawley could see all too easily, they were nothing but the abject pleas of a desperate man.

When he finished, she nodded noncommittally.

Suddenly, the front door opened and Ralph King came in. When he saw the visitors, his face flashed like cutlery and he erupted in a stream of obscenities.

"What the fuck is going on here?" he demanded.

Grady and Williams were taken aback. They had expected a concerned stepfather, not a raging maniac. Grady tried to calm King down.

King turned to the black prosecutor. "You're a motherfucker!" he shouted. "What the fuck are you doing here? You fuck!"

Williams responded peaceably but the tirade continued, and he, too, grew angry. Now everyone was shouting. A chair was pushed back.

A scary thought struck Grady: this might be dangerous. Here was a man who had killed his wife, and he was frothing and pawing like a bull.

There was no stopping him—King's accusations rolled like thunder: the white authorities were covering up for the attackers; they were constantly making statements to the press that undermined the family and put the blame on Tawana; they were not interested in finding the attackers; they had not even followed up on an accusation by Tawana Ward Dempsey that was similar to Tawana's. What were the investigators doing anyway? Why hadn't they arrested somebody?

And, King went on, Grady and Williams had better watch what they say: he was even now tape-recording the whole conversation. Moreover, the police were following him and Glenda around, treating them like criminals. They had even been stopped on the way home from the Westchester County Medical Center one day. It was just plain harassment, he bellowed.

Now Glenda joined in. She charged that St. Francis Hospital had tried to murder Tawana. "They were trying to kill her," Glenda shouted. "Why else was her arm puffed up?" (This was an apparent reference to the slight swelling—nothing dangerous—in Tawana's arm where the intravenous hookup in the ambulance had slipped out.) Grady and Williams had no idea what she was talking about.

King plunged back in. What about Tawana's education? She

was too upset to go to school now. What were the authorities going to do about *that*?

Well, said Grady, at last getting a word in, they might arrange to have Tawana taught at home. Yes, he would do something about that.

King let the point slide. But he and Glenda had Grady in a corner now, and they were not going to let him out. They said they wanted him to assemble a lineup of photographs for Tawana to look at—a rogue's gallery of suspects that would include lots of police officers.

Grady tried to explain the problem: Tawana had not given a sufficiently detailed description for them to come up with a selection of photos for a lineup.

They glowered.

Grady caved in: Well, perhaps he could get something together.

Would it include a picture of Harry Crist?

It could.

Was Crist a suspect?

"We would not concede he's a suspect," said Grady, stiffening. But would the family and Tawana now cooperate? Could his investigators speak to the girl?

They didn't say no.

Finally Glenda said: "Tawana will talk. But we will want a representative there."

"Fine. No problem." Grady's heart was pounding. "You can have anybody you want," he said. "Who is your representative?"

The answer came quickly. "We don't know."

Was she putting him on?

But Glenda now seemed to soften. Perhaps it *would* be all right for Tawana to talk to the investigators. After all, she added, the family wanted the case cleared up, too.

Grady nodded and managed a sympathetic smile.

But it couldn't be done, Glenda was saying, until Tawana was feeling up to it. And it couldn't be done without the permission of their "representative." And it couldn't be done unless the representative was *present*.

Grady nodded.

Yes, said the woman, now with the hint of a smile herself, then perhaps Tawana might speak to them after all.

For the first time in days, Grady allowed his hopes to rise.

Grady hurried to the inquisition in Poughkeepsie. County Executive Lucille Pattison had put out her summonses at the behest of Clarence McGill. They were all there in her office, McGill and the others, to chastise the law-enforcement officials and set them back on the right road.

They closed the doors.

McGill explained the suspicions of the black community.

Grady and Scoralick listened, then said they were doing all they could to win the family's cooperation and break the case. They would be happy to redouble their efforts, they said, if it would help ease suspicions.

When it was over, the sheriff and the district attorney smiled, and McGill said he was pleased. He offered an olive branch, saying he would not use such strong language as "cover-up" to describe what had been going on. "But things have been handled in an unusual way," he said, getting the last dig in.

As soon as he got back to his office, Grady rounded up the press. Then he made some amazing statements.

"There is absolutely no question that Tawana Brawley was sexually assaulted," he said—ignoring the fact that the medical exams had shown no evidence of such an assault and that laboratory analysis of the rape-kit materials sent to the FBI in Washington had not been completed.

"What we have so far is forcible sodomy," he continued, in the face of no evidence to that point whatsoever.

He sailed on: "We have a very brief description of one of the individuals involved in the attack." That description—and perhaps even a composite drawing of the suspect—would "be made public very soon, because there's an absolute need to get as much information before the public."

127

It was as if there had been some magical breakthrough—Grady and his investigators were hot on the trail of the culprits. In fact, Grady was just recycling as a description the few vague details that Juanita Brawley had initially supplied, ones that his own investigators had regarded as almost useless, if not plain false.

The newly resolute prosecutor went further: dropping his earlier stance against showing Tawana pictures of potential suspects, Grady now said it was a good idea. His investigators, he said, intended to show the girl a collection of such pictures, including one of Harry Crist. To be sure, the investigators had "preliminarily" found no link between the Brawley case and the suicide of the part-time police officer. But such a connection was not being ruled out. No, all that the investigators had "ruled out" was the "hypothetical" possibility that the condition in which Tawana was found had been self-inflicted.

As to the case's wider resonance, Grady finally struck the most ominous note of all: "There's no question, based upon conversations with people who have spoken directly to Ku Klux Klan members, that there *is* a Ku Klux Klan organization in this area." Would he identify the people who had told him so? Well, no, he wouldn't.

Even Clarence McGill was taken aback by Grady's sudden turnabout. Whereas only a few days earlier the authorities had expressed skepticism at every turn, now, McGill said, "everyone is convinced that there was a crime." Whereas just a few days ago Grady had scoffed at suggestions of local Ku Klux Klan activity, he was now saying it was real. Perhaps, McGill reflected, the case was even bigger than anyone suspected, so big it could no longer be covered up.

Whatever, as McGill pointed out, the officers of the law had "taken a position that's three hundred and eighty degrees different from what it was a week ago." In other words, they had begun to spin.

That night, to halt the spin and get some facts, the authorities sent their most skilled investigators to the Brawley apartment.

Lieutenant Theodore Cook and Investigator Carol Johnston of the state police and Assistant District Attorney Marjorie Smith presented a sharp contrast to the afternoon contingent. Cook was one of the highest-ranking black officers in the state police and had founded the force's affirmative action program eight years earlier. Johnston, who was white, was one of the finest investigators of sex crimes and child-abuse cases in the state. Smith was Grady's top prosecutor in those fields. All were extremely sensitive to the feelings of the Brawley family. Indeed, Cook had developed something of a rapport with Glenda and Juanita. They had spoken several times by telephone, and through these patient contacts Cook felt a sense of developing trust.

The investigators had hoped to see Tawana, but only Glenda was present. She began by asking them to look into Harry Crist's death; she had read in a newspaper that the police ought to be doing that.

Cook said that Crist's death was being investigated.

Glenda asked that Tawana be supplied with photos of all the police and corrections officers and anyone else who wore a badge in the mid-Hudson Valley.

This request, delivered matter-of-factly, was staggering. It would have required thousands of photos. Besides all the state, county, city, and town police officers and corrections officials in several counties, there were court officers, firefighters, housing and health inspectors, parks and recreation workers, and private guards in hospitals, mental institutions, corporations, and government offices. Even kids had badges—you could buy them in novelty stores. When you came right down to it, practically everyone had a badge.

The investigators told her they needed more information from Tawana to narrow down the field.

But Tawana was still too traumatized to talk to them, said Glenda. Anyway, the girl could be interviewed only in the presence of Alton Maddox.

And that's where they left it. Once again, despite Grady's desperate cave-in, the investigators came away empty-handed.

Still, they were not daunted. Carol Johnston returned the next day with Detective Jerry Schmidt of the sheriff's Juvenile Aid Bureau. This time Juanita was there with her sister, as was King. And so was Tawana, lying on the couch. The talk quickly turned to the subject of interviewing her. When it did, Tawana responded: she got up, walked across the living room, and disappeared upstairs.

Just like that, Schmidt thought. For nearly two weeks, she had been carried everywhere; everyone who had seen her had said she appeared unable to walk. Just two days ago, she had been in a wheelchair on a visit to a psychiatrist. Only yesterday, one of her friends had seen her unable to get up, reporting that she even needed help to wash and dress. But now, she had risen abruptly from the couch and walked away without the slightest hint of a limp. Just like that.

William Grady seemed unnerved as he faced the assembled reporters and television cameras. Today, he looked more like a suspect than a prosecutor—a man about to undergo a terrible grilling. It was the day after his ringing, reassuring press conference. Now he had to take most of it back.

First, the business about the KKK being active locally: "That is not correct," he said. "That was an error. I accept full responsibility for having made the statement." Yes, his office had developed information about people claiming to be affiliated with the KKK, but none of them were local. And there had been no evidence so far to show that the KKK was involved in the Brawley case.

Then, the business of zeroing in on the assailants: in fact, he said, his investigators had only a *preliminary* description—even this was an exaggeration—and further questioning of the girl would be necessary before a real description or composite sketch could be provided.

But he *was* hopeful—hopeful of arranging a conversation with Tawana Brawley through Alton Maddox. Yes, he had had some difficulty getting in touch with the lawyer. (He did not mention that Maddox had refused to return his calls all week.)

Grady had another reason for hope: he was planning to impanel a special grand jury, one that would focus on the Brawley case alone. After the second press conference, he went to see Dr. Ruth Lavites, a psychiatrist at the Westchester County Medical Center who had been talking to Tawana. The girl was not yet sixteen, so the doctor was not bound by confidentiality. She told Grady that there was no medical reason why the girl could not testify. Perhaps, he thought, a grand jury could force Tawana Brawley to break her silence.

11

There were rallies against racism on both sides of the Hudson that Saturday, in Poughkeepsie and Newburgh, but the two events were a world apart. One rally was small and subdued; it drew only local people, and its purpose was to raise questions. The other was large and raucous; it attracted big-name orators from halfway across the country, and its purpose was to raise hell.

Two weeks had passed since Tawana Brawley had been found at the Pavillion, and in the spreading crusade on her behalf two movements had sprung up, each with its own aims, leaders, and methods. One, led by local people like Clarence McGill, emphasized justice for Tawana Brawley, whatever else came of it. The other, led by celebrities from distant cities, like Alton Maddox and Al Sharpton, wanted to use the Brawley case as a weapon in the broader war against racism.

Their differences represented something larger as well about the nature and effectiveness of political action in the United States. On the one hand were people who believed that the pressure of facts alone would force the legal apparatus and public officials to bring about justice. On the other were people who placed little faith in the facts and none in elected leaders, who believed that only enormous pressure by angry masses could force sheriffs and politicians to act for justice. These disparate strategies had often jostled for supremacy in American grass-roots politics. And on this December 12 in two small cities on opposite banks of the Hudson River, their differences were never plainer.

Clarence McGill grasped the podium and looked out over the quiet, attentive audience of one hundred fifty at the civic center in Poughkeepsie. They were local black people mostly, including teachers and preachers who could always be counted on to turn out, who had come today to hear sensible talk about the Brawley case.

McGill was just the person to give it to them. He was one of the most influential blacks in the county, and though unknown beyond its borders, he always drew a small but thoughtful crowd eager for his insights. McGill inspired confidence: his solemn baritone voice, the graying hair, and the salt-and-pepper mustache gave him the aura of an elder statesman. When he spoke there was a ring of truth in the air. He spoke now, with measured scorn: "Our county sheriff, with all his ultra-wisdom, says it could be self-inflicted. Can you imagine the arrogance?" Could anything be more unthinkable than that Tawana Brawley could have smeared herself with excrement and written racial slurs on her own body? Why, McGill asked, would any rational person smear herself with excrement and write such terrible things on her own body? The straightforward explanation—an abduction by racists and rapists— was far more likely to be the truth.

In his calm, reasonable way, McGill mentioned the anger many blacks felt over the Brawley case, a feeling he said he shared. He questioned whether the law was doing its best to solve the case, and he suggested that the appointment of a special prosecutor might be a good idea.

But he did not urge protests to pressure the authorities. Instead, he sounded a note of caution: "I don't think to fight now would be in our best interests. The best thing now is to use the people we have elected."

Polite applause floated up.

Folami Gray spoke too. She was there representing the Dutchess County executive, Lucille Pattison, the county's highest elected official. To more polite applause, she said, "I need not be convinced of the existence of racism in Dutchess County." They all knew what she was talking about: just a few months earlier, Gray had been named executive director of the Dutchess County Youth Bureau, the first black ever to be appointed to head a county department.

The governor had sent a representative too—Eve Carlin. Soothingly, she told the gathering: "I have listened closely to what has been spoken before me, and I will take the message back to the governor of your request for a special prosecutor."

And then they drifted away, heading home with a sense of solid, if modest, achievement: a representative of the governor had promised to speak to him about their concerns.

Louis Farrakhan stepped out of the automobile into the bright wintry sunlight, and shouts of excitement broke from the people in waves. For a few moments, the crowd outside the Newburgh church forgot Al Sharpton and Tawana Brawley and even the rally. All eyes watched the minister of the Nation of Islam, the black man whites feared like death. He stood there momentarily, slender and elegant, the sunlight glinting on his gold-wire spectacles, while his entourage of icy-eyed bodyguards rushed ahead, clearing the way. The vast throng divided like extras in a Hollywood epic, and the revolution's executioner moved through them.

For Lillian Howard, it was a dream come true: Louis Farrakhan and a vast crowd from many parts of the country, here in Newburgh to protest the mistreatment of her boy, to share her anger over the Tawana Brawley case, to stand with her in denouncing racism in all its forms.

From New York City and Chicago, from Washington, D.C., and Buffalo and Albany, from up and down the Hudson Valley, they had poured into town all morning by bus and car for the biggest protest the region had seen in years—a thousand black people with a message for racists. If it was impressive evidence of the growing network of people and organizations available to the Brawley struggle, it also provided a clear window into the rivalries within the loose coalition. And for most of the ordinary people, it was a day of intense and conflicting emotions: while they were outraged over racism, they were thrilled to be there; primed for incendiary tirades, they brimmed with pride.

As they milled about outside the Baptist Temple Church on William Street, Farrakhan strode in to meet the rally organizers. He had been contacted at his Chicago headquarters by his followers in New York a few days earlier and had called his old friend Sharpton to arrange his appearance. His presence at the rally was an enormous coup: it guaranteed major media attention.

Farrakhan was far more than a celebrity. For many blacks, his magnetism and message evoked images of power and pride that no other person, not even Jesse Jackson, had been able to create. But to most whites, he was a monster. His predictions of race war, his anti-Semitic and antiwhite tirades, his praise of Hitler, had made him a terrifying figure. Yet few people knew much about him. The son of an Episcopal minister, born Louis Wolcott in 1933, he had been a calypso singer in Boston when, in the 1950s, he was recruited into the Nation of Islam by its best-known figure, Malcolm X. A religious sect founded in Detroit in 1930, it had been built by Elijah Muhammad, its prophet, into a black-supremacist movement that had once claimed as many as five hundred thousand members. After Elijah Muhammad's death in 1975, his son became leader, renounced black supremacy, and transformed the organization into a more orthodox religious entity.

It was left to Farrakhan and his followers to keep the fires stoked, and in 1977 they broke away to resurrect Muhammad's teachings. But Farrakhan attracted little notice outside black circles until he came to national attention in 1984 as a supporter of Jackson's bid for the Democratic presidential nomination. After Farrakhan termed Judaism "a gutter religion" and praised Hitler as "a great man," Jackson was forced to disavow some of his remarks. Nonetheless, Farrakhan pressed on with antiwhite, anti-Semitic oratory and his calls for a separate black nation within the United States. In 1985 he accepted a five-million-dollar loan from the Libyan leader, Colonel Muammar el-Qaddafi, to establish a business in hair and skin products to help keep black money in the black community.

At the church in Newburgh that day, not everyone was an admirer of Farrakhan. Some Hudson Valley people were there only because of the Brawley case, and many busloads had come from New York City and other parts of the state, people who had known about Tawana only briefly and were there to protest various local cases of racism. Still others from more distant points saw racism large in the foreground; to them, the Brawley case was only an example, though a good one ideologically. In general, the more distance they had traveled, the more radical they were—the more they admired Farrakhan and the less they cared about Tawana Brawley.

Dissension among the factions began immediately.

Farrakhan's paramilitary bodyguards, known as the Fruit of Islam, were frisking everyone—everyone but Sharpton and Farrakhan—at the church door, and Viola Plummer, among many, was upset. "They're taking over our rally," she said.

Farrakhan, Sharpton, Sonny Carson, and the Reverend Timothy Mitchell of the Ebenezer Missionary Baptist Church in Queens had gone in and were talking things over in the office of the pastor, Reverend Saul Williams. They had been at it for twenty minutes when Viola Plummer stormed in. She was hopping mad about being frisked, and she launched into a tirade against Farrakhan. He offered to leave. Voices grew shrill, but then subsided.

When C. Vernon Mason arrived, there was another blowup. Mason was making his debut in the Brawley affair, and he had brought along for the occasion a CBS camera crew that was shooting a day in the life of Mason for the news program *West 57th Street*.

"What are you doing here with a crew?" Viola Plummer demanded. Then, spotting a microphone on Mason's lapel, her eyes went wide. "And you're wired!" she shouted.

In short order, the *West 57th Street* producer was ejected, and Mason's microphone was thrown out too.

But who was to preside over the rally? "These revolutionaries are not getting in my pulpit," Williams declared self-righteously. "My pulpit is sacred. It's a house of God, and these people don't even believe in God." Finally, it was decided: Mitchell would preside, and Sharpton, Farrakhan, Mason, Carson, and Plummer would speak, all but the last two from the pulpit. They were down to one issue: what to do about the media? Sharpton was always in favor of including them in everything, but this time he was overruled, and they were barred from the rally. It hardly discouraged coverage: like any censorship challenge, it only piqued the interest of the press.

Finally, the ruffled feelings smoothed over, they all trooped into the sanctuary, where a thousand people waited, packed into the pews, jammed between the pillars, spilling out the doors with the security guards.

Farrakhan took the pulpit, and his soft voice suddenly became a cracking whip. "You will not do to another black girl in America what you did to Tawana Brawley and get away with it!" he warned the land of racists.

"That's right!" the crowd shouted back.

"We are not anarchists," he boomed.

"That's right!"

"There is life for you in retaliation!"

The crowd roared—Farrakhan was getting to the core of it now: "When the courts won't find a white man guilty for a crime he committed, then *we* try *them*. Then we execute them."

Here it was—the call of the true revolutionary, the unforgiving executioner—and the crowd roared again, clapping hands and stomping feet.

Then it was Sharpton's turn. "Black people around this state," he declared, "are being murdered, brutalized, and sodomized almost on a daily basis."

"That's right!"

The "racial beasts who are terrorizing the state" must be arrested, he went on. And the white leadership was fully culpable, including Mario Cuomo—"a symbol of sophisticated urban racism." The governor, he said, had no blacks in his cabinet (in fact, there were two), which led Sharpton to his withering conclusion: "Mario Cuomo governs the most racist state in the union while he's being touted as presidential material!"

Next to Farrakhan, Sharpton seemed moderate. His call was not for violence but for political pressure against Cuomo and the state to do what was right for blacks. But if Sharpton lacked the fire of Farrakhan, he stayed close to the flame, positioning himself next to him in the church and later marching out beside him with a somber face, well within the narrow-angle frames of the TV cameras.

Alton Maddox wasn't there. He was in Atlanta doing legal work, which he was required to do once a year to keep his license in Georgia. But Sonny Carson, who had brought eleven busloads of people from New York City, might have been speaking for Maddox when he described the NAACP as "Cuomo coons." Then, in deference to the local people, he tried to soft-pedal the differences. "Don't worry about where we are coming from," he yelled to the fainthearted, "but where we're going!"

Then it was Mason's turn. His was a litany of all the blacks who had been beaten, arrested, and killed by white police officers. There was Howard Beach and Jimmy Lee Bruce, Eleanor Bumpurs and Michael Stewart, and the brutality of the guards at the Orange County Jail. "When you violated our law, you took from us all we had left," he told racist America. This was Mason's ground, a blustery confrontation with the absent enemy. It was tough talk, but its meaning, too, was political, for what Mason wanted above all was to be seen—and quoted—as a kind of black statesman. "You've been beating our sons, killing our sons," he concluded. "Now you're taking our women."

They left the church then and marched through the streets of Newburgh, waving placards, raising fists, shouting and chanting their grievances and threats, while the television crews, barred from the church, captured every shriek, every angry gesture:

"What's coming?"

"War!"

"What's coming?"

"War!"

"Black power!"

"Freedom or death!"

"Black power!"

"Freedom or death!"

"No justice! No peace!"

"Tawana Brawley!"

"No justice! No peace!"

"Tawana Brawley!"

"KKK, have you heard? This is not Johannesburg!"

"KKK, have you heard? This is not Johannesburg!"

They wound their way through the back streets of Newburgh. But the farther they got, the more apparent it became that they were marching through deserted streets.

"Who did the routing on this?" Sharpton demanded of Sonny Carson.

"Nobody."

"This doesn't make sense!" Sharpton bellowed. "Why are we marching around some abandoned buildings in Newburgh? There's literally nobody in the buildings. There's literally no one here. And we're not accusing any of these people of doing the rape. What are we doing this for?"

The march did an about-face, back into the church. "We need a black liberation army!" Timothy Mitchell shouted, trying to drum things up again. It was getting late. Many had a long way to go home; the crowd was growing restless. But there was one star attraction left—Juanita Brawley.

She was the only member of the family present, and when she was introduced by Mitchell, the crowd fell silent. Many at the rally—especially those from nearby towns—had come expressly to see her, the doughty aunt, the one closest to the girl who had suffered. And she did not disappoint them. She had on big hoop earrings and a becoming new hairdo, and her face was full of pain. Without ado, she took everyone right back to that terrible moment in the hospital room, where she and her sister, Glenda, had scarcely been able to recognize their girl with "all her hair pulled out, *cut* out." She told them, slightly misquoting, what the police officer had so sadistically said to Tawana—"Are you mad at me?" And as she went on she seemed wrapped in pain.

Sonny Carson stepped up to comfort her. With his arm around her, he announced that there was to be a much bigger protest on December 21 in New York City, the first of a series of civil disobediences to be called "days of outrage." The plan was to tie up the whole town, he said. "Tawana has started a movement that's going to shake up this nation!" The crowd roared approval.

For, of course, it had been about much more than whatever had happened to Tawana Brawley. They had spoken of Jimmy Lee Bruce and the Orange County Jail fracas, of Howard Beach and so many other similar cases in New York and around the country. The mere mention of her name—"Tawana!"—had become another flash point in America's struggle with racism. The case had become less a mystery than the symbol of a larger cause.

And when it was over, when the divisive words and petty rivalries and angry speeches had been vented, and they had got what they had wanted, Minister Farrakhan and his bodyguards headed back to Chicago, and Sharpton and hundreds of people from New York City boarded their chartered buses and headed back down the thruway. The scores of people from Washington, Albany, Buffalo, and up and down the Hudson Valley faded away too. The reporters and television crews packed up and rushed off to meet their deadlines. And as light drained from the darkening sky, Newburgh was left alone again with its drug addicts and deserted streets.

Furious faces, placards held high, Farrakhan shrieking for revenge: this was the spectacle that flashed into millions of homes that night and the next morning, giving much of America its first glimpse of the Tawana Brawley case. But the dignified little gathering in Poughkeepsie drew no big headlines, no replays on television. Indeed, apart from those who had actually gone to the civic center seeking rational discourse, scarcely anyone knew that this rally had even happened.

"Niggers out of control," Professor Mackey was saying at the back table at Edgar's Food Shop, "always have to be watched. The press *has* to cover them. It's a thing that scares the system more than anything else. It was true of Malcolm X. It's true of Farrakhan. It's true of Sharpton."

Hampton Rookard, who had gone to the Newburgh rally with Roy Canton, still couldn't get over something else—the timidity of the locals. "The people who were the residents of this place were afraid to express themselves," he put in. "They pulled the shades down and they peeped around the corners and they would not participate in the march at all. We were the ones that made the parade—the out-of-towners. But the people there—if you were sensitive, you could feel their terror, and it was horrible, horrible. We were there to help them, but they were so terrified they couldn't even help themselves."

Rookard sipped his coffee, savoring the memory of the rally, even the rather pathetic march. Then he said: "The whole deal behind mass demonstration is that you're showing the powerful political group that you are not alone. So you take me out, you've got somebody else to contend with. You take him out, you've got somebody else to contend with. One of the main things you've got to have is the audacity to express *your* fucking power. If you don't have that, give it up."

12

"Press-titutes! Harlots of Sodom! Vile prevaricators!" The heavy-set man, a scowling Dickensian crabstick with goatee and gold-rimmed spectacles, was holding forth in the dark, Victorian parlor of his old gray clapboard house in the south end of Wappingers Falls. His name was Charles McCluskey; he was the editor of the *Hudson Valley Hornet,* and in all the journalistic hysteria surrounding the Tawana Brawley case, he was one rock of certitude.

Slithering things moved in the shadows of the heavy, over-wrought furniture, emerging into the dusty light now and then as cats. So numerous were the piles of books across the floor—thousands of them scattered like rebukes to ignorant visitors—that McCluskey's lair had no discernible dimensions. But his performances to the out-of-town reporters—the "press-titutes" who sought him out during the Brawley affair—were ribald: "I'm a purveyor of intentionally inflammatory journalism," he confided. "My father said shit ain't worth anything unless it smells. I'm trying to get people thinking, to raise hell. I don't give a cup of warm spit what people think of me. I'm four degrees to the right of Jesse Helms. I'm as far right as you can get—thank God! I make the John Birch people look wishy-washy."

Not that the "John Birch people" lacked for exposure in the *Hornet,* the outraged, outrageous weekly that McCluskey had founded with sixty dollars in Wappingers Falls on May Day in 1973. Sprinkled through its thirty-two pages were features distributed by the ultraconservative John Birch Society, the Heritage Foundation, and Reed Irvine's Accuracy In Media. In between were extensive "Observations at Random" by McCluskey and "Editorials" and "More Editorials" in which the irrepressible curmudgeon gave full vent to his right-wing nonsense, reserving many of his sharpest barbs for the "liberal press," in particular his Dutchess County competitors. He called the *Poughkeepsie Journal* "Pravda," and the *Pawling News-Chronicle* "Little Pravda."

McCluskey, it might be said, was the first skeptic about the Brawley case. In his initial commentary on December 4, less than a week after Tawana had been found at the Pavillion, his front-page headline in the *Hornet* asked: "Did the Attack Happen, or Is It Just a Media Show?" McCluskey wrote: "The attack on Tawana Brawley may have happened exactly as she said, and then again it may be a fabrication."

In the gloom of his parlor, McCluskey went further. He said he did not believe Tawana Brawley had been kidnapped and at-tacked by white racists. He acknowledged that he had no proof, but he insisted that Wappingers Falls was not a racist community. He pointed out the window to the Bethany Missionary Baptist Church across the street and noted that its congregation was black. "They are very fine people," he said.

Because of his eccentricities, perhaps, but more likely because he had been so artless as to deny that racism was a reality in Wappingers Falls, the press corps tended to discount McCluskey's views on the Brawley case. He seemed too insensitive to the issues, too glib in his sweeping conclusions. Many local blacks dismissed him as a troglodyte. But many white residents of Wappingers Falls would come to think that he had been right all along—and he was the kind of man who loved having the last laugh.

Only the local newspapers in the Hudson Valley provided regular coverage in the early stages of the case; the *Poughkeepsie Journal*, *The Newburgh Evening News*, the Kingston *Daily Freeman*, and

The Times Herald-Record of Middletown were all on the story. It was noninvestigative and mediocre journalism at best. Stories dutifully regurgitated the charges, countercharges, and conflicting statements of the Brawley family, the public officials, civil rights activists, and others. In an effort to get a Brawley story—any story—the newspapers repeatedly offered themselves as public forums for anyone who had anything to say. But journalistic enterprise was as lacking as proof in the case, and little beyond an occasional paragraph of context was offered to help readers understand what had happened or what it all meant. Even that paragraph was most often missing. The result, for most Hudson Valley residents, was confusion, a sense that something terrible had happened in their midst, even though they didn't know exactly what.

Right from the start, there were wild contradictions. The Kingston *Daily Freeman* quoted Juanita Brawley as saying, "The doctor told us she had been sexually assaulted," and in the same story the paper quoted the chief of Dutchess County detectives as saying that "preliminary reports are to the contrary—there was no rape." In fact, test results were still pending.

As the days passed and the competing claims of the family and the authorities were published and broadcast raw, without illumination, the public's puzzlement deepened. "People are confused about the mixed messages from TV and newspapers," Gordon Hirt, the principal of Ketcham High School, told the *Poughkeepsie Journal* during the first week of the case. "They would like to know what is going on."

Adding to the confusion, of course, were Tawana Brawley's vagueness and Juanita Brawley's running commentary aimed at arousing the public and making it impossible for the authorities to cover up what she believed was a heinous crime.

Despite its vagaries, the avalanche of news seemed proof enough that something awful had happened, and for many Hudson Valley residents that was devastating. Their reactions were not the unfocused antipathies that larger audiences of television viewers and big-city newspaper readers felt when they heard that a girl in a faraway place had been kidnapped and raped by racists. To local people, it was an outrage close to home, the tragedy of a neighbor, a mystery that raised fearful possibilities about the people one saw every day. The familiar now seemed monstrous: the quiet road where the girl had vanished was an ominous setting; danger lurked in every slow-moving car.

Downstate, the New York City newspapers—the *Daily News*, the *New York Post, New York Newsday*, and *The New York Times*—all but ignored the story at the start. The *Post* published an article on the case on December 1, and the *Daily News* ran its first piece on December 6.

The *Daily News* story focused on a fiery press conference by Alton Maddox, Al Sharpton, and a state legislator, Gloria Davis, laying out their sensational charges of police cover-up and Ku Klux Klan activity in the Hudson Valley. The paper used this event as a way to introduce the Brawley story to its readers: "A Bronx assemblywoman called yesterday for a special prosecutor to investigate the alleged gang-rape last month of a 15-year-old black Dutchess County cheerleader by several white men—including one with a badge," it began. The story quoted the Brawley family as saying that Tawana had been approached by three white men, "dragged inside the car, knocked out, driven to a wooded area and forced to perform oral sex on at least six white men."

From the metropolitan desk, John Darnton scanned the block-long newsroom of *The New York Times* like a captain on the bridge, searching for the right reporter for a holiday story. At a nearby desk, Paul Fishleder, his weekend editor, was on the phone to a reporter-trainee down at police headquarters, talking about the Tawana Brawley case.

The newsroom—the nerve center of a global news-gathering operation—was a vast jumble of desks piled with paper, computer terminals trickling luminous green words, wall maps, clocks on pillars, crammed filing cabinets, stacks of newspapers and telephone directories, overflowing in-baskets, television sets, books in tottering piles, paper coffee cups, and here and there a type-writer to show that it was still a newspaper.

Scattered down the room, dozens of reporters and editors labored at their trade, working at telephones and video screens, helping to collect and write up the day's politics and murders, the city's vast entertainments and cruelties. There were unseen legions too: hundreds of other reporters who filed reports from the streets, from City Hall and Albany and Washington, from posts in the suburbs and across the country and around the world.

"Hey, Paul," said Darnton, "what have you got for the weekend?"

Fishleder drew up a chair beside Darnton.

They went over the list of news and feature stories that the weekend metro editor was proposing for the Sunday and Monday editions, December 13 and 14. Some of the stories had already been written; others would be covered over the weekend.

Darnton, the metropolitan editor, listened and nodded. He was an easygoing man with a loose necktie, rolled-up sleeves, and a bony face that wore a bemused expression for the chaotic world. For much of the last decade, he had been a correspondent in Africa, Poland, and Spain; in 1982, he had won a Pulitzer Prize for his *Times* coverage of the Solidarity labor movement in Poland.

It was Fishleder who brought up the Brawley case. Esther Iverem, a young black reporter-trainee working at police head-quarters, had just gotten back from vacation and had seen some wire-service stories on the case. She had checked the paper and asked colleagues and learned that the *Times* had yet to run an article on it. She was surprised and had called the weekend editor to ask if she might go up to Dutchess County over the weekend and do a story.

Fishleder was somewhat uneasy. He knew about the case and regarded the assignment as a delicate one; Iverem was a trainee with little experience. He had told her he would have to check with the metro editor. Now, Fishleder mentioned the matter to Darnton.

Darnton remembered the name Tawana Brawley. He had been backing his blue Hyundai out the driveway in Connecticut a couple of weeks ago when the story came on WCBS radio: a black girl, covered with feces and racial slurs, found in a plastic bag in Dutchess County. There had been cursory news items in the *Post* and the *Daily News* and on television, but the *Times* had published nothing. With crack wars raging on city streets, a municipal corruption scandal threatening to unseat the mayor, and an AIDS crisis overwhelming the city's health care system, Darnton's attention had been focused on other stories. Besides, as he remembered, there had been serious questions about what had really happened to the girl. The police had said there was no evidence of the sexual attack her family was talking about, and the girl had refused to cooperate with investigators. But perhaps the confusion had been resolved and the time had come to do a story.

Fishleder next reminded Darnton that, as Iverem had noted, there had been several instances of racial controversy in the Hudson Valley recently. Iverem, he said, had suggested taking a look at all of them for a "wrap-up." A wrap-up was typical of the kind of article the *Times* gave readers when it had missed a story or had decided not to pursue one initially. The wrap-up was an esteemed vehicle that gave the paper a way to back up and move forward at the same time, covering an old story in a larger context. The *Times* always strived to provide the larger context anyway: a story about racism in a region was sometimes even preferable to an article on one instance of racism because it gave readers depth and context and spared them from numerous, sometimes pointlessly incremental pieces day after day.

Darnton gave his permission and Fishleder passed it along. Iverem was delighted. A bright, eager young reporter, she was hoping during a trial period to show what she could do. She drove up to Poughkeepsie Friday night and checked into the Wyndham Hotel. The rallies were the next day and she covered them. Over the weekend, she also rounded up information on other recent racial cases in the Hudson Valley and wrote the article.

The *Times*, sometimes slow on stories and especially on stories in small towns in upstate New York where it had no correspondents and relied on stringers and police reports, published its first article on the Brawley case on December 14, more than two weeks after the girl had been found.

Iverem's 1,275-word article used the December 12 rallies in Newburgh and Poughkeepsie as a focus to wrap up three recent racial incidents in the Hudson Valley. "Bias Cases Fuel Anger of Blacks," the headline declared. The article appeared on the front page of the metropolitan news section, the second part of a four-part edition. Only eleven of the twenty-eight paragraphs were devoted to the Brawley case. The rest detailed the clash of guards and inmates at the Orange County Jail and the Peekskill incident in which a black man was chased down a road by three white men wielding bats and pipes.

Under a Poughkeepsie dateline, the story began: "Tawana Brawley, a popular 15-year-old high school student, was found Nov. 28 curled in a fetal position inside a plastic bag behind an apartment house in Wappingers Falls, six miles south of here." It went on to say that law-enforcement officials had "questioned the truthfulness" of the girl's statements, while civil rights leaders had accused the police of covering up. The story was a shallow dip into a complex case, merely repeating untested claims that Tawana "had been beaten," that "her hair had been chopped off," and that "she had been abducted and sexually assaulted by six white men."

It was an inauspicious beginning for the *Times*, which did not offer a follow-up story for six weeks and did not pursue the case vigorously for nearly three months. But the confused and lurid elements of the Brawley case, as they were known in December, made it the kind of story the *Times* tended to shy away from. This was not, as its critics liked to charge, a matter of "stodginess," but a reflection of the paper's reserve. If the *Times* was sometimes slow to react to important stories, it was generally because its editors knew that sensational events often proved chimerical. Moreover, they knew all too well how the *Times*, by its unique weight in the news business, could catapult obscure events to the forefront of the nation's consciousness, setting the news agenda each morning for the networks, local television and radio stations, and hundreds of newspapers and magazines. A misstep by the *Times* was more than embarrassing; it could skew the nation's perception of what was really "news."

For much of the century, blacks had been as much second-class citizens in the news columns of white establishment newspapers like the *Times* as they were in public accommodations. If news happened in Harlem or Watts, it might just as well not have happened at all. But the civil rights movement of the 1960s had prompted wider coverage of black life, discrimination, and the struggle for equality in education, housing, and jobs.

In the 1980s, the *Times* found itself reevaluating questions of coverage and fairness on a deeper level. Senior editors regularly critiqued the paper's fairness and balance, asking pointedly whether the extensive coverage of the rape of a white woman was justified if similar coverage was not extended to the story of a black woman's rape, or to what extent black people and issues were represented and black voices resonated in the news columns. Black reporters and editors at the paper were among its harshest critics. They complained that the *Times* missed opportunities to cover blacks and that the paper too readily accepted the word of the authorities in racially controversial cases.

To be sure, the *Times* had covered the Howard Beach case extensively from the start. Even so, some black reporters and editors questioned whether the paper had initially given too much play to the question of what the black victims were doing in the white neighborhood when they were attacked, and not enough to the villainy of the white mob that chased them. Moreover, coverage of Howard Beach quickly became clouded by the politics injected into the affair: almost immediately, the victims' accounts got lost in the debate between their lawyers, Maddox and Mason, and the police over what had happened and the question of whether the authorities were conducting a fair inquiry.

Unfortunate or not, the politics of race could not be ignored. And like much of the American press, the *Times* sometimes chose to cover a racial incident only when civil rights activists or politicians had made a fuss about it, often relying on the versions of the activists on the one hand and the police on the other to detail what had happened. In such matters, civil rights activists were comparable to the public relations functionaries that politicians and corporations, police departments, and other government agencies hired to polish their images and smooth over their miscues. And because reporters who covered race-related news for the *Times* had come to regard civil rights organizations and black political leaders as their main sources, those institutional and political voices—not the less articulate ones of ordinary people—were the ones that most often came through to readers. As a result, rhetoric about "justice" or the lack thereof often relegated the "facts" of controversial cases to a side issue.

At the heart of the problem was the fact that like most news organizations, the *Times* was more often than not reactive rather than predictive about racial flare-ups. Rare were the stories showing how and where and why racial troubles might be brewing. But stories *after* the eruptions of racial violence were endless—along with analyses of the supposed causes. This had been true during the sixties, when urban riots seemed to erupt out of the blue, and it was even truer in the eighties, as the *Times* reactively covered the stories of Eleanor Bumpurs and Michael Stewart, Howard Beach and Tawana Brawley, following them through all the predictable stages: a race-related death or other incident; a period of public outrage; contentious disputes between the authorities and supporters of the victim; and finally, a resolution generally unsatisfactory to blacks.

The fact was—and still is—that the American press was ill-prepared to cover racism in the country. For its part, America's black press had the will but not the resources for the job. Major newspapers and television networks, which had the resources and were potent forces for change, seemed in the self-enriching eighties to lack the will to cover race relations as a major theme of American life. To be sure, members of these organizations—under pressure of lawsuits and adverse publicity—had set up "affirmative action" programs and hired more black and Hispanic staff members. This was true of the *Times*. But for the most part, the coverage of racial incidents was neither aggressive nor insightful.

Television had found it easy to jump at once on the Brawley story; with its vivid cast of characters and horrific ingredients, the case was the perfect stuff of quick-take drama (although after its initial fling with the case, WCBS largely lost interest and did not resume extensive coverage for months). But the *Times* was still wrestling with profound uncertainties about the handling of racial matters when John Darnton assigned Esther Iverem to go up to Poughkeepsie for a first, belated look at the story.

What the press and the public hungered for were facts, and behind the scenes at the FBI laboratories in Washington, D.C., the search was under way.

Agent Joseph Errera, a forensic expert on serums, was at work on the rape-kit samples taken at St. Francis Hospital and sent down with Tawana's clothing, along with other evidence gathered by the Dutchess County investigators. He examined blood and saliva samples and swabs from her mouth, vagina, and rectum that had been preserved on microscope slides. His initial examination found no semen on any of the slides, but these results were regarded as inconclusive. If the girl had been raped or had engaged in sexual intercourse at the start of her disappearance, semen would not necessarily have shown up.

Errera also examined the plastic bag in which Tawana had been found and the gray cottonlike wads from the bag and from 19A Carnaby Drive. They were like the wads seen in her nostrils and ears, though those wads had not been saved. Errera discovered that the material was Du Pont Hollofil, the same material as that which lined the white boots in 19A. It was clear that whoever had stuffed the wads into Tawana's ears and nostrils had gone to considerable trouble to spare her from infection and the odor of the excrement smeared on her.

The blood samples were turned over to Agent Thomas Lynch, an expert in chemistry. He found no evidence of alcohol or any of four hundred other drugs in the samples. Agent Michael Malone, an expert on hair and fibers, also began an examination of the clothing and other materials.

Far more elaborate workups were planned for the clothing and other materials, including the black strap, the burnt cloth, and the gloves found beside Tawana. These were to be subjected to ultraviolet scans and chemical tests to screen for acid phosphatase, prostate antigen, and choline, all of which are found in semen. But these tests were extremely complex and would take months to complete.

And so the findings regarding the absence of semen and the matching cotton wads were the only ones reported by the FBI to the state and county investigators that early winter. Because they were inconclusive (and because the secrecy of the grand jury investigation made it illegal to prematurely disclose such information), they were not announced—which left the public and the press as much in the dark as ever.

13

The celebration was four days late and the mood was hardly jubilant, but there were friends and presents and a cake. Tawana Brawley was finally having her sweet-sixteen party. The birthday girl lay on the couch in a living room strewn with balloons and wrapping paper, with letters and cards from well-wishers. A clutch of reporters had gotten there early, and Tawana cooed to them: "For a while, I wouldn't talk to anybody, but my friends are coming to see me today."

She talked about singing and hanging out with her friends, about doing all the things she used to do, confiding somberly: "It might be a while before I can dance again. I still can't walk."

Learning to drive a car was what she longed to do. "I'm getting my permit soon," she announced, adding, "as soon as I'm able to take the test." She pointed to her legs. "They still hurt," she said, and added that she was undergoing special therapy for her legs at the Westchester County Medical Center. (In fact, she was only seeing a psychiatrist there.)

Eleven visitors showed up that day, December 19, including six of her closest friends—her latest boyfriend, Daryl Rodriguez, with whom she talked a great deal, and Kisha McLemore, Jerome McLemore, Don Waters, Sonya Waters, and Tamala McLain. Chimene Lewis couldn't attend, but she and others telephoned later.

Tawana had managed it all quite well. She had limped in the

presence of doctors, gone mute before investigators, and withdrawn into her shell when lawyers, social workers, and civil rights activists had come to see her. And she had begun to make the transition: to move by fine degrees through the illusion of recovery. But now she began to let down her guard in the company of her friends. Throughout the afternoon, she laughed and gossiped with unconcealed enthusiasm. There were interruptions for the ringing telephone, for cake and sodas, for hugs from her mother and aunt. She was busy constantly, chatting on the telephone, opening presents, beaming at the sight of her new stereo set, hugging everyone with an exuberance of affection.

And at day's end, there were a few quiet moments alone with Daryl Rodriguez, moments in which they found a chance to resume their intimacies and he found the opportunity to ask what had happened to her. She could not tell him yet, she said. But someday, she promised, she would—everything.

Among the crimes of love, betrayal is the hardest to accept. And Tawana could not bring herself to believe what her mother had been telling her—that Todd Buxton was dangerous, that his gentle curiosity might be feigned, that his voice down the wire might be an instrument of the police. She was not home the first time he called from the Orange County Jail. She had been there to take his second call, but Glenda had come into the room, with her suspicions and her scowls, and Tawana had cut the conversation short, asking him to call back in a day or two.

She had awaited his next call with an anxious heart, wanting to open up to him again, as she had last summer, but fearful of the possibilities. She still loved Todd despite her feelings for Rodriguez, but she could not quite *trust* him. He was, after all, in custody—he had almost four months to serve on his six-month sentence for assault—and there was no telling what terrible pressures the authorities might bring to turn him into their secret agent.

When he finally called again on December 22, she was relieved that her mother was not home. But the conflict was there anyway:

she yearned to preserve her relationship with Buxton, but the suspicions set off alarms as his rattling small talk gave out and he drew near to the mark.

Baldly, he asked what had happened to her during the days she was missing.

Tawana bridled: "I don't want to talk about it."

He gave way, and they settled back into pleasantries about each other and their families, comparing their lives of confinement. Gradually Buxton steered the conversation back to recent events.

"Is it true what they be writing in the paper?" he asked.

She wondered what he meant, but played it safe: "No."

"It ain't?"

"Well, part of it is."

"What part is true?"

"I was fifteen and I did go to Ketcham."

The conversation veered off again. They talked about the clothes she had worn the day she visited him at the jail, about his mother and the time Tawana had spent with her that day, about Tawana's recent move from the Pavillion to Carmine Drive.

It was Buxton who raised the name of Thomas Barnes, the passenger on the bus who got off at Fishkill the night she disappeared. Buxton seemed to be steering things again, but it was impossible to tell whether it was his natural curiosity or something more sinister. He asked where she had got off the bus that night. It seemed innocent enough, a fact already in print.

It was on Route 9 at Myers Corners Road, she said. "That's all I have to say. I'm not saying anything else."

But Buxton was walking a tightrope. He pressed with more questions: "What this guy supposed to look like? Was that part true in the paper?"

"They wrote it in the paper?" Tawana said, puzzled. He seemed to be saying the description of an assailant had been published, and she was taken aback because she had never given any detailed description. "I don't know," she said, "what did they write?"

"About, ah, green car."

155

"I don't know nothing to say about it," she said, relieved. It was just the newspapers making things up again. "I don't know where they got that from."

Buxton scoffed, directing the skepticism at her now. "You don't know *nothing!*" he said with an edge.

She gave in a little. "No. I do remember."

But they had come close enough to the dangerous ground for one day. The talk trailed off to the recent rally for Tawana in Newburgh and to her birthday party. In a strange way, she said, she was enjoying all the attention. Finally, the conversation ended. It had lasted twenty minutes and had left Tawana extremely uneasy.

The next day, Buxton called again.

"Is this being taped?" Tawana demanded right off.

Buxton denied it.

She accused him of striking a deal with the authorities.

He denied this, too, begging her to believe him.

His pleas were soothing. Even so, she resolved to be wary. She said her legs still hurt and explained that she had been hopping around on one leg and using a wheelchair. She complained of recurring headaches and of days filled with boredom.

"I don't do nothing," she said.

After a pause, Buxton meekly resumed his probing. "I can't know?" he asked.

"You already read about it," she said.

"What you tell me? Half of that wasn't right, right?"

"Yeah, but most of it—the right [sic] that you read was."

"Now, now listen to you."

"It *was* right. Everything. I can't tell you stuff I don't remember."

Later, as Buxton sought more, Tawana's voice grew exasperated. "But I don't remember the whole thing, so how can I tell you. I don't remember!"

"You don't remember?" he asked.

"No."

"Are you kidding?"

"No."

He pleaded again: "Can't I know?"

He was asking for trust, and she felt she might lose him if she refused. "Yes," she replied, walking her own tightrope. "But how can I tell you something I don't remember?"

"Then tell me what you remember."

She searched for something to give him, and a fragment of Buxton's banter yesterday came to mind. "I can tell you what they lied about," she said.

"What?"

"There wasn't no green car."

Then, as Buxton prodded, she was testy. "I don't remember! So how can I tell you what I don't remember?"

His silence was like hatred, and she conceded a point to drive it back: "I remember more than what I told you. But just a little bit, and it doesn't make any difference what I remember."

Had she recognized any of her abductors?

She mumbled something: ". . . cop killed himself . . ."

Buxton didn't know what she was talking about.

"You know one of them killed himself," she said.

"Who?"

"One of them—killed himself," she said again.

They danced around it awhile.

"One of them?"

"Uh-huh."

"Who?"

"The cop."

"Who? What's his name?"

She couldn't bring herself to say Harry Crist's name. "The cop killed himself, committed suicide. He killed himself!"

"Where was this?"

"In Wappingers."

"How'd he kill himself?"

"He shot himself in the head."

"It was in the papers?"

"No. They put a news blackout on it."

"Yeah," Buxton said, commiserating over the rotten newspapers.

157

"Yup. There was like a little bit on it, an article, you know."

"You know," Buxton pressed, "I mean, you remember the faces?"

"One."

"One of them?"

"Yes."

"Who?"

She had already gone too far and she didn't answer.

Buxton fished around some more. ". . . the one, that what's-his-name, that approached you on the . . ."

"Nobody approached me," she snapped. She was exasperated with his dogged insistence, her own evasiveness.

"Oh," he said, "the one that showed you the badge."

"Yeah."

"And you won't tell on him?"

She tried to veer off: "I remember everything."

"That's what I don't understand," Buxton said, pulling her back.

"What?"

"That's what I don't understand. If they did this to you, why don't you want to tell?"

" 'Cause I don't know who."

"You don't know?"

"No."

"You don't remember—you just remember faces."

"Yup."

"That's what you saying. Is you lying?"

"No." She had to deny it, and that meant making up more lies. "But I remember one of them. I may have touched him—like I remember, like, what he had on."

"That's the one who's supposed to have shot himself in the head?"

"No," she said, taking refuge in confusion. "I'm not gonna say nothing. They didn't do nothing."

Buxton was flabbergasted. "What you mean, they didn't do nothing?"

"They didn't do anything," she said, as if correcting grammar.

Buxton made one last stab: "Where in hell was you during these four days?" There it was—the heart of the matter.

"I don't know."

"You don't remember?"

"I don't know, I told you. I don't remember nothing."

They hung up. After forty-five minutes of sparring, Tawana lay back on the couch and wondered how much damage had been done.

At the Orange County Jail, Buxton handed the receiver to Russell Crawford of the state police. Crawford turned off the tape recorder, a piece of junk that had somehow lost some of yesterday's eavesdroppings. But it had been an intriguing two days, full of glimpses of the girl and tantalizing hints about what had happened to her. In the end, however, the decisive breakthrough Crawford had hoped for had not occurred.

It was helpful, he thought. It was the first time they had heard Tawana Brawley speak about the situation. It gave them a look at her demeanor—what she sounded like, how she acted. She was not as closemouthed as she was being portrayed. Most important, it made them think maybe she did remember what had happened.

There was no get-out-of-jail-free card for Buxton. With less than four months to serve, he had been promised nothing and had given his cooperation freely, believing he might help catch the abductors. No court order was needed for the telephone tap: when one party betrays another, the law says—even if they are lovers—the victim need not be told.

They glared at each other across the cluttered desk, old allies gone sour with suspicion, mistrust, and jealousy. Alton Maddox was seething, and C. Vernon Mason was indignant. Watching them both, trying to play the peacemaker, was the Reverend Al Sharpton. Outside, the traffic of Manhattan roared.

The Brawley defense was at stake. Sharpton had called the two lawyers together for a meeting at Mason's office to keep things from falling apart. Aside from his speech at the Newburgh rally, Mason had played no role at all in the Brawley case. But after the rally, he and Sonny Carson had driven to Wappingers Falls and visited the Brawleys. Mason had left them with the gratuitous impression that he would be working on the case with Maddox, just as the two men had worked together on Howard Beach.

When Maddox, returning from Atlanta, discovered this, he had flown into a rage.

Maddox and Mason had worked together on many cases, but they were not law partners, and they often disagreed on strategy and ideology. Sometimes they even competed for cases. In fact, their aims were different; whereas Maddox regarded cases involving blacks as bludgeons in the battle over civil rights, Mason saw them as assets in a political arena. While Maddox wanted to change or even destroy the system, Mason wanted to make it work and to be a part of it. Maddox, in his talks with the Brawleys, had not even mentioned Mason as a possible partner. Now, Maddox, who was fiercely protective of his cases, came close to accusing Mason of horning in.

The situation was touchy. The NAACP was trying to woo the Brawleys, and Maddox didn't want to frighten the family off by linking Tawana's case to the dispute over what had happened at the Orange County Jail. He suspected that Carson was interested in the Brawley case only as a means of attracting wider attention to the jail episode, and he refused to tolerate interference by Carson—or Mason, for that matter.

Mason scoffed at the notion that he was interfering or being used by Carson. It came down to this, he argued: the Brawleys wanted the whole Howard Beach *team* to defend Tawana.

It was Sharpton who forged the truce. He reminded Maddox that Maddox had always been the one to push for coalitions. Now he was resisting a coalition with Mason. They had all worked well together in the Howard Beach case, and this was another opportunity for them. In the end, Maddox relented. If the Brawleys wanted them, Maddox and Mason would both represent Tawana, and Sharpton would join the team as "spokesman" and "adviser."

But it was far from certain that the Brawleys would make that choice.

C. Vernon Mason leaned back in the high leather chair, folded his hands across his sleeveless argyle sweater and let his thoughts drift back across the years to the cotton fields of northeast Arkansas, to the little school at Tuckerman with broken desks and no white faces.

The teachers, like the students, were all black, and he remembered them as dedicated and resourceful, holding classes in split sessions and giving lessons when they could during the cotton-picking season. Even as a boy, he had been recognized as a promising scholar and given extra work in writing and history, including black history. His father, an agricultural agent who helped farmers and sharecroppers, heartily approved. And when a teacher paid the fee for the youth to take a test for early admission to all-black Morehouse College in Atlanta, he jumped at the chance.

In 1962, only fifteen years old, Mason became a freshman and learned what it meant to be "a Morehouse man," as preached by the college's president, Dr. Benjamin Mays. This gospel proclaimed that a black man had to work doubly hard for academic excellence, not only to overcome his disadvantages in a white society, but also to carry on the fight against segregation and advance his race.

Mason liked to say that Morehouse was the most important influence on him, because Mays stressed what they had to do with their talents. Like Maddox, Mason was also heavily influenced by the writings of Howard University's Charles Houston.

Like Maddox, Mason had framed his future in accordance with Houston's fundamental option for educated blacks: to be a social engineer and never a parasite. After graduation from Morehouse in 1967, he had wanted to go to law school. Failing to get a scholarship, he had earned a master's degree at the University of Indiana. In 1969, with loans and aid, he finally enrolled at the

Columbia University Law School in New York. On graduation in 1972, a prestigious law firm offered him a job, but the spirits of Mays and Houston hovered and he turned it down and took a job instead with the NAACP Legal Defense and Educational Fund. His plan was to work briefly in New York and then return to Arkansas to open a practice in civil rights law. But he soon became convinced that New York was a more volatile civil rights battleground than Arkansas. Working on juvenile-justice projects, he met Maddox, and the two young lawyers discovered they had a great deal in common.

Mason quit the fund after nine months and established a law practice in New York. He took on a range of clients—labor unions, accused narcotics dealers, victims of discrimination in employment, institutions like the Abyssinian Baptist Church in Harlem, and a host of people who had been brutalized by the police, deprived of housing or jobs, or otherwise abused because they were black. Whenever possible, Mason sought publicity to broaden these cases, to raise wider issues. "The game is to try to impact the structure," he liked to say, "because with many of the smaller individual cases you're just putting your finger in the dike." He also began representing blacks in the mid–Hudson Valley as well: a troupe in Newburgh that was fighting for control of a theater, a discharged school principal in Beacon, and the family of Jimmy Lee Bruce, the man killed in a struggle with an off-duty policeman at a movie theater in the town of Wallkill.

It was a full agenda, and some clients complained that their cases languished while Mason focused on higher-profile causes. Mason, Maddox, and the Reverend Calvin O. Butts III of the Abyssinian Baptist Church got a congressional subcommittee to hold hearings in New York on police brutality, and one upshot was a newspaper survey that showed the time was ripe for a black candidate to challenge the Manhattan district attorney, Robert M. Morgenthau, in the 1985 election. There were no black district attorneys in the state, and Mason's pioneering bid was well received. "The people are alienated from the district attorney's office," he declared in a debate with Morgenthau. "John F.

Kennedy said that the law of life is change, and the time for change in the district attorney's office has come." Mason lost the Democratic primary election, but he received a surprising one-third of the vote, including the support of many whites. It seemed an auspicious political debut. And the ensuing two years had brought Mason even greater prominence. He had teamed up with Sharpton in defending the black youths shot in New York City by the subway gunman Bernhard H. Goetz. Then the Maddox-Mason-Sharpton triumvirate was forged in the Howard Beach case. They had turned the case into a national platform against racism, and it had turned them into celebrities.

Mason had come a long way from Arkansas. He and his wife, Thelma, and their three children lived in a comfortable home in Harlem, and his roomy office on Broadway in lower Manhattan was lined with pictures of his family and framed degrees and testaments to his talents. Near the venetian blinds, the filing cabinets bulged with the cases that had won him modest fame, that had fulfilled his early promise. He adjusted his horn-rimmed glasses and stroked his goatee, and when he spoke the South echoed in his mellow voice: "They criticized Alton and me for broadening things like we did with Howard Beach, but we have found that it is absolutely necessary."

It seemed incredible, but weeks into the case, the family had still not picked a lawyer. Maddox had the inside track, since Glenda was referring inquiries to him and telling law-enforcement officials that they could not speak to Tawana outside his presence. But George Hairston, the attorney sent in by the NAACP, was still an option.

Hairston had come to the door one day and introduced himself. He was not just a local lawyer who worked on the side for a worthy cause. He practiced in New York City and around the nation and had compiled a distinguished record in civil rights cases, some of which had made history and headlines. In Alabama in 1980, he had helped overturn the wrongful conviction of Tommy

Lee Hines, a retarded black man who had been sent to jail for thirty years in the rape of a white railroad clerk. In 1983–84, Hairston had won a new trial and then an acquittal for Lenell Geter, a black man unfairly convicted in Dallas of armed robbery and sentenced to life in prison. Now, he had come to discuss the Brawley case.

Glenda and King heard him out and were impressed. They had no firm agreement with Maddox and Mason. Perhaps Hairston could work with them, they suggested. Diplomatically, he said he would think about it. He had known Maddox and Mason for years. He, too, had grown up in the South and had turned to the law to fight Jim Crow. He was a Morehouse man, like Mason, but he had profound differences with Maddox. Hairston believed passionately in the NAACP, and he could hardly justify a partnership with a man who called it the "National Association for the Advancement of Coon People."

Hairston promised a solid legal tack: he would ferret out the facts and marshal them to protect Tawana and help prosecute the guilty. Maddox promised a more political approach: he would withhold cooperation from the authorities to draw public attention and to pressure the prosecution into an all-out effort.

Juanita favored Maddox's approach. The rest of the family was drifting toward Maddox too. There were pitfalls for Tawana no matter what course they took. There might be less hullabaloo if Hairston were picked, but he would focus on the facts. Maddox, on the other hand, would favor a big political fuss. But there was no telling how long the facts *could* be suppressed, and the public attention Maddox pledged might backfire by raising the political stakes to a point where the public demand for facts could no longer be resisted.

While so much depended on their decision, it was never clear that the family really made a choice. Instead, it became a decision by default. Soon it was obvious to Hairston that Maddox and Mason were speaking for the family; soon it was clear that the Brawleys were taking their advice not to cooperate with the authorities.

But Hairston was never told of any decision, though he had several discussions with Glenda and Juanita about it. In the last of these, with Glenda, Hairston broached the subject. He said it appeared that Maddox and Mason were the family attorneys.

There was no response.

He said that he and the NAACP were stepping aside.

Looming up behind the pulpit was the powerful figure of a black Christ crucified against a map of Africa. It was December 20, the first anniversary of the death of Michael Griffith in Howard Beach, and the crowd gathered for the memorial service at Our Lady of Charity Catholic Church in Brooklyn filled the seats and aisles and spilled out into the street.

It was not difficult for the mourners to see Michael Griffith's limp body on that cross, a symbol of every lynching, every beating, every murder of a black person. There were millions who imagined that preserving hallowed words in a constitution or engraving them in the granite facades of public buildings made them real. But what was real was up there, silhouetted against the map of Africa: agony, deceit, and death.

"The death of Michael Griffith reminds us that we are an African people," said the Reverend Benjamin F. Chavis, Jr., executive director of the Commission on Racial Justice of the United Church of Christ. "In South Africa, our people are massacred by white racism, and it is the same here in New York City too."

"Teach!" they shouted. "Right on!"

"You can't just cry freedom—you must fight for it," he said.

To anyone who has ever witnessed it, the evening rush in New York City is an event of almost biblical proportions. Millions of people are breathed outward from the central core, just as they were inhaled in the morning. The system is magnificently efficient and nightmarishly vulnerable.

It took only a few hundred people to choke it off the next day.

They formed the phalanxes in Brooklyn and with military discipline split into smaller groups and moved toward the subways, bridges, and highways to apply human tourniquets on the critical arteries between Manhattan and Brooklyn.

"No justice! No peace!" they chanted as the homebound rush ground to a halt. They sat on roadways high over the East River, and traffic backed up into Manhattan. Underground, eight subway lines packed with riders halted as protesters pulled emergency cords, leaped onto tracks, and held train doors open. The trains, too, backed up for miles in the tunnels. Huge crowds with Christmas packages jammed the stations and grumbled uncharitable oaths. Cars choked the tangled streets, and gridlock spread north toward midtown.

The five hundred demonstrators halted hundreds of thousands of commuters and holiday shoppers in the most disruptive protest the city had seen in years. No one was hurt, but seventy people, including Mason and Sharpton, were arrested on minor charges.

"This is a monumental occasion," said an ebullient and unarrested Alton Maddox. "This is a beginning of a civil rights movement in the city of New York. We're sick and tired of the law being used against us."

The day had seemed an enormous success for the protesters. They had made big headlines and spots on network television news programs. They had set out to be so disruptive that the city and perhaps the nation would take notice of injustice against blacks. But the point was lost on most people, who saw the disruption not as a lesson in racism but as an underhanded, even threatening, gesture by troublemakers.

The long arm of the law may reach out to nab robbers or murderers. But the climate of racial sensitivity aroused by the Brawley case had rendered the law almost helpless. Ordinarily, Grady's ace in the hole was the grand jury, a panel of citizens that heard evidence and decided whether to bring charges in a criminal case.

A grand jury had the power to compel testimony, and if witnesses wouldn't talk they could be jailed. But that was just the theory of it. Grady couldn't jail a black girl who might have been abducted and gang-raped by whites. And that meant he could scarcely force her, or her family, to testify.

Still, he had no choice but to try. His letter arrived on Christmas Eve at 4-D Carmine Drive. There had been no answer to his earlier pleas for help, and he was trying again to win the girl's cooperation. He planned to impanel a grand jury to hear the case in January, and he wanted to help the girl prepare for her appearance. There was no threat to subpoena her. It was only an invitation, a gentle prodding.

"I don't know what Grady expects her to say that she hasn't said already," Glenda said disingenuously. The family did not respond to Grady's letter.

On January 6, twenty-three Dutchess County residents were sworn in as members of Grady's grand jury by County Judge Judith A. Hillary at the Dutchess County Courthouse in Pough-keepsie. No witnesses testified that day, although Grady said two hundred fifty people had been questioned and one hundred might testify. The jurors spent the day being briefed by prosecutors.

Grady, trapped by his own legal processes, had to move ahead, no matter what the Brawleys did, because it was politically unpalatable to stand still. So, late in the day, he issued subpoenas ordering Tawana, Glenda, and Juanita Brawley to appear before the grand jury in a week.

No subpoena was issued for Ralph King because investigators still regarded him as an "open lead." They did not concede this publicly. But because he had a criminal record and had displayed a suspiciously hostile attitude, and because detectives simply did not know if he had played any role in the case, King had not been ruled out as a suspect. Testimony before a New York State grand jury confers automatic immunity from prosecution, and they did not want to grant him that privilege, at least not yet.

Chief Assistant District Attorney William O'Neill went to Carmine Drive that afternoon to deliver the subpoenas for Tawana and Glenda. King answered the door. As it opened, he saw Tawana scoot into the kitchen, where she hid until he left. O'Neill did not see Glenda. King refused to let him in. He also refused to accept the subpoenas, which were placed on the floor in front of him. This was a legal service of the subpoenas, which commanded Tawana and her mother to appear before the grand jury on January 13.

That afternoon, Maddox—having ignored Grady's messages for a month—called the prosecutor. He did not have much to say. He relayed a complaint from King about the way the subpoenas had been served.

Grady, for his part, asked for a chance to talk to Tawana.

"The time is not right," Maddox replied cryptically.

If Maddox was implying that the girl was still too debilitated to come forward, several neighbors on Carmine Drive would have laughed in his face. A few days later they saw Tawana removing suitcases from a car. There was no trace of a limp, and with a bag in each hand she was able to balance on one foot and deftly shove the car door shut with the other.

14

District Attorney Grady slid the Jaguar into its space outside the courthouse, turned off the engine, and stepped into the cold. The remnants of a big snowstorm still blanketed Poughkeepsie, and he crunched ice underfoot as he made his way inside. The storm had disrupted life all over town and even shut down the grand jury's work. But today, Grady thought, it would be different: the storm had passed, thirty witnesses had already testified, and the case was finally moving forward.

Today was crucial. It was January 13, and Tawana, Glenda, and Juanita Brawley were scheduled to appear before the grand jury. Each would be given immunity from prosecution, and with luck, Grady thought, the whole thing might be cleared up by nightfall. He was tense but optimistic as he entered the familiar old lobby: it would be his turf and his rules this time.

In the office upstairs, Grady collected his papers and his thoughts, had a cup of coffee, and met with his chief assistant, William O'Neill. Then he sat back to await developments. Within minutes, he got the news: Ralph King had arrived downstairs. With him were Alton Maddox and an entourage of aides. Tawana, Glenda, and Juanita were not with them.

Grady sent an assistant down to find out what was going on. He found King standing outside the grand jury room, and he made the mistake of putting the questions to him.

King erupted with a stream of obscenities and abuse. If Grady wanted to know anything about Tawana and Glenda and Juanita, he said, let him go ask them himself. (Actually, Tawana had gone to stay with her uncle, Matthew Strong, in Monticello, and Glenda and Juanita had just stayed home, but King offered no clue to their whereabouts.) The prosecutors and the grand jury, King went on, were bogus, and he shrieked his rage at *not* having been subpoenaed—and been given immunity—for he knew the implication: that he was a suspect.

Finally, his anger spent, King stamped out into the cold and went across the street to Alex's Diner.

Grady was shaken. The case was slipping through his fingers. He sent Investigator Carol Johnston of the state police after King. She found him sitting in a booth with Maddox and a couple of aides, including Perry McKinnon, Sharpton's right-hand man. She implored Maddox to talk to Grady about making Tawana, Glenda, and Juanita available to the grand jury.

"I'll see," Maddox replied coolly. It was the kind of remark parents use on teenagers when they mean "no," but want to avoid a confrontation.

When Johnston left, Maddox turned to McKinnon and said he did not intend to let anyone in the family talk to the grand jury. "Tawana Brawley," he told a reporter for *The Times Herald-Record*, "will never appear before a grand jury in Dutchess County without the presence of a special prosecutor."

To Grady, it had all the earmarks of extortion. Six weeks had already elapsed. His hopes of solving the case were growing dimmer—and the cries of cover-up growing shriller—with every passing day.

But to Maddox, a solution to the Brawley case was hardly the point. He was after bigger game: a special prosecutor not only for this case, but for all racially motivated crimes in New York State, a permanent official who would sweep aside local district attorneys every time a black person was victimized in any way. It would be a revolving beacon with a flashing message that the criminal justice system could not be trusted.

The knock at the door was like a gunshot. Grady had time only to blink through his discombobulated spectacles before the door flew open and O'Neill filled the room with his Irish cop bulk and his shock of snowy hair. Bad news was all over the feverish pink face.

The chief assistant was supposed to be downstairs with the grand jury, trying like Humpty-Dumpty to put the case back together without the Brawleys. He looked flushed, as if he had taken the steps two at a time, and he sat down to catch his breath.

"The mailman saw a car," O'Neill said.

Grady gave him a puzzled look. There *was* a postman in the story somewhere, but he was not a very important witness. Tim Losee was his name. He delivered the mail at the Pavillion, and he was scheduled to testify that he had found a full mailbox at Apartment 19A two days after Glenda Brawley insisted she had picked up the mail. That would show she was not telling the truth about what she was doing there the day—the very hour, in fact—that Tawana was found, but it would hardly solve the mystery.

"I have him downstairs"—O'Neill used the present tense, like a Runyonesque horseplayer—"and I'm about to put him before the grand jury to ask him about the mail when he tells me about this car."

"What car?"

Losee had said it looked like a decommissioned police car. It could have been a white, four-door Chrysler or Plymouth with the flasher bar removed. There were four white men in it, Losee had thought, and he remembered it cruising along Scarborough Lane at the Pavillion on November 27 or 28.

Grady frowned: November 28 was the day Tawana had been found.

And there was another thing, O'Neill said. The state police report on Harry Crist had just come back. His death looked like a suicide, all right, but there was a troubling detail in the report: Crist owned a decommissioned police car, a silver, four-door Plymouth.

The room revolved a little.

"Did the mailman ever mention this before?" Grady asked.

O'Neill shook his head. It had come as a complete surprise. Losee had been ready to go into the grand jury room when he mentioned it. The vision of the car had been troubling him for days, he said. He didn't know whether it meant anything, but he thought he'd better tell about it, even if it *was* last-minute.

Prosecutors rarely put a witness on the stand unless they know what he is going to say: it's like turning the cue ball loose. So O'Neill, shocked by the revelation, had quickly postponed Losee's appearance. If the mailman was right, it would change things completely. Instead of casting doubt on Glenda Brawley, he might support Tawana's story—and put Harry Crist on the scene, as well.

Harry Crist.

O'Neill and Grady looked at each other. Winter sunlight through the blinds striped the leather-top desk, the piles of paper, the law books. The Brawleys had been after Grady for a month to investigate Crist's death and possible involvement, and Tawana had accused Crist in her telephone conversation with Buxton.

There had been no evidence, only her claim and the family's suspicion.

But if Crist was involved . . .

The memory of a day in early December suddenly came back to Grady with a chill. He had been sitting in his office, just like now, when a troubled Steven A. Pagones had come to see him. Grady liked the young assistant prosecutor. They were both from Beacon, and Pagones's father, Anthony, was a city judge, a prominent local lawyer, and a former assistant prosecutor himself. Pagones was upset that his dead friend, Harry Crist, was being portrayed in news reports as a possible suspect in the Brawley case. That was preposterous, Pagones had said, because he had been with Crist in Connecticut the day Tawana was found. There was more, but Grady couldn't recall it.

It suddenly occurred to Grady that he needed more details about that trip to Connecticut. If Pagones was telling the truth about it, there was nothing to worry about. If not, Grady realized, there was trouble right in his office—and the last thing he should be doing was talking to Pagones.

He dispatched O'Neill to have a little chat with Pagones.

When he got back, O'Neill looked more troubled than ever. Pagones had said that he, Crist, and two other friends—a state trooper named Scott Patterson, whose father was one of a number of inspectors with the state police, and a utility worker, Eugene Branson—had driven in Crist's 1983 Plymouth, a used police car, to the Danbury Fair Mall in Danbury, Connecticut, on November 28. They had shopped and wandered around the mall all afternoon. It sounded like a good alibi, but what if he was lying? If they were the abductors, it was no alibi at all, just conspirators lying for one another. There were four of them in a decommissioned police car, just as the mailman had said.

And, O'Neill added, there was a devastating kicker: Pagones had a vague recollection that at some point, perhaps that day, perhaps later, one of his friends—and he thought it was Crist— had mentioned a missing girl, as he put it, "a girl in a bag of shit."

Grady was thunderstruck.

His thoughts raced: How could Crist have said that unless he knew about Tawana Brawley? And if Crist was involved, Pagones would have to be regarded as a suspect. And most important of all, it would be a conflict of interest for a prosecutor to investigate a case in which an assistant was a suspect.

"Conflict of interest" . . . Grady immediately suspended the Brawley investigation.

John Poklemba puffed distractedly on a cigarette and looked at the two supplicants across his desk in the State Capitol. One was big and the other small, but they both looked uneasy, like men embarked on a dubious enterprise. Poklemba himself was uneasy. It was January 15, his first day as Governor Cuomo's director of criminal justice, having replaced Larry Kurlander, and it was proving to be a bad day.

"I still want to handle this, but . . . ," the smaller of the two men said, his voice trailing off.

The bigger one with the pink face just sat there.

Poklemba, a forty-year-old protégé of the governor who, like Cuomo, had attended St. John's University Law School, had been surprised to see Grady and O'Neill that morning. The Dutchess County prosecutor and his chief assistant had dropped in, and Poklemba, when he arrived to find them there, had ushered them into his blue-carpeted office and motioned them to chairs.

As the top counsel to Kurlander, who had resigned for a corporate job in Manhattan, Poklemba had followed the Brawley affair as closely as his boss and had even taken a hand in shaping the investigation, so he was familiar with the details when they started talking about the case.

O'Neill outlined the inquiry so far, reaching into his briefcase to show Poklemba the photographs of Tawana, the diagrams of the Pavillion, the other charts and documents. Poklemba knew it was a complicated and difficult case, but the whole thing suddenly tilted on its axis when Grady started talking about Crist, Pagones, a possible conflict of interest, and the likelihood that he would have to step aside. They were here, they said, to explore the possibility of the governor's naming a special prosecutor to take over the Brawley case from Grady.

Poklemba didn't like the idea. He was not convinced that a conflict of interest existed, and he suspected that Grady was trying to get out of the case just because it was proving to be a political liability.

Like Cuomo, Poklemba felt that local prosecutors should not lightly quit a case. Stepping aside over a possible conflict might seem prudent under ethical canons and close readings of the law. But as a practical and political matter, especially in this case, it could be misread. The Brawley case needed continuity and a decisive hand, a prosecutor who would see it through. There had already been too much timidity and ineptitude, all feeding suspicions of a cover-up. And there was a more general policy problem as well. Appointing special prosecutors, Cuomo believed, undermined confidence in elected prosecutors and set a bad precedent. Howard Beach had been an unfortunate necessity. But the governor didn't want to have to face this issue every time a race-bias case arose. There had been only one other time that Cuomo had named a special prosecutor: a 1986 case in which the Jefferson County district attorney begged off prosecuting two sheriff's deputies for perjury after they had testified for him as star witnesses in the prosecution of another officer for beating a prisoner.

It was not at all clear that Pagones was a suspect or that Grady had a conflict. Even if those things proved true, Poklemba reflected, the right course might be for Grady to prosecute Pagones. In any case, Poklemba told his visitors, he would speak to the governor and get back to them.

The solution from Albany a few days later was a creative one: let a local judge decide, and if there was a need for a special prosecutor, let the judge pick one locally. Grady would not be saddled with the case, and Cuomo would not have to name a special prosecutor. They were both happy.

Soon, Poklemba and Grady were on the phone working out the details. They drew up a list of six local lawyers who might serve, and on January 20 Grady gave it to Dutchess County Judge Judith A. Hillary with his application to withdraw. The judge gave them a hearing in her plant-filled chamber, granted the application, and sealed the record. There was only one hitch: Grady could not tell the public why he was withdrawing. To do so would cast Pagones openly as a suspect when there was as yet not an iota of evidence against him.

But of course, the lack of an explanation was fuel for the flames. Grady's mysterious withdrawal served only to reinforce suspicions that something was indeed amiss, that Dutchess County law-enforcement officers might well have attacked Tawana Brawley, that the system had tried—was still trying—to cover up.

The short, unhappy education of David B. Sall began early the next morning. When the telephone rang in his small law office two blocks from the courthouse, Sall answered it and was surprised to hear Judge Hillary on the line—even more surprised to hear what she wanted.

As a former public defender, he had appeared in her court often since moving to Poughkeepsie in 1986 from Brooklyn, where he had been an assistant prosecutor for two years. Now thirty-eight, Sall had a private criminal-law practice, but was not yet well known or well established locally. He was working now on a special inquiry into allegations that a local police chief had been mixed up with stolen property.

Sall knew nothing about the Brawley case except what he had read in the newspapers, but he had a healthy confidence in himself and he quickly accepted Judge Hillary's appointment as special prosecutor. He asked only that he be allowed to take on a deputy who was working with him on the police inquiry, William T. Burke, a lawyer in nearby Rhinebeck who had also once been a prosecutor. Judge Hillary had no objection.

The news of Grady's withdrawal and Sall's appointment got out quickly. Within hours, both were besieged by reporters, photographers, and television crews.

In Albany, Poklemba was taken aback at the news of Sall's selection. He called Grady, only to discover that Grady couldn't explain it either: Sall's name had not been on the list they had compiled. Who was Sall? Poklemba called a friend in the Brooklyn district attorney's office to get a line on Sall, and the news was not encouraging. He was described as headstrong and inflexible, hardly the man, Poklemba thought, for the delicate Brawley case.

In his aggressive way, Sall immediately plunged into Lesson One. He called Maddox, expecting to have a little talk and straighten out whatever it was Grady had stumbled over. But Maddox wasn't in. Sall left a message for a callback. There was none.

He decided to call 4-D Carmine Drive: there was nothing like a direct, upbeat approach. Juanita Brawley was there, and she and Glenda got on a pair of extension phones.

Sall explained who he was and asked for their cooperation. It all seemed so direct, so simple.

"I'd like to look you in the eye and see if you're an honest man," Glenda Brawley told him.

Sall agreed. "Can I come to see you and the child tomorrow?"

Glenda Brawley said he could.

"Eight o'clock?"

Glenda agreed.

Sall was elated at his quick success. He reached Burke and arranged to meet him in the morning to go to the Brawley apartment. Everything was falling into place so easily.

But his blithe reverie was broken by a call from a reporter. The Associated Press was quoting Maddox as saying the family considered the Sall-Burke appointments "a charade," the reporter read. "It is the position of the Brawley family that they would rather go to jail than be part of a whitewash," Maddox had said, adding that the family would continue to snub the investigation. Would Sall care to comment?

Sall summoned up his tact. "Perhaps I could allay his fears. I'm a firm believer that two people sitting down with a common interest can iron out any differences between them and get down to the business at hand." He went on like a grandiose politician: "I don't care what the circumstances are or who is involved. My only consideration is a young teenage girl. I want to look the family squarely in the face and give them reassurance."

Sall was up at dawn the next morning, eager for conquest.

Reflexively, he called his office and activated his answering machine. There was a message from Glenda Brawley: "On the advice of my attorneys," she cooed pleasantly, "I'm canceling our appointment for tomorrow."

Sall slumped back in his chair. He could see it now. It was Howard Beach all over again. He pushed the button and replayed it. "On the advice of my attorneys . . ." So, Maddox and Mason were counseling noncooperation. It was not, as the lawyers were claiming, the family's idea. He considered going to see the Brawleys anyway, but decided against it. That would only make matters worse. He would have to deal with Maddox, but Maddox would not even return his calls.

Swallowing his pride, Sall plunged into Lesson Two. He called
Burke and together they went to see Grady. It was only then that
they learned why the district attorney had stepped aside, that an
assistant prosecutor was a possible suspect in the case. The implication was staggering: they would probably have to investigate
Grady's office, which prosecuted many of the clients they represented. Their private law practices would have to be discontinued
to do it.

Sall felt suddenly as if the wind had been knocked out of him
by a fastball. More wild pitches were rocketing around, coming
straight for his head—and he was paralyzed.

"Let's go back to my office," Sall told Burke. "We have to think
this thing over." They did not stop at O'Neill's office on the way
to pick up the Brawley file, deciding it would be better not to
look at any confidential material just yet.

In Sall's office, they looked at each other like two men who
had just discovered they had the same disease. They mulled it
over awhile, and finally called Judge Hillary. She agreed to see
them immediately at the courthouse.

Judge Hillary listened patiently while they explained the
unanticipated difficulties. For nearly three hours, they reviewed
the facts and examined ethical issues. The cover-up charges against
Grady's office might be spurious, but Sall and Burke both had
clients facing prosecution by his staff. How could they investigate
Grady's office and still represent those clients? Were they to give
up their law practices?

Finally, Judge Hillary agreed to let them drop the case.

The language was bland, vague, and devastating: "After conducting an initial investigation," Sall told the press, "we have
concluded that we couldn't investigate all the possible aspects
involving this case." What was he saying? What couldn't he say?
Was he protecting a suspect in the Brawley affair? As if this
possible implication weren't enough, Sall made things worse: no
local attorney, he added without explanation, could possibly investigate the case.

If Grady's withdrawal had caused consternation, Sall's exit on

January 22—after less than two days on the job—amplified all the unanswered questions into a roar. A local inquiry had become a statewide scandal.

Attorney General Robert Abrams looked out the flawed old pane at purple winter dusk and the dying sun, an orange ball behind the dark tangle of woods. The last light retreated down the empty road. It was always like this: a breathtaking sunset, the sense of peace.

Somewhere madmen poisoned the air, robbed old people, molested children, and killed with drugs and bombs. But here in the rolling hills of eastern Dutchess County, a just God loved the world and Robert Abrams on weekends found deeper meanings in his faith and his family.

Behind him, Shabbas candles flickered at the dinner table, a fire hissed in the grate, and the warm glow of the Sabbath filled the old clapboard farmhouse retreat. It was Friday. Abrams and his wife, Diane, and the girls, Rachel and Becky, had driven up from Manhattan in time to beat the traffic and prepare the meal before sundown. The family kept kosher households in the city and the country, and abided by the Jewish stricture against working on the Sabbath.

It was that stricture that sprang to mind when the telephone rang.

Had it happened a minute or two later, after the sun was down and the Sabbath under way, they might have ignored it. As it was, Diane frowned and shot a questioning glance at her husband. It had to be important state business: his aides, like everyone else, knew not to trespass on the family's religious observances.

Abrams picked up the receiver.

"Bob? Sorry to intrude."

It was his top deputy, R. Scott Greathead, the first assistant attorney general, and there was an excited pitch in his voice.

"We just heard from the governor," Greathead said. "He wants to name you special prosecutor in the Tawana Brawley case."

"Did you say anything?"

"I said I'd talk to you. Obviously, I think we should take it."

"Of course."

After hanging up, Abrams, whose studious face always seemed heavy with worry, allowed himself a smile. He had been paying close attention to news reports on the Brawley case, and after Sall's withdrawal earlier today, Abrams had even expected that the case might fall to him. It was a nasty one, but highly visible, and it would reinforce the perception that when a difficult case came along the governor looked to the attorney general.

A few days later, just before Cuomo was to announce the appointment, Abrams called the governor. They were both liberal Democrats and nominal partners at the top of the state government, but they were still uneasy with each other, like rival executives in a boardroom. A question burned in the attorney general's mind, and he had to put it to Cuomo before finally accepting his offer.

"Will they cooperate?" Abrams said, referring to the Brawleys and their lawyers.

"Yes," Cuomo said. "I just heard fifteen minutes ago that they would."

Abrams had his doubts.

But immediately after Cuomo announced his appointment, Abrams plunged into action. He liked to leave nothing to chance. He made dozens of phone calls around the state, to black ministers, civil rights leaders, and federal, state, and local officials, appealing for their support. He told them he believed Tawana Brawley's story and would go after the criminals with every weapon and all the energy at his command. Many of those he called had kind words for him and promised to back him up. It was not mere public relations by the attorney general. Abrams was an unabashed liberal, and his office was staffed with lawyers and activists who had marched for civil rights in the South, demonstrated against the war in Vietnam, and monitored human rights violations in Central America. It was entirely plausible to them that white racists had kidnapped and raped the black girl. It had happened throughout history. Of course Tawana Brawley's story was true.

Robert Abrams was not a charismatic figure. His voice was quavery, and when he raised it in anger or frustration it sounded at times like the nattering whine of an adolescent with a toothache. His manner was usually mild, but behind the liquid eyes lurked a deep pessimism, bordering on fatalism. He was an eminently successful man, but a lifetime of experience had somehow convinced him that whatever could go wrong would go wrong. His associates squirmed over bad news, but Abrams only shrugged at the confirmation of his expectations. Pessimism was, perhaps, the unhappy fate of a man who called himself a liberal and a reformer in an age of conservatives and cynics.

At forty-nine, he had spent almost half his life—twenty-three years—in public service, a career launched from a Bronx legislative seat and crowned with the attorney generalship, just a step away from the prize he coveted, the governorship.

The son of a Bronx candy store owner who had pointed him toward a life of public service while initiating him into the mysteries of the perfect egg cream, Abrams had graduated from Columbia College and New York University Law School and positioned himself early for a life in politics. At twenty-seven, he had won a seat in the state assembly, becoming the youngest member of the legislature. He quickly made a name for himself, sponsoring legislation to fight child abuse and to let state prisoners out on work-release programs long before those issues became causes. He was a whirlwind, throwing himself into work on behalf of the Anti-Defamation League of B'nai B'rith, the American Jewish Congress, the NAACP, the Knights of Pythias, and many other groups. In 1970, at thirty-one, he had become the Bronx borough president, the youngest in New York City history, in an upset victory over the Democratic machine that was to become notorious in the municipal scandals of the 1980s.

Eight years later, he was elected attorney general, succeeding

Louis J. Lefkowitz, a shrewd politico who had held the post for twenty years and was universally known as "the General." No one called Bob Abrams "the General." But even Abrams's critics admired his performance as the state's lawyer. He recruited top legal professionals and led the office into new areas of environmental policing, consumer protection, and antitrust litigation. In 1987, his office handled twenty-six thousand cases, nearly double Lefkowitz's caseload, yet it did so with the same-sized legal staff of under five hundred. While the attorney general had historically been a civil litigant, Abrams won big victories in criminal law. For the first time, his office brought actions to clean up toxic waste sites in forty major cases, and he prosecuted big-name retailers like Cartier and Bulgari for conspiring with customers to evade sales taxes on jewelry. He was also investigating the billionaire hotelier Leona Helmsley, who was later convicted of evading federal taxes.

But a common perception among Albany watchers was that Abrams was publicity hungry, pushing cases to get headlines and planning to run for governor. And it was an open secret that Cuomo and Abrams were uneasy with each other, to the point, perhaps, of unfriendliness. The earnest, plodding attorney general and the brooding, metaphysical governor clearly didn't mix well. Cuomo was complex and Machiavellian; Abrams was simple and straightforward. Subordinates and friends called Abrams "Bob." Cuomo called him "Bobby," and Abrams wondered why.

The differences went beyond the personal. In 1984, when Cuomo had proposed legalized sports betting to raise state revenues, Abrams said it was unconstitutional. In 1985, Abrams had tried to name a corruption prosecutor for New York City without consulting the governor, and Cuomo had retaliated by holding up the designee's salary until Abrams backed down and, at Cuomo's prompting, named someone else, Charles (Joe) Hynes.

One thing they had in common: Abrams, like Cuomo, was extremely sensitive to criticism. When a commission said he had made "a bald request for money" in his 1986 campaign by soliciting funds from wealthy people at private breakfasts, Abrams reacted with sanctimonious anger. "How do you raise money?" he demanded, thumping his desk. "You solicit it! Twenty years a life of rectitude! Jesus! And now this! All the things that are going on—contributors giving money to state officials they do business with and this and that. And then they single me out!"

As it happened, Cuomo would have liked to put the Brawley case in the hands of Joe Hynes, a savvy longtime friend who was still the state's special anticorruption prosecutor in New York City. Hynes had accepted designation as special prosecutor in the Howard Beach case, but he had turned the governor down on the Brawley case. Hynes's wife was ill and he was unwilling to endure a long sojourn in Dutchess County.

Abrams did not regard his appointment as a drop-everything task. He turned to John M. Ryan, the head of the attorney general's criminal prosecutions bureau, to take charge of the case on a day-to-day basis. Abrams would oversee things, but Ryan would run them.

"Jack" Ryan had just turned thirty-nine. His boyish face was soft and pliant, with chipmunk cheeks and a turned-up nose. His parents had come from Ireland, and his mother had raised her family alone after her husband died young. Ryan, like Cuomo and Poklemba, had attended St. John's University Law School. He had made his name as a tough criminal prosecutor in the Queens district attorney's office. In 1979, he joined the attorney general's staff and became known as a tenacious and careful prosecutor, somewhat self-righteous at times, but zealous—capable, certainly, of handling the thorniest of cases.

Al Sharpton, alerted by Maddox, reached his favorite electronic soapbox just in time.

"What the hell is this?" he said, glancing around the studios of radio station WLIB on Manhattan's East Side. Maddox and Mason were there, grinning broadly, and a flock of reporters and photographers was there, too, panting for another development.

"Cuomo is appointing Abrams today as special prosecutor,"

Maddox told him. Abrams was now in Rochester and they were going to get him for an on-the-air interview, Maddox said. Then, Sharpton would go on and respond.

"Okay," said Sharpton. "What am I supposed to say?"

Maddox, who had accommodated himself to Joe Hynes as the special prosecutor in the Howard Beach case, was doubtful about Abrams. He felt the attorney general had been lackluster in his opposition to police brutality and racial violence. But when Abrams got on the air and said Ryan would be the point man on the case, Maddox was furious and Sharpton picked up the cue.

"He can't delegate this to John Ryan," Sharpton told the black radio audience. "This is an outrage."

"We've got to go after them," Maddox said during a commercial break. Then, he and Mason took turns on the microphone and began the hatcheting of John Ryan. Abrams was passing the buck to an unknown, unworthy underling, they declared.

"We know nothing about Mister Ryan," Mason said, "and that would indicate to us that the governor is skeptical that a crime has been committed. It seems as though the governor does not understand that."

Then Maddox threw down the gauntlet. "We will not allow the governor or the attorney general or anyone designated by the attorney general to continue to inflict emotional traumas on Tawana Brawley," he declared. And referring to Cuomo, he added: "It's obvious he has a vendetta against us. No good-faith prosecutor was going to be appointed by this governor in any case."

Maddox paused.

Someone in the studio control room was waving his hand vigorously, trying to get Maddox's attention. There was a telephone caller and they wanted to put him on the air right now, to talk to Maddox, Mason, and Sharpton.

It was Governor Cuomo.

15

The disembodied voice filled the studio with its fancy grammar and its lofty principles. It was the grating voice of omniscient reason, of Big Brother. It came through the speakers and surrounded Alton Maddox, C. Vernon Mason, and Al Sharpton with its infuriating self-assurance, and then it went out on the airways to pulsate in homes, cars, offices—anyplace where blacks were tuned to WLIB.

"Good afternoon," the voice said. "Thank you so much for asking me to be heard."

Actually, a member of Cuomo's staff had been monitoring the radio station in New York City and had alerted the governor in Albany that the Brawley advisers were on and that this was an opportunity to call up and rebut them in front of their own audience. "Unfortunately, all I heard was, I think, Mister Maddox's last few sentences, so I'm not privy to what you've been saying until now."

Gary Byrd, the moderator of the show, spoke. "The gentlemen in the studio with me this afternoon do take issue with the appointment of the attorney general, Robert Abrams, particularly on the issue that they are questioning: Who is John Ryan?"

"Well," Cuomo said, "they questioned who Joe Hynes was too. As a matter of fact I remember in the midst of our discussion about Joe Hynes—we spent seven hours—people called him a racist, and I remember some rather heated discussion about that,

185

and they of course were wrong about Joe Hynes. He was given a chance to function and he did. Mister Ryan is with the attorney general. The person I appoint is the attorney general. The person I hold responsible is the attorney general. The person whom I expect to conduct this vigorous investigation and prosecution is the attorney general. . . . The people I look to for responsibility in this situation are the people who were elected three times by the people of this state—Bobby Abrams, each time by a greater majority—and I hold him responsible. He can use anyone he wants. But what I want from him is a result, and to make sure we get a result, which is justice, I'm going to give him my top team from the state police, all the investigators he needs. He can call on Joe Hynes. He can call on anybody to get the result we want, which is the truth."

Gary Byrd shifted gears. Before Cuomo had come on, he said, there had been some discussion of a "personal vendetta" by him. "You were quoted as referring to the attorneys as being 'no good.' How do you respond to that?"

"Which attorneys?" Cuomo demanded.

"I'm speaking of Alton Maddox and C. Vernon Mason," Byrd said.

"I said that they're no good?"

"This was a quote that . . ."

"I doubt very much that you could find anybody responsible to make that statement and repeat it and prove it," Cuomo said. "If I believed that, I probably wouldn't say it, and I don't believe it."

Byrd turned to Maddox and Mason: "The governor," he said, "has indicated obviously that he didn't make the remark. Gentlemen, if you'd like to respond I'll give you the chance before we continue."

"Please do," Cuomo chimed in.

Mason took the microphone. "Governor Cuomo, you made the statement several days ago in Brooklyn when you were asked whether or not you were going to appoint a special prosecutor. The person who called me on it was [radio reporter] Joe Bragg. He played the tape of your voice on the tape, in which you indicated that not only would you not want to appoint a special prosecutor but the attorneys that were representing Tawana Brawley were no good anyway, and he asked me to comment on that."

"I don't know with whom I'm speaking," the voice said with its shameless precision.

"You're speaking to C. Vernon Mason now, Governor," Byrd said.

"Mister Mason, Joe Bragg is an old friend of mine and I suggest you listen to the tape again."

"No," Mason responded. "I heard the tape very good."

"I think," Cuomo said, "what you'll find is I said under no circumstances would I agree to a permanent special prosecutor and that's absolutely true."

"Governor Cuomo, would you explain to us why?" Byrd said.

"Oh, yeah, but let me finish addressing Mister Mason's question. I said under no circumstance would I agree to a permanent special prosecutor. I will do it ad hoc, as I did it in Howard Beach . . . ." He described earlier cases in which special prosecutors had been named. "As to Maddox and Mason, I've never had the privilege, I don't think, of a long discussion with you—if I've had a short one. I probably said very clearly, 'It is not for Maddox and Mason to tell the state how its justice system will run' and 'Who are they?' and 'What qualification do they have to tell the government of the state of New York how it should run?' So their opinion that we need a special state prosecutor on a permanent basis does not impress me one bit, and I repeat that statement."

Sharpton jumped in. "I think your statement on tape said that they personally were no-good lawyers—that was the quote . . ."

"Oh, well, I . . ."

"Let me finish," Sharpton insisted.

"No, no, Al, no," Cuomo rejoined. "I don't want you to, to, to finish. What I suggest is you get the tape from Joe Bragg—it's very easy."

For many listeners, the debate might as well have ended with Cuomo's dismissal of the views of Maddox and Mason on a permanent special prosecutor. It was, to them, an arrogant rejection—by a man they had helped elect and reelect—of black people's troubled feelings about a criminal justice system that did not work for them.

Maddox was still fuming. "I believe that the last time I looked on my wall I at least was a practicing attorney in this state," he said. "I believe that should at least mean something to somebody."

Maddox leaned over to Sharpton and whispered in his ear: "Now's your chance. Tear his ass up!"

Sharpton bellied up to the microphone. He accused Cuomo of misconstruing the Maddox and Mason call for a special permanent prosecutor as a personal statement, rather than a widely held view. "There's clearly a trend throughout this state of racial violence. And there has been any number of people, any number of demonstrations, and people even going to jail around this issue. So I think what the people want to be clear on is, why is it so adamant in your mind that—with racial violence seemingly a daily occurrence in the state—why you refuse to do what is necessary to put a permanent special prosecutor in place to try to deal with this?"

Out of the studio loudspeakers came the voice of the patient Socratic lecturer, enlightening the dull pupils with his luminous questions: "You mean I should appoint, personally, a special prosecutor in every racial case, no matter who is elected district attorney?"

"Yes," Sharpton said, falling into the trap.

"I'm flattered that you trust me to do it, but I don't think it's good institutionally," the teacher said. "Let's say Joe Hynes gets elected DA of Brooklyn. Then I should replace *him*?"

Before the pupil could reply, Mason intervened. He, like many in the audience, was still steaming over Cuomo's remark about not being impressed by their opinion. The governor, Mason said, had not merely resisted Maddox's and Mason's view, but had for years rejected the entreaties of respected preachers like Herbert Daughtry, Saul Williams, and Timothy Mitchell, who spoke for many average black New Yorkers.

The governor cleverly turned the argument inside out, saying it would be terrible for black people if he were moved by mere petitions. "What would happen to the minorities if we behaved that way—if every time a loud voice went up I said: 'I'm going to listen to that loud voice'? I will tell you this: most of the time the loud voice will be with the majority. So I'm not impressed with your petitions on the question of a permanent state prosecutor. I don't believe it will do justice."

There were other black radio stations around the country that provided programming devoted to racial matters. There was even the National Black Network. But there was nothing quite like WLIB, either in format or in time given to serious discussions. It was the flagship of Inner City Broadcasting, a national chain headed by Percy Sutton, a former Manhattan borough president; its stockholders included Jesse Jackson and David N. Dinkins, the borough president since 1985 (who became New York City's mayor in 1990).

Black people were WLIB's subject from sunrise to sunset, when its signal went off the air. It billed itself as an electronic marketplace of African and African-American ideas, and it was the station that the mayor and the police commissioner and New York City's black writers, artists, poets, scholars, activists, and politicians monitored to keep abreast of what blacks were saying. They also turned to the station to deliver propaganda, arguments, and messages for the black community.

It was a station that stirred the emotions. Its broadcasts were alive with controversy, and typically thirty thousand people were tuned in. Most of them were not like the casual listeners of other stations, lulled by background music or a drone of light patter; rather, they closely assayed the program's mix of grievance, insight, and thought-provoking discussion, and they understood it all from a unique perspective, bound as they were into a kind of nonpolitical collective well schooled in bias, suspicious of authority, skeptical of goodwill.

Not all the regulars at Edgar's Food Shop were tuned in that day. But one who was, Roy Canton, sat in his custodial office—he was in charge of maintaining Intermediate School 258 in Brooklyn—with the radio at his elbow, listening to Cuomo's legalisms, and he felt the anger rising in him. Had he been deluded all along about Cuomo, one of the few white politicians he regarded as decent? In fact, his admiration and support for Cuomo had begun to erode in the past year when the governor resisted naming a special prosecutor in the Howard Beach case. Cuomo had relented only when it became clear that the worst racial case in years might go unprosecuted. Later, at rallies and protests, Canton had heard other things about Cuomo: that he had said nothing about Michael Stewart's death or the killing of Eleanor Bumpurs.

Now, the voice over the radio was belittling Maddox, Mason, and Sharpton, men Canton regarded as intelligent and dedicated to justice. Canton suddenly recalled another thing: Cuomo had recently been quoted as saying that Maddox, Mason, and Sharpton "have zero credibility with me." How could he say such a thing? Suddenly, it was not so hard to see—Cuomo had for years been talking like a great friend of blacks, but when you came down to basics, his commitment vanished.

Maddox, Mason, and Sharpton, however, loomed larger than life to Canton, even as they spoke now, challenging the governor. It was the secret desire of most blacks, Canton believed, to stand up to white people, to tell them off. And standing up to the governor was especially brave. Canton's admiration swelled. These were real men. No one cowed them, not even the governor, whose disembodied voice came out of the box at his elbow. He was still lecturing the black men with his fancy grammar and his lofty white principles.

Now Cuomo had launched into a testimonial for Robert Abrams—and to many listeners of WLIB it sounded like nothing so much as a sales pitch for a floundering criminal justice system.

"I wanted somebody who is absolutely honest," the voice over the loudspeakers began, and immediately amended itself—"who is regarded as absolutely honest by a large number of people. This man has been elected three times!"

The listeners translated: Abrams has been there forever—he must be a hack.

Abrams was a man committed to civil rights, Cuomo said. "This man has proven it for years and years. Just look at the support he's gotten from progressives and liberals and people in the minority community."

They translated: leftists, Hispanics, and blacks have voted for Abrams—he tries to please everybody but pleases nobody.

Abrams will have all the resources he needs for the case, Cuomo said. "He's going to have my state police. He has his own vast staff. And whatever he needs, frankly—and I've said it to him and I've said it to the public—we will supply."

They translated: Abrams can't do anything for himself—the governor's got to hold his hand.

Finally, Abrams has "accountability," Cuomo said. "Because this man has to come before the voters again, he's going to be accountable. Mister Mason and Mister Maddox and Reverend Sharpton and all the other communities that are watching so closely here and are so deeply concerned, they'll be around and he knows it."

They translated: If Abrams isn't careful, he'll lose his low-paying, high-pressure job and may have to take a partnership in a big New York law firm at quadruple the salary.

Trying to move the discussion along, Gary Byrd, the moderator, asked if it was true that Cuomo had said Tawana might have fabricated her story of abduction and rape.

No, the governor said. "A fifteen-year-old girl was found with defecation over her body and 'NIGGER' written on her breast in a plastic bag. So somebody did something terrible to her. I don't know who did it or who did what, but I don't need to investigate to see if there was a crime committed. That, I assume."

Maddox, still smarting over Cuomo's dismissal of his views on special prosecutors, challenged him again. Was the governor trying to stifle discussion on the question?

The governor said he was not opposed to people speaking out on issues. "I'm saying that your judgment on special state prosecutors doesn't impress me. You have a position on a permanent state prosecutor that I think would be a disaster for your people." But he softened it immediately: he and the advisers actually wanted the same thing, justice. As the father of a girl who had been assaulted by a man who was never apprehended, he said, he understood Tawana's plight. Tawana, he said, had sent word through Reverend Saul Williams the day before: "Governor," she had said, "please help me."

He said he wanted to do just that, but needed the cooperation of Maddox and Mason. "You have a role to play here. You have the confidence of these people. You can help to see that justice is done."

It sounded to the listeners as though Cuomo were instructing them in their duty, as if they were a bunch of unruly seventh-graders and he alone knew what was best for them.

"The greatest security that we have in this system is the rule of law," the lecturer went on. "Unfortunately, it is not perfect. It is a rule of law that many times has condemned innocent people and certainly has many times let guilty people slip through. There's no question about that. But overall, we have decided that the rule of law is a better way to conduct our affairs than depending on public outcry, depending on people raising up their voices."

Now they were furious. It was not only the "we have decided" and "our affairs" and the affected references to imperfection in the rule of law that galled them; the suggestion that black protests against an unfair criminal justice system were nothing more than a "public outcry" was almost too much to take.

It was Sharpton who put it into words: "We're not asking you to respond to an outcry. What we're talking about is the anarchy that exists in terms of racial violence. We're saying, based on the lawlessness, we need a special prosecutor. Not based on how loud the public outcry is. We are saying to you, there is a consistent pattern of cases that are not being prosecuted. That is the basis of appeal to the governor."

Cuomo ignored the reference to a consistent pattern of cases. "Was there a prosecution in Howard Beach?" he said rhetorically.

"That was one case out of about forty I'm talking about," Sharpton shot back.

"Well, that's the one case I dealt with," Cuomo said, as if Howard Beach were all that mattered.

"But we're asking you to deal with *all* of them!"

"Let's be clear," Cuomo said, ignoring Sharpton's touché. "The trail is going cold and you know it. And the more we delay, the more we put it off, the more we spend time discussing, the less chance we're going to do justice here. And if we don't soon come to an agreement where the Brawleys will come forward and tell the attorney general what the truth is, we're not going to get this thing properly prosecuted, and that would be a terrible shame."

Mason responded. How could justice be achieved in the Brawley case when New York "enjoys the peculiar distinction of being about where Alabama and Arkansas and Mississippi and all those states down there were about thirty years ago?"

Cuomo did not take offense. "You are absolutely correct," he said coolly. "There is a great deal of violence that needs to be dealt with. There is prejudice and bias in our society, and we need to do something about it, and I'm trying."

Sharpton tried to turn the discussion to cases of police brutality, but they had been on the air for nearly an hour and Cuomo said he had to end the dialogue. He had other things to do. "We want to see that justice is done, the way you saw it done in Howard Beach," he said. "I'm afraid I will not be able to do it without your cooperation."

From the governor's point of view, it had gone well: he had got his point of view across to a large segment of New York City's black community. But he had persuaded Maddox, Mason, and Sharpton of nothing. If he had been in the studio, looking them in the eye, he might have seen it. But the absence of his physical presence, that voice from far away filling the room like that of the Wizard of Oz, only added to the great distance they felt.

Again, Cuomo solicited their help: "I have appointed Mister

Abrams, who I think is perfectly fit. There will be no other appointment. It is Mister Abrams who is the special prosecutor, and I implore you to go to the Brawleys. Tell them the governor wants to help."

They translated: Abrams is all there is—take it or leave it.

While Ethelyn Smith served the coffee, Roy Canton dished up the black pride. It was a couple of days later, and they were all at Edgar's, hashing over the WLIB debate.

"I'm so impressed with the intelligence and strength of Maddox and Sharpton," Canton said, pounding the table for emphasis. "The governor is bending. Black men is making this man bend."

Professor Mackey wasn't buying it. "It's a trick," he said.

"They have to protect their own," Hampton Rookard agreed. "It's a trick. I can feel it." He noted that the white newspapers were making a big deal of Abrams's reputation among civil rights advocates, saying he had the credentials and record of a liberal.

"The whites I trust *least* are liberals," Professor Mackey put in. It was not easy to say why this was so, he added. Rednecks were rednecks—you could count on that. But liberals were untrustworthy—they pretended to be your ally and almost always disappointed you in the end. You could see it already in the Brawley case: Cuomo was passing the buck to Abrams, and Abrams was passing the buck to John Ryan. And who *was* this Ryan? He had no record in civil rights. He prosecuted criminals. And before joining the attorney general's office, he had been an assistant in the Queens DA's office—the office that later couldn't get the Howard Beach case off the ground.

"Anyway," the Professor said, "my guess is they're trying to do a whitewash. Call it instinct. I trust my instinct because when I don't trust it, that's when I get into trouble. When I try to deal with intellect rather than instinct, my ass always pays the price."

They all felt the truth in it: why should black people keep the faith? They had been waiting for years for elected district attorneys to crack down on racial violence. Now Cuomo had not only rejected their pleas for a permanent special prosecutor for bias crimes, he had apparently not even taken the black pleas seriously.

The Professor was talking again: "If you're going to put a whitewash on something, if the natives are restless and they're not too smart, the thing you have to do first is try to calm them down. You get somebody who has a 'liberal' reputation and hope he can get a couple of black respected people to support him, and then you go with that. It is never about really doing any kind of serious investigation."

16

His recollections of childhood in the slums of north Philadelphia were vivid. There were no presents in the Cosby home one Christmas, only a scraggly orange tree and an eviction notice to mark the dreary day. There was no bathtub, and his mother put him in a washtub and poured stove-heated water over him. His father, a Navy mess steward, was a drinker who squandered his pay and sometimes beat Bill's mother. She was a maid who earned eight dollars a week. The eldest of three sons, Bill shined shoes, played football in the streets, and went home bloody after gang fights.

Except for the ministers, there were no idols. Any white man who came around was an insurance salesman or a bill collector. Bill envied other boys their fathers, especially those with a sense of humor or a gentle affection, for his own was unreliable and Bill looked up to no one.

After a stint in the Navy and college at Temple University, he broke into comedy and got his first big break, costarring with Robert Culp in the television series *I Spy*. The important thing about the show was that it put a black man and a white man on an equal footing. But his crowning success was *The Bill Cosby Show*. It almost singlehandedly turned NBC from the third-rated network to number one. From its start in 1984, it was the biggest show on the air, with an audience of nearly forty million people —roughly a third of the American viewing public.

You could see Bill Cosby any Thursday night, a gentle father and a loving husband, a doctor with a rubbery face and a paunch, surrounded by his squabbling children, fully at ease in his beautiful home, fending off the day's aggravations with his wry humor and an unlit cigar. The tensions of his television family, the Huxtables, were always ordinary—a huge phone bill, the divorce of two friends, a bout of the flu, a daughter who wanted to forgo college because she was in love—and what it took to resolve them in a half hour of airtime were the basic human qualities: patience, trust, sensitivity, flexibility, forgiveness.

There were critics who said that *The Bill Cosby Show* was not representative of black life, that it did not try to address problems of racism or the hardships of the black experience. It was true, in a way. There was no explicit moral message, no ideological content. The Huxtables—Heathcliff, a doctor, and Claire, a lawyer, and several of their five children—lived in an elegant Brooklyn brownstone, had no money problems, and portrayed the values of an upper-middle-class family that was intact and successful, reaping the rewards of education and parenthood.

But nearly forty million people found in the Huxtables an appeal that went beyond ideology or even the problems of black people. What they found was a half hour of something they all wanted—love, warmth, and most of all, an understanding father. And the black experience was there, too, in subtle ways: Cliff's university T-shirt; the walls decorated with African and African-American art; the references to black authors, singers, musicians, and poets; a household alive with black friends and unself-conscious affections. Of course, it was an idealized family. Personal pride, self-assurance, college educations, and success were all taken for granted. The Huxtables were not representative of all black people, but they were the repository of black middle-class aspirations in America—and the favorite fantasy family of Tawana Brawley. Cosby himself—wise and absurd, kind and stern, with eyes twinkling like Christmas lights—was everyone's ideal father, even his own.

———————

Bill Cosby answered the ringing telephone in his brownstone on East 61st Street in Manhattan that February night and was delighted to hear from his old friend Ed Lewis, the publisher of *Essence* magazine. They had collaborated on many projects together. But it was not another business project Lewis had in mind. He was calling about Tawana Brawley.

The case had been festering unresolved for ten weeks, and Lewis said that many of his friends in publishing, business, and politics were worried that it was getting lost in a political tug-of-war between the state and Tawana's advisers. They all seemed to be talking about a special prosecutor and how the investigation should be conducted, and not about the rape of a teenaged black girl. With every passing day, Lewis said, the trail of the abductors was growing colder.

It was Cosby who suggested a reward. Cosby had contributed many millions of dollars to colleges, charities, and black causes, and he proposed that he and Lewis put up a sum of money for information that might bring about a breakthrough in the case. Lewis agreed. Cosby said he would have his public relations representative notify the Brawley advisers and schedule a press conference.

The advisers were ecstatic. Word that America's favorite father would post a reward would put a national spotlight on the case. But Robert Abrams regarded the prospect with mixed feelings.

Late the next afternoon, he put in a call to Cosby. Static crackled over the line from Abrams's end—he was calling from his car. He had heard about Cosby's plan for a reward for information. "This may generate interest and important leads," he said. "I don't know if you're aware, Mister Cosby. We've used all our best efforts to get cooperation from the advisers to the Brawleys. We've gotten no cooperation whatsoever."

Cosby listened as Abrams detailed the efforts that Grady and the Dutchess County authorities and then the attorney general and his staff had made to elicit cooperation from the family. Abrams pointed out that he had repeatedly written and telephoned Maddox and Mason personally, without response.

Abrams had a request. Would Cosby, in making his announcement, ask the public to submit all information on the case to his office? If it went elsewhere—he didn't mention the Brawley advisers—it might get twisted or lost.

"I understand," Cosby said. "You know, I have four daughters."

"Oh, Mister Cosby," Abrams said, a bit breathless, "I have two daughters. I understand what you're saying."

At the New York Hilton Hotel the next day, February 10, Cosby hugged Al Sharpton. They had known each other for years through Sharpton's work in entertainment promotions, and they chatted briefly before the news conference. Cosby ribbed Sharpton about his recent appearance on the *Morton Downey Jr. Show* and about news reports alleging that Sharpton had ties with the FBI and the mob.

But after the laughs, Cosby asked him about the Brawley case: "What have you been able to find out so far?"

Sharpton said something vague about having talked to the family, but he had no answer: he really knew none of the details, he admitted. "But I have one hundred percent trust in Alton Maddox," he said, "and this is what Maddox tells me."

Cosby said he didn't care who was guilty of attacking Tawana Brawley, as long as justice was done.

Moments later, he and Ed Lewis stepped before the reporters and television cameras. Alton Maddox and the Brawley family stood beside them. Strobe lights flashed and the cameras rolled. Cosby made the announcement: they were putting up a $25,000 reward for information that would lead to a solution of the Brawley case.

"Somewhere, somebody knows something," Cosby said. "And perhaps this money will bring someone forward."

There was a brief, testy exchange with reporters. Did this mean Cosby was siding with the position taken by Maddox and the family in refusing to cooperate with Abrams? No, he said, he was interested only in flushing out information to help solve the case, to make sure that what had happened to Tawana Brawley never again happened to anyone in the state. Any person with information, he said, should call the attorney general's office.

When it was all over, the reporters approached Maddox, who had said only a few days earlier that he knew the identity of at least one of the girl's attackers. Would he submit the name and collect the reward?

"I am not interested in collecting a reward," Maddox said evenly. "I want what I know to be uncovered by the investigators, and I want arrests to be made." What he said next was news too: he, Sharpton, and Mason would go to Albany in the morning to talk things over with Governor Cuomo.

17

Mario Cuomo led them like a tour guide through the baronial chambers of Valhalla, nodding past the red-leather chairs and down the richly paneled feudal hall, ignoring the cathedral windows and the elephantine fireplace to pause a moment at Teddy Roosevelt's old desk.

He was casual in shirt-sleeves, a charming, modest statesman showing them the artifacts of the people's history. A weak tea of winter light seeped down from the arched panes. There was coffee and pastry, smiles and small talk. But nobody was fooled.

It was possible to awe some people with the splendor of the Capitol's Executive Chamber, to serve up celebrity and self-importance with the little pastries before sitting down to negotiate. But the four black visitors looked around with the hard eyes of Bolsheviks in the Czar's palace, and they all knew that the niceties meant nothing.

The governor motioned them into the conference room and they spaced themselves around a long table like equals. He studied them while they sipped coffee: Alton Maddox, C. Vernon Mason, Al Sharpton, and Timothy Mitchell, who had been included because he was an old friend of the governor's. They had come on February 11—deliberately an hour late after Maddox insisted on stopping for breakfast at the Albany airport—to talk about the Brawley case and the governor's appointment of the special prosecutor.

"I never trusted white folks," Maddox began truculently. "But the only white man I ever voted for in my life was you, Governor Cuomo. The one person I've tried to trust is you. I hope you don't screw us up."

The planned soft opening surprised them all. Sharpton and Mason exchanged a quizzical glance, and Cuomo, the poker player, caught it.

Maddox went on with his dispensation: they would cooperate with Attorney General Robert Abrams as the special prosecutor, they would make Tawana Brawley available at an appropriate time, they all hoped for an amicable outcome.

It was all beer and skittles, much too good to be believed.

Then abruptly, Maddox shifted to reality. The appointment of John Ryan to run the prosecution was totally unacceptable. Ryan had no demonstrable record of racial sensitivity.

Mitchell seconded the assertion.

Cuomo scoffed. Now they were on familiar ground: confrontation, tactical insults, lawyerly combat. "That's the same thing you told me about Hynes, and look at what he did," the governor said, flexing up. "I was right about Joe Hynes. I don't care what you say, Sharpton. Remember, you were the ones who originally opposed Hynes as a bigot."

The word drew blood, and Cuomo retreated from their scowls. "Okay, you didn't use the word," he said. "But was I right or wrong? Now I'm right again. Why can't you give me the benefit of the doubt again?" The faces were still wary. "Besides, not everyone is convinced that this has even happened the way that it's being told."

He waved a prop like an actor: a letter from the Dutchess County executive, Lucille Pattison, saying many people did not believe Tawana Brawley and were appalled that Cuomo had appointed a special prosecutor to chase ghosts.

"Look," Cuomo said, the shrewd eyes innocent, "I'm on your side against the skeptics out there." He let the letter flutter down to the table.

It was Sharpton who responded, and he framed three demands.

They wanted a voice in the selection of Abrams's investigative team, which should include some of Hynes's trusted staff members but not Ryan. They wanted Abrams personally to present the case to the grand jury. And they wanted Abrams himself to prosecute suspects brought to trial.

Cuomo pondered it. He would have to check with Abrams, he said, and they took a little break.

John Poklemba made the call from an anteroom. The attorney general was miffed that he had not been invited to the discussion. Poklemba explained that the visitors had requested the meeting with Cuomo alone. (A flurry of behind-the-scenes contacts had led to the meeting. Mitchell had reached out directly for the governor even as Sharpton was speaking to Cuomo's inspector general, Joseph A. Spinelli, a former FBI agent whom Sharpton knew from his mysterious undercover work with the feds. Sharpton had met Cuomo only once, and Maddox and Mason, despite their power play on Howard Beach, had never met the governor.) But when Poklemba got around to telling him about the Brawley team's demands, Abrams was appalled. "Look," he told Poklemba, "nobody can tie my hands. I'm the special prosecutor. I'll make the decisions." He rejected outright the suggestion that the Brawley advisers should have a voice in picking the investigative team. And they could not dictate how he should run the inquiry.

Cuomo conveyed the sense of it to his visitors when they resumed.

Mason looked alarmed. Do you mean to say, he intoned, that Abrams would not make the presentation to the grand jury? Would not try the case himself?

"So what?" Cuomo retorted, trying to make light of it. "You hire the head of the law firm but he doesn't necessarily go into court." Abrams would lend his personal presence to the cause, and so, said the governor, would he.

There was grumbling, and they called another recess.

This time, Cuomo went into his small private office and telephoned Abrams himself. "Bobby," he said, "it's getting hairy in there." They still wanted Joe Hynes, he said, and asked if Abrams would take on a few of Hynes's staffers. After all, he said, Hynes was technically a deputy attorney general under Abrams.

There was a groan down the line. Abrams would probably never forget how the governor had dictated the choice of Joe Hynes after rejecting Abrams's selection of another aide as the special anticorruption prosecutor in New York City.

"Please, Mario," Abrams objected, "let's not get into that one." He said he was not fobbing the investigation off on Ryan. He intended to lead the inquiry. But he had to be free to make his own staffing decisions.

"I hear you," Cuomo said.

Abrams said he did intend to impanel the grand jury himself and make some presentations to it. But he would not make a commitment on a trial role. He was not a trial attorney; indeed, he had no background in criminal law and had never actually argued a big case in court.

"But I'll be responsible," Abrams promised. "I always said I'll be the person responsible for each and every phase."

Cuomo went back into the conference room and they reconvened. He had only one good card—that Abrams would make some presentations to the grand jury—but he carefully held it back.

It was Maddox who opened this time. "We don't want Ryan," he said pugnaciously.

"It is Abrams," Cuomo countered, exasperated. Why wouldn't they trust him? He restated his assurances.

They put up a barrage of skepticism.

Suddenly Sharpton took them off on a tangent. The governor's mind, he said, had been poisoned by Sharpton's enemies, people like the journalist Jack Newfield. "He just castrated me in *The Village Voice* with this fictitious FBI story," Sharpton said.

"Oh," Cuomo said, feigning surprise. "You're *that* guy!"

Sharpton smiled ruefully, the straight man conceding the governor's one-upmanship, and the laughter around the table seemed to break the tension.

Cuomo, the master of timing, now played his high card. Abrams would present the case to the grand jury, but they could not count on him for a trial role and they could not dictate his staff selections.

They were not satisfied, but when Cuomo again offered his assurances that Abrams would play a key role in the case, they took it to mean that he would twist Abrams's arm about a trial role. Cuomo intended no such interpretation: he thought one thing and they thought another.

As for staffing questions, Cuomo said he was sure that the Brawley advisers could work out the details with Abrams. "All right!" Cuomo said. "So we've got a deal, fellas?"

Judicious nods rounded the table. It was over.

A bristling array of microphones and cameras were waiting outside, and at the advisers' behest they held a news conference. Cuomo, a broad smile on his haggard face, was the first to speak. "Mister Maddox and Mister Mason have agreed to cooperate in the Brawley matter. The attorney general confirmed to me and will by his own statement confirm his continuing personal involvement in the investigation of this matter."

Then, eager to please his guests, Cuomo started talking about Tawana, and went too far. "We know that someone has violated her in a terrible way. We need to know who did it, and we need to see to it that that individual or individuals are punished as the law provides." He praised the Brawley advisers.

It was like old home week in front of the cameras. Mason, whose political antennae hummed happily beside the governor, praised Cuomo and saved his scorn for the skeptics. "We understand there are people in the community who suggest that maybe a fifteen-year-old girl would rape herself, kidnap herself, sodomize herself, and then put feces on herself and 'KKK' and 'NIGGER' inscribed on her body. We want to say this to those persons responsible for this: your day is coming. We intend to work vigorously so that, as Bill Cosby said, this will never happen to any other person in the state."

Maddox thanked the governor and said shrewdly that it was his understanding that Abrams would personally carry out the day-today investigation and prosecution. He, too, went too far, but nobody was splitting hairs now.

A reporter shouted: Did that mean Tawana Brawley would now testify?

Mason equivocated. She was still suffering and would need extensive psychiatric therapy. "But," he added vaguely, "she will testify at the appropriate time."

Sharpton's turn in front of the cameras arrived at last. He said their disagreements had been laid aside to break a stalemate, and he snapped off a one-liner for the world of television: "Today was a day of *en*-gage rather than *out*-rage!"

Click. Whirrrrrrrrr.

Cuomo repeated the line appreciatively, rolling it around like wine on the palate.

"I might run against you," Sharpton said, mugging for the cameras.

"I should be so lucky," Cuomo retorted amid laughter. "We will keep in touch. Y'all have a good meeting with Abrams."

As they went out, Cuomo shook Sharpton's hand. "You're not as wild as I thought," he said. "But you're not wired, are you? I'm not saying this where it will be heard, am I?"

He wasn't, but reporters' tapes picked up his words.

Then Cuomo headed back to the baronial chambers, to the elephantine fireplace and Teddy Roosevelt's old desk. He could hardly contain his satisfaction. "Good, good, good," the tapes caught him murmuring.

The car carrying Maddox and Sharpton sped down the thruway between fields and timbered hills draped with snow. The polished Hudson lay beyond the bluffs, a knife in the continent, and night gradually walled in the windows as they talked about Cuomo and the day in Albany. The jack-of-all-trades, Perry McKinnon, was at the wheel, silently taking it all in like an operative. He was Sharpton's chauffeur, bodyguard, sounding board, and sidekick.

They were halfway to New York when Maddox abruptly decided to make a detour into Wappingers Falls and report to the Brawleys. The case had been under way for two and a half months, but Sharpton, amazingly, had still not met Tawana Brawley, and he knew nothing about the case except what Maddox had told him. Moreover, Sharpton was convinced that Mason, who had hitched a ride with Poklemba to New York City in a state helicopter, knew even less than he did.

Expecting to find a stone-faced girl stricken with grief and a bad limp, Sharpton was astonished to be greeted at 4-D Carmine Drive by an ebullient, attractive, seemingly ordinary teenager.

"I saw you on the 'big mouth' show," she said with bright innocence, referring to Morton Downey, Jr.'s televised brutality.

Sharpton grinned. He was one of the elect: a man who knew all the big shots, who could hold his own against Downey and the mob, and when Sharpton dropped names like Michael Jackson and Mike Tyson, Tawana went into a rapture of questions and bubbly comments about his sophisticated life. She sat beside him and chatted about school and music and clothes—everything but her case.

But they had come to talk about the case and the meeting with the governor, and when they began to brief Glenda and Juanita Brawley and Ralph King, Tawana suddenly got up and walked out of the room. It was clear that she did not want to be a part of the discussion.

Juanita was impressed that the governor had become involved, but Glenda was more interested in what Cuomo had had to say, and Ralph King scowled skeptically at the whole thing.

"What are y'all going to agree to without talking to us?" he demanded. And there was more: how did the family know the advisers weren't up there in Albany selling them out?

Maddox did his best to mollify King, but television did it better. When the evening news came on, there was footage of Cuomo with the advisers, talking in the Capitol about the Brawley case and what they were all going to do to make things right. In the middle of it, Tawana came back down the stairs and joined them in front of the television.

Afterward, Sharpton tried to bring Tawana into the conversation and to steer it gently toward the assault.

Tawana ignored his probes. Instead, she asked Sharpton what would happen next. Would the family be badgered by more questions, more doubts?

Sharpton tried to reassure her. The advisers were doing all they could to overcome those problems and resolve the case.

Tawana said she hoped they were not wasting their time.

They would fight to the end, Sharpton said, resorting to the first cliché that came to mind. He smiled and invited her to Brooklyn to visit him and his wife, Cathy.

Before they left, Maddox said they would follow the Howard Beach tactic of withholding cooperation. As to the advisers, he said, their division of labor would also be like Howard Beach. "I concentrate on the law," he said. "Sharpton concentrates on riling up the masses."

"I like the way he talks," Tawana said, giving Sharpton a vote of confidence. "I'd like him to speak for me."

But, Sharpton said, he needed more information about what had happened to Tawana. The girl turned away, as if it were somebody else's problem. But Glenda seemed prepared for this. She handed Sharpton a packet of newspaper clippings.

It seemed that was all he was going to get.

At home later, Sharpton sat up all night reading the news clippings. It was about four o'clock in the morning when he ran across a profile of King. Stunned, he telephoned Maddox.

"Did you know this nigger killed his wife?" Sharpton bellowed.

Maddox, who was always suspicious of telephone conversations, cut him off. They would talk in the morning.

Of course, said Maddox when they met, he knew about King's manslaughter conviction. He had learned about it a month ago. His attitude was, "So what?"

Sharpton was not shocked to be representing a wife killer: many people who were active in his circle had criminal records. What bothered him was that he had not known about it until now. What if someone had thrown this at him on the air? And what else did he not know about?

Mike Tyson was miffed.

"Hey man," he said, "you doing me wrong!"

"What's wrong?" Sharpton said. They were in the lobby of fight promoter Don King's building in Manhattan.

"Man, how come you let Bill Cosby jump out here with this girl and didn't let me?"

Sharpton was taken aback.

Upstairs, Don King, his electric hair standing on end, also turned on Sharpton. "Yeah, man, you let this guy get national coverage, and you know Mike should be there. Get on the phone and arrange a meeting, Reverend."

Sharpton frowned, an abused man. "We talking about a girl getting raped here," he reminded them. "We not talking number one on the top ten boxers."

But Sharpton was not one to let an opportunity slip away. If Tyson wanted to get involved, Sharpton would arrange it. Besides, he thought, his old friend Don King had been trying to sign up Tyson for a long time. The vision of a wonderful three-way deal, with himself as the broker, swam into view.

The next night, two stretch limousines approached Wappingers Falls like ocean liners calling at a banana port. In the first car, Don King, swaddled in a floor-length mink coat, rode with his guests, Mike Tyson and Tyson's actress wife, Robin Givens. The second car rode without passengers; it was to take Tyson and Givens to their retreat in the Catskills later.

All the way up from the city, King, Tyson, and Givens had found little to say to one another. Tyson and Givens were having marital problems, and King could not broach his ambitions without a dig from Givens, who did not want her husband under contract to the promoter. Between the long uneasy silences, there had been superficial talk about boxing. Givens had sulked most of the way.

Once off the highway, the chauffeurs got lost, prolonging the agony as they circled the small-town streets. At last they found 4-D Carmine Drive.

As soon as they pulled up, a rectangle of yellow light broke in the doorway and a childish figure ran out to the car. They rolled down a smoked window and she peered in with star-struck eyes. Robin Givens recognized Tawana Brawley immediately. But, Givens realized with a shock, she had run out! Hadn't she been crippled by her ordeal?

"Ooooooh," the girl cooed, "I'm so excited to see you! Can I sit in the limo?"

They opened the door, and Tawana climbed in between them and leaned back in the plush seat. "I always wanted to sit in a limo," she gushed.

Finally, Tawana took them into the apartment. Sharpton, who had set up the meeting, was already there with Maddox, talking in the kitchen to Ralph King. Don King joined them, and all four kept in the background most of the evening, while Glenda Brawley ferried snacks and drinks into the living room. A Polaroid camera was brought out and pictures were snapped.

Tawana, wearing her modeling outfit, an alluring black-velvet dress cut deep in the back, settled on the sofa next to Tyson and began whispering things in his ear as Givens sat sourly on the hard cushions and sipped something that was too sweet.

"I've always wanted to date you," Tawana said, ignoring Givens and all pretense of reserve. They talked for an hour. Tawana told them she wanted to be a model, and Robin Givens said it was a good idea. Tyson told Tawana to let him know if she ever wanted to attend one of his fights.

Words apparently failing her at the end, Tawana took out a pad and printed a note: "I can't express how you people made me feel by coming to visit me in big fancy words and I don't know how to make speeches. But I can say you made me very happy and you are the special people in my eyes."

And at the bottom, she wrote: "I love you too. Tawana."

Now something of a celebrity herself, she added her autograph with a flourish: "Miss Tawana Brawley."

Tyson was touched. He told Tawana he would put up fifty

thousand dollars for her college education and any medical expenses she might be incurring. He also told her he was going to set up a fund to help other crime victims pay for their educations.

Don King, unwilling to be outdone, said he would match Tyson's offers.

But Tyson could not be upstaged. As they were leaving, he lingered with Tawana. Suddenly, he removed the chunky gold and diamond-studded Rolex watch from his wrist—it was worth thirty-five thousand dollars—and clasped it around Tawana's slender arm. "Look," he said, "I want you to do me a favor. I want you to wear this and know that everybody's with you."

Tawana was stunned. She blushed, then broke into tears.

The evening had been an enormous success. Outside, they all kissed and hugged, and Tawana waved them into the night.

Later, Tyson told reporters he had been deeply inspired by Tawana's courage. "How can I complain," he said, "when this fifteen-year-old girl is stronger than me?"

18

Robert Abrams paced his office nervously and checked the wristwatch under the navy blue cuff again. They were already almost an hour late. Where could they be? Was it a tactic? Would they humiliate him by not showing up? He circled the conference table made by convicts and rearranged the electric-blue chairs once more. Then he fidgeted with some papers at his desk. And when he had had enough of that, he asked his secretary to call Maddox's office again. There was still no answer.

He realized suddenly how foolish he was being. If they didn't come, they didn't come. What would be would be. He was still nursing the injury of his exclusion from their discussions with Cuomo in Albany five days ago. But he was pleased with the outcome. They had promised to cooperate, and it only remained to work out the details: at least, that's what the governor had told him. But he wondered how much he could count on that, or even on their coming. They had not responded to any of his five phone calls or his two hand-delivered letters. Indeed, Maddox, Mason, and Sharpton had never actually said they would be here. Maddox's secretary had only told Abrams's secretary that she would pass on the request for a meeting at eleven A.M. on Tuesday, February 16, at the attorney general's office on the twenty-fifth floor of 120 Broadway, in New York City. Perhaps the message had not even gotten to them.

Abrams took refuge at the window. He scanned the petrified

forest of lower Manhattan with solemn, sentimental eyes, like an immigrant passing the Statue of Liberty. Beyond his image in the glass lay all he believed in: history, faith, orderliness, the dignity of human achievement. They were there in the soaring glass towers, the Gothic spires, and Corinthian columns. They were around the corner at Federal Hall and Fraunces Tavern. They were across the bay on Ellis Island and down in the soil of Trinity churchyard with Alexander Hamilton and Robert Fulton. To other people—to Maddox, Mason, and Sharpton—the gloomy canyons meant crooked white men's fortunes, empires built on blood and the triumph of greed and power. But to Abrams, the masses of steel, concrete, and glass were the sentimental truths of America, the rumbling basso profundo of a great Knickerbocker organ.

He was checking his watch under the cuff again—wincing at noon—when the intercom buzzed.

"They're here," the voice said.

Abrams let out a sigh of relief.

They came in without a word of apology, the unsmiling faces betraying nothing. Abrams went across the mottled blue-green carpet to meet them partway. Through the half-open door, he saw Perry McKinnon, Sharpton's disheveled, distracted-looking aide, hanging back in the outer office like a well-trained orderly awaiting command.

The attorney general called in several of his own people, and they all arranged themselves around the conference table like figureheads and bowsprits—Abrams at the head; Sharpton, Maddox, and Mason on the starboard; and opposite them, John Ryan flanked by two black staff lawyers, Heather Williams and Suzanne Lynn.

Abrams had ordered no food, to show that he thought they could finish the business quickly. But there was a flask of coffee in the center of the table. Sharpton poured a cup and thickened it with astonishing amounts of sugar.

Abrams immediately got off on the wrong foot with a lame

attempt at humor. "Okay, fellas," he said with wry Bronx charm. "When do we see Tawana?"

The deadpan faces gazed back at him as if he had just belched at the opera.

Abrams quickly retreated into his undertaker's solemnity. "This case is my highest priority," he said, accenting each syllable like a pedagogue. He wanted to convey sincerity, but he sounded like a prophet delivering a last admonition to sinners. He lumbered on: "I am the one who is going to rise or fall based on the performance in this case. We are very concerned about Tawana Brawley. She has already been victimized once. We do not want to victimize her further."

"Have you ever heard us say anything bad about you?" Sharpton responded.

Abrams didn't know how to take it at first. It sounded flattering, but with these men you couldn't be sure. Perhaps his public statements and press releases had done some good after all: he'd been careful not to express doubts about Tawana's story, to portray himself as deeply concerned. Perhaps they had picked up his signals.

Yes, Sharpton was saying, they were eager for him to handle the case personally.

Abrams beamed, not recognizing the trap.

They were in no hurry to exploit it. Sharpton slid into a lecture about the sacrifices they all had to make to fight discrimination and get the state to live up to its responsibilities to black people. Then Maddox gave a capsule history of four hundred years of slavery, segregation, and humiliation for blacks in the Americas. And Mason expanded these themes with a peroration of his own.

Finally they got down to business. "How will you approach the victim?" Sharpton asked.

It was the question Abrams had been waiting for. His investigators had found a renowned rape-victim counselor who had agreed to interview Tawana and tell them when the girl was well enough to be questioned. "We have consulted a lot of experts," he said, "and have come up with a professor educated at Harvard and attached to Columbia—Dr. Hilda Hutchinson of the Columbia-Presbyterian Medical Center. She created a clinic for rape victims. She is black, by the way. She's ready to see Tawana. No one will go near the girl until she certifies it's all right—if it takes ten visits."

Abrams waited for a reaction. There was none. It struck him as odd. He had expected them to be delighted. Instead, they ignored the point and launched into a question that Abrams thought had been resolved in their meeting with the governor. They wanted a commitment that Abrams would personally handle all stages of the investigation and prosecution.

He was surprised. The purpose of this meeting, as he understood it, was to arrange for Tawana Brawley's cooperation, not to reargue his own role in the case. He had said he would take responsibility for the case, but he was not going to run out and dust for fingerprints. What was going on here?

But Maddox was already charging ahead. The cooperation of Tawana Brawley, he announced, would be contingent on five commitments by the attorney general. First, Abrams must personally direct all the work of the grand jury, and then at the trial he must lead the jury selection, give the opening and closing statements, and examine all the witnesses.

Furthermore . . .

Abrams was astonished. "Look, gentlemen," he interrupted, his baldish pink pate wrinkling in agitation. "I'll repeat from the outset: I'm personally responsible. I'll be involved with the grand jury and the trial. But I will not give you statements now relating to tactics and strategy."

Maddox's eyes looked right through him. And that was just the first point, Maddox went on as if Abrams had said nothing. There were four other points: the advisers wanted a voice in the composition, assignments, and role of Abrams's investigative staff; they wanted a voice in developing all evidence apart from the testimony of Tawana Brawley; they wanted a voice in how investigators would approach Tawana for her story; and they insisted that the FBI and the federal prosecutor, Rudolph Giuliani, be excluded from the case.

Abrams reeled. How could he commit himself to tactics and strategy even before he had a case? It would amount to giving them a veto over everything from personnel to interrogations. He might just as well let them run it. For years he had heard demands for federal investigations, but he had never heard anyone insist on no federal inquiry. Besides, he had already asked the FBI and Giuliani for help in the case. "Why no FBI or Giuliani?" he stammered.

"Because we've been to Morgenthau and Holtzman and Giuliani," Sharpton said, mixing two local prosecutors with the federal official, "and they've shown no commitment to civil rights enforcement."

Abrams shook his head in disbelief.

"Perhaps if we might caucus?" Maddox suggested. The expression conjured up cigars and back-room politics. But a break was just what the worried Abrams needed. He felt like the frail figure of Civic Virtue tottering in a gale atop New York's Municipal Building.

Maddox, Mason, and Sharpton were given a room down the hall, and they went in and closed the door.

Abrams and his team—enlarged now with his deputy, Scott Greathead, and press adviser, Timothy Gilles—stayed in the conference room. From the lit buttons on the console, they could tell that the advisers were making use of the telephone. Who were they calling? Abrams wondered.

As they analyzed it, point one, that Abrams must personally lead the grand jury and any case for the prosecution, was the stumbling block. They could never go along with that. Maybe they could find something else to agree on, Greathead suggested, and use it to create momentum that would help solve the more difficult issues. It was worth a try, Abrams agreed.

But when they reconvened, the advisers wanted to go over the terms of their agreement with Cuomo. Abrams was again uneasy. Cuomo hadn't told him of any agreement, other than a commitment that Tawana Brawley would cooperate.

The advisers insisted, however, that they had a deal with

Cuomo that committed Abrams to handling every aspect of the case personally. It was only point one again in disguise.

Abrams said he knew nothing about it.

Then either Abrams or Cuomo was lying, Maddox said evenly. "Let's call Cuomo."

Abrams passed over the insult and rejected the idea. A call to see whether the governor or the attorney general was a liar struck him as unseemly, he said. Instead, he went into Scott Greathead's suggestion to veer away. "We disagree on point one," he said. "Let's agree to disagree on that and move on to points two through five."

But they refused. They had to solve point one first, they said.

They went around in circles for hours without progress. In general, Abrams was struck by the absence of any more rancor. Indeed, the upbeat, friendly tone of the talks encouraged him to believe that they could eventually strike a deal, if only they could keep at it.

At midafternoon, the image-conscious Gilles entered and urged the group to make a statement to the restless press.

"We're not ready," Sharpton told him.

"They'll think that you are arguing if you don't hurry up," Gilles said.

"But we *are* arguing," Sharpton said.

By late afternoon, they were all exhausted. Abrams suggested that they adjourn until the next day. They wrangled briefly over what to tell the waiting reporters. Like labor negotiators locked in delicate contract talks, they agreed to say nothing substantive, but to describe their discussions as "frank" and "constructive" —the catch words that meant no progress.

Before they went out, Gilles had the two groups mingle rather than stand separately like warring factions. Gilles was a man who thought of everything. He even urged Sharpton to smile. After making their brief agreed-upon statements to the press, Maddox and Sharpton declined further comment. But Mason, evidently overwrought by the day's tensions, blurted out that the meeting had been a flop. Gilles was miffed. Abrams was more philosophical. Tomorrow was another day, he said.

The next day there were platters of sandwiches and pickles on the table with the coffee flask. Sharpton attacked the platters with gusto.

When the discussions resumed, Abrams again mentioned Dr. Hilda Hutchinson and her readiness to counsel Tawana before any questioning by the authorities. It was virtually all he had to offer. "No matter what, Tawana Brawley will see the best specialists," he vowed like a rich uncle.

But again they ignored it. Maddox had a counterproposal. They would drop their demand for putting trusted members of Joe Hynes's staff on the investigation if Abrams would commit himself to point one, handling every stage of the grand jury investigation and prosecution himself.

Abrams restated his refusal.

They talked about it for six hours and got nowhere. When they broke up, Gilles issued a diplomatic statement saying they had been unable to resolve certain issues and that, at this time, there was no agreement to secure Tawana Brawley's cooperation.

But the advisers held their own press conference and Mason summarized the case in unforgettable terms: "This case began with a young, black fifteen-year-old girl who was kidnapped, raped, sodomized. 'KKK' and 'NIGGER' were inscribed on her body—and feces. She was then placed in a plastic garbage bag and dumped on the road for dead."

Afterward, Ryan told Abrams he was convinced that the advisers had never intended to come to an agreement, that they had entered the two days of talks with one objective, to sabotage them.

Abrams reluctantly agreed. If the advisers had felt the slightest willingness to cooperate, he reflected, they would have moved beyond insisting that he personally handle every stage of the case, the one demand he had to refuse. The more he thought about it, the clearer it seemed: they were deliberately placing Tawana Brawley's cooperation out of reach.

For their part, Maddox, Mason, and Sharpton saw little room for maneuvering. Glenda Brawley had insisted that if Abrams did not agree to their conditions, Tawana would not cooperate. But the advisers left the office convinced there was still a slender chance for reopening the talks with Abrams. "We'll put the heat on him and the heat will make him come back," Sharpton said. "If we stand up to him, he'll cave in."

And then began what might be called "the Abrams nightmares." A few days after his doomed talks with the advisers, the attorney general got a call from Robert Morgenthau, the Manhattan district attorney. "We've received information that someone from your office is trying to sell grand jury minutes from the Brawley case," Morgenthau said in his patrician baritone. The culprit's name was Samuel Evans, Morgenthau explained, and he was a printer in Abrams's New York office. Abrams couldn't believe what he was hearing: he was being sabotaged from inside his own office! But the Manhattan DA was all reassurances: We're on top of it, he said. "Don't worry."

Indeed, Morgenthau was almost too on top of it, and within days the whole sorry affair was exposed. Evans, according to investigators, was deeply troubled, an alcoholic homosexual who was having an affair with a man identified only as "Tank." Trying to impress Tank, he had showed him a copy of something he had stumbled on at work: a two-hundred-page transcript of testimony by thirty witnesses who had appeared before the Dutchess County grand jury that had been convened, and then abandoned, in January. Tank, it happened, was an informer for Morgenthau's office and had tried to sell the documents to a prosecutor. The scheme had backfired. Evans was arrested for stealing and disclosing grand jury secrets. (He later pleaded guilty to a charge of petty larceny in exchange for a sentence of three years' probation.) With his arrest, the press jumped in—and Abrams feared he might become a public joke. The Brawley advisers were quick to fuel speculation that Evans had been hired by the rapists to find out what had happened in the grand jury—that Evans had "a friend" close to Abrams.

219

Not missing a cue, Sharpton clucked gleefully: "It's a sad commentary that this is the third prosecutor and they only seem able to prosecute themselves or a member of their staff."

Hardly had the Evans embarrassment begun to subside when Abrams was blindsided again. He had been scrupulous about putting as many black investigators on the case as possible, and he was especially pleased that one of them, William West, had begun to develop a real rapport with Juanita Brawley. Then the news broke: West had been arrested in Brooklyn by undercover narcotics detectives in a buy-and-bust operation, accused of having vouched for a cocaine dealer to facilitate a sale. West was found not guilty months later, but that was too late for Abrams, who was about to get bushwhacked again.

The tipster had spoken of murder, and Alton Maddox was intrigued. He sent his amateur sleuths to Dutchess County to snoop around. What they came up with was a mangled confusion of names and mixed-up facts: a perfect soup that Maddox served up on WLIB.

First, he charged, William Grady had quit the case because a car seen at the Pavillion on the day Tawana was found had been linked to a Grady assistant, Steven Pagones. Next, he said Harry Crist "may have been bumped off" because he was a weak link in the conspiracy and had to be eliminated by the other men who had attacked Tawana. After all, Maddox pointed out, who knew about the authenticity of Crist's suicide note? "Nobody has seen the note," he sneered.

It was another billow of smoke, and the press rushed in, even though the allegations were quite unfounded: the car seen by the mailman, Tim Losee, may have resembled Crist's, but it did not resemble Pagones's; in any case, no links to either man had been established in the case. Grady had quit because of Pagones's friendship with Crist, not because a car—no matter whose it resembled—had been linked to either of them. Finally, Harry Crist had not been murdered. Overwhelming evidence had shown his death to be a suicide. And the suicide note was not missing, but safe with the authorities, as they had said all along. Still, there was little Abrams could do to sort out the titillating confusion. As he well knew, the facts rarely caught up with the lies.

Now the innuendos started to fly. On February 19, the *Poughkeepsie Journal* carried the headline: "Note Scribbled by Brawley Reportedly Mentions Sheriff." Three notes had supposedly been written by the girl on December 1, saying: "I want him dead," "I want him dead," and "I want Scoralick." But the paper mentioned only the last scribbling.

It was the first Abrams had heard of any note. What did it mean?

He was further disconcerted by Scoralick's feeble response: "I haven't commented. That's not the way law enforcement should work, or the justice system. Cases are not tried in the newspapers." Innocence did not have to be proved like guilt, but even Abrams had to allow that it seemed suspicious. The sheriff was practically being accused of rape, and he had nothing to say for himself?

Abrams sent investigators scrambling to find out what had happened. But the results were inconclusive: the notes apparently had been lost—perhaps they had never existed. But was the sheriff being accused in nonexistent notes? It seemed so, but no one was sure.

The *Journal* nosed ahead, forcing Abrams to send investigators to check out another startling report in its pages. A boy of thirteen who lived near the Pavillion said he had seen someone thrown out of a car onto a road near the condominiums on the night of November 27, the night before Tawana was found. He had not previously disclosed this, the paper said, because he was frightened. Was this the key witness they had all been waiting for? But the boy backed down when the investigators showed up. He had not seen anyone thrown from a car, he confessed. He told the glowering detectives he had just made up the whole story to get attention.

The *Journal* corrected the record a few days later, but it was too late. Mason had already woven the episode into new accusations.

To explain how Tawana could have emerged from four days of torment with no clear memory of it all, her family gave the *Journal* a remarkable new story: her abductors had forced her to drink a mysterious milky white fluid that had not only given her amnesia, but had rendered her temporarily speechless and paralyzed. What could that magic potion have been? No one could possibly say.

One allegation in the *Journal* had real staying power. It said that a possible suspect in the Brawley case had gone to a state police barracks more than once to take lie-detector tests. He was Tommy Masch, a blond, mustachioed young man who was a volunteer fireman, a tow-truck operator, a gas-pump jockey, and a police buff. He owned a refurbished police car and loved racing to the scenes of fires and police activity. He seemed to fit the one vague description of an abductor that Tawana had provided. And as if fate had singled him out for suspicion, he worked at Paino's Mobil station on the corner where Tawana had last been seen on the night of November 24.

The press picked up the story, and for a while Masch was hounded by reporters. Bob Herbert of the *Daily News* confronted him at Paino's and described him as a suspicious character. "Just about everybody who takes a look at the Tawana Brawley case, officially or unofficially, takes a good long look at Tommy Masch," he wrote. He said Masch was "scared now, real scared," and noted that "his eyes were full of apprehension." Even Masch's car looked suspicious: "It was the kind of vehicle that could intimidate people, especially young people."

Abrams and his investigators did not consider Masch a serious suspect. They had already checked him out thoroughly. He had alibis for the time of Tawana's disappearance and had volunteered for and passed the lie-detector tests. Indeed, he had called a police bluff in volunteering for them. But the damage had been done, and the mud slinging accelerated.

For Abrams, the worst came when Sharpton and Timothy Mitchell went to Albany on George Washington's birthday. They had hoped to see the governor. But Cuomo, once burned, refused to see them. So they dropped in on his criminal justice chief, John Poklemba.

Sharpton told Poklemba that Robert Abrams and his wife, Diane, owned a farmhouse in eastern Dutchess County, and he charged that they had been contributors to the election campaigns of Sheriff Scoralick. Sharpton promised to back it up with a photocopy of a canceled check. He argued that this amounted to a connection between Abrams and Scoralick, that Scoralick was a suspect in the case, and that Abrams should therefore remove himself from the investigation.

It struck Poklemba as farfetched, but he agreed to consider any evidence Sharpton provided. He cautioned Sharpton, however, against blowing it out of proportion.

"I've got to beat up on Abrams a little," Sharpton said mischievously.

"Restrain yourself," Poklemba urged. "Bring in the evidence first."

"No," Sharpton said. "I've got to take a shot."

"Tone it down then," Poklemba pleaded.

After leaving Poklemba's office, Sharpton ran into an Associated Press reporter at the Albany Mall and repeated his charge against the attorney general. When the reporter asked if the supposed connection between Abrams and Scoralick would prevent Tawana from cooperating, Sharpton let out all the stops: "That's like asking someone who watched someone killed in the gas chamber to sit down with Mister Hitler."

The slur made the reporter's day, and in its wide retelling became characterized as Sharpton calling Abrams Hitler. To Abrams, a gentle man who took his Jewish heritage seriously, it was an unspeakable calumny: Hitler!

But perhaps not the ultimate one. If Abrams was not already thoroughly shaken up, then Maddox was determined to administer the final jolt: in a Harlem church appearance that was broadcast over New York City's radio station, WNYC, the lawyer voiced his outrage that NBC-TV had shown pictures of Tawana partially disrobed with the racial slurs scrawled on her chest at St. Francis Hospital. "You will never see a white girl who is unclothed, a rape and kidnapping victim, being paraded around for all the Jimmy Swaggarts of the world to do the VCR and maybe use it for later purposes," he said. "Tawana cried when she saw that."

Pause. Then he screamed: "Robert Abrams, you are no longer going to masturbate looking at Tawana Brawley's picture! You're no longer going to go into the men's room with your perverted mind and rape our daughters!"

Part Three

ON THE RUN

19

The loudspeaker boomed down the cavernous mall of *The New York Times* newsroom like an announcement to Kmart shoppers: "Ralph Blumenthal—Metropolitan Desk."

At the far end, lost behind pillars the color of decaying oranges and rows of sooty filing cabinets, a bookish, bushy-haired reporter with horn-rimmed glasses and a droopy mustache paused in the throes of composition. He scoured the clutter of his desk for a pad and pen, and then struck out for the Metropolitan Desk. For twenty-five years, Blumenthal had been answering the call of *Times* editors, through assignments in Vietnam and West Germany and on the crime beat in New York, and this was just one more summons.

John Darnton, the metropolitan editor, sat at the nexus of the city room with his usual aura of beatific calm, seemingly oblivious to the swarm of human traffic, the raking bursts of calls that lit up the telephone banks, the swirl of paper that competed for his attention. He was focused on a *Daily News* clipping on his desk: it was marked up with another editor's bold red ink, especially the sensational parts about Glenda Brawley's felonious companion, Ralph King. It had been over two months since the *Times* had carried its first cursory article on the case. Since then, the paper had run several stories on developments in the case—on the appointment of Abrams as special prosecutor, the legal tactics of Maddox and Mason, and the dispute between the advisers and

227

Abrams. But for a combination of reasons, the *Times* had not delved into the case itself: reporters were not regularly assigned in Dutchess County, there was no one in the newsroom pushing for a follow-up, no rival publication was spurring competition, and the big civil rights groups had not made it a cause. Now the case clamored for attention again because of the controversy surrounding Abrams's appointment, and Darnton was troubled by the unresolved questions about what had really happened to the girl.

Darnton looked at Blumenthal and asked if he recalled the Tawana Brawley story.

Blumenthal nodded, but he remembered it only vaguely, a gruesome racial attack on a black girl upstate and a notion that the authorities seemed unable to get to the bottom of it.

"Take a good look at it," Darnton said. "Let me know what you think."

An assistant handed Blumenthal a packet of clippings.

The next day, Blumenthal drove to Dutchess County, intending to ask some questions and retrace the girl's movements on the day of her disappearance. Thirty-five years earlier, Blumenthal as a child had spent a summer with his family at a lake bungalow off Myers Corners Road, not far from the spot where Tawana had vanished. Now, under a blanket of snow, nothing looked familiar. A succession of sprawling shopping malls had sprung up in the once pristine fields: Wappingers Plaza, Imperial Plaza, Dutchess Shopping Plaza, Lafayette Plaza, Poughkeepsie Plaza, Poughkeepsie Galleria.

In the Village of Wappingers Falls, life seemed preternaturally normal. People sat over coffee in the diners, and pickup trucks churned the snow to slush. Blumenthal stopped to buy a copy of the *Poughkeepsie Journal* and a big front-page headline leaped out: "Note Scribbled by Brawley Reportedly Mentions Sheriff." Blumenthal swung the car around and headed for Poughkeepsie.

Sheriff Frederick Scoralick, a tall, pompadoured man looking like a Florida tourist in a white sports jacket, was surprisingly unshaken. "I haven't made any comment yet and I won't start now," he said evenly.

Blumenthal prodded. "Will you say where you were that night?"

"Anything else you want to talk about?" Scoralick replied coolly. There wasn't.

Blumenthal found Market Street and started pumping quarters into a phone in a search for witnesses who might have seen Tawana's note. He came up with Clarence McGill, chairman of the Dutchess County Committee Against Racism.

They met in a coffee shop at the Wyndham Hotel. McGill seethed with suspicions. "Crist's suicide note hasn't been made public," he said. "Why? What are they hiding?" The voice dropped conspiratorially. "A friend of Crist's aunt said she didn't want to be involved but said Crist knew the girl. Crist had a friend, a guard at the Orange County Jail, and a friend in the state police. They got the suicide note. I got a call the day before Crist's obituary ran—said he committed suicide. They only wrote he 'died Wednesday at his home.' I called up the newspaper. I said, 'Hey, didn't he commit suicide?' "

"What about the Scoralick note?" Blumenthal asked.

"I remember her writing something, but I never saw it."

"Who has it?"

McGill shrugged. "I don't know."

People whose names were concealed from the world often called M. A. Farber in the middle of the night. Sometimes these shadowy people met him in an out-of-the-way bar, or picked him up in a car for a ride to nowhere and an anonymous chat. Some of these people were criminals. Some were high officials of government. They all wanted to tell him things that they wanted to see in *The New York Times*.

Farber was an investigative reporter who looked like Shakespeare, with somber eyes, a high forehead, long silvery hair over his ears, and a short beard. One tipster a decade earlier had set him on the track of Doctor X at a New Jersey hospital where patients were dying inexplicably; a notable Farber series, and later a book, detailed a story that had led to the exhumation of bodies, murder charges against the doctor, and a forty-day jail term for Farber for refusing, on First Amendment grounds, to turn over his notes on the case.

Now the voice on the telephone was a familiar one. It was a state law-enforcement official, and he sounded dismayed. What bothered him was the avalanche of misinformation on the Tawana Brawley case.

"For example?" Farber said.

"For example," said the voice, "she was arrested for shoplifting a few months before. She's frightened of her parents. Her father came to the jail and said, 'You can keep her.' Forget the model student stuff. She's not a great student."

The source said he had heard that there was no abduction, that Tawana had come home with several boys from a party and had been hiding from her parents at the Pavillion. "When her mother came to get the mail, she hid in the bag." It was possible, he said, that Tawana's hair wasn't really cut, that it had just looked that way. The FBI was still analyzing the rape tests, but so far the results were negative.

"Negative?" Farber asked.

"No rape." Another thing, he said, "eat" was misspelled.

"Eat?" Farber didn't get it.

"The writing on her chest. 'Eat shit.' 'Eat' was spelled 'e-t-e.' "

"So what does that mean?" Farber asked.

"I don't know," the caller said.

Farber related this conversation to Darnton, and Darnton made a mental note: Farber, too, would be good for the Brawley story.

The young, round-faced woman looked up from the law briefs piled precariously around her and saw John Darnton. The metropolitan editor had an edition of the *Times* open to her provocative news analysis on the tactics of Alton Maddox and C. Vernon Mason. As one of the first participants in a pioneering Columbia University program to award graduate students joint degrees in journalism and law, E. R. Shipp covered the legal beat. Plainspoken, gravel voiced, she laughed easily, but took no guff from anyone, including fellow blacks, who sometimes baited her for working for the "white press."

Darnton asked if she would go to Wappingers Falls for the Brawley case.

She hesitated. She had resisted for years being typecast as a "black affairs" reporter; she insisted that her specialty was law, not blackness.

But Darnton persisted: it was an important story and the paper needed her.

Later, in Darnton's office, another editor dialed the home of a young black reporter-trainee who had just come to New York from Chicago. Don Terry worked weekends and was off that day. He answered the phone groggily.

"Pack your bag, sweetheart," the editor said.

Another of Darnton's deputies roused Craig Wolff at home. A former sportswriter who was in his first month of assignment to the city desk, Wolff was still asleep after an all-night stint covering labor talks.

"They want you on this team," the editor said. "It's a big deal. John sees you as a bulldog. Be here by one."

Shipp ran into Blumenthal on the way back to her desk. "Aren't you part of the team?" she asked.

What team? Blumenthal went to Darnton.

"Oh," the metro editor soothed, "didn't I tell you? I'm sorry. We're starting a Brawley team. You're the leader."

One more reporter was added before the day was out: Fox Butterfield, a China scholar who had just joined metro from the *Times*'s Washington Bureau. A dogged investigative team was almost complete, someone observed. It now boasted a Fox and a Wolff.

As Shipp and Terry drove upstate together, they shared misgivings. Had they been assigned to the team primarily to show some black faces? The answer would lie ultimately in the way the paper handled the story. If they detected any skewing of the facts, any unwarranted leaning toward official versions, they would know.

Terry drove and Shipp read aloud from a packet of clippings on the case. It looked like a white cover-up, they agreed. Terry was inclined to accept Sharpton's version, but Shipp was warier: Sharpton reminded her of Chicago Mayor Harold Washington's comment about an associate: "Slicker than eel shit."

It was dark when they reached the Wyndham, which reared up over downtown Poughkeepsie like a sleek Disney confection. It was too late to reach public officials for interviews, but they buttonholed some staff members at the hotel for their views. No, the employees said, they did not find it farfetched that white racists in Dutchess County might abduct and rape a black teenager and that white cops might cover it up.

High over the Hudson and the snow-dusted rooftops of the city, in her small mauve room with mock-stucco walls and plastic frosted wall sconces, Shipp went to bed that night convinced they were on the trail of the men who had attacked Tawana Brawley.

Craig Wolff was lost. He had driven across the river and into Newburgh before realizing his mistake, and it was late when he reached Wappingers Falls. He stopped at Paino's Mobil station in search of Tommy Masch, who seemed to be gaining notoriety as a suspect.

Wolff approached a pretty, dark-haired young woman at the cash register. He had a boyish face with a beard, pleading brown eyes, and a velvety voice that made him a natural schmoozer. He asked her about Masch.

"Get him out of here!" a voice shouted from the repair bays in the back. "Leave the poor kid alone!"

Wolff smiled, a lost waif, and the young woman rewarded him with a sympathetic grin. "Tommy lives at the White Gate Apartments, across from the Pavillion," she said. "He drives a pickup truck. Lots of time he hangs out at the Dunkin' Donuts."

The doughnut shop was up Route 9 between a pizza parlor and a karate studio. Wolff went in and identified himself. Had anyone seen Masch?

"Enough already!" whined a stubbly-faced man who fixed him with a hard stare.

"Don't jump to conclusions," Wolff said. "I'm just a guy from New York trying to do my job."

"New York!" the man spat. "You might as well come from Mars."

"Get out of here!" another man screamed. "Would you be here if a white girl was raped by six black guys?"

Someone went to the pay phone and made a call.

Wolff ordered a cruller and coffee and sat down. A few minutes later, the door burst open and an enraged voice screamed: "Where's the fuckin' reporter?"

Wolff spun around and faced a tall young man in a denim jacket over long johns. He looked as if he had just climbed out of a grease pit: the grime was everywhere, from the bill of his cap to his boots.

Tommy Masch thrust his blackened face at Wolff. "What is it with everybody?" he roared. "Why don't you leave me alone?"

Wolff tried to hide his fear. "I'm here to find out about your side," he said.

Masch looked Wolff up and down as if he were the grimy one. "My father doesn't want me to talk," he said childishly, but he seemed to be calming down a little. And his hesitation invited a few questions. Wolff tried to block out the cluster of unfriendly faces all around and asked his last question first: had Masch played any role in what happened to Tawana Brawley?

"We've never even seen Tawana," a confederate broke in, and the crowd erupted with denials of racism.

"We've never done anything to black people—we don't think that way," said another youth. But in the welter of voices, Wolff heard the word "niggers."

Masch said he had attended a friend's birthday party the night Tawana disappeared, but he refused to say where. "The authorities know where I was," he said.

Wolff asked about Masch's car, and the doughnut shop erupted in bedlam again. They pointed out three former police cars in the parking lot and said any of their owners might be mistaken for officers.

"We've always collected them," Masch said. "They say we're police buffs, ambulance chasers, looking for glory, but I try to help. I spent four days putting out a fire at a plumbing store." Another youth said they used cars and CB radios to play a vehicular hide-and-seek called "fox hunt." "What else is there to do in this town?" he asked.

Masch suddenly pulled a badge out of his pocket, and Wolff's eyes widened. It had been issued by the Hughsonville Fire Company. Three other youths in the group also pulled out their volunteer fireman badges.

Masch ridiculed Tawana and her allegations. "Look at all the loopholes. She said she gave oral sex and was unconscious at the same time. How can that be?"

From the outskirts, Newburgh looked like a nice town, but as Don Terry drove in, the grim reality set in.

Hoping to trace Tawana Brawley's movements on the day she vanished, Terry went first to the apartment of Geneva Buxton, who had taken the girl to the Orange County Jail to visit her son, Todd. She was a stocky woman with a short Afro. With her was her daughter, Sandra, stylish with jangling jewelry and a ponytail. In the living room where a TV droned, a reporter for another paper was already getting the story. Terry swore under his breath: there went his exclusive.

Geneva quietly narrated the story of Tawana Brawley's visit, and Sandra filled in details. Sandra said she had called Tawana for Todd the night before the trip. Terry listened avidly as Geneva told about the ride to Goshen, the reunion with Todd, and the trip back, including a passing encounter with two white men in a pickup truck who stared at Tawana as they waited for a bus. Geneva recalled Tawana's curious reluctance to go home that night and the trouble she had spoken of—trouble with Ralph King for staying out late. And she recalled how Tawana finally changed out of her miniskirt and left to catch a Short Line bus to Wappingers Falls. That, she said, was the last she saw of her.

Terry next tracked down the bus driver, Todd McGue. He refused to see Terry, but by phone gave the reporter many details of Tawana's ride from Newburgh to Wappingers Falls, the same details, he said, that he had volunteered to the police. He had recognized Tawana as Ralph King's stepdaughter and had chatted with her on the ride. But unlike Geneva Buxton's description of a troubled girl, McGue remembered her as smiling, even ebullient. He said she asked him to take Route 9D instead of Route 9 to drop her nearer to her home, and he had declined. He recalled dropping her off near Paino's station and seeing her walking back toward the rear of the bus as he pulled away.

In the darkness, one of Farber's polished moccasins sank into something squishy on the lawn of the Pavillion.

"Oh no!" he muttered with alarm.

But it was only slush, and Shipp, Blumenthal, and Terry roared with laughter like incompetent burglars.

Residents were arriving home and lights were winking on that night, February 24, as the reporters started knocking on doors, canvassing for witnesses who might have seen Tawana Brawley during the days she was missing.

At Apartment 19B, across a narrow hallway from the old Brawley flat, a potbellied man in a sweatshirt opened the door cautiously. Beyond the crack of light, a slim brown-haired woman in a robe stood by a dinette. The couple, Gaston and Elizabeth Abril, doubted they could add anything to the accounts they had given to the police, but they let Blumenthal and Shipp in.

Glenda Brawley was a nice neighbor, they said, but King seemed to resent whites, so they had kept their distance. The Brawleys had had loud fights, and sometimes there were screams beyond the thin walls, they recalled. They had heard someone in 19A after the Brawleys moved out, and it could have been the week of Thanksgiving, but they weren't sure. Gaston had heard a door slam and voices, nothing that sounded like a party. But, he added, they had seen no one.

But they had seen Glenda's car out front the day Tawana was found and later heard that she claimed to have been there to collect mail. But, Gaston said, the mail was still in the box after she left. And, he added, the police had told them that Tawana had been found with cotton in her ears and nose.

Shipp and Blumenthal exchanged a glance. Neither had ever heard that before.

"I'll bet the farm it didn't happen that way," the criminal justice official was telling Farber. "It's either bullshit or somebody did this to the kid and she told a false story. It's unlikely she spread feces on herself or wrote on herself. But the abduction story is false. People told the state police she was at the Pavillion moving around at least three of the four days she was missing. Something went awry. Drugs? Hallucinogens? I'll bet if she ever does step forward as a sworn witness, she'll say, 'I remember nothing.' "

That rang a bell with Farber: a few weeks earlier, he had asked Al Sharpton if Tawana had really been abducted and raped. Sharpton had not answered. But when Farber turned and put the question to Sharpton's sidekick, Perry McKinnon, he got an answer of sorts. "The problem is that she doesn't remember much," McKinnon had said, and Sharpton hadn't quibbled.

Trying to develop this lead, Farber reached a senior investigative official who agreed to a quiet meeting at a bar off the thruway. They had never met, so the investigator said he would use a code name, "Oscar," and added: "I'll be wearing a pink shirt." Cloak-and-dagger antics were no novelty to Farber; he had a naturally secretive bent, and jittery quirks were common to his investigative sources, who feared professional death from the disease known as public exposure.

The bar, to Farber's dismay, was mobbed with Friday-night revelers. Disco rock blasted over loudspeakers, drowning all but blood-curdling screams. Blinding strobe lights flashed psychedelic nightmares off the walls, turning the place into a flickering old-time movie and robbing everyone of color: it was impossible to tell who was wearing pink. In his brass-button blazer, Farber looked like a detective, and the patrons eyed him suspiciously. He reached for some bar matches to light his briar pipe and stared incredulously at the name on the back.

It was the wrong place.

He called to a waitress and shouted the name of the bar he wanted.

That place was across the road, she said. Farber tore out of the hellish din, jumped back in his car, and screeched across the road. He straightened his tie and went calmly in.

This was more like it. Soft lights. No music. There were a few drinkers at the bar, but none in pink. Farber pulled up a stool and got a glass of red wine. After a while, he noticed a tall man looking at him down the way. His shirt wasn't pink, but Farber tried anyway.

"Oscar?"

The man nodded.

"But you're not wearing a pink shirt!"

He shrugged. "I decided to change."

They found a secluded booth and Oscar sipped a bourbon too rapidly. He was worried about keeping his identity secret. Farber gave his forty-days-in-jail assurances.

What the *Times* wanted, he said, was a reliable source who could verify information the paper picked up in the course of its inquiries into the Brawley case.

Oscar nodded. "I think I can be helpful," he said.

Farber said he understood that Tawana Brawley was not the source of the allegations that she was raped by as many as a half dozen white men.

"That's true," Oscar said. "It's coming from the family and the lawyers."

"And no semen or drugs were found?"

"Not that we know of."

"She was seen climbing into the bag?" Farber asked.

"By two people."

Farber asked about the excrement. "It was all over her? Under her clothes?"

Oscar nodded. "But not on her face."

The answer hung for a moment in the smoky booth like a suspicion. They drained their drinks, shook hands, and agreed to meet again by coded prearrangement.

The small plain house on Garden Drive in Monticello had a scrawny patch of lawn, a short driveway, and a little porch. The shades were drawn, and Craig Wolff wondered whether anyone was home. He rang the bell and waited. Finally, the door opened and a tall bald man with a striking resemblance to the actor Lou Gossett, Jr., filled the doorway.

Wolff expected to have the door shut in his face. But he quickly apologized for intruding and soon found himself in the kitchen. Matthew Strong, Juanita Brawley's ex-husband and a local policeman, was still Tawana's legal guardian, but to Wolff's surprise he didn't seem to know much about the case.

"Tawana and I have a close relationship, and I don't want to jeopardize that," Strong explained. "If she has anything to say, I want her to feel free to do that."

"Have you asked her what happened?"

"No. But I'm here for her if she needs me."

Tawana had taken refuge in this house with her uncle Matthew and cousin Kenya in January, in order to escape the hounding press and the confusing investigations that had closed in on her in Wappingers Falls. Wolff hoped for a glimpse of her new life and perhaps a clue about what had happened to her in November.

"Since she's been here," Strong said, "she has opened up quite a bit. She feels safe and comfortable going to school here. She watches TV and reads the papers about herself. Usually she doesn't say anything, but she laughed the other day when she read that she was in a psychiatric ward."

Wolff asked how Strong felt about Maddox, Mason, and Sharpton.

"I'm upset that they're not moving fast enough, but I guess they have to follow their advice," he said, shaking his head. "I don't know about those guys."

Wolff was puzzled. Didn't Strong believe in them?

It wasn't exactly that, he said. But the case had been dragging on so long, and it had been allowed to fester politically. "What bothers me is when they say it was a cover-up," he said. "I'm an officer and that's pretty hard to believe. I'd be livid if this were happening to my child, and I wish they would hurry it up. I guess you have to have confidence in the lawyers and respect them, but sometimes I wonder why they jumped in. Mostly I wish it had never happened."

Strong looked out the window, and Wolff got the impression he did not want to say any more, but was too polite to ask him to leave. There was no sign of Tawana, and rather than sour his relationship with Strong, Wolff decided to go.

Then the phone rang.

Wolff gathered that Juanita Brawley was on the line. Strong told her Wolff was there, and to the reporter's astonishment Strong said Juanita was in Monticello and would be glad to talk to him.

"She'll meet you at Gager's Diner at two o'clock," Strong said.

The diner was only a few blocks away on Broadway.

Wolff took a table in a roped-off section at the back and waited. By two-fifteen there was no sign of her. He called Strong.

"She'll be there," he said.

Wolff waited until three and called again.

"I'm sure she'll be there," Strong said.

At three-thirty, as Wolff was about to give up, Juanita Brawley, in jeans and a white sweatshirt, bounded in. Wolff recognized her from television. "We're going to get to the bottom of this," she said breathlessly. "I have five minutes. I have something to do. I'm a woman on a mission."

Outside a horn blared for her.

"I'll be right back," she said, and ran out again.

The bewildered Wolff peered through the blinds and saw her standing beside a red car. At the wheel was Sharpton.

Juanita dashed back inside then and sat down opposite Wolff.

"We won't stand for this any longer," she said.

Wolff was thoroughly confused. "We have a team," he began, lapsing into obscurity himself. "We're going to solve this."

"Huh?" she said.

The honking horn beckoned her again.

"Look," said Wolff, "I need to talk to you. We have to talk."

The blaring horn was more insistent.

"Give me your phone number," Wolff pleaded.

She had recently moved from Kingston to Newburgh, and she gave him a number. "If you come later to Newburgh, call me," she said.

"When?"

"Five-thirty or six." She ran out the door.

Wolff, disconsolate that he had let her get away, drove to Newburgh and pulled into a Sunoco station for gas.

A small red car was just pulling out, and Wolff swerved to avoid a collision. Then he did a double-take. It was Juanita Brawley at the wheel. And Tawana—whom he had never seen—was beside her. There was no sign of Sharpton.

Juanita recognized Wolff, too, and stopped. She shook her head in censure. "I thought *The New York Times* was better than this," she said reproachfully.

"You are not going to believe this, but I was not following you."

Tawana smiled at him demurely. She was clutching a teddy bear and looked more like eight than sixteen. As he studied her, the thought of an abduction and gang-rape suddenly struck him; he felt queasy, almost ill.

"Call me later," Juanita shouted between the cars. "I'll be home in a little while." She drove off with Tawana.

Wolff went to a restaurant and killed some time playing video games. Then he dialed Juanita's number.

"I'm sorry," said a synthesized voice, "but the number you

have dialed is not in service in area code nine-one-four. Please check your number and try again."

Wolff hung up slowly and walked to the car, his pride at war with his gullibility.

Later that night, from his room at the Wyndham, Wolff worked the telephone like a man possessed. Finally, he found someone who had a number for Juanita Brawley in Newburgh. It was a couple of digits off from the one Juanita had given him.

Wolff tried it repeatedly, but there was no answer. At last, shortly before midnight, he got an answer.

"Hello?"

Wolff recognized Juanita's voice right away.

"Juanita, it's Craig Wolff."

"Call back in fifteen minutes," she said, and immediately hung up.

Wolff dutifully waited fifteen minutes and tried again. The number rang and rang unanswered. He kept trying, on and on. Finally, someone picked up and reset the receiver without a word.

In the morning, still unwilling to give up, Wolff tried again. This time, Juanita answered and, as if nothing were amiss, calmly answered some questions.

"We have no idea who did it—we just know there's a cover-up," she said. "Am I supposed to know exactly who did it?" She said Maddox and Mason would get to the bottom of it. "I have insight into people," she boasted. "I have a master's in psychology. I've gotten to know them and they're brilliant."

But had Tawana talked to the lawyers?

Juanita skipped over the question. She urged Wolff to look closely at Crist, Masch, Pagones, and Grady. "There was a party," she said conspiratorially.

"What kind of party? Where? When?" Wolff stammered.

But the line had gone dead.

A few days later, on a street in Newburgh, Juanita's car pulled up beside Wolff. She rolled down the window and in a small conspiratorial voice, said: "Look for the man with a missing finger."

"Look for what?"

"The man with the missing finger," she said. "He did it!"

With that, she sped off.

Wolff, bewildered, began asking around. There were indeed stories all over the streets about the man with the missing finger. His name was Mickey Carlton. Sharpton, too, told the press that the advisers' investigation had now discovered that one of Tawana's attackers was a man with a missing finger.

State police investigator Russell Crawford was more than amused when he heard all this: he was enlightened. As he confided much later, Crawford himself had invented Mickey Carlton and his missing finger and had put out word on the street that he wanted to question the mysterious figure in the Brawley case. As Crawford envisioned it, the tale was a kind of truth test for would-be informants, many of whom were simply seeking publicity or currying favor with state and local investigators. If these informants said they knew Carlton, Crawford would know they were unreliable sources.

John Darnton braced himself as the tall, gangling figure in the blue Turnbull & Asser shirt loped toward him like a tropical waterspout churning across the newsroom. The approach of Managing Editor Arthur Gelb often presaged a tidal wave of story suggestions, staffing proposals, and critiques. Gelb, a former metropolitan editor, was the *Times*'s most creative and erratic editor, an arm-waving elemental force whose legendary enthusiasms swamped weaker-willed editors and reporters. He was a man to whom few said no, who turned maybes into yeses.

He was impatient for the results of the Brawley team's news blitz. It was Friday morning, February 26. Little more than three days had gone by since the team had begun its inquiries in the Hudson Valley—an eon for a breaking story, but hardly a stutter for an investigation of a complicated case. It was easy to gloss over the distinction, however.

"So where's the piece?" Gelb asked.

"We've got it," Darnton blurted. He looked at the frowning visage of mercurial moods. "We can have it for the weekend." Gelb was gone by the time he realized what he had done. Darnton wasn't even sure what the team had come up with. What had he promised?

In his room at the Wyndham that night, Blumenthal sorted through his scribbled notes and the memos of his colleagues. It was an unwieldy mass. He flipped on the portable computer, typed "draft" like a hopeful sentiment at the top of the screen, and began:

"Key state law-enforcement authorities have concluded that the recounted abduction and rape of a black fifteen-year-old high school girl did not happen as she and her family and lawyers have claimed and that discrepancies cloud many aspects of the case . . ."

He went on for a thousand words and sent the results over the phone line to 43rd Street.

Darnton scanned the printout. It wasn't bad, but it wasn't right. The lead was too hard. This was a great yarn. It had to have narrative sweep and color. Maybe they were a little too close to it up there in Poughkeepsie. Maybe it should be written here. Darnton's glance moved automatically across the metro desk to a reporter in the front row. This time Darnton didn't use the loud-speaker and he didn't shout over the rising deadline clatter.

He walked over to Robert D. McFadden, the dean of *The New York Times* rewrite bank, and talked quietly about a difficult assignment: to take the compiled findings of the Brawley team's investigation and write a comprehensive story.

In a bygone era of cutthroat competition, the rewrite man with his smoking typewriter and speed-writing gifts embodied the irreverent, rapid-fire romance of newspapering. He took notes from legmen and churned out the hoopla of politics, the drama of a plane crash, or the heartbreak of a child lost in a fire, like a magician working sleeve tricks. But rewrite had evolved into much more over the years; it now meant coping with the intrica-

cies of nuclear power and municipal budgets, detailing the per-
sonalities behind the masks of politicians and celebrities, pulling
together the complex threads of stories on government, labor,
education, transportation, law, the environment, the mass media,
the arts, and a bewildering array of other subjects. And it was still
necessary to pull off the big breaking story, just as in the old days.
For nearly twenty-five years, McFadden *was* rewrite at the *Times*.

Darnton explained the task: Blumenthal would coordinate the
Brawley team's flow of memos from Poughkeepsie. McFadden
would weave it all into one great tapestry.

McFadden swiped a thatch of white hair off his forehead. The
vital thing was organization. He put the memos Darnton had
handed him into neat piles on his desk—they totaled well over
twenty thousand words—and read through them, methodically
underlining the most important ideas, making check marks and
X's like a code, digesting it all.

He tapped the key points into his computer:

. . . serious doubts about major aspects of Tawana's story . . .
no one doubts something happened . . . not held captive in
woods . . . was seen (or heard) around the Pavillion during the
four days she was missing . . . no evidence of sexual assault . . .
indications she was fed . . . no hypothermia . . . racial slurs and
excrement on her . . . others dispute she was a model student
. . . a fight with parents before her disappearance . . . stepfather
violent . . .

Darnton had hoped for Sunday publication. The fat Sunday
paper is a showcase, with a circulation half again as big as that
of the weekday editions, but the need to get the Sunday paper
out by Saturday evening means that the normal deadline for copy
is usually three hours earlier—four P.M. Saturday. Darnton was
standing by, but McFadden was still writing feverishly into Saturday night.

By Sunday, he had several thousand words. They began:

"She vanished on a cold moonless autumn night in Wappingers

Falls, N.Y., not far from Washington Irving's old haunts up the Hudson, where headless horsemen and tombstones in country churchyards seem less sinister now than the racial hatreds hiding in the suburbs of America."

Darnton dispatched an assistant metro editor as his emissary on the story. He was Charles Strum, an indefatigable former night-desk editor who had somehow managed to keep his cheerful sanity through years of a nightly triage of killing and trimming the impossible dreams of the daytime editors.

Strum read McFadden's story with mounting admiration. He called Darnton. "It's great stuff," he said. "We have to fight for the space."

The story had grown to 6,700 words, which would jump from page one, cover an entire inside page, and then spill over onto half of a second inside page. This was an almost unheard-of length in a metropolitan news story. With pictures and headlines, it would require more than nine columns of space, more than many presidential news conferences.

Darnton went into the office as a printout of the story was delivered to Gelb at home. Gelb called Darnton at the office, peppering him with questions. The reporters, down from Pough-keepsie, gathered around McFadden to answer the questions.

At the last minute, an editor wondered whether the *Times* wasn't imputing racial hatred to all the suburbs of America. McFadden quickly reworked the lead: "She vanished on a cold moonless autumn night in Wappingers Falls, N.Y., from a strip of gas stations and fast food outlets that stand as a kind of neon-lit mockery of Washington Irving's quaint old haunts up the Hudson."

The story—"Brawley Case: Stubborn Puzzle, Silent Victim"—on Monday, February 29, summed up the three-month investigation and cast grave doubt on the version of events told by the Brawleys and their advisers. It presented the case as a mystery and a racial question of national dimensions. By day's end, it had become an American leitmotif. In Washington and Chicago and Dallas and Los Angeles, blacks and whites were debating the actions of

William Grady, Mario Cuomo, and Robert Abrams, and Tawana Brawley's relationship with Glenda and Ralph King.

Editors at the *Times* were exultant.

"This is the way to go about it," Arthur Gelb exhorted colleagues at a morning news meeting. "Not to concentrate on small stories day by day. Put it all together into big stories periodically." That meant keeping the team together under Strum's direction.

The next day, the investigative team headed back to Poughkeepsie. They were exuberant over the reaction to the story, but as McFadden had reminded them, there was an enormous hole in it.

They still didn't know what had happened to Tawana Brawley.

Attorney General Robert Abrams, wrapped in a double-breasted topcoat and a wool scarf against the icy wind, stepped briskly out of the black state sedan and crossed the sidewalk to the Dutchess County Courthouse on Market Street in Poughkeepsie. Bounding beside him and clutching a thick briefcase was the prosecutor Jack Ryan. Determination etched their grim faces like Hudson Valley grit.

A new phase of the Brawley case was beginning. For six weeks, since the collapse of William Grady's grand jury inquiry and David Sall's brief appointment as special prosecutor, the state's investigation of what had happened to Tawana had been in limbo, held back by squabbling over a new prosecutor. Now it was time to put aside the wrangling and get down to facts. Abrams and Ryan were to have their own grand jury: its twenty-three members were to be selected here on this rarest of days, leap year day, February 29.

In a courtroom on the second floor, the largest in the building, Abrams and Ryan took their places. The room was already crowded with reporters, spectators, and prospective jurors. On the bench, robed in black, state Supreme Court Justice Angelo J. Ingrassia leaned back and surveyed the rows of veniremen, a pool of 120

Dutchess County residents who had been summoned for questioning about their qualifications to serve on the grand jury. The panel's task would be to hear evidence presented by the Abrams team and to decide whether a crime had been committed and, if so, whether there was enough evidence to bring a formal charge against anyone.

While the grand jury's proceedings were to be conducted in secret, the selection of its members was held in open court, though each juror, to preserve his or her anonymity, was referred to by a number and was questioned quietly at the bench, out of earshot of the reporters and spectators. Ingrassia, Abrams, and Ryan questioned them about their availability to serve and about marital and family status, education, livelihood, and other pertinent background information. All of them had read or heard about the case, but the crucial question was whether they thought they could keep an open mind about the evidence. Some said no and were excused. Others joined the growing panel in the box. At one point, the judge inadvertently spoke aloud the name of Donald E. Perrotte, the man named as jury foreman; his identity alone among the jurors thus became known to the press and public.

It took only a few hours, and when it was over, eleven women and twelve men, including two black men, had been selected and sworn in. One of the jurors was Anthony J. Montanari of Clinton Corners, a former real estate man who was now a computer consultant. He was, officially, "number sixteen." As he drove home that day, Montanari felt a strange mix of apprehension and excitement at the daunting prospect of unraveling the mystery everyone was talking about.

Around the table in the Wyndham's Tudor Room, the plates bore the remnants of trout almandine, Mexican *fajitas,* and chicken Dijon. Farber was about to light up his briar. Blumenthal was sipping coffee when they heard the commotion out in the lobby.

A resonant voice boomed out, and suddenly a bulky form burst into the room. Al Sharpton bore down on the table of *New York Times* reporters. He headed straight for Farber.

"Farber, my man," he growled.

Farber shrank back, imagining he was about to be attacked. But Sharpton pulled him up and enveloped him in an affectionate embrace. A month earlier, Farber had investigated Sharpton's finances and FBI contacts, and his diligence and concentration had left a deep impression on the wayward activist.

"C'mon outside," he said to Farber. "There's some people I want you to meet."

Farber, still wondering what he might be in for, smoothed his beard and followed like a condemned man. Sharpton led him out the hotel's front door. A blast of cold wind buffeted them as Sharpton escorted him to a waiting gold Lincoln. The window rolled down halfway.

"This here's my man, Farber," he boomed. "Farber, meet Ralph King and Glenda Brawley."

Farber peered into the dark interior. "Could I talk to you sometime," he blurted. "I really need to talk to you."

"Sometime, sure!" Sharpton broke in. "Be in touch."

The door popped open and Sharpton eased himself in. The engine revved up and the Lincoln screeched off, leaving Farber still flustered and shivering at the curb.

One investigator sat ramrod straight at the desk. The other slouched in a chair by the wall, smoking, as Craig Wolff and Ralph Blumenthal prodded them for more information about the condition of Tawana Brawley when she was found. They reminded the reporters that they had never spoken to them—didn't even know them.

"Of course not," Wolff said ritualistically.

The investigators exchanged looks, measuring the potential risks against the possible gains.

Finally, they ventured into it. They had found "practice writing" on her jeans, the one at the desk said. It was done with a sootlike charcoal substance. The same material was on the leather gloves they had found on the ground under the plastic bag. The writing was smudged on her pants and on her body, as if scrawled with fingers. They were not ruling out the possibility that she had written the racial slurs on herself. "We requested handwriting samples from her, but of course we didn't get them," he said.

On another point, he said, hospital personnel had found what looked like cotton wads stuffed in Tawana's nostrils and ears.

Why would racists protect her nose and ears before smearing her with excrement?

And some crucial evidence had been lost. Unfortunately, the workers had thrown the wads out. Some blackened cotton balls, burnt cloth residues, and a used matchstick had also been found in the Pavillion apartment.

And there was some kind of smut found under Tawana's fingernails and around her fingertips, perhaps from a marijuana cigarette, the investigator said. The fingernail scrapings had been taken as part of the rape kit.

"But hospital tests showed no signs of drug use," Wolff said.

"Right. But maybe they didn't test for the drug she was using. Maybe if she took it the first day, it was out of her system by the time they tested."

Now the slouching smoker spoke up. A former neighbor boy at the Pavillion, Timmy Dean, had said under questioning that he had had sexual relations with Tawana when she was twelve. And he remembered seeing Tawana with a bloody nose from a beating by her mother. Violence was not uncommon in the Brawley family, the investigator said. When Tawana was arrested for shoplifting in Poughkeepsie a year ago, King had gone at her with fists and had had to be restrained.

E. R. Shipp and Don Terry were on edge. Part of it was the fact that the story *they* were getting was at odds with the one Blumenthal, Farber, and Wolff were getting. As the two black reporters on the team, they had been assigned primarily to interview blacks, and the emerging picture of race relations in the mid–

Hudson Valley was making Tawana Brawley's story all too plausible. But this wasn't the sole reason for their disgruntlement. The white reporters were not sharing all their information with them. It was true that these reporters sometimes did not share the names of their sources with one another or even with their editors. Nonetheless, the atmosphere of the Brawley investigation was becoming unduly secretive, and it was not surprising that Shipp and Terry felt they were being denied information because their white colleagues did not entirely trust them.

And so, Shipp and Terry, suspicious of unnamed white officials and now increasingly suspicious of their fellow *Times* reporters, vowed to scrutinize every word that appeared in the paper about the case to prevent their colleagues from acting as the mouthpieces of unnamed officials who might have an interest in denying the existence of racism. If the white reporters resented any implication that their professionalism was being compromised, too bad. Shipp and Terry were not going to be part of any dissimulation.

Farber called Sharpton in Brooklyn, and again the answering service cut in to take a message. Impatient, he slammed down the phone and stared out his window at the Wyndham at the purple slopes of the Hudson Valley. Since his strange encounter with Glenda Brawley and Ralph King, he had been trying to reach Sharpton to arrange a meeting. But the man simply did not return calls.

There was a knock on Farber's door, and when he opened it he instantly forgot his pique.

"Perry!" he exclaimed.

"Shh," McKinnon whispered. "We're here under other names."

Farber pulled McKinnon into the room and sat him down.

"Perry, I have to know," Farber said. "If you were standing today before the Good Lord and he asked you, 'Perry, do you believe Tawana Brawley was abducted and raped in the woods by a bunch of white racists?' what would you say?"

"Between us?"

"Between us."

"Uh, maybe she hooked up again with Trayon Kirby or maybe she went to Newburgh with some people using drugs," McKinnon said.

"So you don't believe her either!"

McKinnon paused. "If I had to guess," he said finally, "I'd say she went back with some others to 19A at the Pavillion. Maybe they were free-basing and things got out of hand. Maybe the others got alarmed and put the markings on her for a cover story."

Farber was dumbfounded. So he had doubts too?

"Tawana thinks she can fool anyone," McKinnon said with surprising rancor. "But Abrams and Cuomo aren't dumb. They'll get the real story soon if they don't already have it. Then we'll all look like suckers or fools."

"Perry, this is important," Farber said. "Can you bring Sharpton up to my room in half an hour?" If Sharpton confirmed these doubts, it would blow the whole case wide open.

"I think so."

"Good. I'll be waiting."

Sharpton didn't show up.

The next morning, Farber reached Sharpton and made arrangements for a breakfast meeting in Farber's room. Then Farber rounded up Blumenthal, Shipp, Wolff, and Terry and they sat around the room like defendants waiting for a verdict.

By eleven o'clock, they had heard nothing. Blumenthal went down to scout the lobby and found Sharpton talking on a pay phone.

"Farber's waiting for you upstairs," he nudged.

"Be there soon as I can," Sharpton said.

When he didn't show up by noon, Farber tracked him down in his room.

"Later," Sharpton promised.

Farber, alone now, settled down in the room to wait, watching the sky darken and the snow begin to fall. He waited into the night. Finally he called. Sharpton had checked out.

———————

On March 10, the top left corner of the front page of the *Times* displayed a large rectangle of type and a photograph of Tawana Brawley, under the headline: "From Fiber and Smudges, Questions in Brawley Case."

It was another big story. It said new details—cottonlike wads, smudged gloves, and many other clues—had raised fresh questions about the girl's sketchy account of sexual abuse at the hands of white men. And it noted that investigators were no closer to verifying any part of her story than they had been the previous November.

20

They hurried through the vile crowds on 42nd Street, past the hungry beggars and hopeless tourists, past the urine stench from Grand Central and the taxis blaring like Scottish klaxons beneath the stone arch of the Park Avenue overpass. Eyes went for their wallets, and exhaust fumes rolled at them like a gas attack.

But relief lay just beyond the revolving door of the Grand Hyatt Hotel, and they dived through. Suddenly, they were surrounded by music. A piano player in black tie and tails filled the atrium lobby with the syrupy melody of "New York, New York."

The little troupe—Alton Maddox, C. Vernon Mason, Al Sharpton, Perry McKinnon, Glenda Brawley, Ralph King, and baby Tyice— did not pause with the paying guests to savor the atmosphere. They strode past the bar, rode up the escalator, and hurried into the crowded conference room where the press waited in noisy confusion. A rumor, courtesy of the Brawley watchers, had swept the thirty reporters: when the family was present, it usually meant something important would be said.

Maddox and Mason sat at a table bristling with microphones. Glenda and King stood with the baby off to one side, and Sharpton and McKinnon stood at the other, their arms folded like sumo wrestlers'. Maddox removed papers importantly from his briefcase, as if he intended to read them all the riot act. Television lights, cameras, and tape recorders clicked on in anticipation, but Maddox only invited their questions.

There were a few, and he answered them with a testy impatience, as if waiting in vain for the right one. It went on feebly for fifteen minutes, a tedious recitation of peripheral points and old contentions that made the reporters wonder what they were doing there. It was Sunday, and basketball on television beckoned. Sharpton looked bored. McKinnon seemed half asleep. Mason listened abstractedly with his chin propped in his hand.

Then it happened. Maddox said again, as he had many times before, that he had evidence proving who had attacked Tawana. The reporters, who were getting more and more impatient with the advisers' unsubstantiated allegations, now peppered him with questions. What evidence? Who did it?

Maddox leaned forward, the lights glinting on his flat glasses, and said calmly: "Mister Pagones was one of the attackers."

It was like the sound of a crack when you are far out on the frozen lake. A hush fell over the room. Finally, someone in the back whispered: "Does he mean Steve Pagones, the assistant district attorney?"

Sharpton looked quizzically at McKinnon—the master of surprise suddenly caught off guard. They all looked back at Maddox.

"He was one of the attackers, yes," Maddox said, nodding at the puzzled faces.

"Do you have evidence that supports this?" a reporter blurted out.

"If I didn't have direct evidence, I wouldn't be sitting here saying that," Maddox said evenly. "What we have here is an official, an *officially sanctioned,* conspiracy to obstruct and prevent justice in the case of Tawana Brawley."

"Why would Steven Pagones do something like this?" someone asked. It was a silly question to put to Maddox, but the skepticism behind it was the point. Maddox waved it off.

A half-dozen reporters suddenly spoke at once. It had occurred to them, like dull pupils in a civics class, that they could not just ask if Maddox had evidence: an allegation as serious as his demanded that he make the evidence public.

Maddox pondered it. "Steven Pagones had known the Brawley

family for some time," he said. "He lived on the same street as the Brawley family. Less than two years ago, he had eyed Tawana Brawley."

They expected him to go on. But that was it.

They were flabbergasted. These statements—even if they were true—meant nothing. You could ruin somebody's life in five seconds with the right combination of hateful words. There were laws against this, and the reporters were the first line of defense. More questions flapped up like vultures.

But Maddox shot them all down with a single blast. "We don't want to outline to Mister Pagones what evidence we have," he said. "He's still a law-enforcement official and is in the position to retaliate against the family."

They didn't know what to say, but Maddox kept going. William Grady had lied to a judge about why he was withdrawing from the case and had tried to whitewash Pagones's involvement. Governor Cuomo must immediately order the arrest of Pagones and Grady. If he didn't, Tawana Brawley would never testify.

There was more. Maddox charged that no rape test had ever been performed on Tawana, that the FBI had entered the case only when the family had asked it to do so.

A babble of questions crowded in, but Maddox was already on his feet, stuffing the important papers back in his briefcase as if they were the evidence. No, he would not answer any more questions; it was time for the press to clear out. And so they did. But on the other side of the closed doors, Don Terry of the *Times* heard the muffled shouting voices of the advisers, of Glenda Brawley and Ralph King.

Steven Pagones knotted his necktie and examined his round, boyish face in the mirror. It was a happy face, with a football player's big chin and wide, accepting eyes. But a hint of disquiet had begun to creep into the worry lines lately. There had been so much to do: the wedding invitation list, the reception details, the honeymoon plans, a thousand things to get done before June, and it was already March 13.

It was early afternoon in Wappingers Falls, still an hour before the christening that he and his fiancée, Niki, were to attend. She was waiting for him in the living room while he finished dressing. When the call came, they were just about to leave.

It was a television reporter. "What do you have to say about the press conference?" the voice asked.

"What press conference?"

"Maddox, Mason, and Sharpton—they said you were involved in the case."

Involved in the case? The words were like the wail of a far-off siren. Pagones knew that the advisers had recently been bandying his name about in connection with the Brawley case, but it had never crystalized into a serious accusation. Were they now accusing him of telling some lie for Harry Crist?

"What do you mean?" he said.

"They said you were involved in the rape."

The words didn't register at first. It was as though somebody had told him he wasn't Steven Pagones: it just didn't make sense. Niki knew there was something wrong when she saw the confusion in his face. He didn't know what to say, and he said nothing.

Up the wire, the reporter said something about calling back later, but Pagones didn't catch it.

As soon as he hung up, the phone rang again. It was another television reporter.

"What do you have to say?" she asked him.

Pagones struggled to pull himself together. He told her he couldn't respond until he knew exactly what the Brawley advisers had said.

"They said you participated in the rape."

"They actually said I raped her?"

"Yes."

"It's crazy."

The reporter asked another question, but Pagones didn't get it. The blood pounded in his head; his mind raced with the outrage, but no coherent words came to him. He hung up, and the phone immediately rang again. Another reporter was on the line, and this one was specific: "You were just accused of participating in the rape of Tawana Brawley. We would like to know what you have to say."

"I—really have—uh, no comment," he stammered. He immediately knew it wasn't good enough, but everything was happening so quickly and it was all so unbelievable. He tried to get a grip on himself.

"Won't you deny it?" the reporter prompted.

"Of course I deny it. I've never seen Tawana Brawley."

He hung up, and the telephone rang and rang, bullying them with its persistence. He couldn't go on like this all afternoon. He wanted to scream at the fiends who were tearing his life apart. But they were nowhere within reach. He sat down beside Niki.

"Who are these people?" he said. "Are they crazy?"

And he let himself be comforted by her calm voice and sympathetic eyes.

Between rings on the infernal telephone, Pagones called his father in Beacon. The familiar voice meant home and security, birthdays and graduations, the comfort of a scolding when the line had been crossed. Now it assuaged his anxiety with its steady confidence. His father asked him to come home. In a crisis, it was always best to be home with the family. Pagones made another call, explaining that he could not go to the christening. Even in calamity, life was a kind of regimen: you had to cancel plans, you had to explain things and behave civilly. He flicked on the answering machine and he and Niki went out into the dark afternoon.

They drove over to his parents' house in a light rain. It was midafternoon when they arrived. The lights in the windows on Orchard Place were warm and inviting.

The Spanish-style ranch house where Steven Pagones had grown up was set on a hill and gave the impression of having been there forever. The woodwork darkened by time, the fireplaces, the carpets and comfortable old furniture exuded warmth, hominess, respectability. Pleasant lawns and colorful azaleas flanked the walkway in spring, and ancient trees in summer shaded the grounds, the porch, the street where children romped.

As a boy, he had walked down Main Street like a prince, holding his father's hand as people nodded and greeted them with respect. Everyone in town knew them: the handsome young lawyer who had been a football hero at Beacon High School, the little boy with the father's dark good looks and broad, athletic shoulders.

His grandfather had come from Sparta, Greece, in 1922, settling in Beacon to make a new life as a merchant. He had opened a soda fountain on Main Street and called it the Boston Candy Kitchen. He had worked hard, bought the house on Orchard Place, and given his children lives of promise. Anthony, after graduating from Cornell University, had gone to Boston University Law School and returned to Dutchess County to become an assistant district attorney. After a few years as a prosecutor, he had joined the rackets bureau of then attorney general Jacob K. Javits, but had remained in Dutchess County. Anthony Pagones was ambitious and saw opportunities in Albany and New York City, but he and his wife did not want to leave Beacon. They were comfortable in the home on Orchard Place that his father had left him, and Anthony opened a law practice and eventually became a city judge. He took easily to local politics: the city government, the school and zoning boards, the municipal court—they were all family, in a way, working together to resolve disputes and problems for their town. It was a matter of compromises, mostly, letting a contract go through and allowing a building to go up, the little decisions that kept the town prosperous and the people contented. It was in Beacon that Anthony Pagones was happy, and it was there that he and his family would stay.

Steven, born in 1961, grew up with a vision of duty to his family and his community. He volunteered for the local ambulance corps as a teenager and was trained as an emergency medical technician—skills he put to use many times over. In 1984, he helped resuscitate a child who had been pulled from a burning house, but a young black boy had died in his arms one tragic summer night despite his efforts to revive him.

At school, Pagones was taught by some of the same teachers who had presided over his father's early education. Unlike his father, Pagones was a mediocre student. He attended Boston University, where his father had gone to law school, and while his grades were average, the experience was invaluable: the unworldly boy found friends from all over the country and a broader sense of life. After graduation, he was admitted to the University of Bridge-port Law School in Connecticut. It was there that he met Niki Eliades, a fellow student, who would go to work for his father after graduation and become Steven's fiancée. Through a summer job as a clerk for a judge in Fishkill, Pagones secured a summer internship at the district attorney's office in Poughkeepsie. And when he graduated in 1986, he became, as his father had, an assistant district attorney for Dutchess County.

He took an apartment at the Montclair Town Houses at the south end of Wappingers Falls, four miles north of his parents, and like his father he resolved to harness his professional and private life to local ambitions, to family life and good friends, to the career of security and respectability that had been laid down for him like railway tracks.

Pagones had followed those tracks until the day Harry Crist shot himself. Then, troubled by the implications, he had gone to his boss, William Grady, and disclosed that he had been with Crist and two other friends, the state trooper Scott Patterson and Eugene Branson, a utility worker, on the day Tawana Brawley was found at the Pavillion.

They went in and Anthony Pagones comforted him, just as he had done years ago. Steven's mother, Felicia, and younger brother, Timothy, were there. Reporters' calls had been flooding the line here, too, and there were calls from friends expressing outrage and wondering if there was anything they could do. There wasn't. To the reporters, they gave a simple reply: the allegation was a lie, and they were going to sue.

They called Gerald V. Hayes, the lawyer they had hired months ago when Harry Crist's suicide had first raised questions within the prosecutor's office. Hayes wasn't home, but he called back later and they talked, three lawyers deliberating an open-and-shut case of slander: a man was not compelled to prove his innocence; Maddox had no evidence, just ugly charges and a megaphone. It didn't take long to reach some conclusions. No one in the family, least of all Steven, was to say anything more to the press. Hayes would handle all that.

At dusk, they went into the family room and watched the news on television. Somehow, knowing what Maddox would say did not spare them. The sound of his voice, the look on his face, the words of accusation were like knives. To make matters worse, the station did not accurately report his response. It said nothing about a slander suit, only that he intended to prove his innocence in court, as if formal charges were sure to be filed against him. They flipped channels and saw the Maddox report on all the stations.

When Pagones got home that night, he found twenty messages on his answering machine, mostly from reporters, and a note from Craig Wolff of the *Times* under the door. He watched the malevolence again on the eleven o'clock news, but took no more calls. He went to bed late and tired, but didn't sleep. Hour after hour, he lay in the dark, listening to the wind in the eaves and to voices calling for the immediate arrest of Steven Pagones.

The telephone was ringing loudly into the darkness of Room 1033 at the Wyndham Hotel in Poughkeepsie when Craig Wolff unlocked the door. He hurried across the room and grabbed it. The call was from the *Times* metropolitan desk in New York. Bob McFadden needed a reaction from Pagones for the story on Maddox's charges, and pronto.

Wolff had been at the Wyndham eighteen of the last nineteen days, tracking down friends and neighbors of Tawana Brawley and stalking local investigators to pry loose anything he could learn. Now he turned on his portable computer and got busy again. He quickly found himself in a cul-de-sac. He telephoned Steven Pagones, but got no answer. He called Anthony Pagones, and was told that all press calls were being taken by Gerald Hayes. But Hayes's line was constantly busy. Finally, there was a break and Wolff got through.

"Man," the irritated Hayes said, "don't you guys know when to stop? Am I allowed to eat dinner?"

"I need to talk to you and I need to talk to your client," Wolff pleaded.

"I can tell you now that you will not talk to my client."

Wolff was bursting with questions: Was Pagones one of the attackers? Where was he when Tawana disappeared? Did he have alibis for the four days she was missing? And where was he on the day she reappeared? Hayes had nothing substantive to say. But for now, Wolff said, he would settle for the lawyer's reaction to Maddox's charges.

"I can assure you," Hayes said, "that Steve Pagones will not only defend himself against these liars, but we will certainly see them in court. If there's any doubt about what I mean by that last statement, it means that we fully intend to sue them for slander. These are outrageous lies by men whose lack of sincerity and lack of credibility were becoming more obvious on a daily basis to all reasonable people. These lies are apparently made out of desperation by men who will say or do anything to further their own cravings for publicity and whose obvious goal is not to achieve truth or justice, but rather to cause disruption and hatred."

The story of Maddox's charges and Hayes's reaction drew page-one play in the *Daily News*, the *Post*, and *New York Newsday* in the morning. But it was on page three of the metro news section in the *Times*. The papers all led with the allegations and said the advisers had offered no proof. But the *Times* story worked the allegations and the response into the first paragraph, and the headline reversed the emphasis: "A Dutchess Prosecutor Vows Brawley Case Slander Suit."

All the newspapers were laid out on the desk when the lawyers met at Anthony Pagones's office in East Fishkill that morning.

Steven and Anthony Pagones were there, along with Gerald Hayes and Anthony's law partners, François Cross, Eugene Rizzo, and Jennifer Van Tuyl. Besides the newspapers, they had rounded up tape recordings of Maddox making the accusation on television and radio.

The strategy session focused on the most important questions. What were the prospects of the suit? What should it focus on? Where should it be filed? When? Should they hold a press conference? The lawsuit, they decided, should go after all the advisers and should not be filed until after the grand jury completed its investigation. They would go to court in Dutchess County and seek hundreds of millions in damages. There would be no press conference, though the victim wanted one to defend himself. Doing so, they told him, would play directly into the hands of Maddox, Mason, and Sharpton. The facts would be lost in a gutter argument, and if the advisers learned what he had been doing during the four days Tawana was missing they might tailor their story around his alibi.

After the meeting, Pagones went to his office to talk to Grady and make arrangements for a brief leave. A mob of reporters was waiting, but he refused to see them. But when the crush was over, he allowed Craig Wolff in.

Pagones was jammed behind a desk in a small room at the back, and even his blue blazer, taut over his barrel chest, seemed to squeeze him. His eyes flitted nervously around the little room. "I had nothing to do with Tawana Brawley," he said with a quaver. "I've never met the girl." He refused to say any more. Hayes was miffed when he found out about these two unauthorized sentences; he advised Pagones to take some time off and lay low.

Later, Wolff tried to talk to the others whose names had been raised, Eugene Branson and Scott Patterson. Had they attacked Tawana Brawley? If not, where had they been when she vanished? Did they have alibis for the days she was missing? But they refused to say anything.

It was nearly dusk when Wolff found the green frame home of Harry Crist's parents. He hesitated about going in, about intruding on grieving people. He drove past, backed up, circled the

On the Run

block, and parked down the street. Finally, he went to the house
next door. He explained himself and asked the neighbors to call
Harry Crist, Sr., to intercede for him. To his surprise, the response was positive.

He climbed the porch and stood on a faded welcome mat.
Behind the gauze of the screen door, he saw a needlepoint Home
Sweet Home and then the haggard face of Harry Crist, Sr.
Tragedy lay on him like a pall: it was in the gray hair, the ashen
face, the body bent with mourning.

Wolff, who seemed always to be apologizing for intrusions, said
he wanted only to learn the truth. The Brawley advisers were
saying things about Harry, and there was no one else to speak up
for him now.

What the advisers were saying was absurd, Crist said. But he
had no proof. He and his wife had been away when their son had
shot himself.

"We never went away," Crist said quietly. "All these years and
we never took a vacation. But we decided to go then. We come
back and we don't have our son."

He stepped farther onto the porch and looked up at the first
evening stars. He sighed heavily and his breath was visible in the
chill spring night. "I don't know what makes men do the things
they do," he said. "Could they really be this mean? Do they know
these men have families? Do they know it's important to be
sure?"

The tears glinted in his eyes. "I lost my son," he said huskily.
"I lost my son. Something was bothering him and we weren't
here."

The death threats began almost immediately.

"You're a dead man, motherfucker, that's your message," said
the voice on Pagones's answering machine. "You want a message.
Well, you just wait, you're a dead motherfucker."

They came in telephone calls and in the mail at his home and
office. There were bomb threats at the office too. Guards were

263

posted at the doors, and every piece of mail was passed through a metal detector. When Pagones walked down the street in Pough-keepsie, black people gave him furious looks. Calls threatening Pagones were taken by WELK, a local radio station.

Intimidated, Pagones called a friend who was an investigator with the state police. He advised Pagones to file a formal report and then start carrying a weapon. Pagones did so. He had hunting rifles at home, but he began carrying an automatic pistol. The threats declined for a time, but then inexplicably resumed, heavi-er than ever, and Pagones bought a shotgun, which he taught Niki how to use.

Pagones began having chest pains. As he sat in his office one day, he thought he was having a heart attack. His stomach was constantly acting up. He went to a doctor for medication. Was he having a nervous breakdown? His doctors recommended psychi-atric therapy, but Pagones didn't act on the suggestion. What if the press thought he was cracking up?

When the break finally came, it was not from the mouths of Pagones or Hayes, Branson or Patterson. They were planning lawsuits and had to keep quiet to preserve their cases. Instead, the break came from an unexpected source. The *Times* reporters designated him "the Fat Man" because his manner was reminis-cent of Sydney Greenstreet in the movie *The Maltese Falcon*.

What the Fat Man told Wolff in a telephone call on the last Friday in March was that he could not only detail the movements of Pagones, Crist, Patterson, and Branson during much of the time Tawana was missing, but also could show the reporter sales re-ceipts and other supporting documents to back up their alibis. It had all been compiled in a painstaking investigation by state and local officials. But there was a hitch: not many people had access to these facts, and he was afraid that if he went beyond a summary and gave Wolff a very detailed picture, someone might guess his identity. That could jeopardize his career and expose him to criminal penalties for disclosing secret grand jury information.

Wolff requested a meeting. "If nothing else," he said, "maybe you can point me in the right direction."

Wolff drove in a pouring rain to the meeting place. He walked up an echoing stairwell, went down a long corridor, and found a large room. The source was there alone, seated cumbrously behind a desk. Thunder rolled down from the hills, and rain beat the window with a silken lash.

"It's all in here," the Fat Man said, nodding at a folder bulging with papers. It was four inches thick. "I have all the information. I just can't give it to you."

They talked awhile, Wolff pressing for details, the Fat Man refusing to go beyond a sketch.

"It's absolutely incredible that you're going through all this, but not helping me," Wolff badgered.

"I'm sorry," he said. He asked for the weekend to think more about it. Wolff agreed.

The call came on Monday. The Fat Man said he had reconsidered the matter and had decided to give Wolff the details, but Wolff in turn would have to promise him complete anonymity.

He returned to the meeting place that afternoon and the Fat Man opened the folder and began reading what amounted to a chronology of each man's activities during a week spanning the four days that Tawana Brawley was missing. The detail was stunning. Some of it was hour by hour, some of it was minute by minute. There were gaps in the chronologies, but taken together there was a ring of truth to them. These were not the elaborately concocted fronts of people hiding secrets, but the petty lives of ordinary men. And the very ordinariness of the activities, when piled one upon the other, took on what seemed an extraordinary power.

Wolff took notes furiously.

It was a wealth of detail about men who had been seen daily at their jobs at the prosecutor's office, at a local police department, at IBM and a utility; about afternoon and evening shopping trips to local stores, to stores in Newburgh and Vails Gate, to a mall in Danbury, Connecticut; about stops for tacos and chicken wings at nearby fast-food outlets; about nights alone with wives and girlfriends; about breakfasts, lunches, and dinners; about elaborate family spreads on Thanksgiving; about idle hours spent lifting weights or watching television; about telephone calls and casual encounters with acquaintances; about stops for gas and auto repairs; about a busy holiday spent installing insulation in an attic; about casual and serious talks with friends and family members— about a thousand comings and goings.

There were sales receipts. There were affidavits of confirmation from salespeople, family members, lovers, and acquaintances. There were police reports showing that insulation had been installed, that telephone calls had been made at particular times to particular numbers, that certain subjects had been discussed— even certain phrases used—in the conversations of the men.

The alibis were especially strong for November 28, the day Tawana was found at the Pavillion. All four men had driven in Crist's car in the late morning to the Danbury Fair Mall in Connecticut and had not returned to Wappingers Falls until eight P.M. Numerous receipts confirmed their purchases and presence in Danbury. The Fat Man even had details about the men's activities on subsequent days. And finally he showed Wolff Crist's suicide note and the investigators' reports confirming its contents.

That night at the Wyndham Hotel, Wolff sat in Room 1033, reading all his notes to Don Terry and Fox Butterfield.

"Incredible detail," Butterfield said.

It did not all have to be checked, but the *Times* reporters fanned out for most of the next week and confirmed enough of it to persuade themselves that there could be no doubt about the thoroughness and accuracy of the investigators' work.

Unless one conjured up visions of Pagones, Crist, Patterson, and Branson dashing out of the woods to go to work, to go shopping, to eat meals and carry on their elaborately mundane lives between assaults on Tawana Brawley, the portrait of a four-day nightmare of abduction and sexual assault by these men, as portrayed by the Brawley advisers, was out of the question.

Even so, Executive Editor Max Frankel and Managing Editor

Arthur Gelb were not satisfied. It would be a journalistic debacle of the first order to print an alibi story if ultimately some of the men were implicated in any way. Frankel and Gelb insisted on more official documentation, and they would not run the story until the reporters got it.

Blumenthal pondered the problem. There was, he knew, a group of special investigators who had conducted an inquiry parallel to that of the state. He made contact. It had to be strictly confidential, he was told, but a meeting with the investigators was finally set up. They met in Manhattan around a conference table that seemed to stretch half the length of a basketball court.

The investigators confirmed the alibis of Pagones, Crist, Patterson, and Branson in detail, and plugged many of the holes that the reporters had found in the mosaic. There had been, for example, a question about Patterson's whereabouts during one segment of the four-day period. He had not been at work, as scheduled. But the investigators found that his unauthorized absence was the result of a personal problem that had nothing to do with Tawana Brawley. They confirmed that nothing linking Harry Crist to the girl in any way had been uncovered.

The *Times* editors were finally satisfied, even though there was, after all the checking, still one troubling problem that none of the investigators could clear up. It typified the intractability of the case, and the *Times* noted it prominently in detailing the findings in another lengthy article on April 9: it was Patterson's story that he and his wife, Lisa, and Harry Crist had eaten dinner at the Patterson apartment on the night of November 24 and that he had driven Crist home at eight-thirty P.M. It was, Patterson had said, an uneventful trip. But there was a hitch: their route would have taken them near the spot where Tawana Brawley vanished—and at just about the time she said she was abducted by two white men in a car, one of them possibly a police officer.

Despite the overwhelming detail in the *Times* story, adding up to an all but airtight alibi for Pagones and his friends, the Brawley advisers clung to that hitch for all it was worth. Indeed, they now seemed to be grasping at any straw to keep the Pagones myth alive—for example, a WCBS-TV story by correspondent Mike Taibbi that sought to put Pagones in bed with the mob.

It was inspired by this: two men who were seeking a liquor license for a restaurant at the Dutchess County Airport had gotten into an altercation with a State Liquor Authority investigator inspecting the premises; charges and countercharges were filed, and it had fallen to Pagones to investigate. When he dismissed the restaurateurs' charges, they called Sharpton to complain about Pagones. Perry McKinnon had put them in touch with Taibbi, who aired a story suggesting that Pagones's actions were part of a mob move to take over the restaurant.

After planting the scurrility, Sharpton trumpeted it as part of a continuing campaign against Pagones. "We knew he was a rapist," Sharpton declared at a news conference. "We did not know he was a mobster."

The more Robert Abrams thought about it, the more it seemed that the key to the case was Glenda Brawley. Her arrival at the Pavillion on the day—indeed, at the very hour—that Tawana had been found had always been naggingly suspicious. It was important to clear that up. And Glenda probably knew a great deal more. She, more than anyone, probably had been taken into Tawana's confidence about what had happened to her during her four-day disappearance. Since it was politically unpalatable to force the truth out of the girl, Glenda seemed to be the next best option. She no doubt knew the truth, or most of it, and she seemed vulnerable to a grand jury subpoena: a mother seeking justice, not an elusive, secretive teenager.

Glenda Brawley had already ignored a letter from Abrams's top aide, John Ryan, asking for help in the case. She had also ignored a letter from the grand jury foreman asking for her cooperation. But a subpoena had the force of law: it could not be ignored without the risk of a fine or even a jail term for contempt of court.

It was always a gamble to call someone to testify without having a good idea of what they might say, for any witness before a New York grand jury was automatically immune from prosecution on matters covered in the testimony. Even here, Glenda Brawley seemed a good bet: she could have had no role in any crime against her daughter, and there was no one else to summon without running the risk of granting immunity to a culprit or a conspirator. Abrams subpoenaed Glenda Brawley to testify before the grand jury on May 24: the state was finally ready to play hardball.

A couple of days before Glenda's scheduled grand jury appearance, Alton Maddox convened a meeting at the Brawley apartment. He explained the meaning of the subpoena and laid out the options.

She could testify, of course. Glenda immediately rejected the idea.

On the other hand, she could simply ignore the subpoena. This meant risking a fine or jail term, but that wasn't as bad as it sounded. For they could challenge the validity of the subpoena; they could delay in a thousand ways; and that would likely bring months of litigation and jockeying.

To Glenda, that seemed infinitely preferable.

Maddox warned Tawana that she, too, might be subpoenaed. He warned the others that there might be indictments: it could get very nasty before it was over.

Fine, Sharpton said. They might not win in court, stacked as the system was against them. But there was still another option: they could take Glenda Brawley public.

21

Ethelyn Smith hushed the noisy regulars and tuned the little radio on the shelf to the voice of black New York, WLIB. It might have been Roosevelt announcing war or ringside at the Joe Louis–Billy Conn fight, for the platters stopped clacking, the voices at Edgar's fell into radio days silence, and the faces took on the faraway look of people about to hear their fate.

"We have some special guests today," Mark Riley, the announcer of *The Morning Show*, was telling thirty thousand listeners across the city—guests who would finally dispel "misconceptions that many people continue to hold about this case."

The guests were Alton Maddox, C. Vernon Mason, Al Sharpton, Ralph King, and perhaps the most important figure of all after Tawana, her mother, Glenda Brawley. She had been subpoenaed to testify before the grand jury in Poughkeepsie today, May 24. Instead, as Mason put it, she had decided to answer history's summons and testify on WLIB to the people.

With their instinct for the dramatic, they did not put her on right away. Instead, Maddox warmed up the audience with tales of racism in the Hudson Valley, and he made it come alive: "I recently met a black man branded by a branding iron in that area by the KKK, and nothing has been done about it," he began. It was a place where black women were routinely abused, where white cops, white sheriffs, white correction officers, white state troopers, white judges, and white prosecutors all looked out for one another. "This is what Cuomo and Abrams is trying to serve notice on our women: that we will rape you, Abrams and Cuomo included. We will rape you. Our sons will rape you, and you better not say anything."

Sharpton got on: "In the history of the state of New York, a white man has never been convicted for raping a black woman." To the sympathetic crowd at Edgar's, to thousands of other listeners, from homemakers to taxi drivers, this statement was now true—and would be repeated often.

Maddox, Mason, and Sharpton next took turns reciting the litany of "truths" about Tawana: urine had been found in her mouth; the girl had given a full account of the abduction and rape to Dutchess County authorities, both at the hospital and later at home.

"What do you mean, 'let Tawana talk'?" Sharpton said, mocking his critics. "Tawana *has* talked, and no one listened."

"No one listened," Mason said like Amen.

Maddox jumped in: "Once Tawana had the temerity to speak the truth and say who did it, the entire law-enforcement apparatus up in Dutchess County went against her." Indeed, a day after she told the authorities that a white cop was among her assailants, county officials had filed against Ralph King and Glenda Brawley "sexual abuse charges, which we fought and which has been proven to be unsubstantiated." Why, at about the same time, Maddox said, under-sheriff David Cundy "went on national TV and said Ralph King was the person who did this to Tawana Brawley, without no proof or anything."

The crowd at Edgar's was spellbound. The advisers said that Cuomo and Abrams were to be compared to the most virulent racists of the South a generation ago; that they, too, had joined in persecuting the Brawleys and Ralph King. King had lost his bus-driver's job in April, despite an exemplary record over many years. Glenda was being vilified as an unfit mother. Her sister, Juanita, had been arrested for shoplifting. And worst of all, Maddox said, Tawana was being depicted as "a possible prostitute, a definite drug addict—although no drugs have ever been found on her and in fact everybody who knows her have said continuously the same thing: that she is a very beautiful young lady. Many persons have said that—Mike Tyson, Don King, Bill Cosby, just anybody who meets this young lady. She's an honor student. She's a cheerleader. She has done everything that we could ask for."

The next voice was that of Ralph King, who was introduced with heavy sarcasm as "a prime suspect."

"They are still trying in undercover ways to pin it on me," he said calmly. He said the family had been harassed and abused by Abrams and other law-enforcement officials. "Until they are out," he said, "we won't do anything. We will not cooperate with them in no way."

At the back table at Edgar's, the regulars could not have agreed more. They sipped coffee and solidified their resolve: they, too, would hold out for justice for Tawana Brawley.

"All of this," Maddox was saying, "has been orchestrated by Mario Cuomo, who is one of the most vindictive persons on the face of this earth."

"Say it, say it," Mason chimed in.

In fact, said Maddox, it was the governor, not Tawana Brawley, who was perpetrating a hoax. "It *has* to be a hoax because Governor Cuomo is tied up with New York State police. Scott Patterson's father is his number-two man in that department. Steve Pagones is an assistant district attorney. He is supposed to be carrying out the enforcement of the law. His daddy is a city judge. Pagones is connected up with the mob. It's obvious that Cuomo is aware of the mob activity and he is protecting that mob activity. So we have a major scandal in this state. It goes way beyond Tawana Brawley because it talks about the way that government is being conducted in this state, and there are a few people who are willing to put their lives and their careers on the line right now in order to bring that to an end."

At Edgar's, they looked at one another knowingly. They had heard about corruption all their lives, but rarely had it been spelled out so clearly. And when Maddox said that the white community was united behind the assailants—this was the call to arms.

At last, it was time for Glenda Brawley. No one could mistake her for a public speaker, though Sharpton had tried to coach her; she was just a mother talking about herself and her daughter, and what she had to say was not closely reasoned or excessively dramatic. But there was a quiet fire in the timid voice, something that touched the heart, and when she began to speak about her frustrating quest for justice, her listeners were chilled and moved.

"We did ask Dutchess County for help before our lawyers did come into the act," Glenda Brawley said. "We begged them for help. We had them in our home and asked them for help."

From the start, she said, she and her family had been cooperative, had given a full account. From that night in the emergency room at St. Francis Hospital, she said, it was plain that Tawana had been so traumatized that she wanted nothing to do with whites.

"I told her, I said, 'Grit your teeth and let them get you well, and we will fight them'—and so far that's what she has done."

Despite all the information that Tawana and the family had provided the authorities, Glenda said, William Grady had the nerve to come to them and say he had no suspects. There was only one interpretation: Grady was trying to protect the attackers.

They heard something else in her voice now, a soft resolve like the first stirrings of rocks before a landslide: "I am not the type of person that's going to stand back and let them attack my child and not do anything about it. I went to the white community—because most of the people in the area are white—for help. They are the officials there. I could not get any justice, so I went to the black community and got all the power that I need to back me, to help me fight for my daughter."

Her strength, her defiance: that's what they had waited to hear. Now it was up to them to help her see it through.

Sharpton almost pushed it too hard, redundantly trying to tell them what it all meant, something about a mother's "sacred promise." But it was Glenda Brawley who did it; she had brought it all home.

Ethelyn Smith turned off the radio.

"I ain't going to pretend to be objective," said Professor Mackey. "History does not permit it."

Mrs. Smith stacked some plates. No one ever wanted to speak about rape, she said, especially the rape of black girls by white men. Now, perhaps, people will talk honestly about it, men about their fears and women about their anger.

The old Professor had brought along some books and pamphlets on black history, and like a tutor he explained the operations of a grand jury and the meaning of Glenda Brawley's act of defiance. The voices at Edgar's went on, rising and falling, and the morning rode away on recollections and anger.

In all the enthusiasm, however, no one seemed to notice the staunch independent face of the Professor's old pal, "Squire" Bradfield. He had listened carefully, but had not joined in the adulation. Under the wrinkled brow, his eyes showed the beginnings of doubt.

Charlie Mays and Ernie Peck sat in their unmarked car across Central Park West from Maddox's apartment building. They had been waiting for hours for Glenda Brawley to return. It was a soft spring night in the park, and pools of light glowed in the velvet woods beyond the stone wall, where unseen marauders hunted on the winding trails.

An improbable chance had brought Mays and Peck here. Mays, driving on a highway, had spotted Ralph King and his Lincoln, carrying Tawana, Glenda, and Tyice, in the afternoon, and had followed them here like a clever detective tailing suspects. He saw them go in to see Maddox, but by the time he found a public phone that worked and reported in to Poughkeepsie, the Lincoln was gone. Peck had joined him for the vigil and they were keeping their eyes open for the blue-gray, two-door Lincoln.

They saw it shortly before eight o'clock, pulling up with a Ford sedan as escort. The doors of the Ford opened first and out came four nattily attired black men in short haircuts and bow ties. Mays

274

and Peck looked at each other: Louis Farrakhan's bodyguards. So that's where they had been.

Like Secret Service agents, the bow-tied men looked up and down Central Park West, scanning for trouble. They checked the rooftops and the line of trees in the park, but they paid no attention to Mays and Peck, hunched down in the unmarked Dodge. Apparently convinced the coast was clear, Farrakhan's men gave a signal.

Mason and Sharpton alighted from the Ford. Ralph King emerged from the Lincoln. He went around to the trunk of his car and opened it, apparently to get something, and the others just stood there, waiting for him.

Mays saw his chance. He opened the car door and walked straight at Glenda like an assassin. As he drew near, he reached into his coat pocket and pulled out the sheaf of papers. He thrust it toward her without a word, but she drew back as if he were trying to give her a snake. Mason saw what was happening and rushed up. He too refused to accept the papers.

Finally, Mays looked into the Lincoln. He was surprised to see the teenaged girl everyone had been talking about for months. She seemed small and frightened. But Mays did not dwell on it. He tossed the court order into the front seat and walked away as Ralph King screamed obscenities and had to be restrained.

It was an unorthodox but legal service of the order directing Glenda Brawley to appear before Justice Angelo J. Ingrassia in state supreme court June 6 to explain her refusal to testify before the grand jury.

Deborah Wright, Ted Hollensworth, and Roy Canton were there. So were Sharpton, Mason, and several hundred other black people from all over the New York area. The crowd had come to the Friendship Baptist Church in Brooklyn to see the woman whose radio voice had captivated them the day before, and to make a commitment. Here was the tangible symbol they had been looking for.

"Our proud African queen," Sharpton said as Glenda walked among them like a myth transformed. "She stepped out of anonymity, stepped out of obscurity, and walked into history." He compared her to Rosa Parks and Fannie Lou Hamer, and he recited the names of all the martyrs: Eleanor Bumpurs, Yvonne Smallwood, Michael Stewart, Michael Griffith. "If you can allow your daughters in your community to be raped and sodomized, then nothing else really matters," he screamed, rocking back on his heels. "Some of us stood up and said enough is enough."

The congregation erupted with riotous cheers, applause, and shouts. It was as if Rosa Parks had only yesterday refused to relinquish her seat on the bus at Montgomery.

"That's right!"

"Tell the truth!"

"New York is Mississippi," Sharpton said. "The only difference between New York and Johannesburg is geography."

"Yes! Yes!"

When he said he had been moved to tears sitting beside Glenda Brawley at WLIB, they remembered their own tears. When he ended with defiance, they remembered their own defiance.

"No justice!" he shouted, throwing his body into it.

"No peace!" they responded.

"When do we want it?"

"Now!"

"When do we want it?"

"Now!"

Mason spoke. "We are going to fight," he said. "If they think they've seen a fight yet, just let them wonder about the meeting we had with Minister Farrakhan." The mere mention of the name sent a charge through the crowd. Some expected to see Farrakhan materialize, but that miracle did not occur.

When it was over, they contributed money to help the Brawley family resist injustice, and they milled about, talking of their feelings like people released from a curse. It had been much more than another rally. It had cemented a bond between the

Brawleys and a core of followers who would provide money and support for as long as faith endured.

Teddy Hollensworth, the father of five children, including three daughters four to eighteen years old, had heard Glenda's broadcast while driving to work from his suburban home north of New York City and decided to get involved in a case he had only read about. He had been touched and outraged by what Glenda said. Fighting for Tawana, he said, would be like fighting for his own daughters.

Deborah Wright, a customer service representative for the Reuters news agency, had heard the broadcast at work. What she felt were the first stirrings of resolve since the antiwar and civil rights tumult of the early 1970s. It was only a small thing to come to this rally, but it was a beginning. She gave them all the money in her purse and wrote out a check too.

"After a while," she said, "you just can't sit back anymore."

Night sailed along the Hudson and thick clouds settled over Newburgh as they headed for the war zone, crunching over broken glass and broken lives. The detective called Eddie drove the unmarked car and gave Craig Wolff the tour-guide spiel, pointing out the crack houses, the prostitutes, the thugs and informants.

The talk on the street was that Tawana Brawley had attended a party in Newburgh sometime during the four days she was missing. Mike Taibbi had aired a WCBS-TV interview with a sweatshirt-hooded youth called G who, between grunts, said Tawana had asked him for a ride home from a party. That had brought in the circus, and investigators and reporters for days now had seemed more common than drug dealers east of Robinson Avenue, the Maginot Line between the last working-class holdouts and the encroaching other half of the city.

They had already spotted Geraldo Rivera and his camera crew, a *Daily News* reporter posing as a vagrant with a bottle of whiskey, and other newshounds waiting at corners or in cars for

277

clandestine meetings with characters named D-Day and Do-Right, Prune and Q, with pushers and partygoers who were said to have the goods on Tawana.

Every night in Newburgh somebody is shot, Eddie was saying. Most of the dead are under thirty, just kids really. He said he trusted no one, especially if they waved hello. A year ago, Eddie said, he'd been shot in the leg by a woman he'd known for years; she'd gotten mad when he asked a question about her son, a drug dealer.

The night's journey into darkened back rooms and storefronts for drug operations began at Freddie's. The balls clicked and rolled and clicked over the pool table, and glazed stares watched them from just beyond the edge of the smoky light. Eddie had advised Wolff to ignore the stares, but it was easy for him to say: he had a revolver under his jacket and a bulletproof vest under his shirt. Wolff's armor was nothing but a press card. The reporter tried to look tough, but the cheeks were too pink over the beard, the eyes too innocent.

Somebody pocketed the eight ball, and money flashed on the green baize. Eddie pulled one of the players aside and they spoke in whispers under a sign advertising chicken wings and fries that were not available. Wolff saw the shark gesticulate. Eddie nodded. The game resumed and Eddie waved Wolff to follow him out.

They crossed South Street to a store with chalked windows and no name. A pit bull terrier chained to a drainpipe stared at them from the roof. They went in. The place was practically empty. Three shelves held a dozen cans of soup, a few cartons of cigarettes, a couple of moldy candy bars. Eddie went to the back and talked to a man called Shorty. Then he waved again and they left.

"What I'm hearing," he said when they were back in the car, "is that Todd is afraid to talk. Everyone will think he's eating cheese." Wolff smiled at the quaint Runyonesque expression. "Todd rules these streets," he went on. "He's got a Jeep and bodyguards and he's trying to get away from this Tawana Brawley thing because it's hurting his business. Anyway, Todd owes me a favor, so I think he'll talk to you."

Eddie left him at Leewood Boone's Used Furniture Shop. Old sofas and chairs filled the back room, but there was nowhere to sit: they were piled one atop the other, sideways and upside down, exposing the shattered arms and broken springs. A lamp cast a dim yellow light over the mess. Wolff waited.

It was a minute after ten when he appeared, materializing out of the shadows like a Christmas ghost.

"I'm Todd," he said.

"You're a hard man to find."

"All these reporters been following me around. I'd be crazy to meet in broad daylight."

Wolff asked about Tawana Brawley.

"She was my girlfriend. She visited me all the time."

Wolff asked about her relationship to Ralph King.

"Maybe she was mad at him and her mother. She used to say that they brought her back to live with them just to take care of the baby. She was upset about that."

"How was she on the day she visited you in jail?"

"She was fine. But you know there wasn't no time for much. We just wanted to be with each other, you know?"

Wolff went straight to the point. "Do you know where Tawana was during those four days after she visited you?"

"Well, there was a lot of parties. I heard she might have been at one of these parties."

"Who told you this?"

"A girl I know."

"Can I get in touch with this girl?"

"Maybe."

"Where was the party?"

"There was more'n one party. But maybe it was on Lander Street." He paused. "I can't be just talking and talking. It's tough here and I don't need no trouble. I got what I got going. I don't want no one else pissed off."

"If I need you again, will I be able to get you?"

"Yeah. You'll know me. I'm the silver Jeep."

There were more conversations later, with Randolph (D-Day) Davis and other characters involved in drugs, burglary, and larceny. Their information was all murky, all meaningless.

Weeks later, one rainy night in May, Wolff found himself walking in search of the youth called Q. He found him at the appointed place outside a boarded-up building. The boy had a round teenage face and pleasant eyes. He said he didn't want anyone in the neighborhood to see him with a reporter. It seemed to Wolff that there wasn't anyone else in the neighborhood, but maybe there were eyes in the ruins. Q said he knew of a more private place and led the way.

They headed into an alley, past shattered television sets, burned mattresses, and piles of soggy clothing, and down into a dimly lighted cellar filled with more junk. At least it was out of the downpour.

"She was at the party," Q said. "I saw her drinking and talking and laughing."

Wolff asked where and when the party had been held.

"I don't want to talk no more," Q said. He started to leave and Wolff started to follow—a move Q must have interpreted as an effort to stop him. He whirled suddenly, and a switchblade knife gleamed in his right hand.

"I can get pretty angry," he said.

Wolff's heart pounded. "Come on, man. I'm on your side. I don't want to bother you anymore."

"I'll tell you one thing," Q said. "She was very pretty."

And then he was gone.

They raged at one another across Market Street: two hundred black demonstrators who had piled off buses from Brooklyn chanting their grievances while fifteen white men from Poughkeepsie stood their ground, singing "God Bless America."

"Governor Cuomo, have you heard? This is not Johannesburg."

"Land that I love . . ."

"No justice!"

"Stand beside her . . ."

"No peace!"

"Tell Steven Pagones, we shall not be moved."

A white man shouted: "Let Tawana testify."

C. Vernon Mason lost his poise. "Our forefathers testified when they came here in chains," he screamed.

Then it got ugly.

A demonstrator unfurled the black, red, and green flag of black liberation.

"Where's your American flag?" a white man shouted.

"Fuck your flag!" a black demonstrator shot back.

In the middle of the cleared street, a dozen police officers stood ready to beat back challenges from either side.

Down the street at the armory, a large form began rising behind the marchers. It was Al Sharpton's backside, struggling upward in a tight blue suit, trying to surmount a five-foot iron fence outside the armory. Several people were under him, pushing and squeezing and shoving. Finally he tumbled over, plunging onto the grass and tumbling backward like Humpty-Dumpty, stomach in the air, legs kicking.

"This is my bedroom," he boomed. "We'll stay as long as we have to."

Photographers rushed to capture the spectacle as blacks and whites roared with laughter on both sides of the street. Later, when things were well cooled, Sharpton climbed back over the fence with great difficulty. Then he and the demonstrators left like a blustering wind that had ruffled the town but torn off no roofs.

"I'm now going to show you my other side," Sharpton said as he led reporters up the sunny path at Vassar College, a thick folder of notes under his arm. And behind the lectern in the pit of Saunders Hall, with one hundred fifty mostly white students looking on, he might have been a tweedy professor contemplating Shelley and Keats.

There was no bombast, no rhetorical tricks, when he began to speak. On the contrary, his voice was gentle, the cadences modulated. He spoke of the struggle of blacks over the centuries and said he had spent most of his life trying to get people to work together. It was captivating.

Then he turned to the Tawana Brawley case, and the stridency came back: Abrams wanted Pagones to testify before the grand jury, he said, because he would then be granted immunity from prosecution. (In fact, Abrams had urged Pagones to testify voluntarily and waive immunity.)

"There was urine in her mouth when she was found," said Sharpton. "Now you tell me how could someone urinate in her own mouth."

The students squirmed and twittered.

"Now they're saying that Ralph King had a thing going with Tawana Brawley. Well, how can they say that and also say that Ralph King was the one who did all this to her? If all this was so, well then all he had to do was take her upstairs in their house and do to her what he wanted."

The logic held together, but the swirl of suppositions left the young audience befuddled.

"I've lost him," a student in the back whispered to a friend.

Sharpton then ridiculed the *Times* article detailing the alibis of Pagones, Crist, and the other men accused by the advisers. "That story placed them at the scene of the crime," he asserted.

Finally, he promised that Tawana would tell her story in ten days.

But ten days later, when a reporter reminded Sharpton of his promise, he responded by saying that Pagones was a mobster and that Tawana could not hazard a public appearance now because she was in mortal danger, this time from the underworld. The accusation was wild, but coming from Sharpton, not that wild. A few days earlier, he had declared that it was not just the Ku Klux Klan that had attacked Tawana, but the Irish Republican Army, too.

With every passing day, Rosemary Dean found herself resenting the Brawley case—and Sharpton, Maddox, and Mason—more and more. Like other blacks who lived silently with their skepticism, she looked with distaste upon the stridency and buffoonery of the advisers. She was especially pained by their self-righteous attacks on black people who doubted them or their version of what had happened: it was like the black-power movement all over again.

Rosemary Dean had watched the case unfold through newspapers and television and through the living room blinds. Her apartment at the Pavillion was just down the lawn from the Brawleys', and her daughter, Alicia, and son, Timothy, had been friends of Tawana's. The case had intruded on their lives, too, as the reporters and investigators had pestered her and her children for what they might know.

They knew little. But Rosemary Dean had her theories. An independent, thirty-six-year-old divorced mother who was an airplane pilot for IBM's private fleet, she had worked hard to give herself and her children a middle-class life. She took pride in their achievements in school and sports, in their ability to say no to the temptations of drugs. She also believed in the black struggle for equality; she herself had been a part of that struggle in schools, on her job, in her right to live where she chose.

She had first grown suspicious of the Brawley family's character after hearing from Alicia of beatings and fights. She knew Glenda only in passing, but regarded her with compassion as a woman who was disadvantaged and frustrated. But she had asked her children to minimize their contacts with the Brawleys after Tawana had come to her apartment one day about a year before her disappearance with a bloody mouth from a beating by her mother. Tawana begged Alicia to lie for her, to tell Glenda that they had been together all afternoon. Alicia had gone along reluctantly, but Rosemary Dean resented it.

And when she heard the reports of Tawana Brawley's disappearance and of the condition in which she had been found, Dean was dubious. She was not naive about racism: she would not have been surprised if Tawana *had* been abducted and raped. But there were aspects of the story that didn't ring true. The hair was one thing.

"When I heard that her hair was chopped off," she told Craig Wolff, "I sat up and said, no, she wears a hair weave. When I read about the hair, the first thing I thought, though I didn't say it to anyone, was Glenda—Glenda pulled the weave out."

She had watched and listened as the family and its advisers amplified Tawana's story, building it into a tale of horrors, but never once did she feel she was hearing the truth. "Half truths, lies, manipulation—but not the whole truth," she said. And when she heard Sharpton describe black people with doubts as confused or misinformed, she bridled.

"I guess that's a tactic, also," she said. "If they knock down everyone who wonders what they are doing, then pretty soon people will believe them just because they're yelling louder. I don't know. I don't think that's how a movement takes place. I don't know much about this, but I think you have to have a truthful start. You can't just be going willy-nilly saying this and that, trying to blast everyone out of the way.

"But don't go telling me I'm disloyal or I've forgotten my roots just because I reason on my own and question you. That's not right. And besides, eventually you'll be found out."

22

He looked like a dirt farmer scanning the hills for rain. You had to imagine the pitchfork crooked in the elbow and the clouds moving up on the horizon like enormous airships, but the rest was in the man: the parchment skin cracked by the sun, the patient face that had read the Farmer's Almanac under kerosene lamps, the big hands that had dug the soil and cultivated onions and celery and lettuce.

The black robes, the high bench, the formality of the dark-paneled courtroom in Poughkeepsie all seemed incongruous, props for Angelo Ingrassia. But if he had come a long way from the farm to the law, he had kept his values intact—a stern view of life, faith in simple things like being on time, treating people fairly, telling the truth. A farmer, a judge: they were not so different in the qualities that mattered.

His parents had immigrated from Italy—his father, Frank, from Sicily, his mother, Adriana, from Naples. Both arrived at Ellis Island as children. Frank Ingrassia went to work at twelve, a migrant child laborer. It had taken him nearly three decades to climb out of poverty. But when he was forty, Frank Ingrassia and a brother bought a black-dirt farm in Orange County, across the Hudson River from Poughkeepsie, and it was there that Angelo was born in March 1923. He grew up on the farm, working the fields with his father and uncle and attending a one-room schoolhouse that had six grades, no running water, and kerosene lamps for dark days.

He graduated from Virginia Polytechnic Institute in 1943 with a degree in metallurgical engineering. He served with an armored unit in Europe during World War II and stayed on after the war as a civilian administrator, becoming friends with a number of lawyers. When he came home in 1947, Ingrassia decided to take advantage of the GI Bill, to study at Albany Law School.

"You can work for yourself or you can work for somebody else, but if you work for somebody else they will never pay you what you are worth," his mother advised him. To Ingrassia, lawyering was a kind of independence. It wasn't farming. Still, justice, like seasons, controlled the cycles of his life, and not some overseer. He hung out his shingle in Orange County in 1950 and threw himself into local Republican politics. He became an assistant prosecutor in 1952 and in 1967 was elected Orange County district attorney. Two years later, he became president of the New York State District Attorneys Association.

In 1971, Governor Nelson A. Rockefeller appointed Ingrassia to an Orange County judgeship, and in 1982 he was elected to a full fourteen-year term as a justice of the state supreme court, where major cases were tried. Piercing everyday dramas unfolded in his court: the woman who killed her child but had to be let go on a technicality, jail escapees who murdered a *Reader's Digest* editor and her invalid husband in their home, the thug who rushed across the courtroom and menaced Ingrassia upon hearing his guilty verdict.

Despite his prosecutor's past, he became known as a scrupulously even-handed judge who made firm, fast rulings and was rarely reversed on appeal. In court, he was short-tempered with inept or ill-prepared lawyers, and some lawyers said that in his drive for efficiency he sometimes rushed through cases, short-changing their clients. But he was a plainspoken, self-effacing jurist with dignity and a sense of humor. He was also a hard worker. Besides his own cases, Ingrassia supervised the work of seventeen other judges in the five counties just north of New York City. Married, the father of three sons and a daughter, one of the more respected jurists in the state, Ingrassia had been picked to direct the grand jury when the Brawley case arose. And after Glenda Brawley ignored a summons to appear before that grand jury on May 24, it was Ingrassia who ordered her to appear in court on June 6 to explain why she should not be held in contempt.

The black army came down Market Street like a mob looking for the jail, and the white detachment was there to meet them. Outside the courthouse, they faced off across no-man's-land and a thin blue line of peacekeepers. Chants shot across the gulf like gunfire.

"No justice! No peace!"

"No justice! No peace!"

"Arrest Pagones NOW!"

"Arrest Pagones NOW!"

The white people stood their ground and responded with icy, defensive stares. They were badly outnumbered. Many of the three hundred in the black army had come up from New York City in buses; they had heard the appeal for recruits on WLIB and had paid ten dollars each to enlist. But there were sheriff's deputies, Poughkeepsie police officers, and even some state troopers to give an illusion of order.

Louis Farrakhan sat in his gold Lincoln, a general surrounded by a cordon of his bow-tied troops, observing the action, careful not to expose himself to danger. In the next car, also shielded by Farrakhan's Fruit of Islam, was the "proud African queen," Glenda Brawley, the object of all the tumult. Ralph King and Juanita Brawley sat with her like her consort and lady-in-waiting, basking in their celebrity, watching the anger ebb and flow. The strategists—Alton Maddox, C. Vernon Mason, and Al Sharpton—arrived separately.

It was judgment day for Glenda Brawley, who had been summoned to account for herself. She seemed to be in no hurry to leave the car, let alone account for herself.

Mason was the first to go in. He went up the wide marble

staircase carrying several large valises containing papers and law books. On the second floor, outside Justice Ingrassia's courtroom, Mason was stopped by court officers. He would not be allowed in with those cases, they told him officiously. Mason identified himself and tried to explain what the cases were, but the numbskulls were adamant. He tried to brush past them, and they grabbed him and wrenched away his cases.

Fuming, Mason burst through the doors. The courtroom was the largest in the building, but it had only one hundred seats for spectators, and they were already packed, mostly with white people. Robert Abrams and John Ryan were there; so were William Grady and Steven Pagones and his lawyer. Indeed, there were white faces everywhere: white spectators, white officials, white journalists, white lawyers. Even the oil portraits lining the walls portrayed white judges, dignified and dead.

There was no one on the bench. But within moments of Mason's arrival a court officer bellowed, "All rise!" and Justice Ingrassia came in. The dark hair was shot with gray and he was hefty under the robes, but he moved vigorously for sixty-five. Behind the glasses, his keen eyes assayed the room and focused finally on Mason. A stickler for being on time, Ingrassia had called the hearing for one-thirty. He had entered promptly then to find a courtroom full of people. But Glenda Brawley and her lawyers had not been there, and he had called a recess. Now it was after two, and Glenda was still nowhere to be seen.

But it was Mason, not the judge, who began complaining. The court officers had roughed him up and confiscated his briefcases, and hundreds of black people who had come to attend this hearing were waiting outside, unable to get in. Even Glenda's spiritual adviser had been unable to get in, he said. As Mason recited his litany, Maddox arrived and began laying out papers on the defense table. Mason promptly yielded the floor, and Maddox took up the cudgels. He demanded to know why the courtroom was full of white people.

Ingrassia had never seen Maddox and Mason, except on television. He studied them now, scaling the faces down to life-size, the rhetoric down to substance. First, the judge ordered the court officers to return Mason's briefcases to him; then he explained the difficulties of the crowded courtroom. It was the biggest they had; forty-five seats had been reserved for the press, and many others for public officials and people who had been subpoenaed—most of them by Maddox—to give evidence at this hearing. The rest were for the public on a first-come basis.

"That does not fit my definition of a public trial," Maddox said.

"It is not your definition that governs," the judge replied.

Getting down to business, he asked where Glenda Brawley was now.

She was outside, Maddox said, and would not come in unless her supporters could be here with her.

It was not necessary from the court's standpoint that Glenda Brawley be present: it was in her own interest to show up and defend herself, and if she didn't do it, the court could act without her.

Maddox, trying to seize the initiative, asked the judge to withdraw from the hearing. He said he believed Ingrassia had discussed the case with Governor Cuomo and thus could not be impartial.

Amusement flickered over Ingrassia's face. "This court," he said, "will state unequivocally for the record that in all of his sixty-five years he has never spoken to the governor, never spoken to any member of the governor's staff, has never met the governor, doesn't know the governor, and is, quite frankly, of the opposite political persuasion from the governor. You need not pursue it any further. Your next question."

"In any event," Maddox said, "I certainly wanted to bring that to your honor's attention. Certainly you have to search your own mind and soul as to how you would deal with that matter."

"I have dealt with it," Ingrassia said.

Maddox pushed on. He charged that blacks had been excluded from the grand jury, and its summons to Glenda Brawley was therefore illegal.

Not so, Ingrassia said. There were blacks on the jury.

Maddox charged that the grand jury had been impaneled in public and that the names of the jurors had been disclosed, all illegalities.

Not so, Ingrassia said. He explained that the jurors had all been referred to by number during the selection process in open court. "They were impaneled and sworn openly," he said. "All other proceedings have been secret."

Maddox charged that Abrams had leaked to NBC the photographs showing Tawana Brawley nude from the waist up, the ones taken at St. Francis Hospital before the racial slurs had been washed off. They had been flashed across the nation by the network.

That would be a serious offense, Ingrassia said, and asked Maddox to give evidence of his assertion.

Maddox said he had it, but would not give it to the court. He then raised a host of similar allegations: there had been leaks of secret grand jury minutes, an investigator on the case had been arrested on cocaine charges, evidence against Steven Pagones and Scott Patterson had been suppressed. It seemed he wanted to talk about anything but the subject of the hearing, Glenda Brawley.

Ingrassia rejected all the allegations.

Perhaps the judge was not up to handling a case of this complexity, Maddox suggested testily.

Ingrassia did not rise to the bait.

Maddox raised the stakes, trying to provoke him, to show him as a racist and an establishment lackey. He described the judge's unfazed demeanor as cold and likened it to faces in Ku Klux Klan dens.

The judge bolted upright, astonished. "I don't think you are comparing me to . . ."

Maddox backed off: "I am not making the comparison."

"Okay. I didn't think you were," said the judge. "I would hate to draw that inference."

Maddox fingered the glasses on his nose thoughtfully. "I can find no better place than here for us to lay out the entire story," he said.

The courtroom stirred. Was Maddox really going to use this forum to unveil the secrets of the Tawana Brawley saga?

"I would think," he went on, "that it would be most unfortunate if the public was not given the opportunity to know over the course of the next few days as to what happened back in November of 1987."

Reporters scribbled furiously. But their pens slowed as Maddox went on. What happened to Tawana Brawley in November 1987, he said, had to be viewed in the context of history, and he began like a visiting lecturer to recite the lessons.

"Four hundred years of oppression is riding on this case," Maddox said, his voice rising, "and we have reached a point when the African nation in this country, and particularly those Africans in New York, are thoroughly disgusted with the way justice is administered and they are thoroughly disgusted with black victims of racial crimes being told by a grand jury that they are hallucinating and that what happened to them amounts to a hoax. I hope that from this day forward we can wipe clean those four hundred years of injustices and begin to proceed into the twenty-first century like intelligent and civilized men and women. And because of that I would ask you to take all that into consideration and search your heart and your mind."

And, he added, step down from this case.

Ingrassia leaned back in his leather chair. For all of Maddox's self-serving pedantry, for all his efforts to put racism on trial instead of Glenda Brawley, Justice Ingrassia had been moved by his statement.

"This is a very unpleasant task, at best, to preside over a matter such as this," Ingrassia said as Maddox sat down. "Believe me, it's not pleasant. The last part of your statement about four hundred years of oppression is moving, and there is a great deal of truth in it. There is a great deal of right in it, if that's the way you want to put it. But there is no way under the sun that I can avoid my duty. And Mister Maddox, believe me, if I felt there was any legitimate or halfway legitimate or valid reason for me to recuse myself, I would."

Maddox rambled on awhile longer. He spoke of the difficulties blacks faced "in a strange land surrounded by hostile persons." In New York, he said, black people could not turn for help to their governor—"the most vindictive individual who's ever graced the Executive Mansion, and who certainly harbors deep racial hostility to persons of African descent."

It was time to speak of Glenda Brawley, the judge said, but they got sidetracked again on the question of allowing television cameras into the courtroom. Maddox was opposed. Even though Glenda Brawley was outside in the glare of it all, he argued that she would be irreparably harmed if the cameras were allowed in court. "Glenda Brawley," Maddox said, "cannot withstand that kind of media exposure—and it will bring emotional, psychological trauma to her." He droned on about injustice, love, and hate in America as the air conditioners whirred and the afternoon sun beat through the panes.

Ingrassia finally called a halt. He said the press served a vital function and ruled that one television camera and one news photographer representing the press would be allowed in. He called a five-minute recess.

Downstairs, the faithful waited under a cloudless sky for some sign from above. The whites and blacks had begun to mingle on Market Street. The heat made them drowsy.

Sharpton stood beside Glenda Brawley's car and tried to revive the black crowd.

"No justice! No peace!"

"Arrest Pagones NOW!"

But the cheers were languid until Maddox and Mason appeared on the courthouse steps. Then, as the noise rose up, Sharpton hurried over and they conferred in the doorway of a bank. Maddox explained what had happened in court: it had been packed to keep them out and the proceedings were stacked against them too. Sharpton suggested taking Glenda Brawley back to Wappingers Falls. "If they want her, let them come out to the house," he said. "We'll sit in the house. Y'all go back and do what you have to do."

The showdown began a few minutes later.

Maddox and Mason were late getting back into court, and the judge rebuked them: "I don't know how long this hearing is going to take. But one thing I will not tolerate is tardiness."

Maddox, his eyes blazing, took another unpredictable turn. All afternoon he had shouted against racism, seemingly to delay the proceedings. Now he wanted only to bring them swiftly to an end. They all wanted to get it over with, didn't they, he said, and perhaps the judge had a dental appointment or something.

Ingrassia coolly said he was in no hurry.

"There are people here who have to get back to New York City," Maddox persisted. "We're not going to delay them and press people who want to file their reports. So they can do that. So we don't have to waste anyone's time on this." There was no need for legal arguments, Maddox went on, because black people could not get justice. Not in Dutchess County. Not anywhere in the United States.

Mason nodded in assent, muttering as if in church: "Tell it. Tell it. Tell the truth, brother."

Ingrassia urged them to make a case for Glenda Brawley. Like a law professor prompting a student, he said he could think of many valid excuses why she had not appeared before the grand jury, and he even laid out some of the options.

But Maddox wasn't interested. He called the hearing an exercise in futility and said he didn't have any idea what would raise an issue of fact in the judge's mind.

"Well, if you don't, Mister Maddox," said the judge, "if you don't, you shouldn't be practicing law."

"Maybe I shouldn't," Maddox rejoined. "I don't think we should be wasting each other's time."

Ingrassia agreed. He asked for some legal basis for Glenda Brawley's defiance of the subpoena.

Maddox offered none. And he rejected the judge's suggestion that she be brought into court now. "She already knew the

outcome of this," he said. "I do not believe that Glenda Brawley
has a snowball's chance in hell of getting justice in New York. My
own . . ."

"Even if you are correct, Mr. Maddox, even if you are correct . . ."

"May I finish?"

". . . that still doesn't give her the right to defy the lawful
mandate of this court, does it?"

"No," Maddox retorted, "it gives her the right if she's not in
fact a citizen of this country—she's not given the protections of
citizenship—gives her a right not to fool herself as to whether a
government exists for her. The reality of it is that in this country
in 1988 there is no protection for any person of African descent,
and anybody who believes otherwise is out of his or her mind."

Mason was an echo at his side: "Tell it. Tell the truth, brother."

Ingrassia was near the end. "Is it your defense . . ."

"I have no defense," Maddox shot back.

"Mr. Maddox, is it your defense . . ."

"I have no defense."

The judge's voice rose. "Is it your defense to this case that
black people cannot receive justice?"

"Yes."

"Is that your defense to this motion to punish for contempt?"

"Absolutely," Maddox concluded.

Ingrassia then turned to the state. "Mister Ryan," he said, "do
you agree that black people can't receive justice in this case?"

"No, I do not, your honor," he said.

But Ryan asked that Glenda Brawley be present in court before
the judge made any decision on whether to hold her in contempt.

Maddox said he wasn't even sure where she was.

Justice Ingrassia had heard enough. In all his years in the law,
he had never held anyone in criminal contempt. But now, he
said, he had no alternative. He ordered that Glenda Brawley be
arrested and, unless she appeared before the grand jury, that she
be jailed for thirty days and fined two hundred fifty dollars. It was
the maximum penalty.

As his last act, Ingrassia quashed subpoenas that Maddox had issued to Governor Cuomo, Robert Abrams, and M. A. Farber of the *Times*. All these were irrelevant to the question of why Glenda Brawley had ignored her grand jury subpoena.

Maddox, fury on his face, was halfway up the aisle, heading out the courtroom, when Ingrassia rapped his gavel, ending the hearing. Mason remained behind, loading his briefcases and muttering, "Outrageous, outrageous."

Abrams, too, was shocked by Glenda's sentence. He hadn't expected such swift action or the maximum penalty. But once again events had overtaken him. Arresting Glenda Brawley might make matters worse, although he wondered how the case could possibly get any worse. Outside, he denounced Maddox and Mason. "Glenda Brawley," he said, "received reprehensible and irresponsible advice. Her lawyers utterly failed to offer a defense. I point the finger of blame at them."

Maddox and Mason were already leading a chanting horde of Brawley supporters down Market Street, the reporters and television crews chasing after them like puppies.

"Free the land!" they chanted.

"No justice! No peace . . ."

The voices faded in the distance.

23

The fugitive from justice was worn out, but there was no sleep in the cramped back seat with the engine growling in her ear and the wheels lurching at every corner and stoplight. The expressways were easiest on her aching back, but the bridges rumbled under the axles like temblors as they crisscrossed New York City on an agonizing all-night journey to nowhere.

Maddox drove and Mason sat beside him. To Glenda Brawley in the back, it was all a blur of street lamps and lurid neon, the drone of traffic, the clicking blinker lights. They drove carefully, hour after hour, passing the tourist sights, ignoring spectacular skyline vistas, crawling around residential neighborhoods. Periodically, they circled lonely blocks and watched the rearview mirror for any sign of the law on their tail.

The crux of it was a misdemeanor, but they were like spies on the run. Glenda Brawley—wanted for thirty days in jail—needed what they called sanctuary, and Sharpton was trying to arrange it. She had been holed up at Maddox's apartment in Manhattan for more than a day since Justice Ingrassia had imposed the contempt sentence, but you couldn't hide at your lawyer's place: they all agreed that wasn't safe.

They stopped once at La Guardia Airport for sodas and sandwiches, mingling with the late-night stragglers, and then hit the road again. They stopped occasionally at pay phones so Maddox could call Sharpton. Worried that Abrams's agents were tracking

296

their moves and recording their conversations, they had set up a little code.

Maddox dialed Sharpton at home.

"Any luck?"

"We're going to point B," Sharpton said. Never mind that it was Maddox who was on the road. It meant that Sharpton had not yet found a sanctuary for Glenda.

Maddox grumbled his impatience, but for security reasons could say no more. They went back to the road and Glenda Brawley's grousing about the potholes and the cramped back seat.

Sharpton finally got the call he had been waiting for. Timothy Mitchell, the pastor who had accompanied the advisers to Albany to see the governor, had been out of town all day, but he had seen a cable television news report on Glenda Brawley's quest for sanctuary in a black church.

"Which church are you going to use?" Mitchell asked.

"Can we use yours?" Sharpton responded.

Mitchell gagged. His relatively conservative congregation at the Ebenezer Missionary Baptist Church in Queens was already concerned over his two arrests with Sharpton during the "days of outrage" protests.

"Oh, no! No!" Mitchell said.

Sharpton promised they would need the church only for a day or two.

Mitchell, who had been a Brawley supporter for more than six months, said he would have to confer with the chairman of his church board of trustees, who happened to be his brother, James Mitchell.

A few hours later, Timothy Mitchell called back. It was all right with him, but the board of trustees was balky. Sharpton himself began talking with James Mitchell by telephone. Finally, he crumbled. But there were to be strict ground rules for the episode: it was only for a day or two. Only Sharpton, Glenda, Ralph King, and two security guards would be permitted into the church.

There could be no press hullabaloo, and no crowds of Brawley supporters inside the church. And no one—not even Glenda—would be allowed in before seven o'clock the next morning, June 8.

"I agree," Sharpton said. He would worry about the details later. The important thing was to get into the church.

Maddox called back before midnight.

"Any luck?"

"It's point A." Sharpton beamed.

"Good," Maddox said. "Get us in at five o'clock."

Sharpton cut in. They could not get in before seven o'clock.

But Maddox didn't care about the details. He just wanted to end the nomadic night behind the wheel as early as possible. "See you at five," he said, and hung up.

They continued to drive around all night. It was nearly six A.M. when Maddox, Mason, and Glenda Brawley pulled up outside the church.

Sharpton was already inside, trying to persuade the sexton, who had slept in the church overnight, to let them in early. But the man was skeptical when he heard they wanted to come in to hide from the police. He called James Mitchell. Reluctantly, the chairman agreed to let them in early.

Finally, Sharpton went out to the car, took Glenda by the arm, and made a dash for the church door, as if the police were hiding behind telephone poles and parked cars waiting to pounce. Inside, they slammed the door and sighed with relief.

The agreement had already been violated, and Sharpton immediately violated it some more: he called The Associated Press and United Press International to say that Glenda Brawley had taken sanctuary in the Ebenezer Missionary Baptist Church.

Sanctuary is not recognized in American jurisprudence, but the concept is deeply rooted in Judeo-Christian theology. In the United States, it was invoked in the nineteenth century when abolitionists gave protection to escaped slaves, during the Vietnam War when draft resisters sought refuge in churches and synagogues, and in the 1980s when religious men and women harbored Latin

American refugees in defiance of the Reagan administration's tight policy on asylum.

But there were no legal niceties in the concept of sanctuary for Glenda Brawley: it was pure political theater. Cuomo and Abrams could not order the police to storm a black church and drag out a black woman who claimed she was protecting her child. Besides all the bad publicity, it would have risked bloodshed. And it was hard to justify the arrest of anyone on a minor charge when two hundred thousand killers, rapists, robbers, and other malefactors named in state warrants were at large. So Glenda could thumb her nose at the law, and Maddox, Mason, and Sharpton could say whatever they wanted, for there was no chance of a police invasion.

"They will have to come through me," Maddox told reporters at the Queens County Criminal Courthouse in Kew Gardens, where the second Howard Beach trial was under way. "Please have a bullet designated for me. We will stand tall and we will stand as men, protecting the rights of black women."

And Sharpton, surrounded by a huge crowd of reporters, photographers, and television cameras outside the publicity-shy Ebenezer Missionary Baptist Church, crowed: "Mister Abrams, your arms are too short to box with God!"

There was perhaps no institution more important in black communities than the church. Since slavery, it had been the one place where blacks had been free to gather, to seek solace and plan their futures. Many of the old Negro spirituals were encoded messages about slaves planning escape.

And it was to their churches—whether Baptist, Methodist, Pentecostal, or any of dozens of other denominations—that black communities turned for leadership. The churches had long been the focal point not only for civil rights struggles, but for fostering black pride and a sense of self-worth.

Ebenezer, from a Hebrew word meaning "stone of help," had been a fortification for black life in the Flushing area of Queens since 1871, one of thousands of churches in New York City that had comforted blacks down through the decades. The best-known black church in New York was the Abyssinian Baptist Church in Harlem, which had served as a religious and political base for Adam Clayton Powell, Jr. But Ebenezer was the oldest black Baptist church in Queens.

The Reverend Timothy Mitchell, whose father had been the church's pastor until his death in 1949, had led the congregation since 1962. Mitchell liked to make an apt comparison: the Abyssinian Baptist Church had a congregation of sophisticates, the city's black journalists, lawyers, doctors, and college professors, while his own congregation was composed of ordinary working-class people. His congregation preferred to hear about God on Sundays and wanted politics kept out of the pulpit. Mitchell and his trustees knew that many of the church members would disapprove of having the Brawley controversy under their roof—and not a few would be scandalized that Glenda Brawley might be sleeping there with a man to whom she was not legally married.

Sharpton had already violated Mitchell's trust by bulling his way in early and calling in the press. Several dozen supporters, who had heard about it on WLIB, showed up and they went in—another violation of Sharpton's agreement with the trustees. Some brought food, medical supplies, reading materials, and other accouterments of a siege. They were all under the impression that storm troopers might arrive at any minute, and many were ready for bloody combat with the invaders.

With so many people around, Sharpton decided to hold a rally. But that required more negotiations with the trustees. They had already given him a mile, why not another inch? They backed down when Sharpton challenged them to order the whole gathering disbanded. And Sharpton threw them a bone: the rally would have a religious format—the choir would sing and Ebenezer's assistant pastor would be master of ceremonies.

"Well," said James Mitchell, "I guess it doesn't matter as long as they don't spend the night."

They proceeded to spend the night. After the rally, Maddox

and Mason went home. But Sharpton, nearly as exhausted as Glenda Brawley, fell asleep on the floor underneath a secretary's desk in the church's administrative office. Others slept atop a conference table in the trustees' meeting room, on the floors, on any flat surface they could find. Glenda, Ralph King, and little Tyice slept on a fold-out sofa in the pastor's office.

In the morning, when the trustees found the church littered with bodies, they ordered all of the supporters out. Sharpton was told to find another place of asylum for Glenda.

Sharpton did not puzzle over it long—and wondered why he had not thought of his second choice first. He called his old friend from the days of the Southern Christian Leadership Conference's Operation Breadbasket, the Reverend William A. Jones, pastor of Bethany Baptist Church in Brooklyn. Since April, the Brawley advisers had been holding rallies at his church, using it as a base for a political drive that would result, they vowed, in blacks gaining control of City Hall in 1989.

Jones quickly agreed to provide sanctuary for Glenda. Indeed, he had been miffed when Sharpton had chosen Mitchell's church first, giving it a windfall of publicity that he felt was due Bethany. Preachers were notorious for their rivalries: the most fiery orator, the best choir, the largest collection, the best-looking women in the congregation.

Jones, Sharpton, and other strategists met for more than two hours on the morning of June 10, considering various cloak-and-dagger scenarios for smuggling Glenda Brawley ten miles across enemy territory to Bethany Baptist Church. Finally they settled on Sharpton's ingeniously simple idea: they walked out the front door, got in the car, and drove to Brooklyn trailing a ten-car caravan of unruly reporters.

At Bethany, there were no petty rules, and the trustees didn't dictate to Jones. The place quickly took on the look of a fortress preparing for Armageddon. The entrances were sealed off and guarded by members of Sharpton's black army, a ragtag troupe of youths and men who included a rap singer, a mail carrier, a school custodian, retired teachers, a preacher, and several men who lived at a YMCA and found the accommodations at Bethany more amenable. They wore dark pants, white short-sleeved shirts, red bow ties, and sunglasses—just enough like Louis Farrakhan's Fruit of Islam to confuse some members of the press corps. The cognoscenti called them "the Fake Fruit."

Enhancing the sense of danger, doctors, nurses, and other volunteers set up an emergency medical center in the church to treat casualties in case the state sent in the riot troops. The volunteers for guard and medical duty were all screened by Sharpton and his handpicked aides, including an elderly security chief known as Mister Dix. The recruiting guidelines were simple: if they did not know someone, he or she was barred. They were determined to have no spies in their midst.

While the church was being made secure, other volunteers rushed about transforming a choir rehearsal room into Glenda Brawley's suite. It had most of the comforts of home. There was a sitting room for receiving guests and separate sleeping quarters for Glenda and Tyice. Someone brought in four cots. Others brought pillows and bedding. Sharpton's mother contributed a color television set. Someone else gave stereo equipment. Suitcases of clothing, a whole wardrobe for Glenda and Tyice, were brought from Wappingers Falls. Across the hall, another room was transformed into Sharpton's combination office–dressing room–bedroom; several of his garish running suits drooped there on hooks.

Women brought prepared dishes, but the bulk of the food for Glenda and her family, her advisers, and supporters came from black-owned restaurants, including Edgar's Food Shop. John Beatty, owner of the Cotton Club in Harlem, came out nearly every evening with food donated by Copeland's and Sylvia's, well-known Harlem establishments whose owners wanted to show solidarity with the cause.

Not everyone in the Bethany congregation approved. Some thought the church should be used for purely religious activities, certainly not for anything as controversial as the Brawley case. A few days after Glenda's arrival, the grumbling in the neighborhood started:

"What's she doing? This is a church!"

"This is embarrassing the church. . . ."

But Reverend Jones's support for sanctuary silenced most of the critics.

It was like an extended vacation for Glenda Brawley. She watched television, did some knitting, answered scores of letters from across the nation, and wrote thank-you cards to those who had volunteered time, money, or goods to make her life easier. She often took the sun on the church roof, and one day they had a rooftop barbecue. The only thing she couldn't do was leave.

With sanctuary came celebrity, a life of ease, and a respite from her uneasy domestic relationship with Ralph King. Men and women, convinced that their presence was all that prevented the state from invading, waited on her every whim, bringing her sodas, styling her hair, caring for her growing wardrobe, keeping little Tyice entertained.

At five o'clock every afternoon, an instructor stopped in to lead Glenda and her female supporters in aerobics exercises on the roof. Afterward came dinner, and then Glenda received visitors. One of them was the mother of Michael Griffith, the young man killed in the Howard Beach case. The wives of local clergymen visited her, as did Sharpton's mother.

Occasionally, King visited the church. So, too, did Tawana, who often went to the roof to practice dance routines with her new friend, Loryn Canton, the daughter of Roy Canton, one of the Brawleys' most devoted camp followers and an Edgar's regular.

Another of Glenda's frequent visitors was Professor William Mackey, a leader of the Edgar's crowd. She smiled and talked to him in her down-home drawl about the kindness of strangers who were supporting her, and the Professor sensed that she was naive: not quite aware of what was going on around her, not conversant with—indeed, overwhelmed by—the social and political implications of her daughter's case. He met Tawana, too. Her eyes were open and trusting, far from the conniving vixen being portrayed in the white press. It was, he thought, like looking into the unworldly eyes of a granddaughter.

Mackey, who was well versed in the biblical and medieval history of sanctuary, regarded the tactic's use in the Brawley case as ingenious. "It's a brilliant political stroke," the Professor reported back to the regulars at Edgar's, "because now if the authorities go and arrest her, they are violating one of the oldest principles. So they can't do a damn thing. It embarrasses the system. Anything that embarrasses these bastards—that shows up the hypocrisy—I'm for it."

Every night, security was provided by thirty men. They patrolled the sidewalks and the roof and took occasional breaks, watching television or playing cards.

Glenda told reporters she could have stayed a long time. "I like being pampered," she admitted. "I like being spoiled."

But as days turned into weeks and the anticipated police assault did not materialize, tensions faded into boredom and Glenda grew restless. There were family problems: Juanita, somewhat adrift since the breakup of her marriage, had been arrested for passing bad checks and served a fifteen-day jail sentence. Glenda was upset that King was staying away for days at a time, and Tawana wanted to know why no one was paying any attention to her up in Monticello.

There were deeper stirrings in Glenda, too, about the case and her role in it. She began to insist that Maddox and Mason, who rarely came to the church, brief her on what was happening in the case. The long hours of thinking about it, perhaps something in Professor Mackey's wisdom, had begun like a loose tooth to trouble her.

24

Perry McKinnon was exhausted, but sleep would not come. He brooded again in the recliner with the shades down and the numbing television images flickering on his face in the dark. Memories came at him in jumbled rushes like the machine-gun fire in Vietnam, only these were worse: you could bury your face in the mud when a rocket screamed out of the tree line, but you couldn't escape the conspiracies of your friends or Al Sharpton's unforgiving eyes.

He was exhausted. That was the trouble with security work. People thought it was exciting, but it was really long hours of useless watching, a drudgery of waiting for things that never happened. There was too much time to think, to brood. And at night there was no relief from the hammering clock and the TV images of Sharpton, Maddox, and Mason telling lies, from memories of men counting money in the back of a church and burying the truth about Tawana Brawley.

When he went out, the torment went with him. He watched people starting cars, hurrying to work, but life's routine somehow only increased his anxiety, and he took his demons back to the recliner.

It had been more than a month since the collapse of his friendship with Al Sharpton, and it still didn't seem real. Nothing seemed as real as Sharpton. McKinnon's childhood in Reidsville, Georgia, his youthful obscurity in Harlem, even the agonies in

Vietnam were dim and faraway things. But he could recall like yesterday his meeting with Sharpton in 1985 at St. Mary's Hospital in Brooklyn. McKinnon had been a security official there, and Sharpton had come across the hall from his National Youth Movement office to chat.

McKinnon had always had big plans. At that time, he had dreamed of setting up a company that would handle security for the developer Donald Trump, boxing promoter Don King, and other celebrities. Sharpton said he might be able to help: he knew the big shots. But McKinnon would need to be bonded for security work, and that cost money. In the meantime, Sharpton said, why not come to work for me?

Sharpton was like a god descended to transform him. McKinnon's service as his bodyguard, chauffeur, and confidant had been the best time of his life. He traveled around the nation and met the rich and famous. He heard their secrets. He was sought out by New York reporters as an insider and saw his ideas in print and on television. He took calls from congressmen and Hollywood stars. After a lifetime of obscurity, he was finally somebody.

But things began to go wrong in the spring of 1988. Reporters didn't rely on him anymore. Neither did Sharpton or his friends, Maddox and Mason, despite his offers to investigate the Brawley case for them. And he began to see strange things: the piles of money people sent to them, a lack of interest in the facts, a cynicism toward the people who believed in them, and finally, outright lies.

In May, as tensions over the case mounted between them, Sharpton and McKinnon had parted company. Sharpton had gone on with the case, but McKinnon had retreated into his private world and had brooded about it for weeks. He grew increasingly haggard, looking older than his thirty-nine years. He picked up a few odd jobs as a guard, but he spent nights alone, poring over newspapers, watching television, tracking developments in the saga from which he had been excluded. More and more, he was haunted by the vision of America's races being pushed by his old friends toward some cataclysm.

It was hard to say when the idea of giving Sharpton away first occurred to him. In his world of exaggerated dangers, a threat was a crisis and a crisis was disaster, and Glenda Brawley's defiance of a grand jury subpoena in Poughkeepsie and her removal to a Queens church seemed ominous to him: they transported the dangers from a quiet countryside to the heart of racial hostility in the city. And then the advisers had moved Glenda to Bethany Baptist Church in the Bedford-Stuyvesant section of Brooklyn, where law was suspect and riots were only a gunshot away.

On Friday, June 10—the day Glenda arrived in Brooklyn—he resolved to act. He thought first of going to the authorities, but decided against it. The advisers had stalemated the authorities for six months. What good could they do?

McKinnon next thought of M. A. Farber, a reporter he trusted. He called *The New York Times*, but Farber's telephone rang and rang into the busy newsroom; Farber and his colleague Ralph Blumenthal had gone to Albany to interview Cuomo on the case. Later, McKinnon tried again, but there was still no answer.

He decided to call Anna Phillips and Mike Taibbi, the producer-reporter team covering the story for WCBS-TV. He sketched his tale. They were interested, but not so much as to disrupt the weekend. They agreed to meet Monday.

The weekend was a year for McKinnon. He was waiting in Shopsin's General Store, a small restaurant on Bedford Street in Greenwich Village, when Taibbi and Phillips arrived on Monday morning. Nervous, disheveled, perspiring, McKinnon poured out his soul for six hours. They heard him out and arranged to get it on videotape the next day.

They met at the St. Moritz Hotel on Central Park South, and after the taping Taibbi and Phillips said casually that they wanted McKinnon to take a lie-detector test. He was taken aback, especially after a polygraph expert, Victor Kaufman, walked in. The whole thing looked like a setup. Didn't they trust him? They explained that there was bound to be a heavy reaction, and the test results would help them rebut it.

Afterward, McKinnon went home. He expected to see the report on the five o'clock news, and when there was nothing on the air, it occurred to him that they were suppressing it. In fact, by the time Taibbi and Phillips had finished editing the long tape, it was too late for the early evening news, and they decided to hold it for the next day rather than go on at eleven P.M. and let the newspapers grab all the headlines in the morning.

The worried McKinnon, however, had called Richard T. Pienciak of the *Daily News*. Pienciak wasted no time. "Sharpton ex-Aide: It's a 'Pack of Lies,' " the tabloid's headline shrieked in the morning. His story on Wednesday, June 15, quoted McKinnon as saying Sharpton had long harbored serious doubts about Tawana's story and that the advisers were all exploiting a hoax for their own purposes.

Taibbi, chagrined at the loss of an exclusive story he had known about since the previous Friday, rushed his report onto the air at noon. "A pack of lies," a WCBS-TV anchorwoman intoned. "With those brief but explosive words, a member of the team advising Tawana Brawley has all but demolished her story of kidnapping and rape at the hands of six white men in Dutchess County. And he has virtually destroyed the credibility of those who claim to represent her." Paraphrasing McKinnon, Taibbi said: "There was no case, only a media show." The Brawley advisers, as he put it, had been "making it up as they went along."

Sounding and looking more astute than reporters had ever seen him, sounding in fact as if he were reading from a prepared script, McKinnon said: "The Tawana Brawley story may be that there is no Tawana Brawley story. The real story is the political agenda of Sharpton, Maddox, and Mason." As far back as January, he said, he had had a "gut feeling" something was wrong; later, when he tried to warn them that Tawana might be lying, they were not interested. The case was unsupported by facts, and the charges against Steven Pagones, the Ku Klux Klan, the Mafia, and the Irish Republican Army were all lies: "A lot of things that were said at news conferences were instantaneous, unplanned, out of emotion."

McKinnon said he had helped count thousands of dollars solicited for the Brawleys, even after Sharpton expressed doubts about the case. He said sums ranging from $1,500 to $4,300 had been collected at church rallies, and envelopes with money continually arrived at Maddox's and Mason's offices. "And they allegedly gave all of this to the Brawley family," McKinnon said skeptically.

"This case is not about Tawana," he said. "It's about Mason, Maddox, and Sharpton sort of taking over the town." As Sharpton had put it to them, McKinnon said: "We beat this, we'll be the biggest niggers in New York."

"What am I trying to accomplish?" McKinnon said. "The truth. And I don't care if I'm by myself. Let me tell you something: that's where your manhood starts, with the truth."

That afternoon, the crowd clustering at the NBC studios at Rockefeller Center in midtown Manhattan expected a Phil Donahue show on how to sue doctors. Instead, they were herded onto buses, a hundred people, most of them white, and whisked off for an adventure in Bedford-Stuyvesant.

Once there, they filed into the Bethany Baptist Church and joined hundreds of blacks who had gathered in support of Glenda Brawley. For twenty years, Donahue had hosted shows on drug addiction, sexual perversities, and a thousand other human conflicts, but he had never presided over anything like this: an emotional national news story in the midst of a breaking controversy, a perfect coup in his ratings war with ABC's Oprah Winfrey.

With the press hovering and cameras jockeying for position, with a line of black paramilitary skirmishers guarding against an invasion by authorities, the Donahue fans—and a rapt nationwide audience of millions—were treated to the spectacle of Sharpton, Maddox, Mason, and Glenda Brawley entering like gladiators, fists raised in a black-power salute, and a madly cheering crowd.

Glenda Brawley said little, and the advisers managed to deflect most of Donahue's questions.

"That's not the point," Sharpton kept saying. "The point is . . ."

"If Tawana was a white girl, you wouldn't make us prove how the crime happened," Sharpton said. "But because she's black she's got to prove herself. You know it, Phil, and I know it. The fact that you've got five hundred black people in this room and every one of them has got a different complexion means that white rape is a reality in the United States."

Cheers and applause erupted. A few whites who tried to raise questions were shouted down. The advisers finally got around to McKinnon, denouncing him as a liar and a fraud. But they did not waste precious national airtime on him. Instead, they castigated Cuomo and Abrams, trumpeted the rape story, and, not least, got their faces before an enormous public. McKinnon had had a New York audience, but they had reached the American people. "If I die tonight, at least I did my job," an elated Sharpton said later. "At least we made the national media come into the ghetto and deal with race relations in New York."

Later, they let McKinnon have it. "Perry McKinnon is a bald-faced liar and a desperate man," Maddox said. "I never discussed any aspect of the case with him."

Sharpton said that McKinnon had known nothing about their beliefs, strategy, or evidence. "He handled a lot of things for me, like personal stuff, getting me hotel rooms, troubleshooting, talking to the press, coming back to me and telling me what this guy was saying or that guy was saying," Sharpton said. But McKinnon was an incompetent investigator and an unkempt companion: "He just wasn't going anywhere, and I kept getting heat from Maddox and them that his hygiene wasn't proper for what I wanted to do. One of the reasons Maddox and them didn't want him around was his appearance. Perry would tend to wear the same thing for a week. He was not the most fumigated guy around." So, Sharpton said, he had called McKinnon in early May and said: "Man, you've got to take a walk."

By morning, every newspaper and radio and television station in New York—and even the national news agencies and television networks—had run stories on McKinnon's charges and the advisers' reactions. The McKinnon story was a catharsis, not only for the press, but for thousands of ordinary people and even government and law-enforcement officials who had been reluctant to call it a hoax—whites for fear of being seen as racist, blacks for fear of being called Uncle Toms. Mario Cuomo said McKinnon's statements required a whole new look at the case, and Robert Abrams, defending McKinnon, said he was now investigating a possible hoax and would invite McKinnon to testify before the grand jury.

But there was more, and from McKinnon's perspective it was all bad. To discredit him, the advisers produced a cousin, Al McKinnon, from Harlem. He said that Perry was mentally disturbed as a result of his combat experience in Vietnam. Reporters who had heard Perry speak of his three tours in Vietnam and his three bronze stars and other medals for valor were surprised to hear Al McKinnon say Perry had been in Vietnam only a year and had come home shell-shocked and undergone treatment by Army psychiatrists. After his discharge in 1971, Al said, Perry had wandered around for three years. He had then worked as a park laborer and a part-time policeman in Reidsville and had been a security guard at several Brooklyn hospitals before meeting Sharpton.

The advisers also produced a woman who identified herself as Aljetta McKinnon. She had married Perry in Georgia in 1976 and was still his wife. Sharpton said McKinnon had also married Gwendolyn Dingle—and several other women—in New York, and he suggested a prosecution "for bigamy or trigamy." He also had a new version of why he and McKinnon had split up. He said he had demanded from McKinnon an accounting of youth movement funds, and that McKinnon had walked out in response. "The only pack of lies he knows," Sharpton said, "is his life."

McKinnon acknowledged some of this when questioned by the grand jury and reporters. It wasn't true that he had served three tours in Vietnam and had many medals for valor. He had been there once, had won a bronze star, and had suffered a combat-related nervous condition from "grenades and bombs." He had been treated by Army psychiatrists. And he did have two wives. But that, he said, was just a matter of incomplete paperwork for a divorce.

Yet the crucial question was what McKinnon really knew about the Brawley case, and the answer was not much. Reporters had seen him with Sharpton everywhere—at Sharpton's apartment in Brooklyn, at the Wyndham Hotel in Poughkeepsie, at Cuomo's office in Albany and Abrams's office in New York. McKinnon had been Sharpton's closest aide and had often spoken to the press for him—mainly because he had been more accessible than the busy Sharpton.

On closer scrutiny, however, it became evident to investigators and reporters that McKinnon was not the insider he had portrayed himself to be. Nor did he possess any vital evidence beyond his impressions of the case and of the advisers' views. He had not, after all, been present at their strategy sessions; nor had they discussed evidence in his presence. He had picked up a lot of hearsay about Maddox and Mason, but his direct knowledge was limited to Sharpton's private musings.

Moreover, even if Sharpton had harbored doubts about Tawana's story, it did not prove that the lawyers or the family had doubts. McKinnon had not had substantive contacts with the lawyers or the family—so what if the advisers had scorned his warnings? As for the money, he had been careful not to say that the advisers had pocketed any of it. Finally, under oath, McKinnon acknowledged that he knew nothing of what had really happened to Tawana between November 24 and 28.

Like so many others, he had had a "gut feeling," no more.

They met like agents on a rainy night, with fog heavy on the river and the lights of Manhattan glowing in the distance. He was waiting under a street lamp on a corner in Jersey City, a short, jittery young man with his collar turned up against the wind and his hands jammed in his pockets. The car pulled up beside him and he got in. He said his name was Samuel McClease, and he knew a place where they could talk.

McClease took them to the waterside skyscraper apartment of a fashion model, a friend who did not mind late-night visitors with private business. It was after midnight on Monday, June 20, when they settled on the couch in a room alive with shadows.

McClease seemed nervous. His palms were sweating and his eyes kept darting around.

"Show me the subpoenas," Mike Taibbi said. The WCBS-TV reporter and his producer had just been through the episode with Perry McKinnon, and they didn't want to take any chances.

McClease took out some papers. He had already showed them to Anna Phillips, and now Taibbi looked them over: an assistant United States attorney in New York, Federico Virella, had ordered Samuel Milton McClease to produce "all originals and copies of tape recordings and other forms of surveillance work performed by agreement with Al Sharpton and the Friends of the National Youth Movement."

The videotape camera rolled.

"I'm basically a surveillance expert," McClease said. "I bug houses." He described his methods and equipment and said: "I was contacted February third by Al Sharpton." Following instructions, he said, he had gone to Riverside Park on Manhattan's West Side and met Sharpton. Their talk was brief, he said, and he reconstructed it:

Sharpton: "What are you going to do?"

McClease: "I'll do anything you want me to do."

Sharpton: "I'll be in touch."

Two weeks later, McClease said, he planted eavesdropping devices for Sharpton at three locations—Sharpton's Brooklyn apartment and C. Vernon Mason's office in lower Manhattan and the lawyer's home in Harlem. Each device was voice activated and hooked up to a tape recorder, McClease said. There were other details: Sharpton had agreed to pay him eleven thousand dollars for the job; fifteen hours of conversations had been recorded. Sharpton had said he wanted the tapes to protect himself because the Brawley case was coming apart.

Only a brief segment of the tapes was important, McClease

313

said. In it, one of the Brawley lawyers—he did not know who—called Tawana's story "bull," made derogatory remarks about her, and, as McClease put it, "discussed the four days of the alleged kidnapping not to be a kidnapping but actually a four-day party." McClease quoted the voices on the tape as saying there had been no abduction and no rape, that Tawana had been partying with a white police officer.

McClease said his conscience had led him to blow the whistle, but something he had said earlier—that Sharpton had not paid him—seemed a more likely motive. And to Taibbi, there was another hitch: McClease didn't have the tapes—they were, he said, in a safe place with a friend. At Taibbi's urging, McClease went into the next room and made a telephone call. He dialed seven digits—they counted them—and spoke for several minutes.

When he came out, he seemed shaken. He said he would not be able to get the tapes until noon, and the subpoena called for him to produce them before a federal grand jury in Manhattan at ten A.M. It was already three o'clock in the morning. Before they parted, he promised to let Taibbi and Phillips listen to and dub some of the tapes, and they promised not to air the story until later in the day.

McClease did not show up with the tapes, either for the grand jury or at WCBS-TV. He called Taibbi late the following morning and said there would be a delay. The station decided to run the story anyway—that night—over the entreaties of Rudolph Giuliani, the United States attorney in Manhattan, who wanted Taibbi to hold off until authorities could get corroboration by wiring McClease for a talk with Sharpton. Taibbi, who had just learned that a WNBC-TV reporter, David Diaz, was onto the story, and feared that he might be scooped again, refused. And so Taibbi aired his "exclusive"—while neglecting to point out he did not have the tapes, that his story rested solely on his glimpse of the subpoena, and on McClease's word.

"Why come forward now?" Taibbi asked a tired-looking McClease on the videotape, which was broadcast on news programs at five P.M., six P.M., and eleven P.M.

"After, uh, when it first came to me it was, uh, gosh I really can't say," McClease stammered. "Something to do—but I believe for some ungodly reason—something to believe in. I felt that, you know, he was, uh, trying to right something that was basically wrong. That's the way I felt."

For all his inarticulateness, McClease's story of fraud in the Brawley camp was electrifying. It was immediately picked up by the press, and for the second time in a week, Maddox, Mason, and Sharpton found themselves on the defensive.

They emerged from a heated meeting at Maddox's office to reassert their solidarity. Mason raked McClease for "defiling" his home, though there was no evidence that he had done anything but appear on television. Sharpton said he had never even met McClease and posed the question at the heart of it: "Where are the tapes?"

McClease himself was nowhere to be found.

Investigators and reporters quickly discovered that McClease was at best an amiable braggart and at worst an unstable liar who for years had misrepresented his credentials, activities, and means. He had bragged about having been a Navy intelligence expert when actually he had been a mechanic who was discharged for unauthorized absences. He had called himself a "surveillance expert," when what he'd really done was progress from selling tickets in a movie theater in Key West, to operating lights in a disco in Virginia Beach, to selling audio equipment in New York. People who knew him said he liked to look at expensive apartments as a prospective buyer and try out foreign cars like a big spender, but in fact had no money and lived in a Jersey City slum. M. A. Farber tracked down McClease's ex-wife, Linda, in Virginia Beach. "He's a pathological liar, very manipulative, cunning, and a man who always wants to be at the center of attention," she told Farber.

A warrant for McClease's arrest had been issued after his failure to appear before the grand jury, and he surrendered the next day. Another court order was issued, and he was released to get the tapes. The FBI was supposed to tail him, but lost the trail. Two days later, he appeared at Giuliani's office with ten tapes.

While McClease waited in a lockup, Giuliani, Robert Abrams, and other officials met that night at Giuliani's office to hear what was on the tapes. As a routine precaution to safeguard the originals, they had the tapes duplicated on high-speed audio equipment. Then, while Giuliani and Abrams adjourned to the library for pizza and a baseball game on television, agents began rolling the tapes for two prosecutors.

Hours later, the door to the library opened. Abrams knew something was wrong as soon as he saw the prosecutors' faces.

The first sign had been the needle on the monitor. It had not moved throughout the dubbing. They had heard nothing at all.

When they told McClease (who would later be acquitted of perjury and obstruction charges), he looked surprised: somebody, he said, must have switched the tapes on him.

25

There were two "truths": the one offered by the state's officers of the law and reported by the white media, the other offered by the Brawleys and their advisers and reported by black newspapers, including *The City Sun*, and WLIB. The white media was skeptical of the Brawley story; the black press believed that it was another milestone on its long crusade to fight racial injustice and to promote the self-esteem of black people.

The American black press, which Gunnar Myrdal had described in his classic study *An American Dilemma* as "the greatest single force in the Negro race," traced its origins to 1827 with the launching of *Freedom's Journal* in New York, and that paper's credo could still serve the nation's two hundred fifty black-owned newspapers and such nationally circulated magazines as *Ebony, Jet, Essence,* and *Black Enterprise*: "We want to plead our own cause," John B. Russwurm and the Reverend Samuel E. Cornish wrote in the first issue of *Freedom's Journal*. "Too long have others spoken for us. Too long has the publick been deceived by misrepresentations in things which concern us deeply."

Unlike the mainstream press, the black press had never pretended to be objective. For one hundred sixty years, it had been a vehicle of advocacy and protest, and its journalistic quality had never been high. Many readers had drifted away over the years. But as the Brawley case gained prominence, blacks who rarely read the *Amsterdam News* or *The City Sun* found themselves

317

doing so, and a large proportion of New York's blacks came to believe that black news outlets were their most reliable sources of information.

The City Sun, a weekly tabloid founded in Brooklyn by Andy Cooper in 1984, brought an aggressiveness to the coverage of politics and racial issues that had long been missing from the *Amsterdam News*, the Harlem weekly that claimed a circulation of thirty-five thousand, the largest of any black paper in the country. But *The City Sun* was not a circulation success.

Throughout the Brawley case, *The City Sun* had voiced its editorial position in support of Tawana Brawley in news articles as well as editorials. But it was not until Glenda Brawley was held in contempt of court and fled to sanctuary in New York that the case was joined to the old crusade.

On June 29, frustration boiled over into hysteria, with *The City Sun*'s red-letter, front-page banner: "TAWANA WAS RAPED." The story, by Utrice Leid, the paper's managing editor, said: "Documents obtained by *The City Sun* not only bear out major portions of her story, but also point to a concerted attempt by law-enforcement officials to cover up the crime, both at the initial stages of the investigation and very possibly even now in the current grand jury probe."

The story, whose underlying documents had been supplied by Maddox, contained a number of incontrovertible facts. But its bald conclusions rested almost entirely on misinterpretations of medical records and wholesale distortions of evidence. For example: "Tawana, then 15, would say later at a local hospital—where she had been taken by ambulance for treatment—that she was abducted by a group of white men, one of whom had a badge and was wearing a gun holster, and that she was raped repeatedly by as many as six of them. She would identify three of her attackers by name and give physical descriptions of others to the police."

Leid had accepted, without question or qualification, Juanita Brawley's earliest version of the story, as well as the subsequent embellishments of the Brawleys and their advisers. It was *they*—not the girl—who had said six white men had raped her, they who had named suspects.

And another example: *The City Sun* reported that when the scantily clad girl crawled into a garbage bag, "it was probably Tawana's last conscious act in a desperate struggle for survival. Had she not crawled into that bag, she might have died." She had suffered, Leid wrote, extensive burns on her hands and legs and cuts and bruises on various parts of her body. She had a swollen vagina, was unconscious, and had a white material on her tonsils. But none of this was true. Nor was it true, as Leid reported, that Tawana had been given a complete bath at St. Francis Hospital before the rape kit had been administered, that she had been discharged from the hospital "inexplicably," that the rape-kit specimens had not been properly safeguarded.

It was also not true, as Leid wrote, that the Westchester County Medical Center, where Tawana had been examined in December, "had come to believe Tawana was a rape victim." A hospital clerk had merely entered the numeric code for "rape" on a computerized billing form because under World Health Organization guidelines there was no numeric code for the hospital's actual diagnosis of "alleged sexual abuse."

But *The City Sun*'s article had a tremendous impact on other black media, which quickly picked up the story. *The City Sun* was praised for its enterprise by its rival the *Amsterdam News* and by WLIB radio. Even at the *Times*, several black reporters who had been skeptical of their own paper's coverage welcomed *The City Sun*'s account. After reexamining Tawana's hospital treatment and the handling of her rape-kit specimens, the *Times* stuck by its skepticism.

On a WABC-TV program, *Like It Is*, Utrice Leid defended her article against charges of distortion, insisting that there could no longer be any doubt that Tawana had been attacked. Pointing to a pile of documents on which she had allegedly drawn, she said triumphantly: "This settles it."

Ethelyn Smith sold out her first batch of papers by early morning. She usually took forty copies for the Wednesday crowd, but *The*

City Sun was not generally popular and she often had to return many of those copies to the distributor. But at midmorning, she telephoned the distributor and asked for another batch. Later she asked for another. By midafternoon, she had sold three times the usual number. And by the end of the day, it was impossible to find a copy of *The City Sun* at Edgar's or any other news outlet in New York City.

The regulars at Edgar's thought it was the best piece of journalism they had ever seen—by far the most comprehensive and truthful they had encountered on the Brawley case.

Ethelyn Smith was mesmerized by "all the documentation cited." What a difference between the Leid article and those reports in the white press, which had tried to make Sharpton, Maddox, Mason, and Tawana look like liars! "They're never useful to show that this young lady was violated," she said to Wayne Chinnery, Squire Bradfield, Roy Canton, and Professor Mackey. "But you can pick it up here." She waved Leid's article like a read-all-about-it news hawker. "*The City Sun* has given us the story as if we were *there*."

Chinnery was fuming. Never again would he tolerate talk about Tawana Brawley's being a liar. "If anybody ever talks about Tawana Brawley like that again, I will floor them!" he said, and the table shook under the elbows of this six-foot, two-inch lawyer, a former amateur boxer who had once flattened opponents all over the Caribbean.

Roy Canton could not understand why some black people found it so difficult to accept Tawana's story. "Caribbean people have no problem believing Tawana," he said, adding that it might be because Caribbean people were more aware of their history; because they were accustomed to having blacks in positions of authority; because they did not feel inferior, the way American blacks seemed to.

For hours, they sang the virtues of *The City Sun*, and eventually they got around to the McKinnon and McClease episodes.

Canton, as a member of Sharpton's black army who guarded Glenda at Bethany Baptist Church and ran errands for Sharpton, had seen McKinnon many times. Now he spoke with the authority of an eyewitness. From his first contacts with McKinnon back in December, he had had an uneasy feeling about Sharpton's side-kick: he was spooky, perhaps even loony—"he didn't look sta-ble." It was funny how Sharpton could have relied so much on McKinnon. "Sharpton is a very brilliant brother," Canton al-lowed, but he was surprised that the reverend "could not see through *this* brother like I did and a few other people did." Then he got to the charges: "I'll never believe that Sharpton told McKinnon that Tawana lied. Sharpton's life is on the line. Sharpton isn't partially involved. Sharpton is *totally* involved." Anyway, Canton went on, McKinnon had never been part of the inner circle. "There is *no way* Alton Maddox would have shared any information about the case with McKinnon. Maddox may be the most committed black man in America."

Someone mentioned McClease, and his name set off a howl of derision: he might as well have been a black Reagan Republican!

It was Professor Mackey who always tried to put characters and events into historical perspective. When three o'clock found him in the middle of a topic, Mrs. Smith just locked the door and kept the coffee cups filled at the back table so they could go on, sometimes two or three hours past closing time. The Professor had often spoken about what motivated white people, about how they plotted to discredit men like Marcus Garvey, Adam Clayton Powell, Jr., and other black heroes who had stood up to the system. Now he said: "They've done it before and now they're after Maddox, Mason, and Sharpton through McKinnon and McClease. America would do anything to destroy these guys' credibility." The McKinnon and McClease episodes were espe-cially dangerous, he pointed out, because they provided an ex-cuse for wavering blacks to abandon the Brawley cause. For too many blacks had failed to come to grips with racism. Too many deluded themselves into thinking everything was all right: "There seems to be a great reluctance, to put it mildly, on our part to really analyze and deal with the reality of our situation. We keep hoping that we'll wake up one morning and it will go away."

The good thing about the Brawley case, he went on, was that it presented blacks with an opportunity to jar loose suppressed memories. "The memory of our past is so painful to so many of our folks that they cannot deal with it. They prefer to say, like the old people used to say, that shit tastes like sugar. If I say that nothing happened to Tawana, then it's not incumbent upon me to do something about it. I can go on with my life. So the instinct, particularly with these second- and third-generation northern, urban African folks is to say that. Too many of them think that they're free, and they don't want to deal with the idea that this is up South as opposed to down South. The assumption is that this is different."

The others nodded knowingly, and even Squire Bradfield was struck, once more, by the power of the Professor's arguments. All afternoon, Bradfield had said little as the others marveled over the *Sun* article and shook their heads in dismay over the turncoats McKinnon and McClease. He couldn't help thinking that the *Sun* article was full of holes; that McKinnon, even if he *was* loony, had raised important questions about what Sharpton and the advisers believed; that McClease, for all his haplessness, had said something entirely believable: that the shrewd Sharpton had bugged his conversations with Maddox and Mason to give himself an out if things went wrong.

But Bradfield, normally a lively talker, kept his thoughts to himself. For the Professor and the others would ride him unmercifully—perhaps even scorn him as a traitor—if they suspected how troubled he really was.

26

As she entered the cool interior of the church, Tawana Brawley turned her back on the blazing sun and the milling crowds. All morning in the rising heat, they had gathered on Marcus Garvey Boulevard in Bedford-Stuyvesant like a town turning out for a carnival: children running through shimmering waves of radiance, hawkers selling "Justice for Tawana" buttons and the red, black, and green flags of black liberation; adults fanning themselves on the igneous pavement. Around the corner, out of sight, a chartered blue-and-white bus was parked—waiting to take her and her entourage to Atlanta and the Democratic National Convention.

Some of the onlookers were there out of curiosity, to watch Glenda Brawley emerge from Bethany Baptist Church after thirty-six days, to see the girl at the heart of the case. Some were there with a sense of dedication, not just to Tawana, but to a mother many thought of as a woman on a mission, a woman just like Fannie Lou Hamer, the sharecropper who had led the Mississippi Freedom Democratic Party to the Democratic Convention in Atlantic City in 1964 in an effort to unseat the state's all-white delegation. Some were there to "make history," to accompany the Brawleys like freedom riders. Some were there to guard Glenda from arrest. And some were there as spies for the police.

Tawana left the spectacle behind and joined Sharpton, Mason, Glenda, and Juanita at the pulpit. Only Maddox was missing; he had flown to Atlanta earlier in the day to take care of advance work for the Brawley delegation. But his wife, Leola Weaver, was standing in for him.

The crowds had already filled the pews, and the reporters, photographers, and television crews were ready. Some had copies of *The City Sun*, with a front-page picture of Tawana and the fiery headline: "It's War!" That rallying cry had been crafted at a Sharpton news conference a few days earlier, when he declared: "It will be an all-out war between the raped and the rapists of American history. Tawana Brawley will be the last known black rape victim after Atlanta. It's a war that has been building for four hundred years. Now the raped have decided to enter the battle-field and war with those who cover up the rape." And Glenda Brawley had added: "We will be on the move in Atlanta. We're in it for justice for all black people."

At the church, things were already hours late, but nothing on this steamy July 16 was to begin on time.

Sharpton, glittering like a carnival man in a blue sequin-trimmed silk shirt and matching bell-bottomed pants, started it off.

"No justice!" he shouted.

"No peace!" the crowd responded ritually.

Tawana Brawley, he announced, would serve as the delega-tion's "sergeant at arms." Nobody knew what it meant, but the packed church—electrified by the girl's presence—cheered wildly anyway.

Then Sharpton spoke of the "caravan of buses" that would take them storming down to Atlanta. (A few sentences later, he re-ferred to "the bus," and alert reporters knew it would be a caravan of one bus.) "If anybody bothers her or her mother, we will turn this state upside down," he went on, bringing the crowd to its feet. Voice booming, body rocking, hair bobbing, he had them now—in a whirlwind of rage and resolution: "We've got a message that the nation must hear! The Dixiecrats have moved north and they're operating in the Empire State!" Governor Cuomo had pulled the wool over the people's eyes: "He administrates the most racist state in these United States."

The crowd was near frenzy, but Sharpton was not satisfied. He lined Tawana, Glenda, and Juanita Brawley up near the altar, pulled out several pairs of handcuffs and linked them and himself together like a chain gang. They thrust their linked hands into the air. Photographers snapped the freedom fighters, and the audience erupted.

"No justice!"

"No peace!"

"When do we want it?"

"Now!"

Sharpton and the Brawleys filed offstage and went back to the rooms that had been Glenda Brawley's home and Sharpton's office for five weeks. There, out of sight of the crowd, they removed the handcuffs. Juanita kicked off her shoes. King bounced Tyice on his shoulder, Tawana and Glenda relaxed to await the departure, and Sharpton and Mason huddled to lay final plans for the journey.

The small cluster of black newspaper and television reporters were talking quietly among themselves in the church basement when they were suddenly confronted by Brawley supporters, including a bow-tied soldier in Sharpton's putative black army. How, one supporter demanded, could blacks, especially women like E. R. Shipp of the *Times* and Sheryl McCarthy of *New York Newsday*, disseminate news stories suggesting that Tawana Brawley was a liar?

A vague response by the reporters brought on harsher accusations. Voices rose. The crowd grew large. Then it got ugly. "Uncle Tom!" "Aunt Tomasina!" "Traitors!" The accusations struck like machine-gun fire. The reporters shot back: "Naive!" "Illogical!"

One of Sharpton's "soldiers" thrust his face forward, as if to strike or be struck. "Nine times out of ten," he screamed, "when a black woman says she was raped, she *was!*"

"But what about that one time out of ten?" Shipp retorted, eyeball to eyeball. "Shouldn't we question whether *this* is that one time out of ten?"

"Well," said a tall black woman, "Utrice Leid said she was

raped." It was a lot to go into right then and there, and fortu-
nately they were pulled back from the brink with another call to
arms: it was time to board the bus.

Once again, the Brawleys and Sharpton were in handcuffs as
they came out of the church blinking in the late-afternoon sun, as
they made their way through the parting crowd. For the first time
since June 10, Glenda Brawley had left the church. Police surveillance teams had been lurking around all day, but no one moved
to intercept her. Roy Canton and many other men were ready to
stand and fight, and the authorities realized that to seize Glenda
outside the church would risk a riot.

Crowding onto the bus with the Brawleys and their advisers
were forty-nine supporters; four reporters, representing the *Times*,
the *Daily News*, the *Post*, and *Big Red*, a black newspaper; and a
Post photographer. Two bus drivers had been hired to spell each
other and keep the bus moving. Fourteen men—most of them
members of Sharpton's "army"—had no seats and stood in the
aisle.

As the overloaded bus chugged away from the cheering masses,
some of the older men and women on board were overcome with
the historical magnitude of it all.

"What a day!" a woman exclaimed.

"What a memory!" said another.

"Beautiful people! Beautiful!"

They rolled out of the slums of Brooklyn, passed the towers of
Manhattan, and shot into the Holland Tunnel under the Hudson—
the longer, more anonymous route out of New York City. Halfway through the tunnel, they crossed into New Jersey and freedom
for Glenda, who was subject to arrest on the contempt charge
only in New York. There were shouts of triumph and palm-
slapping high fives. Ralph King with little Tyice tooted the Lincoln's horn behind them. It all seemed a bit exaggerated. But
state troopers had in fact been staked out on the Verrazano-
Narrows Bridge that linked Brooklyn and Staten Island, with

orders to intercept the bus and seize Glenda Brawley. To Attorney General Abrams and his investigators, that had seemed the most direct route to the South. What they didn't know was that Sharpton had an appointment in Newark.

As the trip began, Sharpton and Mason—who had just returned from a two-week trip to Africa and was wearing a tan safari-style shirt—led the bus in ragged renditions of the black national anthem, "Lift Ev'ry Voice and Sing," and "Amen" and "We Shall Not Be Moved," old spirituals with the occasional new lyrics, such as, "Tell Governor Cuomo / We shall not be moved." More verses named Abrams, Rudolph Giuliani, Glenda and Tawana Brawley, Maddox, Mason, and Sharpton. Mason added another ("Tell all the press folks / We shall not be moved"), which he reinforced by pointing at the journalists and sticking out his tongue.

In downtown Newark, the bus halted abruptly, and King's Lincoln and a carload of Louis Farrakhan's Fruit of Islam pulled up alongside. Sharpton, Mason, and the Brawleys got into the cars, explaining that they had to run an errand and promising to be back in twenty minutes. Two hours later, they returned. They had all had dinner with Farrakhan to confer on plans for Atlanta. Somehow, during the wait, the bus had gotten a flat tire. By the time it was changed, it was nearly nine o'clock in the evening, as they rumbled back onto the New Jersey Turnpike and headed south.

Standees were illegal on a bus, and every time they approached a toll booth, the men in the aisle fell to the floor. Sleep and normal conversation were out of the question. Several riders had brought boom-box tape decks the size of suitcases, which blasted a cacophony of jazz, Afro-Caribbean music, Louis Farrakhan speeches, and Maddox-Mason-Sharpton talk on WLIB all the way to Washington.

Early in the morning, they pulled into Dulles International Airport, where they failed to find rental cars for the standees. After two hours spent trying to locate National Airport, they managed to rent several cars, and the standees rubber-legged off the bus. South they went—through Virginia, through North and South Carolina, and finally into Georgia.

Sharpton and Glenda Brawley were bright as buttons. They summoned the reporters to the front of the bus for a rolling news conference. "I think it's fantastic," Glenda gushed, eyes twinkling. She looked like a Florida tourist in a black T-shirt and figure-hugging white pants. "The escape plan was excellent. I've never been afraid. I have too much support, too much backing." She ribbed Abrams again. "He has met his competition and he has not yet begun to hear from the black community. This is the tip of the iceberg."

Shouts of encouragement from behind the reporters further inspired her: "Abrams is afraid of me, very afraid of me," she said, "because he wants to know what *I* know, and what *I* know can destroy his political career, along with everybody's that's concerned!"

Sharpton's sights were higher: he vowed to capture the attention of the nation and Michael S. Dukakis, the probable Democratic presidential nominee. He hinted that he was planning a major disruption of the proceedings. And once again he dangled the hope that Tawana would tell her story as soon as the racist grand jury completed its whitewash. Then, he would lead a host to Albany to demand a legitimate special prosecutor.

Throughout the trip, Tawana sat beside Sharpton near the front of the bus. She dozed or passed the hours talking quietly to Sharpton, turning occasionally to speak to Mason, Glenda, or Juanita. She ignored the reporters and the other passengers. Like the other members of her family, she had begun to act like a celebrity. A new aloofness, almost a haughtiness, had been noticeable in her demeanor in the church and on the bus: you could see it in the upturned chin, the cool distant eyes, and the confident step. The role of heroine, the months of publicity, had changed her—the awkward teenager had become a young woman with a mission and a bold presence, and the crowds sensed it. They watched her with a kind of awe, and she gave them a marble exterior, the glazed face that can only be worshipped from a distance. Her reddish-brown hair was pushed up in curls and swept to one side with a stylish adult flair. She wore white shorts and a white T-shirt with "Don't Even Think About Defeat" lettered in red, black, and green on the front. During Glenda's news conference, Tawana sat curled up on the seat next to Sharpton, looking bored to death with all the fierce vows, all the scribbling in notebooks. She hardly bothered to look up. But when Shipp asked what she thought about all this, Tawana found the energy to say: "I hate the press."

And they rolled on into Atlanta.

Most of the true believers had paid three hundred dollars that they could ill afford—some had even taken unpaid leaves of absence from work. They were not starry-eyed idealists. Many of them had lived hard lives and sacrificed enormously for their families. They were courageous people, willing to put themselves and their meager resources on the line for their belief in Tawana Brawley and her cause. To them, justice was not a word in the Constitution; it wasn't a "right." It meant more than glory or even life itself, and if you couldn't get it, you had nothing.

Elsie Brown was one of them. A friendly, rotund native of Barbados in her late fifties, she had lived in Harlem for more than forty years. A great-grandmother, she had raised families, run community service programs in Harlem and the Bronx, and fought all her life for civil rights and dignity. At the last minute, she had despaired of being able to raise the three hundred dollars for the trip. But a favorite nephew had given her the money—it was his way of contributing to the cause, too—and she had taken time off from her job at a company that conducted public-opinion polls.

"This is a very important time in our history," she told E. R. Shipp, her seatmate in the back of the bus. "It's very meaningful, and people have to participate."

Because of her weight and her weak legs, she wondered whether she would be able to keep up with the others on all the marches and demonstrations in Atlanta. But she was determined to try.

"We're going there not only for the Tawana Brawley situation, which is horrendous," she said, "but also for Jesse Jackson." She noted that Dukakis had already named Lloyd Bentsen as his running mate and had not even told Jackson before announcing it to the public. "The way he was treated offended all of us," she said.

"We're going to send a message, no matter how small it may seem," she went on. "We are aware of the shenanigans and also the extremes they would go to to humiliate us."

Elsie Brown, as a mother, was convinced that Tawana had been raped by white men. "The girl definitely had to be assaulted. I mean, no one in their right mind would have done that to themselves."

A light rain began to fall as they drew near their destination. They had endured twenty hours on a bus with cramped, uncomfortable seats and a toilet that stank. Trying to make up for the time lost in New Jersey, Sharpton and Mason had ordered the drivers to go straight through Sunday without stopping. Tempers had flared, and they had relented to avoid a mutiny. Now, as the Atlanta skyline rose up in the distance, the riders were exhausted but buoyant, looking forward to a heroes' welcome in the capital of the New South.

It was sweltering in the massive old Wheat Street Baptist Church on Auburn Avenue. Black people were packed into every seat and along the walls and vestibule on the main floor, and the balcony was filled with more people. The men suffered in dark suits; women in Sunday dresses and colorful African ensembles fanned themselves. The air-conditioning was out.

They had heard several hours of droning from the pulpit, but now they were spellbound: Louis Farrakhan had risen, and his now-soothing, now-menacing calypso voice was guiding them through a netherworld of black history posted with verses from the Koran and the Bible and visions of racial conflict and death at the hands of vicious white men. His face glowed with serenity in the thrall of catastrophe, the eyes calm behind the leaping flames.

This was Farrakhan's show—a daylong Black Agenda Conference, a sort of alternative convention for disenchanted blacks, mostly Muslims and other pan-Africanists. Alton Maddox was there too. The meeting had been planned for Atlanta's Morris Brown College, part of the world's largest consortium of black colleges. But at the last minute, the school's administrators had backed out. Farrakhan had transferred it to this venerable church in the heart of a national historic district a few blocks from Martin Luther King, Jr.'s birthplace and the Ebenezer Baptist Church, which had been led by King's family since 1894.

Farrakhan was well into a new diatribe against Dukakis and the Democrats when word came that the Brawley bus had arrived. He quickly dispatched aides to bring in the Brawleys and their advisers. But their companions were stopped at the door.

They had ridden almost around the clock. And they had expected cheers for their efforts. Instead, at the door, they were body searched, the men by the grim-faced guards of Farrakhan's Fruit of Islam, the women by the auxiliary.

Tawana, still in her white shorts and T-shirt, was beckoned to the pulpit and Farrakhan's embrace. "If Tawana was white, there would be no question about it," he intoned. "But they don't think black women can be raped. This is why the media tries to portray her as a temptress and a seductress." His stentorian voice suddenly boomed: "But we're not going for that. We're going to get justice one way or another!"

Pounding applause echoed from the rafters.

Next, Farrakhan called Maddox, Mason, and Sharpton to stand beside him. "The courts cannot do justice by us," he said. These three men, he told them, had had the courage to challenge the system, and now they were being depicted as wicked by Mario Cuomo and Robert Abrams.

"*They* are the criminals," Farrakhan cried. "You see, the Bible tells us, an eye for an eye!"

"Yeah!" the crowd shouted.

". . . a tooth for a tooth!"

"Yeah!"

". . . a life for a life!"

"Yeah!"

The thunder rolled on: "There's a time coming when we will find the rapists and we will deliver justice," Farrakhan vowed. In the meantime, blacks must refuse to serve in the military forces, refuse to pay income taxes if the white abuses continued. If all else failed, blacks should form their own nation.

He turned again to Tawana. "She's a beautiful girl, a highly intelligent girl who suffered, who for more than thirty days could not walk. But look at her now!" He beamed as the audience applauded. "And look at her mom, who stood so strongly at her side!"

Then Tawana stepped to the microphone and the place fell silent. "I'm a little nervous," she said in her sweet Michael Jackson voice. She thanked Farrakhan, Sharpton, her mother, her lawyers. "I just want to thank everybody for standing by me."

"We love you, sister!" a man shouted from the balcony, and the church rocked with cheers.

Riding the wave, Farrakhan led them all in the Muslim chant: "Allah akbar! Allah akbar! Allah akbar!" God is great!

Finally, they rose, a thousand people who had made a commitment to Tawana Brawley. They moved slowly through the vestibule and out into the hot Atlanta evening, hushed by a just cause and the image of that innocent, violated face.

The Brawley entourage did not stay in Atlanta. Instead, they drove fifteen miles east to Decatur and checked in at a Best Western motel. The Brawleys were given a large suite on the ground floor near the swimming pool. Sharpton also took a suite. But the supporters who had paid three hundred dollars each were packed as many as four to a room. Each day during the convention, the entourage boarded the bus for the ride into Atlanta and back again in the evening. The night before the proceedings and protests began, Glenda Brawley, looking bedraggled, vowed she would never ride the bus back north.

On Monday, the bus arrived hours late at the Radisson Hotel, where Sharpton had hoped to confront Governor Cuomo. But Cuomo, who had taken himself out of the presidential race months earlier, and who made two forays into Atlanta during the convention, had returned to New York by the time the Brawley entourage arrived at the Radisson.

"He should have waited around," Sharpton said, as if the governor had fled to escape the Brawley wrath. "He knew we were on our way."

As Ralph King climbed out of his car and the others descended from the bus, two white Brooklynites in town for the convention rushed up, veins pulsing in their necks, and began screaming: "Go back where you came from!" But Sharpton formed his followers into a ragged line and marched them in a circle for nearly an hour, waving signs and chanting slogans: "Impeach New York's Governor for Rape Cover-up" and "Justice for Tawana Brawley." They attracted a few sightseers. A California man took snapshots, but others were indignant or indifferent.

While the nation watched the Democrats in the convention center, the best show was outside in a parking lot they called the "free speech zone"—the unsupervised arena for abortion foes, neo-Nazi skinheads, gay groups, black nationalists, and the Brawley troupe.

A black coalition had banded together to give the illusion of strength on the convention's first day. For symbolism, they had begun their march at the grave of Martin Luther King, Jr. By the time they reached the free speech zone, they had fallen completely apart, chanting competing slogans and raising contradictory banners. An Atlanta woman in the Jesse Jackson brigade turned to Shipp and said: "What I want to know is why did they have to kill the child?" The *Times* reporter pointed to Tawana Brawley, who was striding with them up Auburn Avenue.

As the throng spilled into the parking lot, Lenora Fulani, a fringe candidate for president, and Hosea Williams, an Atlanta politician and civil rights advocate, scuffled for the microphone on the speaker's platform. Sharpton quickly led the Brawleys off. Huddling with Maddox and Mason, he said, "Both of them are supporting us. There ain't no need for us to get into it." The day was nearly over anyway, and it was best to keep a low profile for now, he advised.

There were other voices on hand to speak up for the cause. Imamu Amiri Baraka, the pan-Africanist and poet, had become an ardent Brawley partisan. "The police, prominent people, raped Tawana," he told Shipp at the rally. "If you can rape my sister and then lock her mother up for trying to get justice, then this is still a plantation."

The next day, seventy Brawley supporters barged into the Radisson Hotel, where the New York delegation was headquartered. For two hours in the lobby, they hurled, to anyone who would listen, insults at Mario Cuomo, Robert Abrams, and a host of blacks, including David Dinkins, who was a Jackson delegate, and Hazel Dukes, the president of the New York NAACP. Cuomo and Dukes were in New York, and Abrams was in another hotel, but that did not stop the protesters, who were especially vociferous against Dinkins, calling him "a handkerchief-head Uncle Tom."

Glenda Brawley was in the front line of the shouting mob with a hand-lettered sign in her hand: "Governor Cuomo. You have unfinished business in New York." Glenda, still wearing slacks and a T-shirt, clasped Ralph King's hand as if to fortify her anger and shrieked at the top of her lungs. Her eyes were a study in rage.

Amid the chants and screams, Glenda suddenly found herself face to face with Lucille Pattison, the Dutchess County Executive, and they fell into a shouting match. Pattison demanded that Glenda "let Tawana talk." Glenda demanded that Pattison and other white officials halt the cover-up. The pugnacious women were almost nose to nose—a little too close for Ralph King's liking. Suddenly, King reached between them and pushed Pattison back, yelling: "Get your finger out of my face."

The New York delegates, black and white, came out of the meeting rooms to complain, and finally Dinkins, a tall stately lawyer with none of Sharpton's bombast, could stand it no longer. "I am sure that most of you, certainly everyone that is a member of the Jackson delegation and probably many of the others who are members of the Dukakis delegation, can recite the litany of injustices," he told the delegates in the ballroom. Then his voice rose: "Eleanor Bumpurs. Nicholas Bartlett. Juan Rodriguez. Michael Stewart. The list goes on and on and on. And no one of us takes a back seat to anyone else in our commitment to resolution of these inequities."

As the delegates applauded, Dinkins went on: "I think it's unjust and unfair to make derogatory remarks about our governor, about Bob Abrams, Hazel Dukes, Roger Green, and now, finally, they have come full circle when they attacked Jesse Jackson. Please let us not confuse these issues. There are several. There are inequities in the criminal justice system we feel we must continue to fight against. Then there is the Tawana Brawley case. Clearly, something happened to this young woman. We don't know what, we don't know how."

The delegates applauded again, but from outside there were cries of "Uncle Tom."

That night, Sharpton and a few aides gave Tawana a sight-seeing tour of Atlanta: its skyscrapers and old streets, its malls and restored historic areas. As they strolled through the Marriott Marquis Hotel, some people recognized them and asked for their autographs. Tawana, obviously flattered, complied with a celebrity flourish of the pen.

On the third day, they took center stage—or at least the platform in the free speech zone. It was billed as the biggest protest to date over the Brawley case. Ten thousand people, said Sharpton, would be there to vent outrage. But it wasn't quite that: when the time came, no more than a hundred people showed up, including more than a few sightseers.

While Sharpton blasted forth from the microphone, two young white women strolled by on their lunch break. "Oh, it's Tawana!" exclaimed one, pointing to the girl on the platform. "I saw it on Oprah!" Her friend lit up: she, too, had seen something about Tawana Brawley, something on the *Donahue Show*. Shipp introduced herself as a reporter and asked what the two thought of the case. The young women smiled, but then went blank. Neither could remember *what* exactly the whole thing was about.

Tawana had dressed for the occasion, wearing a two-piece emerald-green African print dress, matching earrings, stockings, and high-heeled shoes. While Glenda was still in slacks and a T-shirt, Ralph King wore an African kente cloth stole around his shoulders.

As the rally fizzled, Sharpton tried to divert reporters' attention and revive the spirits of his group by announcing that they would march to the grave of Martin Luther King, Jr., to lay a wreath "on behalf of race victims, on behalf of black women such as Eleanor Bumpurs and Yvonne Smallwood that have fallen to racism after Doctor King's death."

Reporters, including Shipp, thought that the march had been planned, and raced ahead to the King Center. There, however, officials said they knew nothing about any wreath-laying ceremony; indeed, the director of security bristled at the prospect of a crowd tramping to the gravesite behind a man he had never heard of. Sharpton, mustering his powers of persuasion when he got there, managed to hold a ceremony anyway. After waiting a half hour for a wreath to arrive, they solemnly entered the grounds of the memorial and gathered around the tomb. Sharpton prayed. Then he, the Brawleys, and their lawyers stepped up and placed the wreath of orange and white carnations near the tombstone. They stood there in silence for a few minutes. Tears streamed down Sharpton's cheeks. Then they all turned away from the grave, and Tawana and Glenda and Juanita Brawley linked arms and led the group in singing "We Shall Overcome." There were tears in Glenda's tired eyes as the last strains of the song floated up.

"The interest and attention nationally is on the rise," Sharpton told reporters as the Brawley entourage prepared to leave on the convention's last day. Certainly, the trip had brought some, if fleeting, national attention to Sharpton and the advisers. And for the dozens of true believers who had paid hundreds of dollars, ridden long hours on an uncomfortable bus, and slept three or four to a room in a motel miles outside Atlanta, the trip had been a triumph.

In any event, the show was definitely over. Before heading home, the Brawley troupe stopped in Augusta to meet Sharpton's old hero, the singer James Brown. It was not the best of times in the entertainer's life: for months, he had been in trouble with the law for beating his wife and possession of narcotics. But for Sharpton and Mason, the stop was worth it, if only to step into the spotlight with the godfather of soul.

When the bus left Augusta for New York, Sharpton and Mason were not on board—they took a car. Tawana and Glenda Brawley had left the group, too, having driven off with King and Tyice in the Lincoln. Indeed, the Brawleys and King did not return to New York at all. They spent the rest of the summer in North Carolina, Maryland, and Washington, D.C., visiting relatives and friends. Journalists tried to find them, but they dropped from sight.

But Sharpton was as visible as he could be in the August doldrums. One day, he and Roy Innis, the leader of the once-influential Congress of Racial Equality, taped a debate on the Brawley case at Harlem's Apollo Theater for broadcast on the nationally syndicated *Morton Downey Jr. Show*. Halfway through, Sharpton accused Innis of "kowtowing" to Abrams.

Innis, a volatile man who believed the Brawley case was a hoax and had described the advisers as "the three stooges," leaped to his feet, rushed at Sharpton, and shoved him over backward. Sharpton reeled and his enormous bulk tumbled to the floor. But he wasn't down for long. With surprising agility, he got back on his feet and seemed about to square off with Innis. It looked like a donnybrook, but Downey managed to cool things down, and the taping went on.

To date, the Brawley case had been assiduously avoided by most high-profile politicians. But in late August, Sharpton and Mason succeeded in arranging a private conference with the highest-profile black politician in the country. The meeting with Sharpton's one-time mentor, Jesse Jackson, took place in the Manhattan office of Percy Sutton, a Jackson strategist and a former Manhattan borough president. Jackson, who had not spoken out about the Brawleys, now seemed eager to get involved. The meeting was all smiles, and Jackson said he would very much like to meet Tawana. Sharpton and Mason left, elated.

They had another big fish on the line as well—Representative John Conyers, the liberal Michigan Democrat who headed the House Subcommittee on Criminal Justice and who had conducted hearings a few years earlier on police brutality in New York City. Maddox and Mason had arranged for several black publishers to go to Washington and urge Conyers to hold new hearings. The meeting was set for August 29, a few hours after the meeting with Jackson.

To Conyers's surprise, it was not just the publishers who showed up. Tawana and Glenda Brawley were there with Sharpton, who had raced down from New York. Conyers and his staff were not sure if they should meet them. As they conferred, the Brawleys waited in the outer office. Finally, Sharpton broke the impasse by telling Conyers that Jesse Jackson had just expressed an interest in meeting with the Brawleys.

"I'll beat him to the punch," Conyers said, and he ushered them in for a three-hour meeting. Through it all, Glenda did not speak, but Tawana volunteered to tell her story at an open congressional hearing. Little was said about the facts of the case, however, and Conyers was noncommittal about any kind of hearing.

Still, Sharpton capitalized on the meeting anyway. He told waiting reporters that the powwow with Conyers showed that those concerned about the Brawley case were "not just radical fringe groups." He boasted, "Conyers can get what Abrams can't— Tawana's testimony."

Part Four

CLOSING IN

27

Anthony Montanari drove down Salt Point Turnpike from Clinton Corners with the early-morning sun at his back. It was already near ninety degrees, and the August day promised no relief from the murderous heat. In Poughkeepsie, he nosed the gray 1983 Toyota Corolla into the municipal parking garage. He got out and walked the last block down Church Street, loosening his necktie in the morning heat.

There was just time for coffee and a cigarette at the Poughkeepsie Diner before being locked up. It was there that he had discovered that George Pelote had almost bought a house from him years ago when he was selling real estate, and there that he had learned that one of the women they were serving with was a teacher who had substituted for his wife, Eleanor, in school. In their few leisurely moments, they had discovered all kinds of connections. But like good conspirators, they never spoke in public about the thing that had brought them together.

After coffee, Montanari went next door into the turreted red-brick castle and, after signing the log, took the dark-stained staircase past eagle plaques to Room 11 on the second floor. It was just the mess hall of a century-old armory, with a brick fireplace at one end, upholstered chairs, a large table, and yellow walls. But it was what the Founding Fathers had in mind when they settled the issues of common defense and the general welfare and due process. There were places in the world where a petty official decided if you would be tried for treason or just shot in the courtyard. But this shabby room was a guarantee against that kind of justice, a place where the officials had to come with proof and ask ordinary citizens for permission to bring charges against an American.

The grand jurors were as anonymous as the dingy mess hall. Anthony Montanari was number sixteen, but they called him Tony and they knew by now that he was a fifty-four-year-old computer consultant and that George Pelote, one of the two black jurors, was a church administrator. They had all been strangers when they were impaneled last February: a mailman, housewives, a bookkeeper, businessmen, people who fancied bad neckties or smoked cigarettes or nursed sniffles. But five long months together with the secrets of Tawana Brawley had wrapped them in a kind of camaraderie, like hostages or soldiers confined to barracks, and they had gradually gotten to know who enjoyed a laugh, who had a temper, who trusted authority excessively or had little use for it, and who among them was afflicted with prejudices.

When they were all inside and the doors were locked, the prosecutor, John Ryan, called them to order and they took their places—twenty-three stuffed black chairs arranged in two horseshoe rows around the witness table and the enormous blackboard where they sometimes drew layouts or wrote lists. The lunette windows had been painted over and the shades drawn for security. The only light was the cold glow from fluorescent tubes on the high tin ceiling.

The room was stifling. It was the hottest summer in years in the Hudson Valley, and the air in the grand jury room was like that of a buried coffin. Two air conditioners churned against the heat, but on days like this they brought the room's temperature down only into the eighties, and the racket sometimes drowned out the witnesses. And so the men doffed their jackets and the women fanned themselves with paperback books: there were never any magazines or newspapers in the room.

Like the other jurors, Montanari had given up newspapers and

342

TV news programs. Justice Ingrassia had ruled news reports on the case off-limits for the duration. Still, it was hard to avoid hearing some things: friends and relatives just blurted them out. But Montanari felt he had kept an open mind through the months of testimony and evidence. And he still recalled how shocked and saddened he had been by the early reports on Tawana Brawley.

But then he had heard Joyce Lloray's account of seeing Tawana climb into a bag and hop around at the Pavillion, heard the testimony of doctors, police officers, neighbors, teenaged friends, and schoolmates—one hundred fifty witnesses in all so far—and he had come to doubt Tawana's story. Dr. Michael M. Baden, the director of the State Police Forensic Sciences Unit, and Dr. Justin Uku, the Erie County medical examiner, had told them there was no evidence of any assault. The business about Harry Crist and his suicide took longer to untangle, and it was Tim Losee, the mailman whose sighting of a car like Crist's had implicated him, who finally put that matter to rest. Losee testified that investigators had showed him Crist's car, and the exchange at the witness stand had been conclusive:

"Was that the car that you saw at the Pavillion during the week of November twenty-third through twenty-eighth?"

"I would have to say no."

Since March, Montanari had gone down all the dead-end trails. For instance, several youths had told investigators and reporters about seeing Tawana at parties in Newburgh during the time she was missing; then, under oath, the tales had evaporated. Two of the girl's boyfriends reported that she had asked them for money for an abortion in the weeks before she disappeared, but state investigators had combed state health records, visited hospitals, and found no evidence of an abortion.

More important, Montanari had come to believe that the allegations of the Brawley advisers were dubious. Despite his shaky past, Montanari thought, Perry McKinnon had been extremely believable about the lying by Sharpton and the others. The most persuasive testimony had come only a few days earlier, on August 2.

The muscular young man had come through the door like a football player bulging out of his blazer. Unlike the other witnesses, he had come before the grand jury voluntarily, not in answer to a subpoena, and had waived his right to immunity from prosecution for all that he said under oath. This was important because the witness was Steven Pagones, the young assistant D.A., whom the Brawley advisers had accused of being one of the rapists. For two hours, Pagones had reviewed his whereabouts and actions during Tawana's missing days, answering every question and substantially accounting for every hour. Thirteen other witnesses had supported his testimony: people who had worked or dined with him, seen him at stores or on the street or in their homes between November 24 and 28. Photographs taken during the four days were also submitted, as were the names of forty-nine other people who could be called to verify his alibi.

When Pagones finished, Montanari and the others had heard enough: there was no way this man could have been involved.

And more evidence was piling up every day.

From his chair in the back row to which the jury's four smokers had been relegated, Montanari now watched as a black man in a business suit quietly entered the room and took the path of all the witnesses: over the brown linoleum squares, around the long table piled with legal papers, and into the chair that served as the witness stand. A court stenographer sat beside him and took everything down, word for word.

The witness identified himself as Dr. Ezra Griffith, a psychiatrist, an associate professor at the Yale University School of Medicine and acting chief of the Connecticut Mental Health Center. He readily acknowledged that he had been hired and paid by Attorney General Abrams to review medical records, testimony, and other evidence in the case and to evaluate it for the grand jury.

In his opinion, said Griffith, Tawana Brawley did not appear to be suffering from any neurological or physical disorder when found at the Pavillion or in the weeks that followed. That left two choices: either she had been severely traumatized or else she was faking.

Prosecutor Ryan asked for details.

Griffith talked about something called "post-traumatic stress disorder." But for that affliction, he said, the symptoms—acute anxiety, nightmares, or flashbacks to scenes of rape or beating— were missing. He spoke of "conversion disorder," which he defined as the mind involuntarily producing physical symptoms, such as the inability to walk or talk. But this could not be the case either: Tawana Brawley had been seen crawling into the bag, squatting, hopping, and functioning "at a sophisticated level," not only on the day she was found but for weeks afterward.

So, Ryan asked, what is your diagnosis?

"Malingering her complaints," he said. That is, the girl had been faking the limp and all the other physical symptoms.

Would Dr. Griffith, asked the prosecutor, review the general characteristics of a false claim of sexual assault?

Such claims, the doctor said, tend to be sketchy about the number of attackers and their actions, about the force used and the time, location, and other details. About all these things, Tawana had been vague.

Were there other such characteristics?

Certainly. People who make false claims often have personal problems and want to hide something, said Griffith. And there were usually inconsistencies in the evidence. In Tawana's case, these were obvious: her jeans had been burned, but not her body; excrement had been smeared on her body, but not her face; indeed, cotton wads had been used to protect her nostrils and ears from infection.

Dr. Griffith was excused and they all took a break for lunch. Some members of the grand jury had brought sandwiches and retreated to a balcony overlooking Market Street. Others joined the noontime crowd at the diner next door to get out of the heat. They talked about the broiling weather, about themselves and their activities away from the grand jury, about anything but what was on their minds—Dr. Griffith's testimony. That was the way it had been for months: the most intriguing subjects were the ones you weren't allowed to talk about.

The witness, a white man, entered and took the stand. He identified himself as Dr. Park Elliott Dietz, a psychiatrist and professor of law and medicine at the University of Virginia. Dr. Dietz said it was he who had evaluated John Hinckley after his attempted assassination of President Ronald Reagan in 1981. He acknowledged that he, too, had been hired by Abrams to review and evaluate evidence in the Brawley case.

Like Griffith, Dietz rejected physical and psychological causes for the condition in which Tawana Brawley had been found. He said that almost nothing biological explained how she could have gone from willful behavior like stepping into a bag, to unconsciousness in the ambulance, and back to alert accusatory writing in the hospital.

Why, he was asked, did sex offenders degrade their victims?

There were two main reasons, he said: anger and sadism. He explained that an angry rapist often beats his victim without mercy, especially on the face. But, he noted, Tawana was not injured at all, let alone struck on the face.

As for sadism, he said, an attacker who used excrement to humiliate a victim would hardly spread it all over her body and stop at the face—and it would be absurd to imagine he would protect the victim's ears and nostrils with cotton wads. Moreover, a gang of men who had held and repeatedly attacked a girl for four days would almost certainly not release her uninjured.

Could Dr. Dietz, the prosecutor asked, identify any traits characteristic of someone who falsely alleged sexual assault?

In his research over the years, said the doctor, he had compiled a list of twenty such traits. As he enumerated them, the jurors noted that many were similar to those Griffith had cited, but Dietz had something new to add: such a person, he said, nearly always accused a stranger, was uncooperative with the authorities, and tried to steer the inquiry into the realm of the unprovable. And one more thing: in an astonishing number of false claims, there was writing on the body of the pseudo victim. Of Dietz's twenty traits, Tawana Brawley's behavior appeared to fit eighteen. The only ones she did not have, the doctor said, were a history of making false allegations and a history of extensive medical care.

Montanari and Pelote, who sat next to each other, found the two psychiatrists' testimony compelling. A defense lawyer might have torn into Griffith and Dietz, asking more pointedly how much they were being paid by the state for their testimony, how they could have evaluated the condition of a girl they had never met. But the work of this grand jury was not to try a case; rather, it was to determine whether a crime had been committed and, if so, whether there was enough evidence to indict someone for it. The questions that Montanari and Pelote and the other jurors pressed were intended to get at the facts, not to be argumentative.

That night, like almost every night lately, Montanari went home reasonably satisfied with the day's work. Unlike those of the first months of blind alleys, he had the sense that progress was now being made. But still there was that hole at the heart of it all: what had happened to Tawana Brawley? What did she have to say? A few days ago, they had sent the Brawleys a letter over the signature of the jury foreman, Donald E. Perrotte. It offered Tawana Brawley a "final opportunity" to come in and tell her story, and it concluded: "In the event you decline this invitation and we complete our work without your testimony, our consciences will be clear that we have afforded you every opportunity to obtain truth and justice in this case."

No one told the grand jurors how difficult it had been for the state and the FBI to report on the elusive scientific evidence. For months, the FBI had been working in the laboratory on Tawana's rape kit, her clothing, and other items of evidence found at the

Pavillion. All spring, the FBI had conducted tests in response to requests by Abrams and Ryan for further information. By early summer, when the state began planning the final phases of the grand jury work, including testimony by federal agents and lab specialists, the FBI noted that vacation schedules might necessitate postponements until autumn.

Abrams, worried about a delay, approached Attorney General Edwin Meese at a conference of attorneys general, explained the urgency, and asked him to intervene. Soon thereafter, an Abrams team traveled to Washington, and the FBI began unloading its information. Later, a schedule of appearances by agents before the grand jury was arranged.

Now, as Montanari and the other jurors watched, Agent Joseph Errera of the FBI removed his jacket in the heat, opened his briefcase, and took out the records of his laboratory work. He put them in order on the witness table and looked up, indicating that he was ready to begin. Once sworn in, he described himself as an expert in forensic serology, or the investigation of serums. He worked at the FBI labs in Washington and he had conducted extensive tests in the Brawley case, including workups on the rape-kit samples taken from the girl at St. Francis Hospital.

What, John Ryan asked, were the samples?

The rape kit, Errera said, included blood and saliva samples, swabs from the girl's mouth, vagina, and rectum that were preserved on glass slides, and fingernail clippings that included material on and under the nails.

And what had he done with all the samples?

Errera said he had conducted tests using microscopes and various techniques of chemical analysis to determine if any of the samples contained blood, sperm cells, or prostate antigen, a substance unique in semen whose presence would indicate sexual activity.

If Tawana Brawley had been repeatedly sexually assaulted during four days, what would be the likelihood of finding blood, semen, or prostate antigen?

It would be extremely likely, provided that the samples had been taken from the girl within forty-eight hours of the last sexual activity and provided that during that time she had not bathed.

And had he found any blood, semen, or prostate antigen?

No, said Errera.

Had there been tests on the other material?

Yes. Errera had also performed tests for blood and semen on the clothing the girl was wearing when she was found, on the gloves found under the bag, on the bag itself, on clothing found in Apartment 19A at the Pavillion, and on the white boots that had been stolen from a next-door neighbor and left in the former Brawley flat.

Would Errera describe his procedures in some detail?

In searching for stains, the forensic expert said, he first used ultraviolet light. When he found a stain, he used various chemical tests to screen it for acid phosphatase, an enzyme or protein found in semen, and for choline, a chemical substance produced in the male's seminal vesicle and also found in semen. If he found either of those two chemicals in the stain, he would examine it under a microscope and test for the presence of P-30, or prostate antigen.

How long could a blood or semen stain last?

Up to thirty or forty years, said Errera, if the clothing or other material had not been washed and had been kept relatively cool and dry.

And had he found any blood or semen stains in any of the materials he examined?

None, he said.

On the basis of all the materials that he had examined, what had he concluded?

The answer was unequivocal. Errera said that there was no evidence—nothing in the physical examination, the rape kit, or the materials found at the Pavillion—of any sexual assault on Tawana Brawley.

He was excused, and another FBI agent came in and took the stand. He identified himself as Michael Malone, an expert on hair and fiber analysis. He said he had examined Tawana Brawley's clothing, pubic hair combings, and fingernail scrapings, the gloves found under the bag, and a variety of materials found in Apartment 19A.

Asked about his qualifications, Malone said he had examined evidence in approximately fifteen hundred rape cases, including several hundred that had allegedly occurred in wooded areas.

The prosecutor asked him to describe the "transfer theory of Locard."

Simply put, Malone said, it meant that if two people came into close contact with each other, there would be a transfer of either hairs or fibers or both.

If three or more white men sexually assaulted a black girl, would there be such a transfer?

Indeed there would, said Malone. A large number of Caucasian hairs, especially pubic hairs, would be found. This would be true even if the men wore condoms.

And what were Malone's findings?

He had found no pubic hairs of any kind, other than Tawana Brawley's, on any of the items he examined. There were no Caucasian hairs in her pubic hair combings, fingernail scrapings, or any of the materials taken from Apartment 19A. The agent said he had found one bleached blond hair several inches long on the girl's black blouse, which had fallen to the floor at the hospital and had been kicked under the stretcher in the emergency room. But in his opinion, he said, the blouse was thereby contaminated and the hair had probably come from the hospital floor.

What, therefore, was his general conclusion?

There was no evidence, he said, that the girl had been sexually assaulted.

But there was, he said in response to another question, abundant evidence that Tawana had spent much of the time she was missing in Apartment 19A. Malone had found fibers from the apartment's carpet on the girl's jeans and pink shoe, on the black blouse wrapped around her head, and on a black strap found with her. In the girl's pubic hair and on the feces on the left glove, he had found more fibers that perfectly matched the insulation cut from one of the white boots found in the apartment. The insulation, he said, was Du Pont Hollofil. He had found it as well on a denim jacket left in the washing machine in the apartment—the jacket she had been wearing the night she disappeared.

Ryan asked what kind of evidence was usually found in cases of rape in the woods.

The most obvious evidence, Malone said, was plant material on the person or clothing. In his opinion, it would be impossible for a person to spend any length of time in the woods without picking up a great deal of plant material, such as grass, leaves, twigs, wood fragments, soil, and pine needles. "Normally," Malone said, "you're going to find it all over the clothes, all over the body, just everywhere."

The prosecutor nodded. And in your examination of Tawana Brawley's clothing, hair, fingernail scrapings, and other materials, he said, what did you find?

"I found absolutely no plant material."

After dinner at the Wyndham Hotel, John Ryan and Agent Thomas Lynch of the FBI ducked into the bar off the lobby for a drink. Lynch was to testify the next day about the feces found smeared on Tawana and the writing of the racial slurs. Lynch had reported that the excrement had been traced through hairs to a border collie named Remi, who lived in 21A Carnaby Drive at the Pavillion, a dog that had roamed daily behind the old Brawley apartment. The pattern of feces on the gloves found with Tawana—on the palms and between the fingers—suggested that they had been used to smear the excrement on her. But there were troubling loose ends about the writing, said the agent. Now he and Ryan talked quietly about them.

They still didn't know what had been used to scrawl the racial slurs that had lifted this case into the realm of the extraordinary. It was not charcoal; lab tests on charcoal briquettes like those littering the Pavillion lawn had not worked, producing illegible results. It wasn't eyebrow pencil; that had proved too shiny. Microscopic examination had finally showed that the writing fibers were burned cotton. Several pieces of burned cotton cloth had been found under the bag, and they had seemed the likely sources. But Lynch had tried writing on a shirt like Tawana's with a burned cotton facecloth, and that had not worked either: the fibers flaked off too easily. In short, Lynch believed the writing had been done with the burned cotton, but he couldn't prove it.

"It was the damnedest thing," he said. "I found the same thing under her fingernails."

Ryan looked at him. "You what?"

Lynch explained: virtually identical burned cotton fibers were found in the writing on the shirt, on the inside of the black gloves, and on Tawana Brawley's fingernail clippings. "They had exactly the same characteristics," he said of the fibers, and apparently all of them had come from the charred pieces of cloth found under the bag.

"Isn't that important?" said the prosecutor.

Perhaps it was, but Lynch couldn't say how. Something was missing, something that would show *how* the writing was done. Lynch still didn't see how a couple of pieces of charred cloth could have produced lettering on the girl's shirt and torso.

Ryan and Lynch finished their drinks and said good-night. It was maddening, thought the prosecutor: all that evidence pointed to one conclusion, and yet the last little link, the final explanation, was missing. For days, Ryan was haunted by the matter of the burned cotton. Finally, over the long Labor Day weekend at his home on Long Island, he decided to experiment a little. While his wife, Barbara, looked on as though he were crazy, he singed the corner of a cotton towel over the kitchen sink and tried using it to write on her stomach. It didn't stick. Then Barbara noticed that a piece of the burned cloth had fallen into the sink, where it had gotten damp. She picked it up and rubbed it on Ryan's arm. Like magic, it stuck, drawing a distinctive charcoallike line just like the ones on Tawana Brawley's torso. Ryan called Abrams at home.

Now it was Abrams's turn to rush into his bathroom, take off his shirt, and after singeing a facecloth over the sink, try writing with it on his chest. The burned fibers just flaked off. Abrams moistened a part of the burned cloth, forming a kind of paste, and tried it again. The results were astonishing—and they set off bells: the smoke detector overhead began wailing and the bathroom door swung open. It was Becky, the attorney general's two-year-old daughter. At the sight of her father standing there with "KKK" scrawled across his bare chest, she giggled.

Two weeks later, after reproducing Ryan's experimental results in the laboratory and using a light-skinned black investigator as a model to write on, FBI Agent Stephen Grantham laid it all out for the grand jury. The conclusion was inescapable: Tawana Brawley had written the racial slurs on herself.

"I almost fell off my chair," Montanari said later. "The stuff that was used to write the slurs. The stuff under the fingernails and in the gloves. I mean, c'mon!"

28

They couldn't go home again. Home, to the Brawleys, meant jail for Glenda, the scorn of neighbors and classmates for Tawana, harassment by investigators and the press, the cheap flat with thin walls, and no work to pay the rent.

As the grand jury closed in, they longed for obscurity again. Glenda had quit IBM. Short Line had fired Ralph King. The tedious journey through the South that had begun after the Democratic National Convention in July had seen them safely through August and early September. But now they were running out of friends and relatives to visit.

And so, the place in Virginia Beach seemed inviting. Its real-estate brochure gushed vulgar snobbery: "The aura of success. It's the pace of your walk. The lift in your voice. The gleam in your eyes. It's part of your style. Like Reflections. Come explore and discover a world far beyond your expectations."

Their expectations weren't that high, and to them, the Reflections Luxury Apartments in Virginia Beach looked like heaven. It was not on the ocean, but it was close enough, and the sand underfoot was soft and warm. Besides, the six-hundred-dollar monthly rent included a place to park and free racquetball, a swimming pool, and the use of the volleyball courts, the jogging trail, and the clubhouse.

The two-bedroom apartment on Diamond Plum Circle was a spacious retreat from an unforgiving world, and it was a short drive from Floyd E. Kellam High School, a large red-brick place with a campus setting among horse farms and a student body that was predominantly white. Tawana was enrolled and began commuting to Kellam. Her fellow students greeted her with a mixture of curiosity and reticence; they all knew who she was, but no one asked her to explain herself, and no one accused her of anything.

Neither Glenda nor Ralph King had a job, and soon money was a problem. Abrams's investigators found that King during the summer had deposited seven thousand dollars in a savings account at Pawling, New York, where the family had had only one dollar in May. The money, it was presumed, came from collections at church rallies and protest marches. But the summer's travel had left the family with depleted funds and a mounting pile of debts, many of them charged on a Visa card.

The investigators had tracked the family all summer on a paper trail of Visa charges and were continually aware of their movements. But they made no move to bring Glenda Brawley back to New York. No one, as far as they knew, had ever been extradited on a misdemeanor warrant, and Glenda was safe from arrest as long as she stayed out of the state. Tawana was under no such constraints. She slipped into New York City a couple of times in August, to attend a wedding at the Cotton Club in Harlem and to see—with Sharpton—the musical *Sarafina* on Broadway.

With cash running out, the only thing left was their story. At the end of August, Glenda Brawley called Mike Wallace, of the CBS program *60 Minutes*.

"Maybe the time has come for us to talk," she told him.

Wallace said he would be delighted to report the story. He invited Glenda and Tawana to meet with him, and he was referred to the lawyer C. Vernon Mason to make the arrangements. But the arrangements immediately fell through when Mason indicated that the Brawleys wanted to be paid for their story. Wallace said there was no money for that. In that case, replied Mason, there was no point in talking further.

Sharpton's hopes for some real political muscle had been dashed as well. Representative Conyers had said nothing about Tawana's offer to testify before Congress, and Jesse Jackson had been a big disappointment on a WLIB broadcast. The most he would say about the Brawley case was that it was part of a growing list of racial antagonisms leading to a loss of confidence in the criminal justice system. When someone asked if he approved of the girl's withholding her cooperation from the grand jury, Jackson had gone all cagey, saying he preferred "not to comment on the strategy and tactics employed by her lawyers." Then, asked if he believed Tawana's story, he had bridled with: "How can I answer that if I don't know what her story is?"

But the quest continued for a television or magazine outlet that would shell out for the Brawley story. At a news conference on September 8, Sharpton was his old self: "They are considering several six-figure offers," he said. He admitted that things had gone awry with Mike Wallace, dropping the celebrity broadcaster's name to give his cause a little cachet. But there were, he said, many other possibilities still in the wind.

As for the family, he disclosed that they had settled out of state to escape their tormentors in New York, but he refused to say where. Glenda and King, he said, were looking for work, and Tawana had resumed her education in a new setting. "We want Tawana to go to school and not be harassed," he declared. "And the family feels that New York has declared war on them. They're leaving, but they will still fight the battle!"

The telephone at Virginia Beach was listed in King's name, and Ralph Blumenthal called the number.

"Ralph King?" Blumenthal identified himself. "Have you now moved down there?"

"I'm here, ain't I?" King snapped.

"Has Tawana transferred to high school there?"

"I don't know," King said coyly. "You'll have to find out. Come over here and find out. You know where I am." But he refused to agree to an interview and hung up.

It didn't take reporters long to locate the Brawleys. They flew to Virginia Beach and converged on the Reflections Luxury Apartments like bees around the hive. The Brawleys remained behind closed doors, so reporters began talking to neighbors and shopkeepers, picking up any tidbits they could. Some of them began following Tawana to Kellam High. The media circus was starting up all over again.

One day, Glenda Brawley was spotted coming home with a bag of groceries. As the reporters converged on her, she bellowed: "I'm sure you all have children, and I'm sure you don't want the black army to come to your house and follow your daughter or son to school."

She turned on Richard Pienciak of the *Daily News*: "They sell guns freely around here in Virginia. Do not call my house again. As God is my witness, I'll shoot first and ask questions later."

In short order, as if in response to her warnings, Sharpton arrived in Virginia Beach with a five-member "protective force." One day, Ralph King, who drove Tawana to school, ran Pienciak's car off the road on the way home.

To Bill Morris, a reporter for *The Virginian-Pilot* of Norfolk, the hullabaloo had a surreal quality. In a guest column for *New York Newsday* that brought a fresh eye to these zany events, he told of being assigned by his paper "to keep tabs on Tawana and the mob of New York newspaper, radio and TV reporters, plus some local TV types with good haircuts who camped outside the family's new home in the plush Reflections apartment complex. Oh, what fun!"

"The story," Morris wrote, "kept getting weirder and weirder. The Rev. Al Sharpton, the dapper preacher who spends almost $2,000 a year on his hair care at the PrimaDonna Beauty Salon in Brooklyn, rolled into town with a contingent of his 'black army' to protect the besieged family. And believe me, when a New York–based outfit called the 'black army' rolls into a nice, quiet Virginia town, people take notice. Then at 5 o'clock one morning, a repo man, operating on behalf of a New York collection agency, showed

up outside the Brawleys' apartment armed with a .45-caliber hand-
gun and quietly repossessed King's gray Lincoln. King, angered
perhaps by the media mob, then threatened to shoot a neighbor's
yappy dog."

29

The man calling Ralph Blumenthal was a government official and said he thought it was important for the public finally to hear the truth. Would Blumenthal be willing—confidentially, of course—to help get the whole story out?

Certainly, said the *Times* reporter.

They met at the Algonquin for a drink, and when the meeting was over Blumenthal realized that the man was a treasure trove. He seemed almost too obsessed with the Brawley case, and he clearly wanted to influence the *Times*'s coverage: that would have to be guarded against. But if he was handled right, if what he had to say passed critical evaluation, he just might provide the final breakthrough.

Blumenthal met two more times with the source and then wrote a 7,500-word memorandum to his editors summarizing what he had learned. It was full of information that had never before been made public—information about the forensic psychiatrists who had been hired by Abrams, about feces that had been found on the girl's gloves, about Tawana's physical condition, about the rape kit's showing no evidence of sexual assault, about scores of other details. The source had also supplied fascinating details about the interplay among Cuomo, Abrams, Giuliani, and others in the case.

"Gee, this is amazing stuff," said John Darnton, the metropolitan editor, and he approved pursuing the source—carefully.

They code-named the source "Massapequa" for no good reason, and M. A. Farber, with Blumenthal's blessing, got the next crack at him. Massapequa, in their first conversation, had recalled Farber's decision to go to jail for forty days in 1978 rather than break confidentiality with his sources. "I hope you won't have to go back," he said.

They began meeting at night: first at Massapequa's home, later at Farber's apartment, but never in a public place. Farber had a thousand questions, and Massapequa answered most of them as the reporter scribbled copious notes. Farber's main objective was to learn what the grand jury intended to do about the case.

After each of his meetings with Massapequa, Farber tried to check what he had learned with other confidential sources, including the man he called Oscar. These sources, their tongues loosened by Farber's knowledge, confirmed much of what Massapequa had said and agreed on the main points of what the grand jury had learned. But some information was still being held back: Massapequa, Oscar, and the other sources acknowledged it.

Farber finally wrote a memo of his findings. It began: "The grand jury has received no evidence that anything was done to Tawana of which she was not a willing participant. In other words, whatever condition she was found in was the result of her own doing or her own doing in conjunction with someone helping her." Copies of the memo went to Darnton, Blumenthal, Chuck Strum, and Bob McFadden.

On September 17, Darnton met with them in his office. They were in high spirits, sensing that they were on the verge of capturing the biggest New York story of the year. They felt they had the substance of it, and they could therefore publish before the grand jury issued its report. But there were two hitches: they were relying on the word of official sources who insisted on anonymity, and the *Times* did not know definitively what the grand jury's ultimate findings would be. There was still time—the grand jury would not make its report public before the end of the month— and they decided to keep digging, at least for a while.

Blumenthal and Farber both met Massapequa for the last time

at an apartment in Manhattan, and it was the most productive session of all. The source explained the reasons why the authorities were so certain that Tawana was not dazed on the day she was found. He explained why her hair appeared short, even though it had not been cut. He said that the grand jury had no evidence linking Ralph King to Tawana's condition. And he said that there was a major piece of evidence he had to hold back. All he could say for now was that it related to the girl's body and supported a conclusion that her condition was—he paused to select the right words—"self-inflicted."

Blumenthal pressed. Farber pressed. Massapequa unbent only to say that the breakthrough was not the result of any handwriting analysis. But he would go no further.

"Forget it," Massapequa said. "I've told you more than I meant to."

They talked on for a while, double-checking some of the points they had already covered, examining a few nuances. Finally, in the middle of an otherwise innocuous sentence, Massapequa mentioned a small point that had been in "the summaries." Then, a little later, he referred to "the summaries" again.

Blumenthal and Farber, avoiding each other's eyes, nodded at Massapequa each time, as if they knew all about the summaries. Finally, Farber broke in.

"Summaries—ah, these summaries—ah, they cover all the evidence gathered, don't they?" he said tentatively. "I mean, they're pretty damn complete, aren't they?"

"Oh, yes," Massapequa said. They even included a lot of evidence the grand jury *hadn't* seen—after all, only a quarter of the material gathered had been presented to the grand jury.

The reporters were staggered. For six months, they had worked this story like blind men. How could they have missed the existence of "summaries." When you thought about it, the sheer volume of evidence was staggering. How could anyone hope to digest it without something like summaries?

"Well," Blumenthal said with a prayer, "no one's seen these summaries except the investigators and, I guess, Abrams and his staff, right?"

"I suppose so," Massapequa said. "I really don't know."

"Do any reporters have them?" Farber asked, afraid of the answer.

"How would I know?" Massapequa said. "You tell me."

Summaries.

For three hours after their meeting with Massapequa, the two reporters drank coffee and talked of ways to get the summaries. Who would have them? And who would part with them?

Blumenthal looked depressed. "You know, if *Newsday* or CBS or anybody gets their hands on these summaries before us, we're cooked. Boy oh boy oh boy."

Farber caught a taxi home. The streets were nearly deserted, and he felt sick and alone. But on the way, he got an idea. Abruptly he told the driver to pull over. He went to a telephone booth and dialed information. The woman had an unlisted number. Farber looked at his wristwatch: it was two-forty A.M.

He called home, roused his wife, Sabine, and told her exactly where to look. She gave him the number and he dialed it. It rang and rang. He was just about to give up when he heard the click.

"Hello?" the sleepy voice said.

Farber didn't give his name. He didn't have to. "I've got to see you right away," he said.

She was still grumbling when he hung up.

Farber opened his apartment door, the briar pipe jutting from his smug mouth. Blumenthal stepped in. Morning sunlight streamed in the windows, illuminating the cluttered table, the books in rows, the piles of newspapers containing a million words that meant nothing. Gently, as if handling a bird, Farber put the hefty pile of papers down on the dining table.

Centered on the cover page were the words, "The Tawana Brawley Matter," and below, "A Summary of the Events."

Blumenthal grabbed it, kissing the front page. "Where did you get these?"

"C'mon, Ralph," Farber admonished. "Let's go see the team."

They headed for the office. Blumenthal gave McFadden a two-page memo on the previous night's meeting with Massapequa. Now the summaries put the hundreds of little pieces, the whole ten-month-long puzzle, into place.

They were in a mood of almost childish glee. Darnton ushered them into his office. It was McFadden who brought them down to earth. There were two sets of summaries, one dated in June and the other in July. Were there later ones for August or September? Were these out of date? They looked at him as if he had said there was no Santa Claus.

Farber was stricken. Why hadn't he noticed that? Excuses rushed in: he had been too tired, too elated, too . . .

"Can you go back to the source?"

"She's too scared."

Blumenthal had an idea. Massapequa had raised the subject of the summaries in the first place. Why not go back to him, without saying they had these, and check on the dates? Farber nodded and hurried out.

Later in the day, he was back and he had the answer. The July summaries were the last. None had been prepared after that. These two overlapping documents—together 186 pages long—contained the vast bulk of what was known by the grand jury.

McFadden wrote the story, and as usual the whole team was credited unobtrusively in a box on the jump page inside.

"Evidence Points to Deceit by Brawley," said the headline on the story, which occupied the whole upper-left quarter of the front page on September 27. The article—a six-thousand-word compendium of all the major evidence and the probable conclusions of the grand jury—signaled the beginning of the end of the case. The sixth of the *Times*'s periodic blockbusters about the Brawley affair, it was a mosaic that began: "A seven-month New York State grand jury inquiry has compiled overwhelming evidence that Tawana Brawley fabricated her story of abduction and sexual abuse by a gang of racist white men last year. . . ." The opus ended with the recollection of a Brawley neighbor on Carmine Drive who had told the grand jury of hearing Glenda Brawley say, "They know we're lying, and they're going to find out and come and get us."

Robert Abrams was livid. He pounded his desk and cursed as he read the word "summaries." How, he demanded, had the *Times* gotten hold of the summaries, which included reference after reference to secret grand jury testimony?

With news organizations besieging him, the attorney general issued a four-page statement that neither confirmed nor denied "the accuracy of any aspect" of the *Times* story. He said he had asked Joe Hynes, the state's special corruption prosecutor, to investigate whether there had been any "unauthorized disclosure" of grand jury secrets.

Governor Cuomo solemnly joined in. "I have spoken to Joe Hynes simply to impress upon him the urgency of the matter he is now investigating."

Hynes began a flurry of interrogations that led nowhere. The *Times* reporters declined to be questioned, citing Constitutional protections and a state shield law aimed at ensuring the public's right to know.

30

The *Times* story had caught Sharpton off guard completely, and he quickly got on the phone with Maddox and Mason. Sharpton argued that Tawana should respond immediately and forcefully, if only to reassure her black supporters. Maddox disagreed; he didn't want her to say anything specific about the case. Mason was middle-of-the-road.

They finally came around to Sharpton's view. Sharpton called the Brawleys and pointed out that the New York–based national press would not go to Virginia for a simple reaction story, so the Brawleys would have to come north. Glenda could not set foot in New York, so Sharpton rented a conference room at a hotel in Newark, New Jersey, just across the Hudson from Manhattan, and set up a news briefing.

The next day, Sharpton met the Brawleys and Ralph King at Newark Airport and took Tawana into a coffee shop. He hurriedly scribbled a dozen sentences for her to read to reporters waiting downtown.

Yes, she agreed, that was what she wanted to say.

Fifty reporters crammed into the conference room at Newark's Quality Inn. A platoon of photographers jockeyed for position with ten television cameramen. Wires snaked over the floor. Chairs were bowled over in the crush.

Finally, Tawana Brawley made her entrance. She looked as if she had just breezed in from Santa Anita: sunglasses, sneakers, a white, red, and black sweatshirt emblazoned with the words "Kamikaze Racing Team."

"I am not a liar," she began, her soft voice more defiant than ever. "And I am not crazy. We have said that I would cooperate with an impartial grand jury—impartial. Why won't they let me?"

It was a poignant, disturbing moment, especially for reporters who had covered the case for most of a year and who hoped to write an end to it. It was nearly over, and still Tawana was apparently content to leave a vacuum.

She fixed her large dark eyes on the piece of paper and Sharpton's flamboyant scrawl. God had saved her life, she said, reading it to them. God would see her through. All she wanted was justice and to be left alone. She had deceived no one—certainly not "my people." It was just that she had had "no *New York Times* to leak to."

She looked up for the last time, and her eyes seemed inspired by a vision of the attorney general floating over the reporters' heads. "Mister Abrams," she said, "you know the truth and I know it too. Why don't you step aside and let me speak to people I know will help me?"

Sharpton took over. Cheered on by fifty supporters, he described the *Times*'s article as "beneath a porno magazine to print." Mason joined him at the podium and they vowed to lead another demonstration that would shut down New York City. But now it had a hollow ring: there had been so many protests that had come to nothing, so many claims and counterclaims that had canceled one another out, so many vicious accusations and self-serving denials. How many times could you warn of apocalypse before people stopped listening?

They rushed out without answering questions, leaving the reporters flustered and wondering about a hundred unasked questions. Tawana and her family and Sharpton piled into a car and headed for Newark Airport. Speeding up the airport ramp, Sharpton noticed three cars pulling in behind them. He thought he saw a gun and badge.

"Hit the gas!" he yelled. "Hit the gas!"

Sharpton's driver hesitated—he already had too many tickets. But with the preacher screeching in his ear, he slammed on the accelerator and the Brawleys sped off the ramp, south to Philadelphia, once more on the run.

"Based upon all of the evidence that has been presented to the grand jury, we conclude that Tawana Brawley was not the victim of a forcible sexual assault by multiple assailants over a four-day period. There is no evidence that any sexual assault occurred. The grand jury further concludes there is nothing in regard to Tawana Brawley's appearance on November 28 that is inconsistent with this condition having been self-inflicted."

On October 6, 1988, the grand jury issued a one-hundred-seventy-page report based on six thousand pages of testimony from one hundred eighty witnesses and on two hundred fifty exhibits. Except for some forensic details—notably the way the racial slurs had been written on Tawana—there were no surprises.

Only one grand juror did not agree with the report. He was Jimmy Lee Powell, one of the two black jurors. A Mississippi-born engineer who had moved to Wappingers Falls in 1970 to work for IBM, he said too little was known of what happened to Tawana during her four missing days; he alone felt there was insufficient evidence to conclude that she lied. "I really do believe something did happen to Tawana," he said. "It could have been some family members or friends."

But Justice Ingrassia, who read the grand jury report to verify that its conclusions were justified by the evidence, said he had never seen a more rigorous presentation to a grand jury. "It was done thoroughly, competently, and, this is important, I thought it was done fairly," he told Abrams and Ryan in a brief court session. The conclusions "were not only beyond a preponderance of the credible evidence, but beyond any reasonable doubt—beyond any doubt."

Leaving the court, Abrams strode down Market Street to the armory, where a hundred reporters were waiting. Surrounded by law-enforcement officials who had toiled on the case for eight months, he was dapper in a dark suit, white shirt, and striped tie and more animated than anyone had ever seen him. It was like commencement day for the long-suffering attorney general. He waved the report, read from it, commented on it. When he talked of fecal matter and fibers, he gestured extravagantly.

The report, he said, should convince anyone, "whether you believe in the criminal justice system or not." It was not up to the grand jury to say *why* Tawana Brawley had lied, he observed, brushing the air with his hand to show the question was futile. "It's in the mind."

Finally, he tore into his chief tormentors—the Brawley advisers. "Their outrageous acts have increased the atmosphere of tension between the races throughout this nation, because of the celebrated nature of this case, because of their antics, because of the irresponsible charges they have made." It would be their fault, he said, if some legitimate victim of racism now was not taken seriously.

With the Brawley case over, he said, it was time to look at the conduct of these men. He handed out copies of a ten-page letter asking state judicial authorities to investigate Maddox and Mason, with a view toward suspension or disbarment. And his parting shot was unequivocal: "By counseling the Brawley family not to cooperate with law-enforcement authorities, by spreading lies and false information, and by advising their clients to defy and evade the mandate of the grand jury and the court, Mister Mason and Mister Maddox have made every effort to prevent the criminal justice system from uncovering the truth of what happened to Tawana Brawley."

"Get the hell away from my door," Ralph King screamed at the reporters who flocked into Diamond Plum Circle the day of the grand jury report.

Tawana had no comment.

The next day, the Brawleys and their advisers flew to Chicago for the annual convention of the Nation of Islam. There, Tawana was received in triumph by ten thousand members of the sect. When Louis Farrakhan took the stage, it was as if there had been no investigations, no grand jury, no evidence of a hoax, no lies. There was only his powerful voice rising to the rafters, vowing to dismember the white racists who had attacked Tawana Brawley, and the crowd's thundering roar of assent.

In the spring of 1989, C. Vernon Mason received a standing ovation at a Harvard Law School forum sponsored by black and women students when he declared: "I want to repeat to everyone within the sound of my voice that Steven Pagones, Scott Patterson, and Harry Crist, amongst others, kidnapped, raped, and sodomized Tawana Brawley."

Pagones, as promised, sued the Brawley advisers for eight hundred million dollars. The sum was absurd, but the prosecutor hoped to force them to account for the calumny they had heaped on him. "Every time they hold a news conference, every time they slander me," said Pagones, "that's an additional cause of action." (Pagones, citing disillusionment with a legal system that could be manipulated by the advisers' circus-like tactics, later quit his job as a prosecutor and became a private investigator.)

In June 1989, Sharpton was indicted on state charges of income tax evasion and grand larceny. He was accused of diverting to his personal use at least $250,000 in contributions to his National Youth Movement. The indictment stemmed from an investigation by Abrams begun almost a year before the Brawley case. Maddox called the charges a "political witch-hunt" stemming from the Brawley affair. Sharpton ridiculed the charges and the indictment as his "induction into the activist hall of fame."

Two months later, when a black teenager, Yusuf K. Hawkins, was surrounded by white youths and shot to death in the Bensonhurst section of Brooklyn, the dead boy's father turned to Sharpton to advise him and organize demonstrations. Governor Cuomo had to deal with Sharpton when he wanted to attend Yusuf's funeral, and Sharpton was soon on the march with crowds in Bensonhurst, chanting, "No justice! No peace!"

Angry whites picked up the rhythm, but with a twist:

"We want Tawana!

"We want Tawana!

"We want Tawana!"

At the next Nation of Islam convention, in October 1989, Farrakhan bestowed upon Tawana the Muslim name Maryum Muhammad. By then, she had graduated from Kellam High and she, Glenda, Tyice, and Ralph King had moved to Washington, D.C. By early 1990, Glenda Brawley and Ralph King had moved to Delaware, where Glenda took a clerical job with an accounting firm and King found work with a construction company. Juanita Brawley had returned to Monticello, though not to Matthew Strong, and was working for a youth agency.

Tawana, showing no legacy of trauma, had begun her freshman year at Howard University in Washington, her tuition paid by Sharpton's United African Movement. Her enrollment was front-page news in the school newspaper, and in an interview with the paper she called Alton Maddox her inspiration. She said she wanted to be a lawyer and was glad to be at a black college. "Being around your own people," she said, "is much better." There was no more talk about her case or the four days that had made her famous.

In May 1990, a court suspended Maddox from practicing law in New York State for refusing to cooperate with an official investigation into his conduct in the Brawley case.

One friend is known to have heard the truth from Tawana. Her confession took place in the spring of 1989 in a rented room in Virginia Beach. Glenda and Ralph King had insisted that she have nothing to do with the young man, her last boyfriend from Wappingers Falls. So when he arrived to see her, they had been forced to meet secretly. And it was in that room in Virginia Beach that Tawana kept her long-standing promise to tell Daryl Rodriguez everything.

31

The alarm clock pealed in Tawana Brawley's brain like a jester's rage. She threw back the covers and groped in the dark for the merciful lever, then dropped back to the edge of consciousness and slowly let the walls of her room swim into focus. Behind the frosted pane, purple dawn caught the branches, the eaves, the line of the porch, and stole in to paint the mirror frame, the bedstead, the jar on the dresser.

She hurried for the bathroom, as always, to beat the rush. But she had a special reason for wanting to be up and out early, for this day—November 24, 1987—was not to be just another school day. Her hair was more fuss than usual: it was quite short, about three inches, but a new hairpiece called a weave gave her shoulder-length tresses that had to be brushed out. She put on stone-washed jeans, a yellow sweater, black shoes, and an acid-washed blue-denim jacket she had borrowed from Trayon Kirby. The final touches were a gold necklace and two rings.

The rest of the household was beginning to stir, but Tawana bustled about as always, primping for classmates, hiding her intentions. She would tell them lies if they got up and asked any questions.

Atop her schoolbooks, she neatly folded a green-black, acid-washed miniskirt and a black blouse, and she picked out a small black pocketbook with a delicate thin strap and put a pair of black stockings in it. Shortly after seven o'clock, Tawana crept silently downstairs, threaded her way through the jumble of un-packed boxes in the living room, sipped some juice from the refrigerator, and went out with the stealth of a burglar. Mauve streaked the sky, and the first light like smoke drifted in the woods above the Hudson.

In a little while, she saw the car, a blue Dodge Omni. It had been stolen in Poughkeepsie not long ago. Trayon Kirby was behind the wheel, and next to him was another Ketcham stu-dent, Paul Franco. Tawana had known Kirby as a classmate and neighbor at the Montclair Town Houses and had even had a short romantic fling with him. Ketcham was only a ten-minute walk from her apartment, but since her recent transfer from John Jay High, Kirby had been giving her a lift to school.

This morning, however, she asked him to drive her to New-burgh.

They sped the six miles down a winding river road and across the Beacon-Newburgh Bridge into Newburgh, into streets of run-down row houses and graffiti-scarred storefronts. Kirby let her off outside a three-story apartment building at 88 Clinton Street. The place was painted a garish turquoise, but anything was possible in this war zone.

Tawana Brawley knocked at the door.

Sandra Buxton was surprised to see her. They had spoken by telephone the night before about her visiting Todd, but no date had been set. It occurred to Sandra that Tawana should be in school, and the encounter began on a false note.

"Why aren't you in school?" she asked.

"I'm on Thanksgiving break," said Tawana. It was so difficult to be guileless: one had to anticipate the question, consider what was plausible, then find the right-sounding words.

Sandra knew it was a lie. She had brothers in school, and they were not to be dismissed until Wednesday, the day before Thanksgiving; this was Tuesday. But she didn't argue the point. She was too sleepy. Besides, this was not such a bad day for Tawana to visit Todd. Sandra explained that her mother, Ge-neva, intended to visit Todd at the jail today. Perhaps Tawana could go with her. Sandra had some errands to run, but she too wanted to see Todd and maybe she would join them later at the jail.

Sandra's boyfriend, Kelvin Morris, drove Tawana to Geneva Buxton's apartment, a few blocks away at 150 Smith Street. It was a red-brick housing project that loomed up two blocks from the river, a place that rumbled when the freight trains rolled by on the Conrail tracks. The Buxton apartment had no river view: it overlooked an asphalt parking lot where youths hatched plots in the twilight and children in shabby coats played basketball under broken hoops.

Geneva Buxton, a stocky woman with a short Afro, opened the door. She recognized Tawana from previous visits.

"Are you going to see Todd today?" Tawana asked meekly.

"Yes."

She beamed. "I'm going too."

While Tawana had visited the Buxton apartment many times during her steady relationship with Todd, her appearance now surprised Geneva. She had always come before in the evening or on weekends. Geneva realized that she was skipping school, which surprised her because she had thought of the girl as conscientious, almost bookish. But she knew Tawana was infatuated with Todd, and she agreed to let the girl accompany her to the jail.

As Geneva dressed for the trip, Tawana—normally talkative— was oddly silent. But over the next hour, as the time to leave drew near, her mood swung sharply up. She bounced on the sofa, waved her hands, and bubbled excitedly about Todd. She helped dress Geneva's infant granddaughter, Janell. The girl had always been helpful and respectful, almost like a member of the family, which now included five boys, two girls, and various grandchildren. She had washed the dinner dishes sometimes, had called Geneva "ma'am," had even asked for permission when she wanted to use the bathroom. Geneva regarded her as a sweet, lovely child.

As Geneva Buxton finished dressing, Tawana changed from her

jeans and sweater into the acid-washed skirt and black blouse. She also put on the black stockings. Tawana carried Janell and they took a taxi driven by Geneva's son, Gary, to the Short Line bus terminal, where they caught a ten-fifteen bus for Goshen. They slept most of the way and arrived at the jail about one P.M.

They immediately ran into a problem. As a minor not related to an inmate, Tawana could not be admitted under jail regulations. But Geneva told a matron that Tawana was her daughter, that she had come all the way from New York City and forgotten her identification. The matron did not believe her, and Tawana began to pout. It worked. "Just this once," the matron said sternly, unlocking the passage.

They were ushered past two metal detectors and two locked, barred doors into a Spartan, brightly lighted visiting room with hard chairs and a bare table. Todd was there, smiling crookedly, hope and despair etched on his shallow adolescent face. A guard hovered. Tawana tried to hold Todd's hand, but he pulled away: he had already been trained in the terrors of jail. Todd showed them bruises where he said he had been beaten. The mood of the jail was ugly, he said. Only last Sunday, some guards and inmates had clashed and he had heard tales that white-sheeted guards had shackled and beaten prisoners.

After a while, Todd asked his mother to wait outside so he and Tawana could talk alone. She did.

For twenty minutes, they talked quietly about the past, about their relationship, about what they would do when he was freed in the spring: poignant musings unbound by bars and walls. Tawana took out her wallet and tried to give Todd some photographs of herself, but the guard stopped her. It was the kind of pointless denial that strengthened a prisoner's resolve.

Geneva finally came back in; Sandra Buxton had arrived and they all chatted for another half hour. Sandra stayed when Tawana and Geneva left at midafternoon to catch a bus back to Newburgh.

Outside, as they waited for the bus, there occurred one of those

strange events—perhaps innocent, perhaps menacing—that are
hard to gauge, even in retrospect, and that made wonderful grist
for Alton Maddox's righteousness. Geneva was standing at the
curb and Tawana was seated on the grass, cross-legged in the miniskirt, holding the baby Janell in her lap, when it happened. A
red pickup truck with gray stripes and twin vertical exhaust pipes
drove slowly past. They saw two white men inside, a heavyset
driver with a dark beard and long hair, and a companion they
could not make out clearly. As they cruised by, both stared hard
at Tawana. The truck made a U-turn down the road, came back,
and made another slow pass. Again the creeps stared at Tawana.
It was unnerving, but they saw the men no more.

The bus finally pulled up and the women headed back to Newburgh. The trip was uneventful and it was late afternoon when
they arrived. Several of Geneva's teenaged children were home.
As she began to fix supper, Geneva suggested that Tawana hurry
if she was going to catch the six o'clock bus to Wappingers Falls.

But Tawana was in no hurry. She settled down on the sofa and
began watching television.

Geneva had been vaguely worried about her all day. There were
little hints that something was wrong. She had taken nothing
to eat or drink, and now as the family sat down to dinner she
refused even a glass of juice. She just sat there, watching television. The next bus was at eight, and she showed no inclination
to take it, either.

"Is anything wrong?" Geneva asked.

Tawana was reluctant to go home, she said, because she hated
her family's new apartment at Leewood Arms. "The people aren't
very friendly. They act prejudiced," she explained.

It occurred to Geneva that Tawana wanted to stay overnight.
But she didn't know Tawana's mother and she didn't want to
be blamed for keeping the girl out. Nor did she want to tell her
what to do. And so while she offered Tawana the couch for the
night, she also offered a word of warning, suggesting that the girl
might be better off going home. "Tawana," she said, "if you
don't catch the bus you might get into trouble."

"I'm already in trouble," the girl replied.

It was Ralph King, Tawana explained. He was still furious with her for staying out until five in the morning after a party a few weeks ago. Her mother had forgiven her, but King was still upset and had been scolding her for days.

"He's been ranting on and on and on about it," Tawana said. "He won't let go." She said nothing about his leers, nothing about the fears that had plagued her at home for months.

"I want to leave home," she confided, and she went into flights of fancy: perhaps she could move into Todd's bedroom until he got out of jail. Then they could get an apartment together; they could get married.

Surely she was only joking, Geneva Buxton suggested.

But the girl went on. She might become a model and make lots of money. A modeling photographer had already taken pictures of her—the ones she tried to give Todd at the jail—and she pulled them out like evidence, as if they somehow proved the wonderful possibilities of her dream. One showed her in a black dress, cut low in the back. Geneva didn't like it: the dress was pretty, but not for a young girl.

Once more, Geneva urged her to go home, to keep matters from getting worse and incurring the wrath of Ralph King.

Still the girl hesitated.

But Geneva did not. Now she said: "I don't want to get into trouble with your parents. Maybe it would be best—for both of us—if you went home."

Tawana got up. She changed from the green-black skirt into her jeans and pulled the denim jacket on over her black blouse. She put the other clothes, the skirt and the yellow sweater, into a white plastic grocery bag Geneva gave her. Geneva called Bob's Taxicab Service and in a little while a taxi driven by another of her sons, Dwain, pulled up and took Tawana to the Short Line bus terminal.

Newburgh's main street, Broadway, is preposterously wide. Its scale suggests a procession of elegant theaters, cosmopolitan hotels, and awning-draped department stores. But the reality is the grim front of a desperate town: rows of shabby storefronts, boarded-up buildings, and fleabag hotels, staring at one another across the gulf. The Short Line terminal was as unappealing as all the rest—a dim light behind the dirty windows, a big room with broken seats, dust motes scurrying over the floor like mice. It was closed for the night, but it was better out in the cold anyway, and that's where Tawana waited. There was no moon, but stars flecked the galactic night.

A freezing wind scythed off the Hudson as the northbound bus from New York City pulled up with Todd McGue at the wheel and one passenger sitting way back in the dark, bound for Poughkeepsie. Waiting at the bus stop in the chilly night were two more passengers, Thomas Barnes, who was heading home to Fishkill just across the Hudson, and Tawana Brawley.

As Tawana paid the $2.10 fare for the twenty-five-minute one-way trip to Wappingers Falls, Todd McGue greeted her. It was a pleasant surprise for both of them. McGue, a Poughkeepsie resident, knew Tawana both as a passenger and as the stepdaughter of a fellow Short Line driver. She sat up front behind McGue. So did Barnes. The other passenger (whose name was never learned despite extensive efforts to find him) remained in the back and spoke to no one.

McGue pulled out at eight-fifteen on the last run of his thirteen-hour day.

Barnes quickly struck up a conversation with Tawana, who seemed open and friendly. But McGue brashly intruded from the driver's seat and warned Barnes off. Tawana was the stepdaughter of another driver, Ralph King, he said, and he warned: "King would kill you."

Barnes did not pursue it, though he had the impression that McGue, a young man, was himself trying to flirt with the girl. Barnes got off in Fishkill just after eight twenty-five.

Now they were alone except for the other rider. Tawana and McGue talked quietly on the trip to Wappingers Falls. She seemed to be in good spirits, smiling and joking.

She asked him if he would mind driving her home. She explained that she had moved recently from the Pavillion Condominiums to an apartment on Carmine Drive in Wappingers Falls.

McGue said he was sorry, but he couldn't do it. Dropping the rider in Fishkill had forced him to go north to Poughkeepsie along Route 9, instead of taking 9D, a parallel road that went through Wappingers Falls and right by Carmine Drive. The route he was on would take her no closer than a mile from home. But Tawana took this lightly, sighing and settling back. McGue asked what she was doing out so late. She told him she had visited a friend at the Orange County Jail.

As they rolled north, McGue recalled that she had often met his bus near a 7-Eleven at Hopewell Road, near the Pavillion. It occurred to him that she might want to get off there. But when he approached Hopewell Road and began pulling over, Tawana asked him to drive on. She said she would get off farther up, at the next crossroad, known as Myers Corners Road to the east and Middlebush Road to the west.

It was a busy intersection. Traffic was light on the crossroad, but heavy on the six-lane Route 9, which at Wappingers Falls became a strip of neon-lit service stations and fast-food joints. On the northeast corner was Paino's Mobil station, an all-night oasis where arc lamps pushed back the darkness. Everything else was shut: a bank on the northwest corner, an abandoned music shop with a steep chalet roof to the southeast, a squat office building that concealed a cemetery to the southwest.

It was eight-forty P.M. when McGue pulled the bus over.

Tawana got up. Slung over her shoulder was the black purse with the thin black strap. She hugged her schoolbooks to her chest and carried the white plastic grocery bag containing her extra clothing.

McGue, still worried about her long walk down a dark untraveled road, had a suggestion. "There's a telephone over near the corner," he said. "Why don't you call somebody at home. Maybe they could come and get you."

Tawana told him the phone at her family's new apartment had

not yet been connected. (In fact, the telephone had been hooked up for four days, and she had been using it regularly.)

She stepped off the bus, serene, vulnerable.

They said good-bye, and McGue shut the door.

As he pulled away, gathering speed, moving out into the flow of traffic bound for Poughkeepsie, he glanced into the sideview mirror and saw her for the last time. She was walking back along Route 9 toward Myers Corners Road, getting smaller in the quivering mirror, vanishing into the cold, moonless night.

She walked along the shoulder of the highway, facing the onrushing cars, oblivious of the murderous fenders, lost in the greater dangers of home and family. The girl seemed magically to appear and disappear as the glaring headlights splashed her with blinding light and raced away, leaving her in darkness.

She knew she was in trouble. Ralph King had been badgering her for weeks, complaining of her late-night escapades and threatening her with his crude words and his powerful hands. Now she had skipped school two days in a row and it was another late night. How could she explain it this time? Did another beating await her? Would her mother never wake up to the evil triangle they lived in? Perhaps the right lie would save her again. But she needed, first, to know the prevailing mood at 4-D Carmine Drive.

There was a phone near the corner, as McGue had said, and she dropped in a coin and called 298–0381. Her mother answered.

Furious, Glenda erupted: Where was she? Why hadn't she called? She ordered Tawana to get home—no, Ralph would pick her up.

Tawana didn't try to make excuses. She hung up. She crossed Route 9 and began walking west on Middlebush Road.

King's car soon pulled up beside her and he got out. He struck her just behind the left ear, raising a small bruise. She got in the car and sobbed all the way home.

At 4-D Carmine Drive, they demanded to know where she had

been and what she had done. She muttered explanations between sobs, but they did not satisfy King.

The anger died down at last. But Tawana had already made up her mind: she could no longer stay in this house with this man. King had killed a woman once before, and she had been the target, too many times, of that same fury. She fled upstairs to her room. The humiliation was always harder to bear than the pain: the bruises and the welts went away, but the shame went to bed with you. The plan formed itself in the dark. She listened for the sounds of the household to die. Then, after her mother and King had gone to bed, she changed her clothes and crept downstairs. After taking some food from the refrigerator, she left the house, closing the door softly behind her.

The wind was up and dead leaves rattled over the ground; invisible branches swayed and clicked like things alive. She walked until the yellow pools of light from the street lamps gave out at the edge of town. There were a few illuminated houses down the road and finally the garish highway to cross, then a country lane where only stars lit the lonely way. It was a little more than two miles to her family's vacant former apartment at the Pavillion, and it took her about half an hour to get there.

A window latch at the rear of Apartment 19A was broken, and she opened it and climbed in. The place was bare, except for the little pile of green plastic garbage bags her family had left. The electricity was still on, but she didn't turn on the lights. There was a baseboard electric heater, though, and she got that going. She also plugged in the refrigerator and put her food inside. She spent the night on the carpeted floor, a jacket for her pillow.

The next day, she slipped out and called home.

Glenda Brawley answered.

Tawana cursed King and his violence. She cursed her mother for allowing it and for her blindness to King's advances toward her. She was tired of being abused. She would not come home while there was any chance that King might do it again.

Glenda was taken aback at the forcefulness of Tawana's appeal.

She softened and tried to comfort her daughter. Glenda said she was sure something could be worked out, but perhaps not right away. King had awakened to discover that Tawana had run away again, and he was in no mood to listen to reason. She asked her daughter where she was.

Tawana was reluctant to disclose her hideaway for fear that King might come and get her. But Glenda persuaded her that they would have to trust each other and work together if ever Tawana was to get back into the house. Tawana finally told her mother that she was staying at the Pavillion, and they agreed that she would have to remain there for the time being, until King calmed down.

Did Tawana need anything?

She had enough food for the day. The heater was working. She would need a few things, but not right away. They agreed to meet early the next morning, Thanksgiving Day, at the Pavillion.

In the meantime, Glenda would pretend to know nothing. It was the only thing she could do if she wanted to keep both King and her daughter.

The conspiracy began modestly.

First, Glenda made a series of telephone calls to Tawana's friends—Stacey and Cheryl Kelly, Trayon Kirby, and others. Tawana was missing, Glenda said. Had any of them seen her?

Only Kirby knew anything. He said Tawana had skipped school Tuesday, and Monday for that matter. He admitted he had driven her to Newburgh instead of to school Tuesday morning, at her request, and had dropped her off on Clinton Street, near South and Liberty Streets.

Glenda next mustered her courage and called her older sister, Juanita. "Nit, Tawana didn't come home," she said. "We're worried. Ralph's crying. We don't know what to do."

"What do you mean she didn't come home? Where was she last seen?"

"Trayon picked her up yesterday."

Glenda said Kirby had been able to supply only scant information on Tawana's movements, so Juanita called Kirby herself.
He told her he had dropped Tawana off at Sandra Buxton's house
in Newburgh, that he had taken her there so she could see Todd
Buxton.

Juanita was deeply worried. Tawana was hardly an innocent:
she had run away several times, skipped school, and stayed away
overnight. But the neighborhood around South and Liberty Streets
was rough. She had a feeling that something awful had happened to the girl. From her home in Kingston, Juanita drove down
the Hudson twenty-five miles to Newburgh and went straight
to police headquarters, arriving at dusk.

A sergeant was behind the bulletproof glass when she walked
in, distress on her face.

"We don't have anybody to talk to you right now," he said.
"Could you come back later?"

"No, I won't." She told him her niece was missing from
Wappingers Falls and had last been seen at Liberty and South
Streets. She offered the sergeant a snapshot, but he didn't
take it.

"Teenagers run away," he said. "Give it another twenty-four
hours."

"It's not like her," she lied.

"Well, the best we could do right now is to put her name in
the computer."

The sergeant took a few notes, but did not make out a formal
missing person's report. He said something about making a report in Wappingers Falls, but Juanita didn't get it.

When she left the station, she was under the impression that
the police were proceeding on the case, though without much
enthusiasm. She headed for Clinton Street: whatever the police
might be doing, it could not hurt for her to hunt for Tawana
too. She rang the bell at Sandra Buxton's apartment, but there
was no answer.

She decided to scour the streets and soon found herself in "crack
alley." Courageously, Juanita went into four or five crack houses,

asking addicts and pushers if anyone knew or had seen Tawana Brawley. She showed them the snapshot.

"Who is she?" a boy asked. "We've never seen her around before."

No one had.

After hours of fruitless searching, Juanita returned to her youth-counseling office in Kingston and enlisted the help of a street-wise teenager from Poughkeepsie who knew all the dens and hideouts of crack alley.

"We got to go back," she implored.

The youth warned her it was dangerous, but she insisted and he went with her. They returned to Sandra Buxton's apart-ment. Juanita banged on the door, and this time she was home.

"Are you Sandra Buxton?"

"Yeah."

"Do you know Tawana Brawley?"

"No, I don't know any Tawana."

"Tawana hasn't been here?"

"I haven't seen her! Didn't I tell you I don't know any Tawana."

"Let me tell you something. Tawana is a minor, and if I hear or know of any way at all that you're involved in any foul play, I'll have you arrested for endangering the welfare of a minor."

Juanita stormed away, nursing her suspicions. She and her es-cort searched for hours, but found nothing. Finally, she took him home, but was too upset to break off. She returned to New-burgh, but found only more crackheads, more criminals.

Although it was late, she enlisted the help of Kermit Thorpe, a middle-aged member of the Jubilaires, the gospel singers who had become "big brothers" of Tawana. She and Thorpe worked opposite sides of town to cover more ground.

"I haven't seen her," Thorpe reported when they met later. "No one has seen her. No one has even heard of her."

"Kermit, did you describe her?"

"Juanita, I've looked everywhere."

They went on for another hour, but it seemed hopeless. When

they gave up, it was four-thirty A.M. on Thanksgiving Day. Juanita went home and called Glenda.

"Ralph is out looking," Glenda said. "He is crying. He is very upset. No one knows where she is. No one seems to have any idea."

Thanksgiving dawned cold and clear, and Frank Backer was up early at 14A Scarborough Lane. It was sometime before eight-thirty that he chanced to look out the rear glass doors, out across the broad faded lawns of the Pavillion Condominiums.

What he saw was a black teenaged girl in an acid-washed denim jacket standing at the back door of 19A Carnaby Drive. Her hair was longish, almost to her shoulders, but it stuck out on the sides and was matted in the back, as if it had been slept on and unwashed for days. As he watched, the girl stepped to the corner of the building, crouched down, and peeked around onto Carnaby Drive. Then, she stood up, walked back, and entered Apartment 19A through the rear door.

Backer turned away, puzzled, and fixed the details in memory.

Glenda entered 19A from the front. Tawana had expected her mother, but it had occurred to her when she saw one of the family cars pulling up that King might have discovered her hiding place—and she had cautiously gone outside to peek around the corner, ready to run if necessary.

Glenda had brought a radio, some crackers and milk, a toothbrush and toiletries, a washcloth, a few things to relieve the boredom and hunger. She cautioned Tawana to play the radio softly and to keep the lights low at night lest some nosy neighbor learn of her presence and notify the Pavillion's management office. But Tawana cared nothing about the neighbors or the management; she worried only about keeping her whereabouts a secret from Ralph King. Later, the neighbors did hear music and see lights in the supposedly vacated apartment, but they did nothing about it.

The inspiration came from a similar ruse pulled by her name-sake acquaintance, Tawana Ward Dempsey. Dempsey's story had been easily punctured by the police. The Brawley story wouldn't have to go that far. It would only have to fool King. But it would have to be persuasive. She would pretend she had been abducted and raped by a gang of white men. King's anger would melt to sympathy, clearing her way to return home.

She began to work out the details. It would require a razor blade, a pair of gloves, and a few other items. Glenda agreed to fake the discovery of Tawana on the Pavillion lawn. Tawana started assembling the materials that night. She had seen the next-door neighbors, Gaston and Elizabeth Abril, drive off early, apparently to spend the holiday away. The Abrils often left their patio door unlocked. Tawana slipped in and stole a pair of women's jeans and a pair of white boots.

Juanita was more frantic with every passing hour. After a little sleep in Kingston, she returned on Thanksgiving morning to police headquarters in Newburgh and was shocked to hear that the police were not looking for Tawana, that a missing person's report would have to be filed in Wappingers Falls by parents, not an aunt. It seemed useless to tell them that she had virtually raised the girl and was still her legal guardian, and disgustedly she went out again to search.

Ralph King, still angry, went out to look for the runaway on Thanksgiving Day as well. He got Trayon Kirby to drive him to Newburgh and show him where he had dropped Tawana off. He knocked on Sandra Buxton's door, but there was no one home.

By evening, Juanita and King had broken off their separate searches. King went home; Juanita drove to Monticello to have a holiday dinner with her teenaged daughter, Kenya, and former husband, Matthew Strong.

Outrage

The next day, while Juanita searched the streets of Newburgh again, Glenda and Tawana met to lay their final plans. Glenda had brought a razor blade and a pair of black leather gloves. She helped Tawana unbraid the hair weave, leaving her hair short and matted, looking as if it had been cut. They packed up the hair weave and the camp remnants, the extra clothing, the underwear and one of Tawana's pink slip-on shoes, the rest of the food, and the trash that she had accumulated for Glenda to carry away.

They agreed that Glenda would return Saturday afternoon about one-thirty and would discover Tawana in a dazed, degraded condition out on the lawn and take her home. They would tell King that Tawana had been abducted after running away from home, that she had been taken to a woods where five or six white men had raped her, that she had been knocked out for days and then dumped in a garbage bag at the Pavillion, smeared with excrement and scrawled with racial slurs. She would not be able to remember the men or where it had all happened because she had been hit on the head—and had a bruise to prove it. King might suggest calling the police, but Glenda and Tawana were sure they could talk him out of that. It would be a needless hardship on an already traumatized girl. Besides, the police might want to question King about how the girl had suffered the bruise on the back of her head—the bruise he had inflicted the night he picked her up. King would want to avoid any trouble.

Finally, it came time to part. There were no pretenses between them now: they knew one another—they were reliant upon one another—as never before.

That night, Tawana began the final preparations. She used the razor blade to carve "NIGGER" into the side of her lone pink shoe and to cut one of the white boots to pull out some wads of the cottonlike insulation material. When she was done with the razor blade, she hid it under a radiator.

Using the stove's flame, she scorched away the crotch and inner thighs of the stolen jeans. Finding the right thing to write

386

with was a matter of trial and error. She lightly burned parts of
the washcloth her mother had brought and tried to write with
that. It didn't work. But she discovered that by wetting the
charred cloth, she could use it to scrawl letters on her body
with an effect similar to charcoal. She used it to write racial slurs
on her pink blouse and across her chest and torso.

Before dawn on Saturday, Tawana sneaked out onto the lawn
and, using the gloves her mother had brought, gathered dog
feces into one of the green plastic bags her family had left behind. Late in the morning, she stuffed wads of the boot insulation material into her nostrils and ears to protect herself from
infection and foul odor, and again using the gloves, smeared the
excrement into her hair and onto her arms and legs and on the
inside and outside of her clothing, which included the jeans with
the scorched inner thighs. She left the denim jacket and her
own jeans in the washing machine. Finally, she opened another
plastic garbage bag and threw in the feces-smeared gloves, the
charred facecloth, and the unused portions of the cotton wads.
As the hour of rendezvous with her mother approached, she
took up the bag and went out onto the lawn and into the cold.

She crouched at the corner of the building and glanced around
furtively to see if anyone was watching. The coast seemed clear.
Then she crawled into the bag so that just her head was sticking
out. She hopped twice and then toppled onto the wet, mushy
ground and lay there, still as death.

Glenda, who pretended she was driving to the Pavillion to pick
up the mail and look for Tawana, arrived a little late. And so,
instead of being found by her mother, Tawana was found by Joyce
and Lorenzo Lloray and Gary Lanza. When Glenda looked out
the rear window of 19A and saw them all clustered around the
girl, it was clear that their plan had gone awry. Perhaps
the police had been called. Backing off, she sat in her car out
front, pretending to read the mail, waiting to see what would
happen, considering her options. She could walk out into the
yard and join those who had found Tawana, but that might seem too
much of a coincidence. Or she could drive away and file a missing

person's report with the police. But that was risky, too, for she and Tawana wanted to keep the police out of it. Besides, it would seem peculiar if she reported the girl missing just as she was being found. Then a siren began wailing in the distance, and her options narrowed to one: to report the girl missing and obscure the plot between mother and daughter.

As Glenda Brawley pulled away, Deputy Sheriff Eric Thurston pulled up. In time, it would come to be seen as a strange, suspicious coincidence, one of many circumstances that would have to be exploited to trick the local authorities, the FBI, the politicians, the insatiable press, the anguished blacks, the horrified nation, all soon to be swept along on a great river of folly.

THE
SQUIRE
WALKS
OUT

"What do you think about this, Mary?" Squire Bradfield asked his elderly neighbor as he headed for the diner.

He showed her the newspaper.

She paused beside him on the steps and shrugged as if another decade of war and pestilence had come to an end. "Well," she said wryly, "the white folks say it's over . . ."

Bradfield smiled and hurried on.

In a way, it was over, he thought, but not just because white folks through their grand jury and their newspapers had said so. He made his way to Nostrand Avenue. Just beyond Dick Tracey's Bicycle Shop, he turned in at the familiar steamy windows.

The regulars at Edgar's had gathered in the back for the post-mortems, wearing the glum faces of soldiers caught in an exposed foxhole. Ethelyn Smith brought coffee and stood beside them, a hand on her hip.

"We knew it was coming down," Roy Canton muttered.

Professor Mackey, his elbow propped on a book, scowled defiantly. "Everybody who ain't deaf, dumb, blind, and stupid can see that white folks were protecting their own."

Hampton Rookard shrugged at the old, old story: the whites had done it again and the blacks had to take it. You couldn't tell Rookard there was anything new in this. "Look," he said, "I've been in the struggle since I was born."

"I don't think we're going to get justice," Canton said. "I really don't believe so anymore. I don't think that this society has the capacity of giving us justice. I really don't believe so."

"The game never changes, sweetheart—only the names," the Professor said.

"It's over with," said Squire Bradfield simply.

Mrs. Smith arched an eyebrow. "The media says it's over, but in the black community it is not!" They looked at her. She went on: "It will remain because the case—whatever the verdict on whether she was lying or not—opened up the minds of black people."

Spring had arrived on Nostrand Avenue, and through the windows at Edgar's they could see the shoppers and do-nothings, the families and drug pushers moving in the yellow afternoon sunlight: men and women in African hats called crowns and bright kente prints from Ghana, people with dreadlocks, teenagers in the baggy pants, high-top sneakers, and reversed baseball caps of in-your-face hip-hop, a streaming medley of bright colors to put away the dreary winter.

The calendar by the cash register showed that it was Saturday, April 22, 1989. More than six months had gone by since the Brawley case, and they hardly mentioned it anymore. Today, business had been slow, but Ethelyn Smith had been glad of it. She was tired after a hard week at the stove and the tables, and there had been time to mingle and chat, to think about summer and a holiday somewhere far from Nostrand Avenue.

A few of the regulars were there—Squire Bradfield and his friend Dallas Smith; Oswald Cumberbatch and Shirley Hall—lingering over coffee at the back. A couple of customers had just left, but the old-timer called Pops was still at the counter. Mrs. Smith surveyed the row of empty tables and vacant stools and glanced at the clock—it was only two-ten, but she shrugged: perhaps she'd close early.

She put away a stack of dishes and came around the counter to lock up and reverse the OPEN sign on the front door. She might have made it if she hadn't paused to say something to Bradfield. When she looked up again the two black men were standing near the register—a tall one and a short one.

The short one said nothing. He stayed at the front, near the cash register, and his eyes swept the tables, the counter, the back, the few patrons, in a swift assessment.

"What do you have good for dinner?" the tall one asked, stepping toward the counter. He was about six-feet-four and he looked powerful.

Mrs. Smith began telling him what was left on the menu, but she let it go when she saw the gun. The tall one was pointing it straight at her.

From the back, she could hear the others, still jabbering.

"This is a robbery," the tall one said. "Give me your money."

Now there was silence.

The short one locked the door and the tall one strode to the table in the corner where Bradfield sat with Dallas Smith, Cumberbatch, and Shirley Hall. He put the gun to Bradfield's head, and the short one finally spoke up.

"Give me the money from the register," he said, looking at Mrs. Smith.

"I don't have any money," she said.

He went past her, around behind the register and banged open the till. He scooped out the bills. It didn't amount to much, about fifty dollars, and he scowled.

"I want all your money," the tall one said to the others.

The old man called Pops suddenly panicked and started shouting, "Police!" The tall one reached out with one hand and knocked him to the floor. Then he waved the gun in their frightened faces.

Shirley Hall slipped off two gold rings, one with diamonds and the other with a topaz birthstone, and handed them over. Dallas Smith took out a wallet and surrendered one hundred thirty dollars. Bradfield gave up a hundred dollars.

Up front, the short one reached for Ethelyn Smith's gold earrings, the ones she'd received for Christmas from her eldest son. She drew back and then took them off herself so he wouldn't rip her earlobes open. He stuffed them in his pocket. Then he grabbed the front of her white waitress dress and ripped it open. He reached inside her bra, but found nothing hidden. He checked her pockets: again nothing. Cursing, he ordered her to lie face-down on the floor behind the counter. She thought: We're all going to be shot.

Then she heard the tall one shouting at Bradfield, Cumberbatch, Dallas Smith, and Shirley Hall. He was moving around them, waving the gun, using his free hand to pull out their pockets, rifle a purse, open a wallet. "If I find any more money on you," he said, "I'm going to kill you."

The search turned up nothing. Cursing, he ordered them all to lie on the floor.

"Is this all I got?" the short one was complaining. "I'm not goin' nowhere until I get some more money."

They searched the toilet, the storage room at the back, Mrs. Smith's little office. They found nothing of value. Mrs. Smith didn't dare look up. The others, too, pressed their faces to the floor, listening to the banging desk drawers and the obscenities, watching the feet move across the linoleum between the chair legs.

Suddenly, they were gone.

Pops was first on his feet. He hurried to the front door and saw them at the corner jumping onto a number 44 bus going south on Nostrand.

The rest of them got up slowly, still shaking. They called the police then and submitted to the pointless questions. "It was a bad scene," Mrs. Smith told the detectives.

The afternoon light had gone when they finally left, and she sat alone for a little while at the counter. She'd done it a thousand times at closing without really seeing the shabbiness of the place. But it was easier to take stock when someone has just pointed a gun at you. She looked around at the rickety tables, the empty register, the paper napkins, the chipped dishes, the pastry going stale under the cover. She was forty-one years old. She'd been robbed before, and she'd be robbed again, probably even shot if she went on.

The Squire Walks Out

The sign outside said Cafeteria, and the inside was as anonymous as a railway waiting room. Gossipy servers dished overcooked food from steam tables. Someone stuffed bent spoons and forks into metal draincups. The coffee was invariably bitter.

The place was anonymous, like the clientele, but it was out of the cold autumn wind that blew up Nostrand Avenue, and not far from the vacant shell that had been Edgar's until a few months ago.

They had been talking for an hour at a table near the front, exiles who had found one another in the diaspora. Most of the old crowd had gone elsewhere, and while they still met on the street they rarely sat down anymore to take up the anything-black agenda. The Brawley case had ended a year ago, and as Ethelyn Smith had said, it was time to move on.

Rookard with his awesome spiked dreadlocks was the first to go. He had attended all of Sharpton's United African Movement meetings at the nearby Slave Theater since the Brawley case, and he would go on attending them; he had marched on the protests and the days of outrage, and he would march again every chance he got. If they were out there, they would see *him* around. "If it's black and it's for black people, I'll do what I can," he said. "Whether I'm walking with Sharpton or Daughtry or Farrakhan, it doesn't matter. If it's for *black*, that's where I am."

Professor Mackey was the next to leave. His judgmental eyes scanned the little circle of friends as if wondering what might become of them. He was sixty-nine, but he had his life as a lecturer and counselor, and he had his unshakable faith in history. He finished his coffee, said farewell, and went out without looking back, carrying his books like confidence.

Marilyn Grier, who also attended the meetings at the Slave Theater, seemed in no hurry to go. She and Roy Canton lingered with Squire Bradfield over a last cup of coffee.

Confession was not on Bradfield's mind, but something about the moment was ripe: Mackey and Rookard had taken their strident black patriotisms out into the cold, and now they were alone.

"I hate to go against my friends," Bradfield said quietly. "But I really don't believe Tawana Brawley."

Canton looked at him as if for the first time. The talkative Squire had said so little about the case or his feelings, either while it was going on or over the past year. He was talking now about black women who gave themselves willingly to white men, and Canton cut him off sharply: "You're talking about a fifteen-year-old, okay?"

But Bradfield had begun something that had nagged at him for a long time, and he was determined to go on: "I really don't believe her. I believed her at the outset. Naturally, I was outraged. But when they couldn't bring any substantial evidence, my skepticism grew. I didn't see any evidence that this happened. I mean, that she's in the garbage bag and all this. I started putting all this together and it just seemed to me that this wasn't the case."

Canton turned to Marilyn Grier and said with an edge: "He would not make that statement back at Mrs. Smith's place. He's talking about death!"

But Edgar's was gone and Bradfield was going on, recalling how quickly—how miraculously—Tawana had recovered from the ordeal her family and advisers had described. Like Mackey and Canton and Rookard, he had gone to Bethany Baptist Church. Like them, he had seen the girl.

"She's standing up there like a queen, shaking people's hands. Hundreds of people! Saying, 'How do you do? How do you do?' With the poise!"

"God held her hand," Grier said. "What did you expect?"

"He would not come to the Slave and make that statement," Canton said.

"No," Bradfield admitted. "I wouldn't be indiscreet."

Canton still believed passionately in Tawana; as far as he could see, the outcome of her case meant the police were free to kill his son and rape his daughter. But he cared about the Squire, too.

He asked him whether he'd ever told any of the Edgar's crowd how he felt.

Bradfield's reply was quiet, almost bemused: "What would have happened if I had?"

The scorn, the ostracism, didn't have to be spelled out. Besides, what good would it have done to speak up: people heard only what they wanted to hear.

But now Bradfield felt emboldened. Black people, he said, could be just as dishonest as whites. It was wrong to think that you could fight centuries of white hatred with black lies. "We are not clean," he said solemnly.

Canton nearly jumped up: "Don't say things like that." He glanced at the black faces all around. "Believe me, one of them guys could seriously hurt you."

"I know the passions," Bradfield said, getting up. "But I can't help it. I want to be objective." He turned and strode out onto Nostrand Avenue.

His friend watched him go, shaking his head sadly. No, the Squire had it wrong. But he, Roy Canton, would never change his mind about Tawana Brawley. There had been far too much pain for that.

A Word About Sources

This book is based on more than one thousand interviews with well over one hundred investigators, witnesses, and key participants in the case. Many details have also been taken from the report of the grand jury and other official documents, including police and medical reports, and from the confidential summaries of evidence compiled by investigators for the special prosecutor who presented the matter to the grand jury. These summaries were obtained by the authors in reporting the Brawley story for *The New York Times*.

Our accounts of meetings and events that took place in private—including conversations and details ranging from the participants' thoughts to nuances of their behavior—have all come from participants themselves; wherever possible, we have obtained accounts from several of those involved, especially concerning encounters that proved to be disputatious. Details of closed-door meetings the Brawley advisers had with Governor Cuomo and Attorney General Abrams, for example, come from Cuomo and Abrams and from various members of their staffs, as well as from the Reverend Al Sharpton. On some points, the versions were in conflict, and we have evaluated the competing claims and presented an account based on our considered judgment of what happened.

Accounts of strategy developed by Alton Maddox, C. Vernon Mason, and Al Sharpton, and of meetings, conversations, and other events involving the Brawley advisers, as well as their views and attitudes, were provided by Sharpton. In nearly twenty hours of interviews, Sharpton also gave behind-the-scenes details about events and attitudes within the Brawley family, as well as about rallies and protests, radio and television appearances, contacts with the press, confrontations with politicians, accusations against Steven Pagones and others, Glenda Brawley's defiance of a subpoena, and the family's ultimate defiance of the press and the grand jury. As was the case with all other sources in this book, Sharpton's information was checked, wherever possible, with other available accounts. Maddox and Mason refused all requests to be interviewed.

Details about Tawana Brawley's actions and conversations in the company of friends and acquaintances came in each case from one or more of those present, including her boyfriends Todd Buxton and Daryl Rodriguez. Tawana, Glenda and Juanita Brawley, and Ralph King declined to be interviewed for this book. Just as they refused to cooperate with the authorities, they have declined steadfastly to provide a verifiable account of what happened to Tawana during her four missing days. But Glenda and Juanita Brawley gave interviews to *The City Sun,* WLIB, and other segments of the black media, providing details about Tawana and her family's history and about their own actions and observations in the case. Juanita Brawley and Matthew Strong gave the *Times* several interviews prior to the grand jury report and the authors have drawn on these, and on the accounts in the black press, principally for background information.

Chapter 31, in which the authors set forth an account of Tawana's missing days, is based to a large extent on the report of the grand jury and the investigators' summaries of evidence, as well as on the authors' own investigation and interviews. Events that only Tawana and Glenda Brawley know firsthand have been reconstructed in this chapter primarily from interviews with Daryl Rodriguez.

Index

Index

Index

Index

Racism (*cont.*)
  and Maddox, Alton, 78–84, 270–271, 291–292, 310
  and Mason, C. Vernon, 162, 310
  media and
    American press and coverage of, 150
    American black press and, 317–322, 399
    New York Times coverage of racial issues, 148–151
    WLIB's programming and, 189, 270–274
  in Wappingers Falls, NY, 30–32
  racial incidents and legal cases
    Tawana Brawley case as, 34, 40, 58–59, 60–67, 87–88, 106, 132–141, 150, 306–309, 310, 320–322
    Jimmy Lee Bruce, Jr. case, 32–33, 57
    Eleanor Bumpurs case, 33, 57, 150, 190, 276, 335, 336
    Rev. Lee Johnson case, 81–82
    Orange County Jail incident, 65–66, 138, 148
    Peekskill incident, 148;
    Jonah Perry case, 83
    Michael Stewart case, 33, 57, 82–83, 150, 190, 276, 335
  rallies
    Friendship Baptist Church rally, 275–277
    Newburgh, NY, rally against, 86–87, 132, 134–140
    Poughkeepsie rally against, Dec. 12, 132–134, 140
    rally/protest on anniversary of Michael Griffith's death, 165–166
  special prosecutor's issue and, 185–195
  See also Edgar's Food Shop; Howard Beach; Ku Klux Klan; Maddox, Alton; Mason, C. Vernon; NAACP; Sharpton, Al
Radisson Hotel, Atlanta, GA, 333–334
Ramsey, B. Harold, 67, 71, 74, 85, 86
Rape
  as racial issue, 271, 324, 325, 330, 331, 334. *See also* Brawley, Tawana
  rapist's behavior, 346
Reagan, Ronald (President), 42, 43
Reflections Luxury Apartments, 354–355, 357, 368
Reidsville, GA, 305
Reuters news agency, 277
Riley, Mark, 270
Rivera, Geraldo, 277
Rizzo, Eugene, 262
Rockefeller, Nelson A., 286
Rodriguez, Daryl T., ix, 102–104, 153, 154, 370
  account of abduction/rape incident, 371–388
  and *New York Times* investigation, 398
Rodriguez, Juan, 335
Rookard, Hampton, 4, 6, 7–8, 70–71, 86–87, 141, 194, 391, 395
Rosewhite, Carlos, 31
Ross, Joseph D., 90
Roy C. Ketcham High School, 97, 98, 103–104, 144, 372
  Tawana cheerleader at, 98
Russwurm, John B., 317
Rustin, Bayard, 111
Ryan, John M. (prosecutor), viii
  and Abrams as special prosecutor, 183, 184, 213, 246–247
  controversy over, 202–206

  discussed in Gov. Cuomo's phone call to WLIB, 185–186, 194
  grand jury, 288, 294, 342, 345, 348, 351, 352–353, 367–368
Ryan, Katheryne, 21, 51

Sall, David B. (special prosecutor), 175–179
Saltzman, Jonathan, 61
Sanctuary, 298–299
Sandiford, Cedric, 83
Santucci, John J. (prosecutor), 84
Schmidt, Jerry (detective), 21–22, 48, 130
Scoralick, Frederick A. (Sheriff)
  alleged campaign contributions by Abrams, 223
  alleged racism, 42–44
  and Brawley case, 57–59, 75, 123
  doubts crime committed, 123, 133
  Tawana note implicating, 76, 221, 228–229
  WCBS interview, Nov. 19, 65
Sharpton, Al (Rev), ix, 78
  appearance, background, and character, 107, 108, 109–112, 284, 324, 357
  and James Brown, 111–112
  and Bill Cosby, 199–200
  and FBI, 113–114, 204, 206, 232
  Hawkins, Yusuf, case, 369
  Howard Beach and other racial cases, 57, 107–108
  indictment for income tax evasion and grand larceny, 369
  media and, 108–109, 114–115, 116
  mother, 302, 303
  wife, Cathy, 208
  and Tawana Brawley case, 207–208, 236
    and Abrams, Robert, 212–219, 220, 223–224, 282, 299
    account of case, 271, 273, 282
    accusation of Pagones, 253–255, 268, 282
    and Conyers, John, 338, 356
    and Cuomo, Mario, Gov., 183–184, 185–195, 201–206
    after exposure of hoax, 355–357, 369
    and grand jury, 287, 292, 328
    and hoax allegations by McKinnon, 305–309, 310–312, 320–321
    and hoax allegations by McClease, 312–316, 320–321
    and Jesse Jackson, 337–338, 356
    and media, 145, 205–207, 220
    and *New York Times* Investigation, 236, 248, 250–251, 398–399
    noncooperation tactic, 208, 218–219
    press conferences and interviews: (WLIB) 183–184, 185–195, (Mar. 13) 253–255, (WLIB, May 24) 270–274, (Vassar College) 281–282, (*Phil Donahue Show*) 309–310, (Bethany Baptist Church, June 10) 323–326, (*Morton Downey Jr. Show*) 337, (after *Times* expose) 365–366
    rallies, (Newburgh) 12, 136, 137–140, (Friendship Baptist Church) 275–277, (Atlanta) 331, 333, 335–336
    sanctuary for Glenda Brawley, 296–304
    special prosecutor issue, 201, 328
Shipp, E. R., 230–232, 235–236, 249–250, 251, 325, 326, 329–330, 333, 335–336
Shopsin's General Store, 307
60 Minutes 355

407